INTEGRATING MANAGED CARE AND ETHICS

Transforming Challenges into Positive Outcomes

INTEGRATING MANAGED CARE AND ETHICS

Transforming Challenges into Positive Outcomes

DENNIS A. ROBBINS

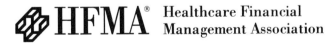 **HFMA**® Healthcare Financial Management Association

Educational Foundation

McGraw-Hill

New York   San Francisco   Washington, D.C.   Auckland   Bogotá
Caracas   Lisbon   London   Madrid   Mexico City   Milan
Montreal   New Delhi   San Juan   Singapore
Sydney   Tokyo   Toronto

McGraw-Hill

A Division of The McGraw·Hill Companies

Copyright © 1998 by The Healthcare Financial Management Association. All rights re-
served. Printed in the United States of America. Except as permitted under the United
States Copyright Act of 1976, no part of this publication may be reproduced or distributed
in any form or by any means, or stored in a database or retrieval system, without the prior
written permission of the publisher.

1 2 3 4 5 6 7 8 9 0 BKM / BKM 02 01 00 99 98

ISBN 0-07-053083-1

Printed and bound by Book-mart Press, Inc.

This publication is designed to provide accurate and authoritative information in regard to the
subject matter covered. It is sold with the understanding that neither the author nor
the publisher is engaged in rendering legal, accounting, or other professional service.
If legal advice or other expert assistance is required, the services of a competent professional
person should be sought.

> *—From a Declaration of Principles jointly adapted by a Committee of the American
> Bar Association and a Committee of Publishers.*

McGraw-Hill books are available at special quantity discounts to use as premiums and sales
promotions, or for use in corporate training programs. For more information, please write to
the Director of Sales, McGraw-Hill, 11 West 19th Street, New York, NY 10011. Or contact
your local bookstore.

Library of Congress Cataloging-in-Publication Data

Robbins, Dennis A.
  Integrating managed care and ethics : transforming challenges into positive
positive outcomes / by Dennis A. Robbins.
    p.   cm.
  Includes bibliographical references and index.
  ISBN 0–07-053083-1
  1. Managed care plans (Medical care)—United States. 2. Medical
Ethics. I. Title.
  RA413.5.U5R58   1997
  362.1'04258'0973—dc21   97-48804
                                                            CIP

To my wife and long-time confidente, Lora, my daughter Lynne, but particularly to my daughter Diana and others whose lives have been imperiled by the painful evolution of American healthcare.

FOREWORD

Today's healthcare environment is characterized by unprecedented challenges in which patient trust and confidence are being severely constrained. When people purchase health insurance, whether through fee-for-service or managed care, they wish to purchase peace of mind, not uncertainty. They trust that their medically appropriate needs will be met and that their lives as well as those they love will not be jeopardized by perverse financial considerations. Major legal actions, such as the *Fox v. Healthnet* case I argued, involve great personal loss; behind the headlines and headnotes and possible verdicts are real people with real needs that must not be ignored. An $89.3 million jury verdict can neither bring back my sister nor account for the loss of life and pain that so many suffer when financial concerns supersede trust, integrity, and accountability.

New legal actions, such as tortuous interference with the doctor-patient relationship and breach of fiduciary trust, are arising in increasing numbers. Even the shifts in caregivers' traditional roles create new and often impossible challenges. For example, when health plans export risk to capitated physicians, irresolvable conflicts arise, for how can the physician serve as both insurer and caregiver? How can the physician properly care for and advocate for his or her patient? Also, when incentives are based on doing less rather than what is right, something is wrong!

We have needed a guide or resource to help patients, caregivers, and anyone else who needs guidance through the tortuous paths of today's healthcare system. It is important to have a resource that can help empower persons so that they can understand how to face challenges endemic to healthcare today. As the financial mission threatens the care mission, caregivers and patients alike must recapture some sense of control. At the same time, those managed care organizations that base their decisions on integrity, accountability, and trust can look to a better model of what to pursue and what to avoid by examining various scenarios and cases in this text.

Dennis' book, *Integrating Managed Care and Ethics,* is a long awaited resource for identifying and addressing many of the complex legal and ethical issues that arise in managed healthcare. The experience and insights that Dennis brings to the playing field not only blend important insights from the fields of law, ethics and managed care, but also yield a compelling result. His approach offers a balanced treatment in a field so dominated by caricatures and denial that it is difficult to get clear answers and at times difficult even to formulate the right questions. His insights into using ethics as a problem-solving tool as well as identifying and examining of the roots of ethical conflicts that arise in managed care settings are captivating. His discussions of capitation and its attendant incentives not to treat, of the insured life as an asset and the patient as a financial liability, of fiscal arrogance, advocacy and inclusion, and of the major legal cases in this field are state of the art. In my own work as an advocate for patients and advisor to caregivers in managed care, my greatest success has come from helping people get what they need in a timely fashion and providing direction to caregivers to make a better, safer and more reliable system. Yet, a comprehensive resource to which the caregivers, healthcare executives, attorneys, and general public can look to get clarification, insight and direction has, until now, not been available. Dennis' book is a giant step in filling this previously unmet need.

Mark O. Hiepler, J.D.
Partner, Hiepler & Hiepler, Oxnard, CA

P R E F A C E

This book is the result of my work as a health systems specialist dealing with clinical ethics and health law over the past twenty years. It draws upon my experience as a lecturer, consultant, advisor, change agent, and educator. I have taught healthcare clinicians and executives, and currently teach *Ethical and Legal Issues in Managed Care and Healthcare Reform* to fourth-year medical students at Loyola Medical School in the Chicago area. I have also worked as an in-house consultant, dealing with many managed care issues at the Joint Commission as well as with the American Board of Quality Assurance and Utilization Review Physicians, The Case Management Society of America and the National Managed Healthcare Congress.

This book will treat a broad range of issues surrounding managed care, focusing primarily on the development of legal and ethical issues in managed care. It also addresses challenges that arise in managed care. Trends and recent legislative initiatives are examined, as is the guidance offered through several of the major healthcare trade associations. The goal of the book is to help the reader develop increased talent, tools, and technique to help transform challenges and change into more positive outcomes.

This book identifies ways to help physicians and other healthcare providers to maintain the standards of their professions as well as to negotiate with payors as active partners rather than passive recipients. It also serves as a resource for payors, health administrators, case managers, and managed care partners seeking better ways of addressing and solving the problems posed by the rapid transformation of the healthcare industry, the emergence of nontraditional healthcare, and new healthcare financing models. The text also helps impart a heightened awareness and sensitivity to ethical concerns and emerging challenges in healthcare so readers can respond to these challenges as agents in the process of change rather than as victims.

An important motivation for the creation of this text developed from working with diverse healthcare professionals, some of whom are involved in direct care, and others of whom influence the delivery of care and see the need for some framework for bridging the gap between fiscal concerns and clinical standards. This is obviously no small challenge. I have worked with large groups of clinical and financial professionals, including payors, case managers, risk managers, outcome specialists, employers, financial officers, quality assurance specialists, and utilization review specialists, and have seen increasing tension in the cost-quality tether that requires diverse disciplines working together to define creative alternatives and solutions at the interface of fiscal and clinical concerns.

The text will stimulate a dialogue that will enable us to blend financial and clinical concerns in such a way as to enhance rather than undermine the way we deliver care. It is also intended to serve as a resource for medical students and residents as well as other healthcare professionals who may have minimal training in health organization and administration and have no clear baseline from which to address cost control and cost containment initiatives and their relationship to managed care. Understanding basic managed care principles and how to work in managed care settings will become increasingly important for caregivers and administrators alike.

Besides providing a better understanding of the legal and ethical issues in managed and marketplace models of care, this text also focuses on the process of "doing ethics," or the manner in which we approach and define issues, examine those issues, make provisional decisions, and test, revise, and justify those decisions.

Non-traditional healthcare environments offering nontraditional care are raising many questions and concerns. At the same time, the law is shifting in response to these new roles. We are seeing, for example, the focus on negligence cases shifting from the failure to perform a procedure or to perform it properly, to cases involving the failure to refer or the failure to diagnose. Traditional relationships are being dramatically modified by managed care and there is an increased incidence of lawsuits in specialties that have been for the most part immune in the past. Guidelines that accommodate the reasonable and exclude the improper are a good starting point in the quest to make better decisions when faced with conflict, controversy, or uncertainty. Developing more comprehensive and dependable problem-definition and problem-solving skills will help us deal with the clinical, financial as well as legal and ethical issues that arise in managed care. The models and alternatives I offer have proved effective in teaching others to enhance their strengths and expertise and in helping find ways to resolve or preclude conflict when dealing with these difficult ethical and legal issues.

I hope this book will provide the guidance to allow caregivers and payors to take better care of patients and to partner together to achieve common goals rather than working at each other's expense. My hope is that this book will serve as a resource for training, educating, and sensitizing delivery system leaders, healthcare professionals, payors and patients alike. Accordingly, I have included an extensive topical bibliography and a wide array of case studies.

The book is designed to equip the reader to identify issues, define alternatives, and gain skills in solving and preventing problems and conflicts from arising. Before adopting the suggested policies and techniques in the book, you should tailor them to fit your organizational needs with the assistance of a quality assurance representative or risk manager, and ensure that they are consistent with controlling state and federal laws and regulations. While this book offers general guidance for your attorney, it is neither intended to provide legal advice nor to substitute for professional legal services.

ACKNOWLEDGMENTS

I would like to thank those who have been instrumental in helping me create this book. First, I would like to thank the publishing staff at McGraw-Hill, whose support, enthusiasm and professional manner was so important in the production of this text. It is important to have a publisher who not only meets but also exceeds my greatest expectations. Specifically I would like to thank Kris Rynne, who spearheaded the publishing endeavor, as well as Tom Sharpe, Laura Callo and Jeannie Miller, who instilled more confidence in me than any author could hope for.

I would like to thank many healthcare and health law professionals for the content suggestions and insight. First I would like to thank my new friend and colleague, Mark Hiepler, J.D., of Hiepler and Hiepler, Oxnard, California, not only for his insight and superb foreword, but also for his pioneering work in advocating for patients and caregivers in managed care, and for helping us to get behind the headlines and headnotes of an $89.3 million jury verdict and share in the depth and humanity of a very complex issue that real people often face. I would like to thank my long-time friend and colleague, Paul Armstrong, for the distinctive perspectives he shared as counsel for Quinlan, Jobes, and Baby M, as well as his involvement in the Cruzan case and *Vacco v. Quill*. I would like to thank Martin Hatlie, J.D., Director of the National Foundation for Patient Safety at the AMA, formerly director of liability and insurance at the AMA, and former executive director of the Health Care Liability Alliance, for his supply of ideas, perceptions, and critical information regarding emerging liability issues and trends in managed healthcare. I would like to thank Larry Hipp, M.D., Vice-President for Managed Care at the Joint Commission (JCAHO), for his insights on the purchaser's and business sides and for his unique perspective as medical director of AT&T for 14 years. I would like to acknowledge and thank Arnold S. Relman, M.D., for his insight, support, and friendship. I would like to thank all others who have supported my endeavors in word and deed or by serving as models for how we might proceed. I wish to acknowledge the insights of the Case Management Society of America's executive director, Jeannie Boling, and the current president of the CMSA, Nancy Skinner, for exposing me to the intricacies, challenges, and future direction of case management.

I would like to thank Linda McCormick of Glaxo-Wellcome for her company's support over the years in enabling me to share my ideas with medical and healthcare audiences around the nation and to learn from those organizations, their members and their leadership. I appreciate their having the vision and motivation to offer something truly valuable rather than limiting their sponsorship to someone talking about their specific pharmaceutical products. I would like to thank my wife, Lora Robbins, especially for her unending assistance in providing cutting-edge research and resource materials to me. She has been an important catalyst for content and laid the foundation for many of the creative directions this book has taken. I am also grateful to her for developing the user-friendly bibliography at the end of this book, which is an important resource for the reader. The time and energy she spent in compiling such a helpful resource is greatly appreciated.

I would like to thank those organizations, facilities, and individuals with whom I have worked as an advisor, consultant, educator and problem solver. Finally, I would like to reaffirm my thanks to the National Fund for Medical Education, who underwrote my postdoctoral studies in clinical ethics and health law at the Kennedy Interfaculty Program in Medical Ethics at the Harvard Schools of Public Health and Medicine, and helped create the intellectual and clinical foundation for this work.

CONTENTS

Chapter 1

Setting the Stage for Integrating Managed Care and Ethics   1

What is Managed Care?   2

The Development of the Health Maintenance Organization (HMO)   3

Market Forces in Managed Care   5

Federal Initiatives in Managed Care   5

Trends in Healthcare   7

The Tension Between Perceptions and Realities Involving Marketplace Models   8

Identifying Core Ethical Issues and Challenges in Managed Care: An Overview   9

Gatekeeping   11

New Implications of Changes in Healthcare Delivery Paradigms   11

Ethics as a Useful Tool   13

Lying and Gaming: Recipes for Failure   14

Creating Architectures in Which We Can All Comfortably Co-exist   14

Good Motivations Surrounding Managed Care: They Really Care!   15

Bad Apples Taint the Barrel—Why Don't They Care?   16

Shared Accountability   17

Care-setting–Specific Issues and Errors   18

Maxing out   19

Administrative Ethics and Network Guidelines   20

Mission and Policy   21

Serving Aggregate Populations Rather Than An Individual   22

Issues Endemic To Managed Home Care and Long-Term Care   22

Legal Guidance Involving End-Of-Life Concerns: An Overview   23

Futility   24

Deselection Issues   25

Inadequate Care   25

Experimental, Advanced, and Costly Procedures   25

Ethical Constants   26

Conclusion   27

Chapter 2

The Cost-Quality Interface   29

Introduction   29
Ethics on the Cost-Quality Interface   30
Medical Necessity and Fiscal Integrity   31
Integrating Fiscal Integrity with Medical Necessity   32
Aggregates and Ethics   33
Efficiency and Evidence-Based Decision Making   33
Precision Instruments for Measuring Quality and Performance: Is Our
Enthusiasm Premature?   34
Ethical Concerns Endemic to Capitated and Cost-Driven Care   35
Shifting from Fee-for-Service to Capitation   37
Identifying Hidden Agendas   38
From Care to Services   39
Purchasers Perspectives on the Cost-Quality Tension   40
Who Should Take the Initiative for Ethics and Ethical Responsibility?   41
Efficiency, Quality, and Ethics: Can They Be Integrated?   42
Leadership and Ethics   44
Initiatives in Performance Measurement and Quality   44
Some Differences Between HEDIS and the IMSystem   46
The Agency for Health Policy and Research (AHCPR)   48
Ethical Issues in Quality Measurement and Data Collection   50
Benchmarking and Reducing Error   51
Making Strides in Quality Measurement and Assessment   52
AMA, JCAHO, and Other Trade Association Quality Initiatives   52
Fiscal and Medical Arrogance   54
Conclusion   55
Case Studies   56

Chapter 3

Gatekeeping and Other Issues of Special Concern for Physicians   59

Introduction   59
Gatekeeping   60
Negative Gatekeeping   61
The Physician Gatekeeper   61
Ethical Dilemmas Posed by Gatekeeping   62

Healthcare Liability, Referrals, and Managed Care   62
Gag Clauses and Informed Consent 63
Beyond Gatekeeping: Issues of Special Concern to Physicians   64
Challenges to Providing Routine Care   65
Rationing   65
The Oregon Plan   66
Financial Incentives to Limit Care for HMOs and Independent Practice
Associations (IPAS)   67
Deselection Issues   68
Legal Remedies and Deselection   69
Advice Regarding Deselection   69
Conclusion   70
Case Studies   70

Chapter 4

Ethical Issues in Managed Care Contracting, Negotiating, Partnering   73

Introduction   73
Partnering   74
Partnering With Sharks   74
Management Service Organizations   75
Point of Service (POS) and Partnering   77
New Pressures in Physician Practices   77
The Spirit Of Partnering: Positive and Negative Dimensions   78
Carve-Outs   79
Provisional Outliers   80
The Capitation Learning Curve   80
Conclusion   81
Case Studies   81

Chapter 5

Managing Information and Communications Technologies: Ethical Concerns   83

Introduction   83
Ethical Dimensions of Information and Communication Technologies   83
Data Warehousing   84

Confidentiality and Privacy: Beyond Encryption and Firewalls   84
Archiving   85
Electronic Medical Records and Errors   86
Information and Economic Profiling of Physicians   88
Networks, Business, and Privileged Information   88
Limiting Disclosure: The Right Not to Know   88
Information "Haves" and "Have Nots"   89
Management and Measurement Systems: Limitations   89
The Seductiveness of Technology   90
Information, Telemedicine, and Liability   90
Related Ethical Concerns About Telemedicine   92
Conclusion   92
Case Studies   92

Chapter 6

Legal Frameworks, Liability, and the Regulation of Managed Care   93

Introduction   93
Overview   94
Legal and Ethical Concepts   95
Consent and Determining Decisional Capacity   97
Fluctuating Capacity   97
The Major Cases: Legal Issues and Media Perceptions   98
    Wickline v. California   99
    Wilson v. Blue Cross of California   99
    Fox v. Healthnet   100
    Ching v. Gaines   101
    DeMeurers v. HealthNet   102
    Adams et al v. Kaiser Foundation Health Plan of Georgia   104
    McClellan v. Long Beach Community Hospital   105
Fear of Legal Liability   106
Negligence and Malpractice   107
On Consent   108
Continuity of Consent   109
Conflicts Between Clinical Judgment and Cost Containment   109
The Cost of Liability and Defensive Medicine   110

Liability Issues Associated with Integrating Cost and Quality 112
Hold-Harmless Clauses 113
Remedies for Liability: Trends in Risk Management 113
The Employment Retirement Income Security Act (ERISA) 114
Chipping Away at the ERISA Preemption: Recent Legal Backlash 115
A Coalition Aimed at Tort Reform and Quality 117
Growth in Liability Concerns 118
Tort Reform and Managed Care 120
Regulatory Issues 121
Antitrust and Related Regulatory Concerns 121
The Joint Commission Ethics and Leadership Standards 122
Medicare and Medicaid Fraud and Abuse 125
New Initiatives in Health Care Fraud and Abuse 126
Referrals and Fraud and Abuse 127
Conclusion 127
Case Studies 128

Chapter 7

Advocacy in Managed Care   129

Introduction 129
What Is Advocacy and Why Is It So Important in Managed Care? 129
Physician-Based Advocacy 131
Case Management: A Model for Advocacy and Partnering 131
Payor-Based Advocacy 132
Trade Associations as Advocacy Forums 133
"Best Practices" Advocacy 134
Advocacy as Empowerment 135
Advocacy and Public Policy: Regulatory Initiatives 136
State-Based Consumer Protection Advocacy 136
A Coalition for Advocacy 137
Conflicts Between Patient Decisions, Caregivers' Preferred Course
of Treatment, and Medical Association Advocacy Policies 137
The AMA Managed Care Guidelines 138
The National Patient Safety Foundation of the AMA 141
AMA Advocacy Policy Regarding Formulary Issues 141
Recommendations About Formularies 141

Advocacy Related to Discharge Criteria and Standards   143
Conclusion   144
Case Studies   146

Chapter 8

Clarifying and Applying Ethics 149

Introduction   149
The Process of Applying Ethics, Morals, and Ethical Theory   150
Ethics and Bioethics: Clarifying Ambiguities   151
Consequentionalism and Nonconsequentionalism   152
Ethical Pluralism   153
Understanding Key Ethical and Legal Concepts   153
Rights and Wishes   154
Informed Consent and Knowledge   155
Knowledge and Ethics   156
Making Sure We're Talking About the Same Thing   157
Establishing a Framework for Using Ethics to Enhance Decision Making   157
Framing the Issue   157
Justifying Your Position   159
Right and Wrong Answers   160
Conclusion   161
Case Studies   161

Chapter 9

Applying a Model for Decision-Making   165

Introduction   165
A Decision-Making Model   166
Applying the Model   168
Conclusion   173

Chapter 10

**Tools for Conflict Resolution: Ethics Audits, Guidelines, Medical
Management Policies and Procedures, Ethics Committees,
and Ethics Rounds   175**

Introduction   175
Establishing a Baseline and Direction Through an Ethics Audit   176

Clinical Ethics Rounds   177

The Benefits of Ethics Rounds   178

Clinical Ethics Rounds and the Ethics Committee   179

Developing Policies and Adjudicating Conflict   180

Evaluating Conflict Resolution Techniques   181

General Clinical Conflict Resolution Guidelines   182

Conflict Resolution in Managed Care: Guidelines for Appeals of Utilization Management Decisions   183

Recommendations for Reducing Conflict and Liability Exposure in Medical Management Determinations   184

The Ethics Committee in Managed Care   186

A Historical Perspective on Ethics Committees   187

Ethics Committees and Advocacy   188

Non–Hospital-Based Ethics Committees   188

Long Term Care and Home Healthcare Ethics Committees   189

A Response to Managed Care From Care and Service Provider Organizations   190

Payor-Based Ethics Committees   190

Some Advantages of Ethics Committees   191

Responsibilities of Ethics Committee Members   192

Educating Committee Members   193

Educating Other Staff Members and the Community   193

Committee Composition and Membership   194

Case Consultations   194

Conclusion   195

Case Studies   196

Chapter 11

Community-Based Ethics Committees   199

Introduction   199

A New Marketing Concept   200

Ethics and the Community   201

Sharing Risk, Accountability, and Vision   202

A Scenario for the Community-Based Committee to Address   202

Assuring Continuity Across the Continuum   203

Better Ensuring Continuity of Patient Wishes   205

Community-Based Ethics Committee Membership   205

Coordination and Networking   207
Community-Based Ethics Committees and Advocacy   207
Conclusion   208
Case Study   209

Chapter 12

**Managed Care and End-of-Life Decision Making:
Tracing the Legal Legacy   211**

The High End Cost of Health Care and the High Cost
of End-of-Life Care   212
Ethics and Policy Development   214
The Right to Privacy   216
Consent and Determining Decisional Capacity   218
Fluctuating Capacity   218
Guardianship   219
Patients Lacking Decisional Capacity   221
The Common Law Background: Tracing the Legal Legacy   221
Legal Cases Involving The Withholding/Withdrawing of Life-Prolonging
Medical Procedures   222
   In re Quinlan   222
   Superintendent of Belchertown State School v. Saikewicz   224
   In re Dinnerstein   226
   In re Spring   226
   In re Eichner and *Eichner v. Dillon*   227
Withholding Artificial Nutrition and Hydration   228
   In re Conroy   228
   Cruzan v. Director, Missouri Department of Health   230
   In re Michael Martin   231
Physician-Assisted Suicide: *Vacco v. Quill* and *Washington v. Glucksberg*   232
Summarizing the Legal Legacy   233
Conclusion   236
Case Studies   236

Chapter 13

Consent-Based Policies and Procedures   239

Introduction   239
Policies and Consent   240

Consent as a Dynamic Process   241
Confusion About Consent   242
Consent and Duty   243
An Integrated Consent Policy: An Overview   245
The Integrated Policy   246
Opinion of the AMA Council of Ethical and Judicial Affairs on Withholding or Withdrawing Sustaining Medical Treatment   249
Conclusion   255
Case Studies   256

Chapter 14

Advance Directives: Possibilities and Perils   261

Introduction   261
Advance Directives   261
Living Wills   262
Durable Powers of Attorney   263
On Surrogacy and Surrogacy Laws   266
Problems Associated with Advance Directives   266
A Way to Highlight the Importance of Advance Directives   268
Compliance with Advance Directives   271
Lag Time Between the Identification of Advance Directives and Orders to Comply   271
Telephone DNR Orders   272
Policies and Polemics Regarding Advance Directives   272
Creating Sensible Policies   273
Documenting Controversy   274
Matters of Conscience   275
Conclusion   275
Case Studies   276

Chapter 15

Transforming Outcomes into Ethically and Socially Responsible Health Care Plans: An Unfinished Chapter   279

Topical Bibliography   295

Glossary   321

Index   327

INTRODUCTION

What should a book on managed care and ethics be? It would be easy to mirror the popular press and attack the sensationalistic topics of drive-through deliveries and premature discharge, or focus on spurious plans with spurious practices. On the other hand, the book could champion the strides that are being made in performance measurement, evidence-based decision making, and creative attempts to solve problems that have been avoided in the past. This text will try to be fair to managed care's advocates as well as its adversaries, without watering down important issues. The goal is to stay away from the extremes (but not to ignore or excuse them) and try to identify core ethical issues that are common to many managed care settings. Thus, this text will neither be a diatribe against the "evils" of imposing cost controls, efficiency and performance measurement models on caring for sick people, nor an uncritical celebration of the strides that are being made through outcomes assessment, creative healthcare delivery systems, and reducing error by identifying best practices, best products, and redesigning systems. It will neither be a one-sided discussion from the clinicians' perspective about all the perils of managed care, nor an exercise in finger pointing from the payor side at caricatures of an unreasonable media, cost-be-damned physicians, and other healthcare professionals.

All too often, discussions of ethics and managed care are no more than fault-finding exercises, assigning blame to one side or the other for all the ills of healthcare, including those inherited from the past as well as the challenges of today. The treatment of such issues is characterized by preconception, prejudice, and uncritical assessment by the horde of self-proclaimed crusaders bent on correcting the ills of today's healthcare.

There are also the issues themselves. On the one hand, the very question of whether cost and care can be integrated appears to be quite convoluted and ambiguous. On the other hand, waste and inefficiency are themselves unethical. There is sometimes the perception that these issues were spontaneously generated along with the advent of managed care rather than being problems with which healthcare has grappled for some time.

Then there are those insidious aspects of managed care that, while ethically neutral, are assumed to have intrinsic ethical dimensions.

Gatekeeping, for example, is uncritically thought by many to be a major ethical issue in managed care, as are fixed templates for performance and cost, and denial of designated care and services. However, gatekeeping and even denial of specific care are ethically neutral. How they are applied determines whether the application is ethical or unethical. It is not whether one controls the gate, be it for protecting the patient from over-treatment and/or undertreatment, or negatively to impede, delay, or restrict in such a way that is financially motivated and not in the patients best interest, that is the root of ethical concern. I am not suggesting that there are no normative ethical standards that apply here; instead, I am suggesting that the principles and motivations behind these ethical issues and the ways in which they are determined constitute the grounds for deciding whether an action or policy is ethical or unethical. These ethical questions pivot on how one deals with such issues, not the issues of gatekeeping or denial themselves. Often the practices and concepts themselves are ethically neutral. Questions about whether a denial is fair and appropriate are ethical questions. Denial of payment or services is not an ethical issue without knowing whether integrity, trust, and accountability were ignored and that such a decision was made for less than medically appropriate reasons. Thus, an exhaustive analysis of denial or gatekeeping has little merit. Another question often raised is the question of whether the imposition of marketplace models in healthcare is intrinsically unethical. If by virtue of a marketplace-driven model, increased efficiency and improved outcomes arise and money is saved without compromising (and perhaps even improving) patient care, is that unethical? Again the issues are the manner in which one applies the model, not the model itself. It is the application or index one takes in relation to something, not the something, that is unethical or ethical. The manner in which one applies efficiency models and marketplace models is where the ethical dimensions arise, not the models themselves. Yet trust, accountability, and integrity are still the fulcrum on which such issues must be balanced.

There are those who say that many of the so-called ethical problems in managed care are not generated by managed care but instead were inherited from fee-for-service. This is sometimes used as an excuse to avoid dealing with such problems and as a license for a particular species of intellectual fainting. There are also those who argue that all the ethical issues in healthcare that arose prior to managed care should not be included in a book on ethics and managed care. I have even heard the argument that because the entire legal history, from Quinlan to Cruzan, arose prior to the introduction of managed care into the healthcare system, managed care is exonerated from looking at those issues. According to this reasoning, the very foundation of how we look at privacy, self-determination, and sub-stituted judgment should be excluded from this book. I contend that re-visiting these issues in light of managed care is indeed important, because they graphically emphasize an opportunity to reduce costs while better en-suring patient autonomy, and underscore how evidence-based medicine can offer guidance in achieving that goal.

In response to some of these concerns, I believe that a good start in addressing issues of ethics in managed care would be to highlight impor-tant ethical issues, perceptions, and concerns, and examine them in the managed care context. As already noted, while gatekeeping, consent, per-formance measurement, defining outcomes, mission and leadership, in-formation systems, and confidentiality are not ethical issues, the way in which they are approached or dealt with can have dramatic ethical impli-cations, and these implications are what this book will address. The goal in doing so is to equip the reader with an understanding of how such issues should be addressed and how missions, policies and procedures can be created to appropriately deal with these issues to preclude problems, or at least to understand the potential of some of the emerging ethical issues in managed care.

Managed care is both a payment system and philosophy of care. Its incentives, the changes it stimulates and the challenges it poses require ongoing assessment, direction and creative interventions, as does any other payment system, for that matter. Yet a fresh look at how to offer something different will be scrutinized more than will the status quo. A philosophy of care aimed at reducing waste and inefficiency and collect-ing data to document its success should be welcomed rather than dis-dained. At the same time, incentives that merit doing less when less is not always more and where cost considerations supercede concerns of in-tegrity and accountability must be checked. Hopefully, this book will fill an unmet need, providing guidance in an area infused with misunder-standing.

The book is organized in such a way that each chapter builds upon the last. For those who wish to "try out" new information gleaned from a chapter, case examples containing discussion questions follow the con-clusion of most chapters. These are either actual cases that have been modified for reasons of confidentiality or examples of types of cases that recur in managed care contexts.

The book will provide the reader with an examination of both fundamental concepts in managed care and future issues that will likely arise in the field. The heavy focus on ethical and legal issues makes this text distinctive, particularly because many of the discussions of ethics are more practical in application than theoretical. Discussions of how to evaluate problems, frame issues, make provisional decisions, and justify one's positions will be treated in detail. A model for dealing with complicated problems that require one to break such issues into components will be introduced as a methodological tool to assist the reader. Other practical strategies, such as the development of clinical ethics rounds, ethics committees, community ethics committees, and medical management plans to deal with appeals to coverage decisions, second opinions, and related issues will be included to give the reader better options for approaching conflict resolution and conflict preclusion rather than offering one vehicle to the exclusion of others.

It is the author's hope that this book will be a step forward in terms of better understanding as well as addressing if not resolving some of the tensions on the cost-quality interface, and will blaze a trail towards working together rather than against each other.

A great tension has been developing as a result of attempts to add fiscal efficiency and cost concerns as a routine and integral factor in the practice of medicine and healthcare delivery. The issues of containing and controlling costs will continue to play an important role in medicine and other sectors of healthcare. In working with diverse medical audiences and national healthcare organizations, I find heightened concern with blending fiscal and clinical concerns, but the situation is not improving. In fact, it appears to become more difficult if not impossible to achieve any more than a facile integration of these two aspects of healthcare delivery. When physicians spend large amounts of valuable clinical time securing approvals for coverage, it is seen as a liability and often an "unnecessary and inefficient evil." At the very least it is perceived as an inconvenience that undermines and delays the provision of medical care and services. At the same time, when administrative layers of gatekeepers insulate and separate the physician from the patient, something suffers.

Part of the difficulty in blending the cost-quality interface comes from the fact that there is little understanding of or sensitivity to what each perspective's primary components, concerns, or important ingredients offer. Currently the payor or financial side knows that clinical services cost money but not a lot about the clinical enterprise and what is at stake.

At the same time, the clinician feels that cost considerations are often there to impede, compromise or otherwise complicate what should be un-fettered care based on the doctor's experience and clinical judgment in de-termining medical necessity, which must remain a medical and not an eco-nomic decision. Cost efficiency should be part and parcel of a reasonable and appropriate medical care model, but not the driving force.

NAVIGATING *INTEGRATING MANAGED CARE AND ETHICS*

This book is organized in the following way: Chapter 1 will introduce the topic of ethics and managed care. It will address such questions as what is meant by managed care and the development of the HMO, as well as the market forces that have shaped its development and growth. This will in-clude discussion of the primary forces driving managed care and health-care reform. The chapter will then identify technical issues involving gate-keeping, changes in our perceptions of care, and good and bad scenarios of managed care with respect to the ethical issues they generate. The chap-ter will highlight the importance of shared accountability in a variety of healthcare settings as well as the importance of developing system-wide and organization-wide policies and procedures to offer guid-ance and create architectures that can accomodate caregivers, members, and plans. The remainder of the first chapter will refer to future discus-sions of legal issues as well as ethical issues associated with end-of-life decision making. It will speak more generally to ethical issues on the cost-quality interface. This chapter will serve as an overview of issues to be ad-dressed and set the tone for the remainder of the book. For convenience, often the term "patient" will be used in this text to refer to "members," "insured lives," and "enrollees."

Chapter 2, deals with quality-cost tension, perhaps the most chal-lenging and important topic the book will treat. In this chapter, issues of integration, efficiency, and quality will be discussed in the context of sig-nificant changes in our perception of care and caregivers. Discussions of who has ethical responsibility, and what vehicles can ensure that the cost-quality tension will be examined carefully are included in this chapter. Also addressed are both sensible and aberrant responses to this challenge, ranging from sophisticated measurement systems to fiscal and medical arrogance.

Chapter 3 is dedicated primarily to gatekeeping but will also address other issues of special interest to physicians, including gag rules, deselec-tion, and practical ways to insulate against deselection and liability. The discussion of gatekeeping and its relationship to cost and quality issues will be explored in detail, as will concepts of multiple gatekeepers and their implications for care.

Chapter 4 is of special interest to those interested in contracting with managed care organizations, and to managed care organizations planning contracts with healthcare professionals. It will discuss various ways to assure healthier partnering and share or carve out risk. It will also discuss the increasingly valuable role of MSOs in defining the process by which partnering can be a value-added, cost effective enterprise in which each partner benefits from the relationship. It will also discuss fiscal uncertainty and capitation and ways to more effectively deal with these issues using performance and outcomes information to better negotiate a contract or relationship

Chapter 5 is a specialized chapter dealing with ethical dimensions of information and communication technologies. Confidentiality, security issues, archiving, liability issues, and error will be treated in this chapter. It will discuss the right to know as well as the right not to know. It will discuss the cost of technology and the technology of cost. Finally, some of the emerging technologies such as performance measurement technologies and telemedicine, and the advantages and disadvantages they pose, will be addressed.

Chapter 6 is laden with material dealing with a wide range of legal issues in managed healthcare. This chapter begins with a discussion of key principles required for understanding the topics and cases treated in the text. It also lays the foundation for more detailed discussions of these topics later in the chapter. Issues of privacy, self-determination, surrogacy, consent, fluctuating capacity, and continuity of consent will be raised. An extensive look at major legal cases dealing specifically with managed care will be discussed along with general discussions of legal liability, negligence, and malpractice. Other contractual issues such as "hold-harmless clauses" and "gag rules" will be discussed as well. Emerging concerns related to tort reform will be discussed as well as regulatory and antitrust issues. An array of case studies will conclude this chapter

Chapter 7 addresses foundations and applications in ethics. The goal of this chapter is to give the reader practical tools for addressing ethical issues and prepare the reader to use the decision-making model in Chapter 9. Chapter 7 deals with how we address ethical problems and what tools and techniques we can develop to address them more comprehensively and effectively. A short discussion of ethical theory is coupled with clarification of key concepts in ethics such as rights, wishes, and informed consent. A practical guide on how to evaluate and address an ethical issue follows. This will include making sure we are talking about the same thing, framing the issue, and then justifying the position you have taken. An examination of what role clinical ethics rounds and the development of policies and procedures play in precluding conflict will set the stage for the series of case discussions that conclude the chapter.

After the discussion of general principles in Chapter 7, Chapter 8 will focus on more action-based activity involving ethics and advocacy. Advocacy will be examined from a variety of perspectives, some of which we expected would exist and others we might be surprised to learn of. Accordingly, physician-based and payor-based advocacy will be discussed. Public policy, state-based advocacy, and guidelines for how to pursue advocacy initiatives will be included as well. Examples such as the AMA managed care guidelines, the AMA discharge criteria, the JCAHO Leadership and Rights and Responsibilities Standards, and the AMA's work in the area of pharmaceuticals and formularies will be discussed.

Chapter 9 offers a model for decision making that can be used to investigate multifaceted problems or issues. The model offers a step-by-step process to resolve conflict and to better address ethical issues in a systematic way. An illustration will demonstrate how the model can be applied. The model can eventually become a kind of algorithm that one uses in daily decision making. The illustration used will examine topics that build upon much of the foundation the reader will have already established earlier in the text. The example illustrates the tension between best practices and central operations constraints. This involves issues of consent, fraud and abuse, medical standards, and cost quality tensions (all addressed in Chapter 6).

Chapter 10 is another practical problem-solving tools chapter. It is dedicated exclusively to a potpourri of conflict resolution techniques. Ethics audits, ethics rounds, policy development, ethics committees, medical management policies, and utilization management policies will be discussed. These can be extremely useful for a wide range of caregivers, helping them shape their relationships with managed care partners and advocate for their patients. This section builds heavily on previous chapters. Ethics committees will be explored in detail in this chapter, including institutional ethics committees, ethics committees in managed care, payor-based committees, hospital and non-hospital committees, and specialized committees. Particular considerations of who should serve on an ethics committee, frequency of meetings, and educating ethics committee members and other staff will be discussed in detail. Selected cases will illustrate the techniques and topics discussed in this chapter.

Chapter 11 deals with community-based ethics committees pursuant to the earlier examination of more traditional ethics committees in Chapter 10. This chapter examines the community ethics committee's distinctiveness in light of more traditional models. Issues related to ethics and marketing, education, and membership will also be discussed. A detailed example of how this committee can address a community-wide issue that is not handled well by individual institutions will be treated in some detail. Also, how this committee can enhance the continuum of care will be discussed, as will networking and advocacy

Chapter 12 will trace the legal dimensions of consent and end-of-life decision making and some of the challenges they pose for managed care, which affect not only the terminally ill but provide guidance for a wide range of other issues in healthcare involving self-determination, or the right to determine what shall be done to one's own body. This chapter will focus on the major legal cases that have carved out the privacy and liberty rights, including some discussion of the common law background surrounding autonomy and substitute decision making. It will also extensively treat withholding/withdrawing life-prolonging medical procedures by tracing the legal legacy from Quinlan to Cruzan and then building upon more recent legal controversies involving physician-assisted death (physician-assisted suicide) recently before the United States Supreme Court. An array of related case studies will test the readers' use of principles discussed earlier in the chapter.

Chapter 13 transforms the concepts and discussions of earlier chapters into concrete policies and procedures. This chapter on consent-based polices and procedures examines consent and then explores a well developed policy and its provisions that can protect patient's wishes and at the same time better insulate clinicians from potential or perceived liability than most policies currently in place. Special procedures involving documentation and medical assessment are included.

Chapter 14 will examine the strengths and weaknesses of various types of advance directives and will discuss some of the problems associated with their acceptance or implementation. It will also help the reader to better identify what to consider when drafting his or her own directives, including what caveats and concerns he or she might need to entertain. Learning the value and relative strengths of these instruments, as well as their limitations, can reduce uncertainty and better afford one's wishes. Managed care's challenge in this domain is to do what is medically appropriate rather than prolong the dying process, particularly when pursuing futile efforts that are discordant with good medicine as well as patient wishes.

The concluding chapter is an attempt not only to integrate discussions that have occurred earlier in the text and offer some vision of the future of ethics and managed care, but also to offer a challenge for managed care to be more rather than less of what it can be. It will discuss many of the key ethical issues in managed care and consider the future directions managed care will likely pursue and the attendant ethical issues. It also suggests a preliminary model of an ethically and socially responsible managed care organization or health care plan.

An extensive topical bibliography is also included.

CHAPTER

Setting the Stage for Integrating Managed Care and Ethics

Managed care is sufficiently mature to face both the ethical challenges it has inherited and those it has created. Yet, in order to create an authoritative resource on the subject of ethical issues in managed care, one must first be clear about what is meant by the terms *ethics* and *managed care*. Finally, the goal of a book on integrating managed care and ethics should be defined. This book will clarify concepts and identify ethical dimensions in their application in order to facilitate understanding and improvement. This chapter will define managed care in its breadth, discuss the development of the HMO and its historical roots, and discuss major federal initiatives that spurred the HMO movement.

Next, some of the market forces and trends that have shaped the development of the HMO and managed care philosophies of care will be discussed. Many ethical issues that have been associated with a variety of processes adopted by managed care will also be examined. As noted previously, the ethical questions are generated less by concepts and processes themselves than by the emphasis afforded them. Gatekeeping, capitation-specific issues, economic profiling, de-selection, maxing out, access and availability of care and services, and denial of coverage are issues that commonly arise in managed care contexts. Other issues involving broader questions that arise on the cost-quality interface will also be introduced in this chapter, such as leadership, mission, and accountability. These will often be examined in light of traditional fee-for-service models and discussed in the contexts of both strides made by managed care and its real or perceived deficiencies that need to be addressed. Legal guidance surrounding end-of-life decision making (where costs can be controlled but past behaviors undermine that process) will be discussed, as will advance directives as a way of facilitating that process.

A model for addressing some of the more complex, multifaceted ethical issues that arise in managed care will be also be introduced, which will permit the reader to apply what will be learned in later chapters and learn to better use ethics as a resource tool. Ethics can further serve to help create architectures that can accomodate managed care organizations' (MCOs) central operations and their care and service provider organizations, as well as practitioners and the members they serve. Part of this can be accomplished by enhancing consumer confidence, which has been compromised or eroded in the recent past. Managed healthcare can allay the uncertainty patients face and more effectively integrate clinical and financial concerns while making the patient a partner in that process.

This chapter will provide a better understanding of these issues, so that further improvement can be made while addressing public perception and consumer confidence concerns. Following the conclusion of each chapter are a series of discussion questions through which the reader can rethink and apply concepts addressed in the chapter.

WHAT IS MANAGED CARE?

Managed care is an ambiguous term that is used inconsistently. While it assumes many forms and complexions, fundamentally it is a type of healthcare delivery system that attempts to manage and control the cost, delivery, quality, access, and availability of that care. It achieves these goals by creating provider panels, often using a variety of gatekeepers to regulate access and availability, and to determine medical necessity. It has prescribed benefits and limitations and often contracts with a variety of providers to offer services.

Managed care was created as a viable alternative to the medical delivery models of its predecessors. Employers working in concert with payors felt that increasing healthcare costs needed to be controlled, and that there was little incentive in the fee-for-service system for physicians to assist in the process of controlling them. In fact, until quite recently, considering cost as a factor in evaluating the kind of care being provided was thought to be unethical by physicians. Now, however, there are new pressures to control healthcare costs. Many argue that such pressures compromise care. Others argue that efficiency and the measuring of performance and outcomes can enhance effective care and reduce waste.

THE DEVELOPMENT OF THE HEALTH MAINTENANCE ORGANIZATION (HMO)

The rapid rise of managed care can be attributed to a perceived need among employers to reduce financial exposure associated with rising employee benefit costs. Managed care offered employers more control over their financial exposure, with fixed costs and specific benefits, terms and conditions. Cost reduction, not quality improvement, was the predominant motivation for the switch to managed care. Quality was the concern of the physician, and for the most part, both indemnity insurers and the payors accepted the physician as the locus and determinant of quality. Cost was the concern of the employer, and accordingly, the payor. "In the early 1970s, managed care was essentially limited to, and defined by, health maintenance organizations . . . A dramatic boost was provided by Congress . . . HMOs first appeared in the 1940s but failed to spread beyond California and parts of the Midwest until law makers passed the HMO Act of 1973 (P.L.93-222) The act promised financial support to HMOs that offered a minimum level of benefit to enrollees, charged premiums based on community-wide healthcare costs, and met other criteria for federal qualification. The new laws gave federally qualified HMOs the right to require employers to offer the HMO option to employees, a critical factor in ensuring enrollment growth"[1] Federal financial support, coupled with employer mandates, clearly has fueled the growth of HMOs.

The HMO Act of 1973[2] spearheaded the dramatic rise of HMOs in the United States. HMOs promised many benefits to enrollees, including the following:

1. Greater access and availability of care
2. Cost savings through a refocus on health promotion rather than disease management

---

[1] Kongstvedt, Peter R. *The Managed Health Care Handbook,* 3rd edition, Gaithersburg, MD: Aspen Publishers, Inc., 1996, p. 583.
[2] *United States Code Annotated Comprising all Laws of A General and Permanent Nature under Arrangement of the Official Code of the Laws of the United States with Annotations from Federal and State Courts.* Title 42 Section 300E The Public Health and Welfare Chapter 6A Health Maintenance 1973, p. 146.

3. Proactive caring rather than tourniquet solutions

4. "Reasonable promptness . . . in a manner which assures continuity and when medically necessary to be available and accessible twenty-four hours a day, seven days a week"[3]

5. Physician, inpatient, outpatient, emergency services, mental health services, referral services and diagnostic and laboratory services

6. (A guarantee) not to expel or refuse to re-enroll any member because of his health status or his requirements for health services[4]

The HMO act defined *health maintenance organization* as "a public or private entity which is organized under the laws of any state and which provides basic and supplemental services to its members . . . without limitation as to time and cost."[5] The rallying cry for HMOs was a shift from the previous focus on sickness interventions to something that was perceived to be better. It could be argued that managed care offered a utopian alternative to the status quo—health promotion and sickness prevention rather than delivery of sickness services. It also stood in sharp contrast to a fee-for-service system in which there was little incentive for the physician to diagnose quickly or refer outside of the cost center of an individual medical practice. Our health insurance system was in fact not health insurance but rather sickness insurance which paid for episodic events of sickness. Inconsistency, dramatic variations among practice patterns, and geographical variation prior to the advent of managed care might be aptly characterized as "unmanaged care."

The HMO philosophy centered on the premise that by keeping people healthy through regular checkups, monitoring, well-baby checks, patient education, prophylaxis, and targeted services, care could be provided more economically and people could be kept healthier than under the more traditional system.

Some argue that many of today's managed care models have sacrificed much of the health promotion and health maintenance elements of the early HMOs, and that cost concerns, not health maintenance or health promotion, now predominate.

---

[3] *United States Code,* p. 146.

[4] *United States Code,* p. 152.

[5] *United States Code,* Sub-chapter XII, Health Maintenance Organizations.

MARKET FORCES IN MANAGED CARE

Many forces have contributed to the success of managed care, not the least of which are employers who have adopted a variety of strategies to reduce or control their increasing healthcare costs. One writer characterizes managed care as a "response of the free market to two decades of runaway medical inflation caused by a cost plus system that encouraged unlimited use of medical services."[6] Employers have been quite vocal about the need to reduce employee benefit costs, the largest of which are healthcare related. Employers have worked closely with insurers and healthcare plans to work out ways to control rising healthcare costs. Employers have moved from minimal interest in managed care to increasing involvement and even activitism, for they see it as a realistic way to control employee benefit expenditures. Managed care is seen as a vehicle that can effectively control rising costs and also enhance quality. Some employers active in the move toward managed care see it as an opportunity "truly to manage their health benefit expenditures for employees and for employees to become better educated healthcare consumers and have access to quality-driven accountable healthcare providers."[7]

As a result, employers have become much better informed about healthcare costs and healthcare quality, access, and outcomes, as well as of the importance of fitness and exercise in making employees healthier and more productive.

FEDERAL INITIATIVES IN MANAGED CARE

Employers are not the only players in the cost control process. The federal government has had a dramatic impact on healthcare and healthcare costs since the 1940s through hospital construction initiatives, the advent of Medicare and Medicaid in the 1960s, and the continuing growth in military and other government healthcare systems The drivers of federal healthcare concerns and initiatives are manifold and their impact upon virtually all other forms of healthcare is dramatic. While there are yearly fluctuations in the figures cited below, such as the U.S. budget and the Medicare Trust Fund, the following list describes the most important drivers of federal health policy:

---

[6] Kongstvedt, *Managed Health Care Handbook*, p. 216.
[7] Kongstvedt, *Managed Health Care Handbook*, p. 580.

- The U.S budget deficit: $203 billion annually
- The public debt: $5 trillion and growing
- The Medicare Trust Fund: approaching insolvency by 2002
- State budget shortfalls, strapped by an average 12 percent Medicaid growth rate
- Public perception of change and reluctance to accept larger roles for the government
- An aging population and changing demographics, represented by a 23 percent increase in the over-85 population[8]

These factors have dramatically affected the federal government's role in healthcare in the past and will do so in the future. There are some implicit assumptions about these drivers, particularly the Medicare Trust Fund, which has never *not* been in "danger of impending doom or insolvency" since its inception, since it is for the most part no more than a checking account funded by the former year's payroll taxes. Uwe Reinhardt, the Princeton economist, says this is an example of political doublespeak, in which politicians "structure information felicitously."[9] He believes that the Medicare Trust Fund, just like any other checking account, will be adjusted according to the changing needs of the country. Yet these concerns remain, fueled by the perception that a vast majority of older citizens, particularly the wealthy, are milking the system. This is a suspect assumption, because fewer than five percent of the elderly have over $25,000 in Medicare expenses per year, and most use less than $1000 per year from Medicare coverage. Most Medicare enrollees use about $1300 a year of this fund. However, 25 percent of enrollees account for 91 percent of all Medicare expenditures.[10] Reinhardt also reminds us that Medicare is not a generous plan when compared with the healthcare plans of many other industrialized nations. Each eligible Medicare recipient is responsible for over 37 percent of the cost of his or her medical care, and the full cost of prescriptions is paid out of pocket by the elderly.

One means of reducing Medicare expenditures has been to increase the use of case management to coordinate the care of the high-end users, to identify ways of meeting their healthcare needs, and to provide continuity

---

[8] Kongstvedt, *Managed Health Care Handbook*, p. 17.
[9] Reinhardt, Uwe, *Mediscare: What's Wrong With Medicare?* National Managed Care Congress Northeast, NYC, November 14, 1996.
[10] Reinhardt, National Managed Care Congress, November 14, 1996.

of care. Many employers believe case management is the most successful model for insuring quality while controlling costs. Others believe this provides incentive for unhealthy behavior and punishes healthy participants, who are denied the customized help and direction of the case manager. A current national initiative to evaluate case management interventions and outcomes should add both spice and content to this area of discussion.

This new incentive to gather information to improve performance and outcomes (both clinical and financial) is not without its caveats. Some insidious ethical issues involving confidentiality and what information should be accessible to the employer and what should remain privileged between the doctor and patient arise here. For example, a patient who uses a disproportionate amount of medical resources, (such as someone who requires costly pharmaceuticals to manage a chronic disease) might be identified by a less-than-scrupulous employer as an economic liability. The employer might then look for any reason whatsoever to get rid of that employee. Confidentiality has great impact here, because information on medication and other formerly privileged information can be accessed by an employer more easily than in the past.

The government, as the largest single payor of healthcare costs, also wants to control and reduce its financial exposure. This will likely involve increased payroll taxes and decreased benefits. There is also the likelihood that means testing of the Medicare benefit will occur. It is not likely that their concern will be diminished, because creative ideas and interventions are needed to rescue underfunded systems that are in jeopardy of bankruptcy. These are major national priorities.

It is important to understand trends in healthcare, for without a baseline from which to examine change, change has little meaning. Examining what has been tried, what has worked and what has not, and the reasons for success and failure enables us to work for positive change. A knowledge of trends can provide us with a better indication of what might be feasible and how best to achieve it.

TRENDS IN HEALTHCARE

Cost containment efforts in the United States have relied on various mechanisms and taken different directions in addressing the problem of how to control or to contain rising healthcare costs. There are often dramatically different perceptions of how such goals are to be achieved, without any overriding principles or policies to coordinate them. Attempts to reduce healthcare costs in the United States have been going on for some time. For the most part, our nation has no comprehensive healthcare policy. Instead, health policy makers and caregivers "concentrate their energies on their particular part of the system, trusting that someone else will make the right judgments for the system as a whole."[11] Cost, for example, has only recently been explored in light of outcomes, performance data, and quality measurement indicators. Reducing the number of beds, reducing major capital expenditures and other kinds of purchases, reducing construction investment in major equipment through certificate of need (CON and HSAs), reducing payment for certain kinds of services, shifting from retrospective reimbursement to prospective reimbursement and from fee-for-service to managed care all have been tried and in many cases did little to achieve their intended goal. Even managed care's claims to save money are still open to debate. Costs have continued to rise, and, some argue, quality has deteriorated. Some are responding with a call for greater accountability with regard to outcomes, patient satisfaction, and resource utilization.

The 1990s and beyond offer more complicated and, in many ways, more creative transformations in our healthcare system. The coming years may also herald the development of a true healthcare policy rather than tourniquet solutions. We are looking at the very foundations of healthcare. We are looking at scarcity in new ways and new ways of allocating and prioritizing resources. Cost, which was anathema to the physician of the past, is now an integral component of the clinical decision-making process, as indicated by the increasing use of evidence-based medicine. Patients are concerned that the long-established right to healthcare is now in jeopardy, being challenged by criteria that are other than medically justified. Initiatives for measuring and improving quality, a new impetus towards evidence-based medicine, and new pressures for fiscal efficiency are characteristic of the 1990s and the coming millennium.

THE TENSION BETWEEN PERCEPTIONS AND REALITIES INVOLVING MARKETPLACE MODELS

The balance between marketplace profit and efficiency models and meeting patient needs is an uneasy one. The profit motive has been accepted as

---

[11] Williams, Stephen J. and Paul R. Torrens, *Introduction to Health Services* 2nd edition, New York: Wiley and Sons 1984, p. XV.

a reasonable and necessary component of doing business. On the other hand, when healthcare providers are seen as profiting excessively from the illness or disability of their clients, the resulting negative perceptions have to be taken seriously and addressed. Many patients feel that they are not getting their money's worth; they believe that their care is in jeopardy of being compromised for financial reasons. They believe that money, and not care, drives the system and threatens their well-being and security.

Caricatures color our perceptions, and while we hear about terrible things happening in managed care, fee-for-service created its own litany of horror stories and breaches of ethics. This does not excuse managed care from meeting challenges effectively, but in fairness, fee-for-service never generated the public backlash or the media attention that managed care has unwillingly spawned. Still, many physicians still see involvement with managed care as a necessary evil rather than as a welcome opportunity. Many physicians think they are calling 1-800-DENY rather than a healthcare partner to get approval to administer medically necessary and covered treatments. They envision having to routinely fight to get what they need for their patients. The result is erosion of confidence in the healthcare system. At its worst, when doctors acquiesce too easily, they become adversaries rather than advocates of the patients.

IDENTIFYING CORE ETHICAL ISSUES AND CHALLENGES IN MANAGED CARE: AN OVERVIEW

Not since the advent of abortion has an ethical issue in healthcare received as much attention and heat as managed care. Ethical issues in managed healthcare are emerging for a variety of reasons in response to an increasing awareness of shared risks, shared responsibilities, and shared accountability among those who operate within the context of a managed care system.

Most healthcare, business, and insurance professionals do not have sophisticated tools to address the complex array of ethical and legal challenges that managed care is generating. Also, we often presume incorrectly that the purchasers of healthcare have a solid understanding of the intricacies of healthcare. Even those who have had the benefit of a survey course in ethics may not possess the necessary skills to define an ethical issue, break it down into simple components, and deal with those components individually. It is hoped that identifying some of the core ethical issues and learning how to evaluate them will be a starting point in the process of problem definition and problem solving. In addition, the decision-making model and other guidelines offered in subsequent chapters will strengthen the reader's ability to address these issues more rigorously and comprehensively. This will be achieved through teaching healthcare professionals how to better frame issues, use decision-making models, evaluate a wide range of alternatives, define solutions, and justify their positions using the most appropriate legal, ethical, clinical, and management principles.

Advocacy is an important tool for carrying out a wide range of professional duties in managed care, and arises as a consistent theme from a variety of perspectives. Because of the pressures of managed care, rationing, gatekeeping, and cost constraints, caregivers must expend additional energy to advocate for those who fall under their care. Knowing what their own professional duties are, including their ethical responsibilities, allows caregivers and other healthcare professionals to determine what they can and cannot do on behalf of their patients.

At the same time, obtaining appropriate guidance and direction for addressing conflict, challenging changes that seem incongruous with appropriate care, and otherwise adapting to a rapidly changing healthcare environment are not easily accomplished tasks. Treating a wide range of ethical and legal issues that arise in managed healthcare environments is equally difficult, since the ethical standards and trade-offs are often unclear or untested and case law is still being formed. When ethical and legal resources do exist to help the caregiver and patient, they are often not known of or not easily accessible. Part of this stems from the fact that the healthcare system is changing so dramatically that policies and procedures that were once helpful may no longer be of use due to the changes that have occurred recently, let alone those looming on the horizon. When dealing with ethical challenges that threaten the very core of what it means to be a healthcare professional or a patient advocate, guidance is even more elusive.

A major concern with such guidelines is the question of how much medical input is involved and how much number crunching occurs without regard for clinical criteria and medical realities. It is not uncommon that arbitrary numbers and guidelines are created by less than forthright healthcare plans in hopes that physicians will cut corners to meet these predetermined goals (while physicians assume that there is some dependable, clinical justification for doing so). In fact, the AMA Council on Scientific Affairs is publishing guidelines to create standards based on scientific foundations to discourage such practices. Also, the Patient Safety Foundation at the AMA, developed in late 1997 and dedicated to reducing error and enhancing patient safety by making the healthcare system safer, will play an important role in this process.

GATEKEEPING

From the patient perspective, gatekeeping is perceived as one of the most insidious elements of managed care. The patient feels that he or she needs to go through a series of hoops just to see a physician, and more hoops to get a timely referral for specialty care. Now, however, triage tactics developed on the battlefield have been instituted in the managed care environment. On the battlefield, where there are often fewer doctors and nurses than are needed, available medics or other personnel make medical decisions that would not be acceptable under normal circumstances. Cost savings, not quality concerns, have fostered this environment of changing accountability and treatment.

The physician gatekeeper, however, is not intrinsically negative. He or she is there to determine medical appropriateness, and can open the gate and direct the patient to specialty services, pharmaceuticals, durable medical equipment, and the like. The physician gatekeeping role can be a facilitative one. On the lower level, the role of administrative gatekeeper is a bureaucratic one and is often associated with delays, difficulties, and frustration. The positive element of gatekeeping is physician-based, because the physician can identify and coordinate appropriate services. Care is not fragmented, for in theory someone is putting the pieces together and coordinating them. This has the potential to be a vast improvement over fee-for-service, in which the incentive is not to refer but rather to keep the patient as long as possible in order to maximize reimbursement. Similarly, coordination between physicians to act in the patient's best interests was often absent.

NEW IMPLICATIONS OF CHANGES IN HEALTHCARE DELIVERY PARADIGMS

If the roles of patient, provider, and payor continue to become more adversarial, we run the risk of devolving into further distrust between the involved parties and turning the field of healthcare into a field of battle. There is no more compelling reason to provide a more solid underpinning for our changing healthcare delivery system and its priorities than the chaos in which we are all currently mired. At the same time, while ethics will not instantaneously and magically solve the wide range of healthcare dilemmas we face, it can offer a more reasoned approach to the evaluation and consideration of possible solutions available to us.

Managed care, particularly capitated care (care for which a physician is paid per person per month in advance of delivering services) has generated drastic changes and ambiguities in the way that patients and providers are viewed. It also poses distinct ethical dilemmas for both patients and providers. Providers are being forced to integrate their operations, the operations of MCOs, and subject their caregiving procedures to the scrutiny of these organizations. Meanwhile, patients feel that they are at risk for inappropriate care, inordinately delayed care, or at times, denial of care, even when it is medically necessary.

The friction between the dual obligations (quality care and cost containment) of managed care is a major challenge that presents difficult ethical issues and is perhaps the common thread found in most issues that will be discussed in this text. Ethical issues that arise in the very process of partnering are to a great extent unprecedented in healthcare. Now the very formation of contractual arrangements entails diverse ethical issues surrounding utilization and medical management, cost sharing, risk sharing, and accountability. Other issues that are not as new to healthcare assume new dimensions in managed care.

Healthcare traditionally has been a dynamic enterprise in which cooperation, collaboration, and sharing were standard. This paradigm has shifted, however, and now for some the controlling force has become cost. This does not preclude sharing, but until providers are seen as collaborating primarily in order to improve the quality of care rather than exclusively to cut costs, negative perceptions will persist. Confidence can be earned by actions, not words and packaging. Employers are demanding greater accountability and better outcomes, and thus are increasingly becoming more interested in whether the plans they pursue offer the quality and services they expect or were promised in their negotiations.

Hidden by the focus on cost and efficiency are presumptions about the roles of the caregiver and the patient. The caregiver-patient relationship, one of intimacy and shared trust, is being replaced by an employer-payor model in which the enrollee is merely a passive recipient in the process of delivery or non-delivery of services. Similarly, the caregiver is transformed into a mere supplier of services, which shifts the caregivers' role from compassionate advocate and teacher to a functional agent whose job is to control costs for the payor. In that role, how do healthcare professionals maintain the autonomy necessary to perform their traditional mission of caring without becoming an adversary of the patient, or at the very least falling prey to the sequelae of mixed allegiances? This conflict is exacerbated in capitated environments in which advocacy and cost control via gatekeeping often clash and undermine the possibility of an effective doctor/patient relationship, transforming advocates into adversaries.

ETHICS AS A USEFUL TOOL

Some major questions have arisen about the effectiveness of ethics as a useful resource tool to help address many of the complex challenges that will be treated in this book. How can an understanding of ethical guidance and principles better equip us to deal with these emerging challenges? Despite the focus of medical ethics in the past on the edges-of-life issues, ethics can be a superb tool to help address the thorny issues we face with the new economics and cost-quality tensions.

It is perhaps even more challenging to apply ethical principles with any degree of consistency across the healthcare continuum. New care settings are creating distinctive and new problems that pose new ethical challenges. Anesthesia problems that haven't been seen for years because of such superb quality control standards are beginning to emerge in some outpatient surgical settings. The transformation from inpatient to outpatient models is intrinsically problematic. The postacute setting also creates some problems for managed healthcare, particularly regarding continuity of care and seamless delivery. The lack of coordination among healthcare settings can be improved, particularly with more aggressive case management, and can be used to identify and advocate for the most effective care. Until that is put into place, however, the needs of patients are falling through the cracks. At the same time, we are seeing dramatic technological improvements that enable better and faster care. Using telemedicine, whether via telephone or the TV, allows clinical information to be transmitted and evaluated in real time parameters and monitored effectively. It is not uncommon, for example, in home-based asthma management, for the patient to log in numerical levels by telephone to computers that tell the patient to modify treatment or to call the physician. Simultaneously, the patient's physician and insurers can be called to discuss follow-up or intervention. These and similar modalities will help us successfully identify patient needs and fill in the gaps in diverse healthcare settings and environments. Nontraditional care requires nontraditional solutions with extra monitoring to ensure quality and safety amidst relatively inflexible regulatory constraints. It is critical that we create resources for developing and enhancing tools for early identification of ethical issues associated with these concerns and for addressing such issues with the goal of developing workable solutions.

LYING AND GAMING: RECIPES FOR FAILURE

Often the most basic ethical concerns are overshadowed by more dramatic and sensational issues. One of the most fundamental issues, lying, is absent from most discussions on healthcare ethics, and yet it is a pervasive concern. Some clinicians perceive lying as a precondition for their interactions with the MCO; it is a customary process in "getting what the patient needs." There is often a fine line between knowing how to package information so it may be readily accepted and lying in order to obtain what the physician wants for the patient. While not the same as lying, gaming is often closely linked to the lying process. Gaming, or learning the way the system works and learning how to "work" it to address your desired ends, involves the intentional process of manipulating people and processes to achieve goals that might otherwise be unachievable. It uses tools such as creative writing and relies on ambiguity, obvious and intentional omissions, and half-truths. When a physician is thought to be gaming the system, there is reluctance to respond favorably to his or her requests for additional time or services because, from the payor side, he or she is untrustworthy. A physician who is known as a consummate gamer may actually jeopardize patient care because his or her recommendations become increasingly suspect. Lying cannot replace good systems and processes for appeals and quality assurance. Sound medical management, conflict resolution, and appeal policies are a necessary part of the architecture of a healthcare system. Lying, communicating false information, or omitting critical information is no substitute to formal means of getting the same thing done honestly. Similarly, when the reviewer manipulates the physician in a sort of bartering or bargaining enterprise, this manipulation and gaming is suspect and should not be tolerated as a modus operandi for business.

CREATING ARCHITECTURES IN WHICH WE CAN ALL COMFORTABLY COEXIST

It is important that we develop caring environments into which patients and providers can more comfortably fit and into which payors are motivated to invest. This cannot be achieved without a guiding mission, a high degree of integrity, appropriate policies and procedures, and a sense of vision. The insured party in a managed care plan must understand that the goal of the organization is to be more efficient and that such efficiency should be in the patient's best interest as well as in the health plan's financial interests. Patients need to know that more conservative medicine, which tries less costly but at the same time less invasive procedures, has value for the patient as well as for the plan. Reducing errors from false positives and false negatives, reducing human error, reducing uncertainty as to whether the patient should call the HMO before dialing 911 in an emergency situation, or using a reasonably prudent person's sense of emergency fall under the ambit of this concern. Patients need to understand the restrictions of their healthcare plan, as well as how to access needed services in a timely fashion. Patients are only informed of what they will receive if they enroll in an HMO, and not what they won't receive. They never get the opportunity to see the elusive master contract. People need to feel confident that they will be taken care of. Managed care organizations can either address this need and correct those problems from within, or they can look forward to lawsuits and increased regulation. In an ideal healthy managed care arrangement, the patient and the provider work together to strike a balance in the delivery of care, avoiding excessive and inappropriate care. If managed healthcare can allay the uncertainty patients face, it can more effectively integrate clinical and financial concerns and make the patient a partner in that process, rather than a warring adversary.

GOOD MOTIVATIONS SURROUNDING MANAGED CARE: THEY REALLY CARE!

MCOs and healthcare plans have much to be proud of. They have offered financially successful healthcare delivery models and stimulated an unparalleled focus on concerns for quality, performance data, and outcome measures. They respond to pressures to provide better care by reducing waste and focusing resources on prevention and broader health concerns than more traditional plans have offered. They have been successful in educating physicians and promoting a range of behaviors toward enhancing quality and efficiency, often doing so at a lower cost. They have shifted from unmanaged to managed care. Partnerships are being formed to get special pricing and support. Data are being collected on a wide range of activities, and information systems and electronic medical records are being developed to provide a seamless continuity of consent and of care.

Subacute care settings that offer appropriate and high quality care for more patients at less cost are flourishing. Duplication and waste are being significantly reduced. The hospital is no longer the locus for most healthcare, and other, more appropriate, care settings are available to more conveniently meet patient needs. Physicians who were rarely concerned about costs are now not only integrating economic considerations into their daily practices, but performing differential assessment of outcomes and appropriate interventions to negotiate rates for care. Cost becomes a factor in the algorithms and decision trees that physicians employ. Even the type of physicians that medical schools are training has been shaped to a great extent by managed care. Ways to intervene to help physicians deal better with capitation have been established and negotiating procedures are more data-based than in the past, so that reasonable carve outs, sharing a reasonable amount of risk and shared accountability, are the rule rather than the exception. Evidence-based medicine is on the rise, and measurement and data collection about a range of healthcare and cost factors are being done at an amazingly rapid rate. With all these developments, many MCOs are making record profits, but with all these good motivations, many of which the public supports, why are these organizations receiving so much criticism?

BAD APPLES TAINT THE BARREL—WHY DON'T THEY CARE?

There are good payors, innovative and thoughtful managed care organizations, and caring physicians working together to improve our healthcare system. There are others, however, who have shortsighted and less-than-laudable goals. A growing number of ethical issues are being discussed in managed care today, not the least of which is the question "Why Don't They Care?" Payors wonder why physicians haven't cared enough about cost to change practice behavior to meet the criteria the payors use to measure effectiveness. On the other hand, both caregivers and the public wonder why some shortsighted payors will sometimes concoct arbitrary guidelines that bear no resemblance to clinical reality in hopes that physicians will modify behavior and save money in the process.

When health plans change clinical standards, apparently without medical input, the public wonders why. Don't they care? When plans are unwilling to provide care that is covered under their plan, or gatekeepers impede or delay access and availability of care, the public wonders: Don't they care? When 4 of the 10 most costly court settlements in the United

States in 1996 dealt with managed healthcare, eyebrows were raised. Don't they care? Hiding behind the Employers Retirement Income and Security Act (ERISA) pre-emption, which limits financial recovery to the amount of the benefit denied and no more (for more on this topic see Chapter 6), and the "corporate medical practice shield," while covering over 100 million people in the United States for healthcare and precluding those who are injured from fair and just compensation creates the question, Don't they care? When caregivers are asked to perform procedures for which they are not equipped in order to save money because of pressure from the payor/plan side, Don't they care? With words like greed, coupled with death, dismemberment, pain, despair, and paralysis arising with great frequency and an increasingly voracious press seeking the horrible and inconceivable for its fodder, Don't they care? What about the studies showing that managed care puts some patients at greater risk than they would be in fee-for-service? Don't they care? When payors and plan administrators say that the reason for complaints, eroding confidence, and dissatisfaction is jealousy of their success or unreasonable expectations on the part of the public, Don't they care? Does threatening de-selection to the patient or the physician who doesn't conform to your standards, even if it is done for valid medical reasons, seem fair? Don't they care? Doesn't the fact that thousands of legislative and regulatory initiatives have been generated to regulate managed care send a message? Don't they care? Should anyone care about the effect on patients of policies that ignore need and designate costly interventions as "investigational" or "experimental," yet split millions of dollars set aside annually for transplants and end up splitting the same amount among the four top executives of the plan as a Christmas bonus? Don't they care? When profit and pleasing Wall Street are perceived to be achieved at the expense of quality, security, and patient safety, Don't they care?

SHARED ACCOUNTABILITY

Many insurers and MCO representatives don't seem to understand the implications of these strong public reactions. They often fail to reflect on the causes of eroding public confidence and increasing regulatory initiatives to control managed care. At the same time, report cards show a high degree of satisfaction and many argue they are an indication of managed care's success. The combination of high scores and high distrust should call the grading system into question. Success cannot be measured by market share and profit alone. Public perception, patient satisfaction, and partner satisfaction are important measures of success as well. The American Association of Health Plans (AAHP), the major managed care trade association, *does* seem to care and in fact is attempting to refocus emphasis on customer satisfaction with its recently drafted philosophy of care.

This philosophy of care states, "We represent a philosophy of care that emphasizes active partnerships between patients and their physicians. . . . We believe that comprehensive healthcare is best provided by networks of healthcare professionals who are willing to be held accountable for the quality of their services and the satisfaction of their patients. We are committed to high standards of quality and professional ethics and to the principle that patients come first."[12] (The full text of the AAHP Philosophy of Care appears in Chapter 7 on Advocacy.)

The AAHP statement reflects the importance of working as partners rather than as adversaries. If all parties have a plan for realizing common goals, the outlook can be quite promising. It has been suggested by some that partnering should offer physicians some way to benefit from the work they do to improve efficiency while using innovative ways to meet patient needs. Achieving a better financial outcome while meeting patients' needs is an example of the kind of clinical accountability that serves patients, the health plan, and the doctor well. Similarly, the health plan should allow the physician to be sufficiently flexible in treating each individual even though projections and cost figures are based on aggregates. Also, it is important to have reasonable mechanisms in place for dealing with special circumstances in ways that might cost the plan less and serve the patient better, even when they cost the plan more yet serve the patient better.

CARE-SETTING–SPECIFIC ISSUES AND ERRORS

There are other issues that arise in managed healthcare that are unique to specific care settings. Acute care settings are, for example, very different from long-term care settings. Care provided in an outpatient surgical center is not the same as that provided in a tertiary care hospital. As mentioned previously, anesthesia-related errors and their attending lawsuits,which have not been seen for years given the tight controls and standards in hospitals, are beginning to appear in outpatient surgery. The home health setting in particular is seeing new cases arise because subacute care in the home is often very complicated and technologically intensive. Cost-saving

---

[12] Guglielmo, p.186.

strategies have resulted in some serious problems. For example, nonprofessional packaging of IV bags has resulted in incorrect concentrations or dosages, which has in turn caused deaths and increased morbidity. Errors resulting from the failure to refer and the failure to diagnose are increasing dramatically. Shifting roles and duties have given rise to problems as well. In many managed care organizations, psychiatrists are relegated to prescribing medications rather than being able to observe subtle changes and then determine appropriate interventions that may involve medication, hospitalization, or continued counseling. Now, less costly personnel (e.g., entry-level social workers) provide that service, and errors that have occurred as a result have led to a barrage of lawsuits being brought against psychiatrists. Even the image of each care setting influences the way the public (and regulators) perceive care. While the hospital is a place where people go to get well and then return home, long-term care often occurs indefinitely. This can create the impression that long-term care is somehow outside the continuum of care. The ethical issues are different as well, for long-term care is associated with legal and political problems from which hospital care, to some extent, remains relatively insulated.

Providers are increasingly required by their own professional standards and ethics, as well as by regulators and state agencies, to provide a certain level of care, yet are compelled by managed care contracts to provide that care at reduced costs, allegedly without compromising quality. They are sometimes asked to limit care in situations in which they perceive patients to be at risk. As a consequence, they need to develop a framework for addressing such challenges, and they must also create formal mechanisms to prevent patient care from being compromised. The problem is that they want the cadre of patients that a managed care contract offers but are afraid that deviations from the predetermined and fixed ceiling of utilization will jeopardize their managed care contract, meaning that it will be withdrawn, or that they will be de-selected.

MAXING OUT

An ethical issue that case managers and physical therapists often raise involves cases in which a patient exhausts his or her insurance benefit and still requires care. These cases may involve severe accidents that require extensive rehabilitation, ongoing chronic disease, care for severely compromised and handicapped newborns, and so on. These cases create enormous problems that could be avoided through appropriate reinsurance for catastrophic benefits or riders for catastrophic benefits. Employers have an ethical duty to ensure that their employees are aware of the risks or shortcomings of the products they offer to them. Employers need to provide (either directly, through reinsurance, or through optional coverages) ways to reduce individual financial risk for catastrophic events, and should integrate such coverages into their negotiated benefit packages. In this way the risk to the individual can be spread over all insured lives. The financial devastation that accompanies a catastrophic event or illness cannot be borne by the individual and should be integrated into the broader coverage of a health plan.

Other ethical issues involved in maxing out include spurious financial tactics, such as when a hospital may charge a patient (for example) $300,000 for a costly admission, but because the hospital is a preferred provider organization, it receives a negotiated discount of, say, 30%. The patient pays his or her 20% coinsurance requirement based on the full $300,000 fee, and furthermore the full fee counts against his or her lifetime maximum. When financial resources are exhausted through extensive rehab or repeated hospitalizations, the maximum is determined by inflated figures rather than what was actually spent. When public aid kicks in, the taxpayer suffers from the inflated financial gain of the third-party payor. Medicare has protections against this activity, but other payors and payment associations are sometimes overlooked and not scrutinized as carefully.

ADMINISTRATIVE ETHICS AND NETWORK GUIDELINES

The renewed emphasis on addressing ethical issues in healthcare has been stimulated by a variety of factors, not the least of which are the aforementioned Joint Commission guidelines for organizational ethics, networks, PPOs, and managed behavioral healthcare, and specifically the rights, responsibilities, and ethics section of the Network, PPO, and Managed Behavioral Healthcare Standards. The standards address such areas as the relationships that delivery systems, networks, or even PPOs have with other organizations or with their own care and service provider organizations. Patients, enrollees, insured lives, and members all need to understand their relationship to the MCO. They must have access to all information that will affect access, availability and quality of care. This, coupled with the comprehensive performance measurement and improvement systems, will help develop standards for risk management tools that can reduce error and improve outcomes.

Failure to comply with these mandates can be viewed as negligence, and in some cases, a regulatory violation that may affect continuing accreditation. Accordingly, these issues will receive even greater administrative scrutiny than in the recent past. Corporate or systemwide mission statements and principles provide administrative direction as well, particularly when such statements are integrated into policies where their importance and impact are clear. Policies can be an excellent means of integrating clinical with organizational priorities. They protect caregivers from liability by providing guidance and ensuring consistency. They can be a source of appeals and consistency when there is a crisis or challenge. At the same time, it does not make sense to create mission statements or to develop policies if the clinical and administrative staff are not made familiar with their existence, their content, and how they differ from previous organizational policies.

MISSION AND POLICY

Supporting ethical standards and sponsoring an ethics program can dramatically shape the way in which caregivers and other staff members interact with their patients and associates. Doing something because it is right has different implications than being forced to comply with a mandate. Regardless of the institutional or organizational setting, if staff see that administrators treat others well and honor their wishes, they will be confident that they will be treated right, and may feel a greater allegiance to the organization.

Clear guiding policies help clinicians and healthcare executives cope with ethical issues, thereby better insulating themselves against legal liability. A primary benefit is a reduction in the number and severity of lawsuits, in which thousands or millions of dollars are at stake. Enhancing quality of care while making timely decisions can result in substantial cost savings. Integrating the clinical and business elements with policies that are understood and followed can create an architecture that can both protect and serve.

A guiding policy can often give clinicians the support they need to appeal a coverage decision, or to proceed with or discontinue a course of treatment. It gives clinicians confidence that they have satisfied their duty to act in accordance with professional standards, ethical responsibilities, and the wishes of the patient. Furthermore, it maximizes liability protection by ensuring the existence of appropriate documentation that clinicians have reasonably pursued an appeals process and informed the patient of what is medically most appropriate, regardless of what the plan pays for. This will help potential enrollees who are interested in getting high-quality care without emotional discomfort. By developing partnerships with patients and their families and gaining their trust, caregivers can engage in joint decision making rather than usurping all patient care responsibilities or forcing them all onto family members. Ethics can be an excellent marketing tool. Organizations should communicate their willingness to honor the wishes of their patients, so long as those wishes are medically appropriate and consistent with the ethical integrity of the profession.

SERVING AGGREGATE POPULATIONS RATHER THAN AN INDIVIDUAL

Serving a population can certainly have positive planning and public health implications, but when it comes to the clinician-patient relationship, clinicians never care for populations—they care only for individuals, and only one at a time. This by no means diminishes the importance of public health concerns; immunizations, cancer rates, and other population studies are valuable tools for physicians, healthcare statisticians, and planners. Viewing populations for trends, public health information, or cost data is, of course, appropriate. Nevertheless, clinicians care for individuals, not aggregates, and they deal with each individual in his or her particular circumstances.

While providers apply statistical measures, outcome data, quality measurements, practice parameters, clinical pathways, decision trees, algorithms, and the like, ultimately they care for the individual patient. These tools exist, in fact, to enhance patient care. The AMA has addressed the need to care for individual patients in a variety of memoranda and policy statements, particularly in its discussions of formularies, prescription drugs, physician duties, and a wide range of ethical and advocacy issues. Many other professional and healthcare trade associations have dealt with these issues as well.

ISSUES ENDEMIC TO MANAGED HOME CARE AND LONG-TERM CARE

Cost-containment efforts and reductions in length of stay have provided strong incentives for early, and sometimes premature, discharges from acute care settings. This has led to a greater focus on delivering health services and caring for patients outside of the hospital setting, a trend that will not only continue but become even more prominent. At the same time, non–acute care settings are experiencing an influx of sicker patients.

Accommodating this change in healthcare delivery will require caregivers to revise old problem solving methods, develop new ones, and consider ways of applying acute-care–level standards in the provision of non–acute care. Subacute care has its own problems in the home health and long-term care markets, many of which deal with unreasonable regulations that are incompatible with real needs and patient care. There are more restrictions in subacute care, which is based on less costly LTC reimbursement models, than in acute care. Because of cost savings factors, most managed care organizations will only reimburse within a long-term care model, rather than a hospital-based model, which includes costly medical visits. For this reason, most managed care organizations contract for services in the less costly settings. The professional caregivers must often coordinate inadequate support, sometimes provided by persons incapable of completing assigned tasks. Identifying appropriate personnel and integrating clinical treatment and rehabilitation requires more coordination in subacute care settings than in the hospital, where everything is already in place. Several of the safeguards and protections that exist in hospitals are either diminished or lacking in less traditional care settings, including quality assurance and risk management committees, morbidity and mortality conferences, numerous attending physicians, fellows and department heads, task forces, ad hoc committees, and so forth.

For example, one distinctive problem in long-term care is that many emergency and medical procedures cannot be performed in long-term care facilities, so patients sometimes need to be transferred to a hospital. This may take decision making out of their control. Hospitals have different perceptions, policies, and procedures from long-term care facilities, and the disparities manifest themselves quite clearly. The inability to obtain medical information in a timely fashion can delay decision making and cause additional anxiety for all involved. If sophisticated diagnostic equipment is needed and the patient must return to the hospital for a specific test, the situation becomes even more complicated and costly.

LEGAL GUIDANCE INVOLVING END-OF-LIFE CONCERNS: AN OVERVIEW

No area of medical ethics and health law has received more attention than issues that arise at the end of life, though ethics and managed care are beginning to take center stage. Readers of this text who are seeking guidance in forming or invigorating an ethics committee, developing an ethics program, or serving on a community-based ethics committee will find that this material has been the fodder of ethics committees since their inception in the 1970s. Those already familiar with these topics or those focusing on negotiation or other business concerns may bypass the case discussions and go to the Chapter 6 discussion on consent and capacity.

While advance directives have been touted as administrative and legislative panaceas, caregivers still struggle with personal and professional conflict under a cloud of perceived legal liability. Recent studies don't offer a glowing report card for the effectiveness of advance directives or of physician compliance with such directives. Chance often determines whether a patient in a hospital or a resident in a nursing home is treated by caregivers who do not disenfranchise him or her, and who enable decision making by the patient or his or her surrogate.

FUTILITY

The issue of medical futility is increasingly being discussed in healthcare ethics and legal contexts as a costly and wasteful way of utilizing limited financial resources. Futile procedures are those that provide no benefit to an individual and often are associated with prolonging the dying process. The issue arises when a person has suffered a serious insult for which there is no appropriate treatment and multisystem failure is occurring. Any last-ditch efforts will be futile and probably will be performed only because of an adamant request on the part of the patient or fear of potential legal liability for the failure to "do everything" on the part of the caregiver. The issue also arises when the natural course of a disease prohibits caregivers from doing anything more than minimally pushing back the moment of death.

In cases of medical futility, the caregivers should focus on doing whatever is in the patient's best interests. Symptom control, keeping the patient out of pain, and ministering to the spiritual needs of the patient and the family are the most important goals. Creating mechanisms for dealing with anticipatory grief will be far more helpful than last-ditch efforts that do no good and could cause harm. Medical futility provisions will become more prevalent as the need to reduce the use of marginally beneficial services becomes greater.

DESELECTION ISSUES

Perhaps the greatest fear physicians in managed care arrangements experience (even more than the fear of being sued) is the potential of deselection, that is, being removed or not renewed to participate in a program from which they derive a significant portion of their income. The fear is more real than at any time in the past, for physicians are being judged on a variety of factors that have been peripheral or unimportant to them in the past. How many patients they see how quickly, how effective they are when they do see them, their frequency of referrals, and other aspects of economic profiling, including frequency of malpractice actions and complication rates, are examples of these factors.

INADEQUATE CARE

Another important ethical issue in managed care arises when a caregiver is providing inadequate or inappropriate care, or when a patient is prevented from having access to care or from seeking alternative care from an out-of-network or delivery system provider. There are emerging issues related to negligent referral and perhaps even to fraud and abuse in which physicians could be liable if they refer to a panel or a PPO that they know maintains unacceptable standards of care.

EXPERIMENTAL, ADVANCED, AND COSTLY PROCEDURES

A misplaced priority in managed care is perceived to be one of the greatest threats to the advance of medical knowledge. Managed care leaders attempt to contract with the most efficient and ideally the best physicians. By enlisting talented clinicians with great diagnostic and prognostic capacities who can provide efficient and timely interventions, MCOs reduce risk and meet patient needs more effectively. Such clinicians also often are the ones who are willing to try new techniques and procedures and want to be able to benefit from developments in the field. If the annual contract does not contain approval to utilize the most recent medical innovations, the physician may be put in a very uncomfortable position. Whereas the physician has a duty to expand the realm of medical knowledge, managed care organizations have often impeded this process and denied "investigational or experimental" procedures. The impact that fiscally driven initiatives are having on our medical education system and innovation is dramatic.

Interestingly enough, clinical experimentation (therapeutic or nontherapeutic) in healthcare is highly regimented. There are phase I and phase II trials, human subject committees, several varieties of oversight committees, and so on. Economic experimentation, on the other hand, has been relatively unregulated, and this double standard needs to be more carefully scrutinized.

ETHICAL CONSTANTS

Whatever course the future takes, there are several constants (some of which are being bent, strained, or reconfigured) involving professional duty, individual responsibility, and ethics, as well as personal and professional integrity and accountability. Caregivers must develop consistent and well-developed foundations for decision making and policy development to reduce the agony of change and provide a proactive forum for problem solving and problem preclusion. Trust, accountability, and integrity should be the foundation for determining need. Decision making should not be based on unrealistic contractual provisions that have been created with little or no medical input from specific provisions, or a master contract that remains hidden from the beneficiary of these services. (These considerations will be treated in greater detail in subsequent chapters, specifically Chapters 6–8.)

Caregivers need to reevaluate their responsibilities and the extent to which they are obligated or willing to advocate on behalf of their patients and their professions. Such responsibilities are not job-specific; they are profession-specific. For example, from the payor side, the nursing-trained external case manager who works for the insurer often serves as an advocate for the patient to obtain the right care in a timely fashion. Too often, we think that the insurer's role is to avoid or delay payment. Many times the professional responsibility and strong advocacy position of the nurse carries over in these contexts and protects the patient when others, including the physician, don't go far enough to provide appropriate care. Insurers can promote efficiency and reduce waste, but must do so by enhancing care and quality through data collection and analysis and involving medical personnel as partners in a process of change and improvement.

Without policies and methods of enhancing one's capacity to deal with complex issues, ethics ultimately boils down to individual opinions. While opinions have an important place in ethical discourse, they must be opinions that have been examined, tested, and revised, and they must always be held provisionally and be open to further refinement. For this reason, this book devotes several chapters to defining ethical issues and justifying and testing provisional decisions. A step-by-step model for addressing complex ethical issues and making justifiable decisions is featured in Chapter 9.

While for some time people have been afraid to avail themselves of healthcare, now even more are afraid that healthcare won't be available when they need it. They may be precluded from getting what they need, whether it is a specific service or procedure, pharmaceuticals, durable medical equipment, confirmation of a diagnosis and prescription for treatment, or even assurance that they are healthy and need not worry. Managed care must better address the needs of the noncompliant patient as well. Often, as people get older, they may become forgetful and may fail to keep up with follow-up care. Though such lapses in care are financially beneficial in the short run for the payors and plans, good medical care mandates that the care be maintained. Also many patients dread medical settings and are worried that their wishes will not be honored. Plans and provider organizations need to develop a viable forum for discussing and resolving ethical issues to ensure that patients are treated with maximum respect and are given the opportunity to refuse or avail themselves of appropriate and timely medical services.

CONCLUSION

Ethics can be a positive force for change. Learning how to deal with legal and ethical issues will reshape the way health professionals provide care. Ethical deliberation can clarify what obligations caregivers have to their patients, enrollees, or whomever they serve. By developing better tools to address ethical issues and justify their decisions, caregivers will become more supportive of their patients and be able to meet the challenges they will face in the future. It is hoped that the exposure to understanding pivotal legal and ethical principles will demythologize what are perceived to be impossible and insurmountable issues and allow caregivers to address ethical challenges of the future.

2 CHAPTER

The Cost-Quality Interface

INTRODUCTION

This chapter will address a variety of issues that arise on the cost-quality interface; it will attempt to integrate cost and quality, when possible to enhance rather than compromise care. When this is not possible it will address the conflicts and tradeoffs that cost-quality dilemmas generate. In many ways this chapter is the pivot upon which the remainder of the book turns. Issues of fiscal and medical integrity, medical necessity, capitation, integrating cost and quality, and ethics comprise the core of this discussion and the debate they generate. The chapter will include discussions of efficiency, evidence-based decision making, and fiscal integrity, and will raise leadership issues. Such questions as "Who is to take the initiative for ethical responsibility?" will be explored in light of considerations of mission and vision. This chapter will include discussions of organizational initiatives to develop standards for quality measurement and performance, and will discuss whether and how efficiency, quality, and ethics can be integrated. The chapter will focus on new initiatives of the Joint Commission on the Accreditation of Healthcare Organizations (JCAHO), The National Center for Quality Assurance (NCQA) and The Agency for Health Policy and Research (AHCPR). Ethical issues associated with performance measurement and information collection, including a discussion of validity,

benchmarking, and confidentiality, will be treated as well. While it is important to have quantifiable measurements to help us better determine and
agree upon what we mean by quality, the ethical dimensions of those issues
often revolve around what we do with that information and how valid and
consistent our measurement tools are. The chapter will focus on the need to
emphasize consideration of the ethical issues associated with measuring
performance data and outcomes, and the need to determine how that information can be used to enhance efficiency and clinical care. Trade association initiatives focusing on the cost-quality interface will also be included. A
discussion of fiscal and medical arrogance will precede the concluding remarks, which will be followed by case studies that will allow the reader to
test new knowledge or new perspectives on the cost-quality interface.

ETHICS ON THE COST-QUALITY INTERFACE

How to integrate cost with quality so that cost considerations do not strangle
quality is the question at the heart of the cost-quality controversy. Amidst
the media blasting of managed care and a host of sensationalized horror stories, there are also legitimate ethical concerns that are often not addressed
adequately. These concerns come from the payor side and the plan side as
well as from the public and through the popular press. Dramatic changes
and innovations in the way we perceive healthcare and healthcare services
are occurring. Many of these would not have occurred without managed
care, which is itself creating a potential for higher quality and more efficient
care. Yet these changes are accompanied by a plethora of emerging ethical
issues. The ethical issues are spawned by the perception that care is being
jeopardized by costs, that gag rules prevent patients from knowing what
they need to know, that physicians are being threatened or thrown out of
health plans for providing such information, or that physicians are hard
pressed to get patients what they need when they need it. All of this colors
the way in which we view innovation and the efficiency that the new healthcare offers. This is further exacerbated by increasingly eroding public confidence and serious provider concerns. The greatest ethical challenges we
face involve integrating fiscal efficiency with quality.

The drive for evidence-based medicine, quality measurement patient
report cards, practice parameters, clinical pathways, and so on all provide the basis for more efficient care, while at the same time providing
a potential for quality improvement in patient care. Yet many of the

physician-generated attempts to arrive at evidence-based criteria are spawned by the fear that if they don't determine these criteria themselves, someone less knowledgeable will do so. These guidelines are created reluctantly with great discomfort as to their validity. In the meantime we must work out the bugs in the system caused by those less-than-scrupulous managed care partners interested in a quick buck at the expense of both their patients and their own long-term survival.

In dealing with ethical issues in managed care, this text will focus less on the managed care's successes than upon its shortcomings, and will then develop some improvements and safeguards. The goal of identifying such problems is not a covert managed-care–bashing crusade, but rather an exercise to help identify core ethical issues and learn how to deal with them more effectively. This is a positive step to help reshape the image, direction, and future of managed care and the many assets it can offer. In achieving this, managed care can be perceived as serving and enhancing, rather than jeopardizing and undermining, our healthcare. What is encouraging is that the managed care markets are becoming more mature about facing potential ethical issues and doing something about them through actions such as eliminating gag clauses, more forthright contracting, and developing better medical management criteria for appeals, second opinions and gatekeeping. At the same time, there remain some suspect business practices, or at least the perception of them, that must be ameliorated to save managed care from being so hyperregulated and so micromanaged that it will lose the flexibility it has enjoyed in the past.

This in no way constitutes an endorsement of a return to the fee-for-service model of healthcare, in which there was little incentive to control costs. But it does advocate changing the incentives of a capitated system that can compromise patient care through unreasonable delay or impediments. To ignore the numerous legislative and regulatory initiatives spawned to control managed care, or the increasing liability and unprecedented numbers of legal verdicts and settlements against managed care, would be a serious mistake that could result in a giant step backwards for MCOs.

MEDICAL NECESSITY AND FISCAL INTEGRITY

One of the pivotal concerns in examining the cost-quality interface involves questions of "medical necessity." Medical necessity for the most part means medical "appropriateness" but the very word "necessity" betrays some of the difficulty involved with this term. The idea of necessary entails "what *must* be, that is, what is *necessary*." Medical necessity is not governed by clinical judgment and examination but by coverage provisions; if something is clinically necessary but not a covered service, it is often been designated as "inappropriate," "investigational," or "experimental" by the payor or plan. In fairness, a similar problem of refusal to pay arose in fee-for-service in that if a procedure was reimbursable the patient would receive it. If, however, managed care is really concerned with quality, it should be concerned with changing old ways.

INTEGRATING FISCAL INTEGRITY WITH MEDICAL NECESSITY

Perhaps the greatest challenge of managed care is to integrate fiscal integrity with medical necessity and high quality. For years, patients have been injured because of unnecessary testing and procedures as well as from delays and impediments to care used as tactics in the practice of defensive medicine. As medical necessity is redefined, we will improve our fiscal situation through minimizing unnecessary testing and procedures, helping the patient in the process. This is a high priority that will reduce clinical uncertainty and unnecessary fiscal exposure. There is an immense amount of waste in the healthcare system, and identifying ways to reduce waste and duplication makes sense. Yet the public must be better informed about why and how this waste can be reduced. The public also needs to know not only why waste costs them money but also that it can put their health at risk. This can help offset the fear that money talks and the patient walks if he or she is aggressive about getting what he or she needs. If the patient is educated about the issues, he or she is more likely to become a participant or partner in this endeavor and become a constructive force in the process.

A model or matrix must be developed for integrating clinical and financial concerns. There is nothing endemic to clinical care that makes it fundamentally inefficient, nor is there anything inherent to financial efficiency that makes its inappropriate for the clinical forum. It's a question of how one integrates these components and considerations. "Integrated" suggests that each of the components helps the other; they become mutually supportive and interlinked rather than blended; it ideally should involve a symbiosis, where each contributes to the other's support, and in so doing, both thrive.

AGGREGATES AND ETHICS

One of the major ways in which managed care attempts to measure and control cost, quality, and the manner in which they negotiate contracts is through consideration of aggregates or populations rather than individuals. Keeping this in mind, the reader will see that many of the ethical and legal issues that arise within the field involve the difficulty managed care has in dealing with individual variation. When working with numbers or aggregates there may be a tendency to focus on the numbers, with insufficient regard for the people those numbers represent. The average cannot be allowed to overshadow the individual. While this dimension is not exclusive to managed care, it can be attributed to the way MCOs often view the populations they serve. In many ways this is a significant difference from fee for service, which views individual patients and episodic illness. To ensure greater trust, MCO medical directors can guard against patients feeling that their individual needs are not being met when they seek care. Ways to realistically account for individual variation and needs can be accommodated in various ways by the MCO as an important ingredient its continued success.

EFFICIENCY AND EVIDENCE-BASED DECISION MAKING

Efficiency is intrinsically good; there is nothing about efficiency to make it negative, yet many feel the healthcare industry strives for efficiency at too high a cost. It is what we sacrifice for efficiency that generates ethical problems and concern. Efficiency suggests doing something better, doing it for less, and getting something more. We compare efficiency with inefficiency. Inefficiency suggests waste, inappropriateness, and inferior quality. Making medicine more efficient is indeed a worthy goal, for there is an immense amount of waste in the industry. We spend in excess of $25 billion per year on defensive medicine[1] that has little clinical rationale and in many cases may actually injure the patient. Efficiency suggests making medicine better, and in so doing better serving the needs of the patient. There is a problem only when efficiency supersedes other factors, such as quality or access to care.

One of the most powerful managed care driven initiatives to reduce waste is its focus on evidence-based medicine and evidence-based

---

[1] *Tort Cost Controls: An International Perspective,* Tillinghast-Towers-Perrin, 1995, from HCLA website.

decision making. We have always been told that the practice of medicine is an art and not a science. In many ways, however, the artists have had unlimited flexibility and sometimes that judgment translated into inconsistency. Too often in the past, medical decisions were based primarily on where the physician was trained or what he or she had recently read. Standards, guidelines, practice parameters, and clinical pathways had little impact on a physician's practice. Managed care has stimulated the injection of data into the art by attempting to put more scientific measurement and consistency into medicine. As data are accumulated and patterns are identified, important goals can be achieved. Best practices can be established for various procedures based on information and data and not just on gut feeling. In the future, it is hoped that justification can be made for discontinuing ineffective and costly procedures that offer limited or no positive results. Having objective standards and information by which to make more informed decisions levels the playing field for all stakeholders.

PRECISION INSTRUMENTS FOR MEASURING QUALITY AND PERFORMANCE: IS OUR ENTHUSIASM PREMATURE?

As one peruses the literature dealing with evidence-based decision making, typified by clinical pathways and guidelines, practice parameters, and formal algorithms used to measure performance and enhance efficiency, the impression gained is that we have much more sophisticated tools than what we actually possess. Most managed care plans are at the level of mean, mode and averages, and do not utilize sophisticated biostatistical and epidemiological assessment tools such as multivariate analyses. The same is true for clinical pathways or guidelines, which are often little more than written articulations of the author's own preferred procedures, which are then tested with other colleagues. The problem is not the effectiveness of the system, or that their data cannot be transformed into helpful information, but only that we are at the beginning of this new process of measuring performance and identifying best scenarios and best outcomes. However, when we begin modifying patient encounter criteria based on information that is crude rather than precise, ethical problems arise in terms of justifying the basis upon which a change is made. Therefore, concerns of drive-through deliveries and dramatically shorter hospital stays for a variety of procedures, if based on crude supposition rather than scientific data, have serious implications.

ETHICAL CONCERNS ENDEMIC TO CAPITATED AND COST-DRIVEN CARE

Capitation has served many physicians and plans well, but has likewise fueled the ire of many others. It needs to be modified to remove some of the disincentives it can create. Just as fee-for-service offered little incentive to refer early but motivated physicians to keep the patient under their own reimbursement umbrella as long as possible to maximize reimbursement, capitation also has a built in incentive to withhold treatment or discourage access. For the physician working in a capitated environment, the "insured life" remains an asset until he or she begins to utilize services. In becoming the "patient," he or she becomes a financial liability—a threat to profits. Worse, the patient may be spoken of as a "moral hazard," a long-established insurance term that refers to the hazard of overutilization to get a greater impact for your investment, that is, more bang for the buck. It seems strange to suggest that customers are immoral when they use what they need and are entitled to. Because it comes out of another's prepaid pocket, are the recipients of the care to be considered immoral? In what other business does the customer, who is the root of the business's financial health, walk in the door and becomes a financial liability rather than creating a financial opportunity? Our capitation system should be adjusted to preclude this perception, which many physicians hold. Some modification of the current capitation system is required to meet initial basic patient needs without the physician being incentivized to not treat. Perhaps a mechanism drawn from earlier HMOs, which provides a certain number of routine visits for "well-person checks" or even "sick-person checks," in which there is an incentive to see patients, check on their health, and promote their well being, should be added to the new paradigm. It may even save money and make people healthier in the long run, consistent with the spirit of the original HMO concept.

Mark Hiepler is the architect and litigator in several of the most influential cases involving managed care, capitation, breach of fiduciary duty and related issues. He is also a major legal pioneer whose initiative and instinct are shaping the direction of managed care liability. His success lies not only in the courtroom but also in offering us insight into 140 cases in which he has helped people get what they need when they needed it without having to go to court. He receives over 150 calls per month for guidance. He is best known for receiving the largest managed care liability verdict for breach of fiduciary duty, in *Fox v. Healthnet,* which rendered a verdict of 89.3 million dollars in a case involving the death of his sister. The doctor–patient relationship was at the core of his sister's tragedy, because her expectation was that she would receive quality care, and that her covered medical needs rather than financial considerations would drive her care. Mark Hiepler argues that *capitation, and its incentives not to treat, transform physicians from advocates into potential adversaries* or at the very least put them in circumstances of conflict of interest that they did not realize they contracted for.

While the ability to influence utilization is not new, the fact that it may cost the person making the decision money is new. In fact, the more a system is capitated, the more likely that capitation can become a perverse incentive. Hiepler uses a brilliant illustration of why capitation creates this problem. He reminds us that 77 percent of Americans are insured through private employers, for whom managed care has a favored status because it is insulated from punitive damages and recovery, being limited to the amount of the benefit denied). (The ERISA pre-emption and MCO's favored status will be treated in greater detail in Chapter 6.) Hiepler speaks to this issue through the example of a bank robber: A bank robber has an obvious incentive to steal. But what if, upon being caught, the only penalty was that he or she would have to return the money already stolen? There would be incentives to steal and no incentive not to steal. In the absence of trust, integrity and accountability, self-interest reigns supreme. When judgment is rendered on the basis of cost rather than medical appropriateness, problems will arise: Patients will be injured and medicine compromised. Medical necessity should never be superceded by cost considerations. If a patient is a good candidate for a procedure for which he or she is covered, then not to proceed in a timely fashion can only be considered blatant fiscal arrogance. Hiepler believes that there are some insidiously unethical elements endemic to capitation.[2] In light of the *Fox v. Healthnet* case and other, examples of breach of fiduciary duty and fiscal arrogance, the California Supreme Court has indicated that:

> The physician has a duty to make a full and fair disclosure to the patient of all the facts which materially affect the patients rights and interests and to take all prudent actions including proper diagnosis or referral to a specialist. A physician is not a patient's financial advisor. The reason why a physician must disclose possible conflicts is not because he has a duty to protect his patient's financial interests but because certain personal

---

[2] This material was drawn from meetings and discussions with Mark Hiepler on November 2, 7, 8, 10, and 21.

interests may affect professional judgments more than just within the standard of care.[3]

SHIFTING FROM FEE-FOR-SERVICE TO CAPITATION

Increasing pressure to reduce healthcare expenditures has generated several questions about the cost-quality interface. These questions pivot on how the delivery of healthcare services will be changed from the patient-centered focus of fee-for-service to the population-based approach of managed care. Will the individual and individual variation be jeopardized at the expense of this change in orientation? The major question is whether quality will be undermined by excessive consideration of cost reduction and control missions. A component of this question involves whether integrating cost and quality will be done in a rational and consistent manner based on accepted and proven principles, rather than haphazardly. Capitation may pose the greatest challenge here, for it may provide incentives to reduce utilization on the basis of cost savings for the physician and at the expense of the patient. Of all the issues discussed in this text, capitation poses the greatest potential for abuse. Many would challenge this assertion, arguing that capitation, which pays the physician in advance per member per month and provides the physician with financial certainty, may outweigh the advantages of fee-for-service. However, capitation has an inherent flaw: Whenever the *insured life* becomes a *patient,* he or she exhausts some of what the physician "already has in his/her pocket." To some extent the patient is a financial hazard. Capitation has a propensity to influence gatekeeping as well, in terms of underutilization and delay. Some contracts even have under-utilization clauses, which focus on cost often to the exclusion of needed and covered care, creating such potential conflicts of interests as incentives not to treat, denials, and even breaches fiduciary duty.

It has been observed that capitated managed care as "orthodox managed care is not a market-oriented approach to reform but rather . . . a form of private sector collectivism"[4] that forces physicians to act not as caregivers but rather as insurers. Emery argues that the real consumer is the HMO or MCO. In capitation, the plan exports all risk to the physician,

---

[3] I am indebted to Mark Hiepler for sharing this information at the American Board of Quality Assurance and Utilization Review Physicians Meetings in New Orleans November 7, 1996 in our *Session on Integrating Managed Care and End of Life Decision Making.*

[4] Douglas W. Emery, M. S. C. Fawson, and Roberta Herzberg, "The Political Economy of Capitated Managed Care." *American Journal of Managed Care* 3 (3) p. 398.

who serves as the insuror, gatekeeper, and caregiver. The authors also note that "it seems odd that in an age of specialization, managed care seeks to swim against the tide of modern capitalism by subsuming specialization into generalism."[5] In this model, gatekeepers, who are generalists, are required to act as if they were specialists. Emery believes that actual risks, which are the realm of insurance, are conflagrated with the risk and cost of rendering care, which he refers to as a conflagration of probability and technical risk. His approach uses economic theory to demonstrate the unethical conflicts capitation poses from an economic perspective.[6]

IDENTIFYING HIDDEN AGENDAS

To better understand the various pressures created by imposing a marketplace model on healthcare delivery, it is necessary to examine some of the covert issues associated with managed care. First, the employer uses the insurer or payor of services under managed care as the driving force behind cost reduction. The employer is insulated by the plan from the frustrated patients and providers; the vehicle for access and denial is the managed care plan itself. Unfortunately, the plan often perceives the patient as an over-utilizer and the healthcare provider as a cost-be-damned, unmanaged, out of control, yet moldable entity. Both the patient and the caregiver in these caricatures are obstacles to maximizing profit. It is not uncommon for the patient to be perceived as fundamentally acquisitive and eager to take as much as possible from the system. Viewed this way, the patient simply wants *more,* not necessarily what is best or most appropriate. Further, use is perceived as abuse, and hindering access to services is perceived as a legitimate protection against overuse. This is perhaps overstated, but if there were no truth to the analysis and no merit to this assumption, there would be no gatekeepers! Patients no longer have the comfort of knowing that their needs will be appropriately met and that quality will not be sacrificed for cost. This is ethically problematic. While marginally beneficial services should be carefully evaluated, there should be no incentives to withhold, discourage, or unreasonably delay appropriate care.

The patient who requires healthcare is neither a moral hazard nor an abuser. When the patient uses medical services, such as having an uncomfortable diagnostic procedure performed, it is not because the patient

---

[5] Emery, p. 401.

[6] This material was drawn from telephone conversations with Douglas Emery on December 1–2, 1997.

enjoys the discomfort or sequelae of the procedure and its preparation. It is done because of prophylaxis, because the patient needs it, or because the caregivers need information to evaluate or diagnose a problem. The patient does not have the procedure performed for the sake of exhausting costly medical resources or to get more play for the buck. In fact, most would rather forego an uncomfortable procedure if it didn't "need" to be done. People use medical services because they don't want to die or compromise their health through failure to receive appropriate care. This is the confirmation patients seek. If patients could confirm or rule out their own suspicions, it is highly unlikely that they would avail themselves of such uncomfortable, time-consuming, or invasive procedures.

FROM CARE TO SERVICES

Notice how even the way we speak about care has changed. Although this is not the direct result of managed care, it comes at a time when people are increasingly concerned that their heathcare is in jeopardy, and accordingly, it must be considered as a factor that shapes the ethical issues that managed care faces. We have transformed our language from talking about "utmost care" to "medically necessary care," to "covered services," down to "ya get what ya get and ya better like it and not complain about it." For many, cost control and cost reduction have become the primary missions rather than considerations to be integrated into the decision-making process.

Again, it must never be forgotten that in a capitated system, while the insured life is an important financial asset, the patient is a financial liability. Without the dollars that patients and employers pay to the insurer, the insurer will cease to exist. Yet, if the patient is not treated as a partner in healthcare, the ability to control costs through motivating healthy behaviors is lost. Caregivers need to think positively about those whom they serve. Patients should be perceived as partners involved in a shared endeavor, not as adversaries or unwelcome intruders.

The physician has been transformed from a professional to a supplier of clinical services. This smacks of the commodity model to which we have just referred. This demeaning reduction represents a dramatic departure from the physician's historical role. The physician is also viewed and evaluated as a profit center. Economic profiling of physicians includes identifying their utilization patterns; data accumulated through profiling is often used to exclude or deselect physicians from participation in a given health plan. As a result, caregivers are more sensitive to costs than they have been in the past. They also recognize the need to integrate the caveats of excess as well as what it means to be a professional into their decision-making processes.

There are two opposing views of human nature at stake here, the negative one already referred to (according to which patients and care-givers are profligate wasters of money and resources) and a more positive one. In the positive view, the caregiver–patient relationship is based on trust and on a commitment to a common goal, the patient's health. The patient is a partner in the care process, and the patient and caregiver jointly attempt to meet needs appropriately while minimizing unnecessary expenses so that the patient's premiums will not go up and the caregivers' profits will not decline. This model sets the stage for better care management, reduces duplication, and serves as a foundation for proactive rationing instead of thoughtless limit setting.

Having confidence that their needs will be met while knowing that some delays in access will occur (which is characteristic of managed care) may be something that patients will have to accept. Both caregivers and patients must try to balance the cost of proposed interventions against their efficacy in achieving desirable outcomes. Cost should simply be a factor to be reckoned with, not the primary driving force or mission. It is important that caregivers nurture a positive role for patients, because if they are only passive spectators, they can expect a backlash of spiraling overutilization. It is also important that caregivers resist the attempts of others to redefine their roles and responsibilities in a way that compromises their professional duty and integrity.

PURCHASERS PERSPECTIVES ON THE COST-QUALITY TENSION

The purchasers of healthcare services often define quality in terms of their own expectations, which are based upon their specific corporate culture and needs. One tool to deal with both cost and quality for large employers as major purchasers of healthcare is disease management, which can help identify trends that can suggest interventions for improving performance. "Disease management is a process driven, defined population based approach that identifies an at-risk disease specific group."[7] It could, for example, refer to an asthma management program covering all beneficiaries in a given company, or more broadly, all members in a managed care

---

[7] "Disease Management Purchasers' Perspectives" by Larry L. Hipp, M.D., M.Sc., 1997, p. 1
  (Drawn from materials to be published in Couch, James, *Chronic Disease Management for 21st century,* Gaithersburg, MD: Aspen Publishers, Inc. (in press).

plan. The dilemma disease management poses for the benefits manager is how to balance the needs of its employees and keep them healthy, happy, and productive while simultaneously pleasing their chief financial officers. The market influence of large employers must not be underestimated. The market is heavily driven by employers and employer coalitions. As of 1995, purchaser coalitions covered more than 30 million insured lives.[8] There are national coalitions as well. In many ways employers don't want to be bothered with health plans. Yet they don't want a benefit to become a grievance; they want to keep their employees happy. Many employers have began to realize that the promise of managed care to deliver quality while reducing cost has focused too heavily on cost and too little on quality and ease of use. Their unions and their memberships are becoming increasingly dissatisfied with their MCOs. Employers want to reduce healthcare expenditures, but not at the cost of creating disgruntled employees. This will be a continuing challenge for managed care until the right recipe can yield the outcome an employer and his/or her employees seek. They must supply what their employees need while controlling rising costs. Business leaders need to become activists and advocate for their employees. To do this they must know enough about the system to make choices that satisfy both their needs and expectations.

WHO SHOULD TAKE THE INITIATIVE FOR ETHICS AND ETHICAL RESPONSIBILITY?

Both the physician and the healthcare organization must take responsibility for both efficiency and clinical integrity. The controlling ethic of how this should be done pivots to a great extent on the discipline and roles of those involved in the organization. Those responsible for fiscal responsibility should act in accordance with their professional standards. At the same time, clinicians need to create environments where care can be provided in an appropriate and timely fashion. A method of identifying ways in which common goals can be achieved is an important part of this process. Communication and creative problem solving can be components in this endeavor, as can the creation of policies and procedures. Organizational policies should be created that are reflective of both medical and efficiency missions, but not to the extent that appropriate care suffers or is undermined by cost-cutting modalities that are inconsistent with what

---

[8] Hipp, p. 14.

patients can reasonably expect to receive. This involves both organizational and clinical commitments to do the right things for the right reasons. If fees need to be restructured to accommodate clinical integrity, then so be it. Being competitive financially should in no way mean being clinically compromised.

EFFICIENCY, QUALITY, AND ETHICS: CAN THEY BE INTEGRATED?

Many in the healthcare industry really believe that efficiency can only be achieved at quality's expense. Interestingly enough, while efficiency and improvement have been long-term mainstays in our commercial environments, significant resistance to such models has been experienced in a wide variety of healthcare contexts. However, greater emphasis on recognizing and learning from our own mistakes, as well as the mistakes of others, is beginning to generate an increased willingness (or at least a decreased reluctance) to improve what we do. Cost-quality tensions are causing us to reevaluate and rethink what we do and how we do it. Ultimately, they challenge us to look at not only whether we should be doing it differently but also whether we should be doing it at all.

The climate of how efficiency is viewed and how measurement and outcomes are integrated into our decision making is rapidly changing. We are being challenged to become agents in shaping our destinies rather than being victimized by novelty and change. Several factors have contributed to our current circumstances, not the least of which is a greater emphasis on accountability for effectiveness, value and quality. There has been intense scrutiny of the very foundations of what we do and why we do it. This tugs at the very definition of what it means to be healthcare professionals and challenges us to rethink our mission, values and vision. As already noted, we are no longer obsessing over whether to use the term "utmost quality" or "highest quality," but are instead looking at what we mean by quality and how we can consistently agree to what quality is and how we determine it. Only after an agreement has been reached can quality be measured and improved. While some we are aiming at identifying the root causes of human error, others wish to go one step beyond and explore the multiple ingredients and variables and their interplay, all of which lie at the heart of this concern. And we are no longer satisfied with mere data collection; we are concerned with transforming that data into information, and then into knowledge, and finally into action. Fortunately, we are no longer satisfied with dealing with symptoms; we are moving towards the underlying foundations themselves. At the very least, there is a shift from quality being what the doctor says it is to looking at evidence-based decision making, practice parameters, clinical pathways, performance assessment and measurement, outcomes, and both clinical and financial efficiency.

Speaking of cost and quality is the same breath was taboo for many years in many healthcare professions. Now, however, these words and their interplay have become part of a vocabulary that many have resisted for years. As already noted, many physician colleagues agree that in the not too distant past it was considered "unethical" to consider cost as a factor in clinical decision making and patient care. There are still those who consider cost and quality considerations inherently opposed to one another. Many feel that the focus has shifted to the point that cost has become a mission rather than a consideration. Critics point to economic profiling, withholds, as well as exporting insurance risk to the physicians via capitation, which they believe have moved the pendulum too far in one direction at the expense of the other, with care being sacrificed for cost.

Despite such caveats and concerns, both purchasers of healthcare and consumers want more rather than less value. This new emphasis on value has generated a demand for greater accountability, effectiveness, and demonstrated value. To meet this need, our tools for assessment and measurement need to be accurate, if not razor sharp. We have sometimes ignored or denied the bluntness and lack of precision of our current instruments; we must evaluate and assess them critically and carefully before uncritically placing our confidence in their merit and validity. This is particularly the case when such instruments have been calibrated to deal with populations and do not account for individual variation and needs. If measurement is aimed at efficiency, and we can get greater returns for the energies and resources invested, all is well. If, however, consumers of healthcare believe that efficiency is achieved at the expense of quality, the inroads that quality improvement can make may be imperiled.

To the surprise of many, looking at what we do and how it can be improved has already yielded some exciting innovations and information. These advances enhance quality and identify best practices while reducing cost, error, and waste. Measurement criteria to achieve and insure continuous quality can be taken from the best of Total Quality Management (TQM) and Continuous Quality Improvement (CQI) and translated into guidelines, standards and parameters that will give us better information and better results. Increased efficiency, less waste and better ways to determine effectiveness are on the horizon. Many of these initiatives have been spawned and nurtured by managed care, measurement, and assessment initiatives.

LEADERSHIP AND ETHICS

Among the most critical challenges we face in this area are of an ethical nature. Leadership imbued with mission integrity, vision, values and accountability lies at the heart of these issues. This means letting data honestly shape improvement and reduce risk to patients rather than cutting costs at all costs. We must avoid extremes where either fiscal or medical arrogance prevents innovation and creates an unwillingness to try to create a better mousetrap. The demand for increased fiscal efficiency and clinical certainty lies at the heart of our challenges today.

INITIATIVES IN PERFORMANCE MEASUREMENT AND QUALITY

It is important to have quantifiable measurements to help us better determine and agree upon what we mean by quality. The ethical issues concern what we do with that information. We need to consider ethical issues when measuring performance data and outcomes. The knowledge we gain, however, must be used to enhance the efficiency and quality of clinical care rather than being used as a justification to compromise it. At the same time we need to be realistic about how refined our tools are and what they can and cannot currently offer.

The Joint Commission has been proactive in promoting the role that performance measurement plays in both the accreditation standards and in its effort to do real-time CQI and TQM through the Joint Commission Indicator Measurement System (IMSystem). The JCAHO was among the first to recognize that performance is tied to leadership commitment and vision. They also understood the importance of finding ways to reduce risk through measuring and identifying areas for improvement in response to complications, risk, and error. If we can transform such data into useful information, we can improve rather than compromise quality and help create a brighter, more manageable future.

NCQA, the leader in the managed care quality assessment and measurement field, recently (August 1996) launched a "Quality Compass" program that provided a wealth of data on health plan quality. Quality Compass is "a national database of comparative information about the quality of the nation's managed healthcare plans."[9] These reports allow key decision makers in the member plans to compare data to enhance quality and outcomes for plans that cover over 28 million Americans. This will allow NCQA to develop benchmarking criteria and to identify regional averages and aggregate performance data that will "help employers and plans set performance goals, monitor improvement and establish overall accountability."[10] The ability to have such information at their disposal will allow for more dependable tracking of improvement and areas to be improved in the managed care industry, through benchmarking and data interpretation. By putting both Health Employer Data Information Sheet (HEDIS) measures and accreditation information in an easily accessible database, employers will be able to assess the quality and performance of their own healthcare plans using reliable national and regional sources.

In March 1997, the Joint Commission launched an initiative to blend measurement with accreditation, called ORYX, which it markets as "the next evolution in accreditation." The goals of the ORYX initiative are to use a flexible, affordable approach to increase the relevance and value of accreditation, to support organizational process improvement, to enhance comparative evaluation, and to strengthen and focus the standards development process to insure quality. The idea behind ORYX is to integrate performance measures into the accreditation process. The data collected will be used as a stimulus for intracycle monitoring and to help evaluate compliance with performance improvement and IM standards. ORYX will offer standardized profiles of each contracted system. The Joint Commission will filter the data to validate format and provide a phased implementation process aimed towards integration. At this time, ORYX only applies to hospitals and long-term care organizations and is in the process of developing ORYX network standards. It is expected that other types of Joint Commission accredited organizations will submit data by the year 2000, including clinical laboratories, behavioral healthcare and ambulatory care organizations. By December 31, 1997, the Joint Commission will have required each of their accredited hospitals and long-term care organizations to select or participate in an accepted measurement system. There are currently 60 such systems. Comparative data for monitoring is required by these accredited entities by 1999.[11]

---

[9] NCQA, *First Release Quality Compass Reports* http://www.ncqa.org/news/qcompass.htm 1996, August 21, p. 1.

[10] NCQA, p. 1.

[11] ORYX Information Bulletin Press Release JCAHO, Oakbrook Terrace, IL, March, 1997.

SOME DIFFERENCES BETWEEN HEDIS AND THE IMSYSTEM

Some of the problems with HEDIS revolve around who is providing the data and how they are packaging it. Also, it can be convincingly argued that other plans with more personnel and time to dedicate to correcting problems and deficiencies can outperform a governmental agency generally not known for rapidity and cutting-edge interventions. A competitor to HEDIS will likely be the Joint Commission, which uses an independent panel outside of the institution to perform a review of outcomes measures and prepares a list for purposes of accreditation. (The HEDIS studies are conducted internally.) "The Joint Commission's Indicator Measurement System (IMSystem) is an indicator-based performance measurement system designed to help healthcare organizations measure and to improve their performance."[12] It includes 31 indicators and those who participate in the system continuously evaluate their data. The Joint Commission envisions that each accredited organizations will be required to participate in a measurement system as a condition of accreditation. The ORYX[13] and ORYX Plus systems are a major step in this direction.

Major corporations are driving the move to managed care much more quickly than anyone might have anticipated. Today, nearly 74 percent of the American work force is in managed care. Less than a decade ago the situation was reversed, with 71 percent of the population insured by indemnity plans. Today, the dominant tool for encouraging competition by making comparison of quality is NCQA's HEDIS, which is perhaps more important to NCQA than even its accreditation process. The Joint Commission has been a leader in accreditation for many years because of its heavy emphasis on the integrity of clinical decision making, as well as its evaluation of health plan sites like long-term care facilities and surgi-centers. Some employers worry about HEDIS' substantive flaws, for HEDIS measures are "upstream" and "process" measures. Also, HEDIS measures are not derived from an independent, established, risk-adjusted, episode-of-care database. This is why successful organizations like Medistat are increasingly asked to perform audits of encounter data. Another difference involves the measures themselves. The IMSystem has a database and HEDIS does not; this is a critical difference. Let us suppose that Health Plan A and Health Plan B submit their own data to HEDIS. HEDIS data are not objective; in fact, they are

---

[12] IMSystem General Information, Oakbrook, IL: JCAHO, March, 1997.
[13] ORYX Information Bulletin Press Release, JCAHO, Oakbrook Terrace, IL, March, 1997.

often prepared by the plan's marketing department rather than driven by episode-of-care data. On the other hand, the IMSystem provides dependable data that can be audited and can serve as vehicle to improve performance by identifying and then ameliorating problems.

Employers are beginning to understand the importance of measures for clinical acute care. They understand this because of a very simple fact: The money is going to cover clinical, acute care. Moreover, more money— lots of it—needs to be spent when clinical care goes awry, and when perioperative complications arise (e.g., costly complications for newborns).

The novelty and advantage of IMSystem over HEDIS is that it is a continuous dynamic process; it is not a front-end–loaded process. It is linked to TQM and CQI standards. It's a process that seeks to identify outliers as well as inliers and to measure and thus enhance quality of care through appropriate outcomes assessment and benchmarking. The benchmarking is external; unlike with HEDIS, it is not performed from within and can serve as a reference point for quality that is external to the institution. IMSystem involves an indicator measurement system in various areas such as obstetrics, anesthesia, trauma, oncology, cardiovascular, medication, and infection control. It looks to establish episode-of-care data as benchmarking data that is compared across the system:

> The IMSystem is national reference database designed to measure organizational performance, stimulate improvement in patient care, and generate reports on quality to meet the needs of patients, purchasers and regulators. It is unlike any other database being national in scope and composed of tested data elements and indicators. It allows hospitals to collect data through existing information systems and minimizes data burden. There are currently 220 hospitals participating in the database. The IMSystem has a help desk and 24 hour technical support.[14]

Another difference between HEDIS and IMSystem is that HEDIS is heavily oriented towards routine services and spending issues, while the Joint Commission's IMSystem is concerned with complications, outcomes, mortality, and adverse reactions. HEDIS is heavily oriented towards process measures, upstream towards populations and with the processes

---

[14] I am indebted to both Dr. Larry Hipp M.D.M.Sc., Vice President for Managed Care, and John B. Laing Ph.D., former Vice President for Corporate Strategy, at the Joint Commission for the information and support provided about the IMSYSTEM and ORYX though several conversations in 1996 and 1997 as well as the copies of overheads from which this information was taken.

within an organization, while the IMSystem is concerned more with what really happened. Another distinction is the focus of the two measurement systems. The HEDIS is oriented towards measurements for health plans, and the IMSystem focuses more on hospitals and acute settings. HEDIS measures tell nothing about outcomes or results in themselves.

THE AGENCY FOR HEALTH POLICY AND RESEARCH (AHCPR)

Another major actor on the performance measurement and quality improvement stage is the Agency for Health Policy and Research (AHCPR), the agency of the federal government charged with supporting research designed to improve the quality of healthcare, reduce its cost, and broaden access to essential services. The agency was established in 1989. It is actively engaged in research, the development of clinical guidelines, and technology assessment, and it is charged with bringing current, dependable, and practical information that is "science-based" to medical professionals, healthcare consumers, and other healthcare professionals and purchasers of healthcare.

Among its 14 major functional components, the agency includes several major components oriented towards quality improvement, measurement, and performance, including the:

- Office of Policy Analysis
- Office of Scientific Affairs
- Office of the Forum for Quality and Effectiveness in Healthcare
- Center for Healthcare Technology
- Center for Outcomes and Effectiveness Research
- Center for Primary Care Research
- Center for Organization and Delivery Studies
- Center for Cost and Financing Studies
- Center for Information Technology[15]

What is particularly interesting about this agency's work is that even if their recommendations could affect only one patient in five the cost savings would be substantial. For example:

- Employers and other private sector payors could save $370 million in treatments and tests for low back pain . . .
- Stroke prevention therapies could save $132 million a year

---

[15] From *Better Quality Can Cost Less: The Evolving Role of AHCPR.* http://www.ahcpr.gov/offices/quality.htm.

- Reduced use of acetaminophen could limit kidney damage and save $100-140 million a year for Medicare's ESRD program
- Optimal antibiotic treatment before surgery could reduce the risk of postsurgical infections and save $22.5 million in hospital costs each year
- Moving appropriate cardiac catherizations to an outpatient setting could save at least $13 million a year
- Urinary incontinence therapies could save at least $7.2 million a year in hospital costs for the under-65 population alone
- On-call medical care to terminally ill patients living at home could reduce hospitalization rates and save up to $27 million a year
- Following acute pain management protocols could shorten hospital stays and save as much as $81 million a year in hospital costs for hip replacement patients alone
- Reducing unnecessary interventions for otitis media in children under the age of two could save up to $170 million a year in medical and indirect costs
- Preconception care and enhanced prenatal care for pregnant diabetic women would net savings of 8.5 million per year
- Using an injectable drug in lieu of surgery for ectopic pregnancy could save $55 million a year in reduced hospital stays and other costs
- Early drug interventions for a common AIDS-related pneumonia can save $48.2 million a year in hospital costs[16]

Obviously, these figures are encouraging and can help chart a path for improvement. What is somewhat unnerving from an ethical perspective is that the emphasis in the way in which this data is presented is on cost savings. This has clear merit, but the most important "savings" amidst the litany of cost savings cited above are found in the reduction of pain and suffering. Reductions are possible in the areas of:

- Pain
- Risk
- Urinary incontinence
- Stroke

---

[16] From *Better Quality Can Cost Less: The Evolving Role of AHCPR.* http://www.ahcpr.gov/offices/quality.htm, pp. 1–2.

- Postsurgical infection
- Loss of work time associated with surgery using drug therapy
- Unnecessary interventions
- Morbidity
- Death

ETHICAL ISSUES IN QUALITY MEASUREMENT AND DATA COLLECTION

The exciting work the AHCPR is doing is both important and laudable. Yet it highlights one of the missed opportunities to bridge the cost-quality gap by showing we can save patient suffering and save money by being more efficient. We need to show how reducing waste and cost is something we should welcome rather than fear. Interestingly enough, while these data and advance measurement and evaluation techniques can be quite helpful, there is scant evidence that one can generalize from one set of symptoms and diseases to the quality of care of another set of symptoms and diseases. It takes skill, time, and money to evaluate the scientific literature, update criteria as science changes, develop and administer data collection instruments, and analyze the results with appropriate methods. It is not surprising, therefore, that the most widely used system for measuring the performance of health plans, the Health Plan Data and Information Set (HEDIS), is based mostly on readily available administrative data. The system contains nine indicators of quality, seven of which are process indicators; five of these process indicators are related to prevention. We do not know whether plans that perform well on the basis of these preventive measures are likely to perform well in the diagnosis and treatment of serious and chronic diseases. The developers of HEDIS understand this problem and recently issued a call for measures other than traditional administrative records. More detailed clinical data will be needed, as will the patients' perspectives on the quality of care received.[17]

Many providers, particularly physicians, "doubt that the current emphasis on quality is really aimed at improving their patients' health."[18] Instead, the regulatory and accreditation agencies "agenda has typically consisted of checking, documenting, study(ing) credentialing processes,

---

[17] Brook RH, McGlynn EA, Cleary PD: *Quality of healthcare,* part 2: Measuring quality of care. New England Journal of Medicine 335(13), p. 969.
[18] NEJM, 335(13), p. 1060.

reviewing the work of oversight committees in hospitals and the like . . ." This is coupled with a skepticism that QA programs may not have done much "to improve outcomes for patients."[19] Interestingly enough, CQI is identified by many physicians as a way of justifying a reduction in length of stay and that quality of care is "made to play second fiddle to the imperative to reduce expenditures . . . *centers of excellence* are essentially schemes to negotiate low-cost package deals for specific services in return for the funneling of more patients to the chosen institutions. Any attempt to document excellence in outcomes and efforts as improvements is little more than window dressing."[20]

BENCHMARKING AND REDUCING ERROR

Data collection and benchmarking aimed at improvement are not without concerns and caveats. A major concern pivots on how information will be used and who will have access to it. While these concerns are far outweighed by the ability to identify and ameliorate problems, to reduce error, and to profit by the use of quality data collection instruments that can inform, improve and significantly reduce morbidity and increased mortality, they should not be ignored. Benchmarking raises some profound ethical and liability issues that may not have been originally envisioned. In may ways such endeavors are unprecedented in that concerns of quality, continuous quality improvement, and ethics supersede concerns about potential liability and exposure. In the past, most of the discussion of error was privileged and protected information. Now its potential to be readily accessible is dramatically increased. If we are truly interested in quality, this is a necessary step in the right direction. The concern may not pivot upon the process of benchmarking, but instead on audit trails with patient identifiers. The idea of providing a real-time way of identifying problems and deficiencies and correcting them promptly has merit but at the same time it may invite dramatic potential liability exposure for the hospital. Let us say, for example, that one facility has a success rate on a given procedure of 4 out of 12 with a high complication rate, and another facility has a success ratio of 10 out of 12 with minimal complications. Assuming that the levels of acuity are similar, does this not blaze a potential trail to liability? This invites scrutiny of the facility with inferior numbers, or at least makes it a likely target for investigation. If it

---

[19] NEJM, 335(13), p. 1060.
[20] NEJM, 335(13), p. 1060.

also leads to efforts to make our facilities safer and better, it may very well be a good tradeoff.

MAKING STRIDES IN QUALITY MEASUREMENT AND ASSESSMENT

The dramatic strides being made in quality measurement and assessment, taking outcomes and new scientific information about medical care and blending them with clinical judgment to provide practical guidance to practicing physicians, is unprecedented. Concurrently, performance and outcome measurement techniques and tools have the potential to offer significant input into how we can improve patient care. Clinical critical pathways and guidelines, and practice parameters and guidelines can provide not only direction but also consistency in how we administer care and how we measure the improvement in our performance. They will afford us better tools and techniques for identifying best practices, identifying and reducing errors, and determining outcomes to enhance efficiency and effectiveness in the way in which patient care is provided. David Blumenthal notes that "the very language of current discussions about the quality of care leaves many physicians tongue-tied and uncomprehending: observed and expected mortality, SF-36, case mix and case severity adjustments, profiles, HEDIS measures, control charts, continuous quality improvement, total quality management, critical paths and appropriateness criteria. None of these terms showed up on the blackboards when most physicians now practicing attended medical school. Few of the terms seem, at first glance, to be related to the day to day realities of providing care for individual patients. . . . (yet) physicians owe it to themselves and to their patients to master the substantive issues of quality of care . . . and elevate the performance of our healthcare system."[21]

While payors and health plans are most vocal about controlling and reducing expenditures and costs, physicians and other healthcare professionals are still in the best position to make the case for improving quality.

AMA, JCAHO AND OTHER TRADE ASSOCIATION QUALITY INITIATIVES

In order to bridge the cost-quality gap, some common ground must be found between payors and providers. The American Medical Association

---

[21] David Blumenthal M.D. M.PP. "Quality of Care: What is It." *New England Journal of Medicine* 335(12) 1996 September 19, p. 891.

provided some suggestions for physicians and other providers for dealing with the revolution in healthcare, as the Joint Commission has in dealing with quality issues as related to leadership, the environment of care, and the management of human resources. "Medical societies, many other private sector organizations, accrediting agencies and government agencies such as the Agency for Health Care Policy and Research [AHCPR] are working at creating the tools necessary for the revolution."[22] Some of these "tools" appear below:

- Practice guidelines that synthesize medical knowledge about a topic to assist physicians in the management of patients. Outcomes research and technology assessment are important sources of information for the development of practice guidelines.

- Utilization review or coverage decision-making systems that review medical decisions made or recommended by physicians. They are based on practice guidelines or algorithms.

- An electronic medical record that allows the measurement and aggregation of outcomes information

- Outcomes research to develop a base of information about what clinical practices are truly effective in helping patients

- Technology assessment to determine what medical technologies are effective in helping patients, and the conditions under which those technologies are effective. Outcomes research is essential to technology assessment.

- Profiling systems to evaluate the quality and effectiveness with which a physician manages patients. Ideally these are based on practice guidelines and algorithms.

- Outcomes reports by providers and health plans that inform the public abut their performance.[23]

The AMA report continues with the importance of:

- Developing standards for outcome measurement and reporting, including the content and format of electronic patient records, and guiding and coordinating efforts to gather outcomes data

- Developing standards for coordinating effectiveness research and technology assessment

---

[22] *Transforming Medicare,* American Medical Association. Chicago: June 22, 1995, p. 2.
[23] *Transforming Medicare,* pp. 2–3.

- Coordinating technology assessment and establishing standards for technology dispersion and use
- Establishing priorities for guidelines development through analyses of variations in practice or important procedures
- Creating guidelines form coordinating the development dissemination of practice parameters[24]

These concerns exemplify the significance of providers and payors working as partners, and represent a clear way in which efficiency and clinical care can be integrated to assure higher quality at less cost.

Interestingly, recent responses to Dr. Blumenthal's articles have been mixed.[25] Many are little more than an individual's opinions about managed care and accountability, and have very little to do with evaluating what the author is discussing. A first step in addressing ethical issues in managed care is to hold our preconceptions and prejudices in abeyance, and evaluate novelty on its own merits. We need to let data speak for themselves rather than to transform them to meet our own interpretations.

FISCAL AND MEDICAL ARROGANCE

One cannot avoid discussing quality in managed care without raising issues of patient satisfaction and confidence. The root of the problem of eroding consumer confidence and provider discomfort is based on "fiscal arrogance." Arrogance is defined as "an offensive exhibition of real or assumed superiority."[26] It involves digging in; it is characterized by inflexibility and an unwillingness to see the other as equally valuable or having something to share. Arrogance is a type of prejudice that precludes undertaking any further examination or investing the time, energy, or interest in exploring other options or alternatives other than those which the arrogant person creates and values. It involves placing the blame outside of one's self and one's control. Fiscal arrogance not only involves making cost the priority, but also includes an unwillingness to be receptive to the importance of other alternatives that are not endemic to the model the fiscally arrogant person adopts. This type of person will, for example, examine statistics, explore outliers, create projections, and make changes

---

[24] *Transforming Medicare*, p. 5.
[25] Letters to the Editor, New England Journal of Medicine, March 13, 1997, 36:(11), pp. 804–811.
[26] *The Random House Dictionary of the English Language, The Unabridged Edition*, ed. Laurence Urdang. NY: Random House 1971, p. 83.

with conscious exclusion or preclusion of medical expertise in determining the clinical viability of such changes.

Fiscal arrogance may also involve a kind of "intellectual fainting." The fainting analogy is borrowed from the French philosopher, Jean-Paul Sartre, and is a wonderful example of the seductiveness of the arrogant posture. Imagine, for example, that a car is heading towards you at high speed. You have no way of avoiding its path. Yet you do not relish the conscious experience of injury or death, so you faint, and qualitatively, at least, you avoid the insult: Qualitatively, it never happens! Fiscal arrogance arises not out of regard for those served but rather a disregard. Fiscal arrogance looks beyond the patient to financial efficiency with little regard for either clinical integrity or patient autonomy.

Medical arrogance bears obvious similarities to fiscal arrogance. The medical arrogant, like the fiscal arrogant, is full of self-importance. For the medically arrogant, malpractice arises not because mistakes or errors are made; it's merely a case of a patient trying to get an easy annuity. The medically arrogant person, rather than trying to reduce uncertainty to a comfortable or manageable realm, ignores its existence. The medical arrogant is often equipped with such phrases as "Are you an idiot?" "Where did you get your medical license?" and, "Is this your patient?" When such approaches are used it creates distance rather than helping the patient. Superseding fiscal and medical arrogance and dealing with cases on the basis of risk and health is a much more acceptable alternative.

Both the medically and the fiscally arrogant shun community. They do not solicit or enlist the support of others; instead, they wallow in their own self-importance. Curiosity and inventiveness are stifled unless they serve the interest of the arrogant person.

CONCLUSION

Addressing ways of solving problems on the cost-quality interface requires collaboration, sharing and communication. We must identify a middle ground on which disparate parties can move without compromising their professional integrity. We must also identify impediments we face so that our creative energies can be enlisted in addressing, not avoiding them. The challenge of integrating legitimate costs with legitimate quality concerns lies at the heart of the ethical issues that arise in managed healthcare. Focusing on fiscal integrity and medical necessity requires working in concert rather than at odds with each other. Superseding arrogance and whining, while identifying better solutions should be our goals. The managed care organizations that can achieve this will be the survivors as well as the victors.

CASE STUDIES

CASE 1

The Quality Assurance Department of the "We Want to Do It Better" health plan wants to initiate a program aimed at physicians they feel have been gaming the system and doing a lot of "creative writing" to justify medical expenses. The goal is less to "catch someone" than to change behaviors and to help determine when there is really a health or risk issue and when there is not. They are taking these steps because of a meeting they had with their utilization reviewers, who have expressed concerns about certain physicians. They know that when a physician is continually perceived to be gaming the reviewers that it is difficult to determine when a case that is "really medically necessary" arises.

The plan wants to require selected physicians to receive some training to deal with this issue, which they see as a matter of quality.

Discussion Questions

- How should they approach this issue?
- Can they address these physicians as a group or must they deal with them individually? Why or why not?
- Should such interventions be discussed up front in contract negotiations with physicians?
- Why is this an ethics of cost-quality issue?
- What can be done to keep such a problem from arising in the first place?

CASE 2

A patient needs relief from severe foot pain. Repeated tests are unable to confirm the source of his pain and discomfort, though it may be related to a condition that requires a surgical intervention. This surgery is a covered medical procedure by the managed care plan. However, if possible, the patient would like to try something more conservative and avoid surgery. He is reluctant to put himself in the hands of a surgeon and lose work time if an orthotic device could solve this medical problem. The orthotic device made by the preferred provider organization was not adequate, so the patient already had another orthotic device, which exhausted the once-in-a-lifetime provision of payment for such devices by the plan.

Discussion Questions

- What duty does the physician have to inform the patient that due to so many complaints about the devices made by the former provider, they have changed providers in an effort to insure quality even though the patient has already exhausted his benefit?

- How can quality assurance within the managed care organization intervene to solve the problems?

- Does the organization have a duty to inform people of inferior or inappropriate devices so that patients can seek alternative solutions to their problems?

3

CHAPTER

Gatekeeping and Other Issues of Special Concern for Physicians

INTRODUCTION

This chapter will focus on topics that are of special concern to physicians, for they affect physicians and their patients most directly. A discussion of gatekeeping and the ethical issues that have been associated with it will open the chapter. An extensive discussion of gatekeeping will focus on exploring what gatekeeping means, "negative" gatekeeping, physician gatekeeping, as well as other gatekeepers, and the ethical and clinical challenges they pose. This will be followed by discussions of challenges to providing routine care, rationing, financial incentives to limit care, gag rules, and associated liability issues. (A more extensive discussion of liability issues can be found in Chapter 6.) For the physician, questions involving potential deselection, how one can reduce the risk of deselection, and polices and procedures dealing with deselection will also be included. In many ways the fear of deselection has become a greater fear than malpractice liability fears of the past. After some concluding remarks, some gatekeeping discussion questions will be included to enhance the reader's understanding of the dimensions of these issues.

GATEKEEPING

Gatekeeping is most often thought of in terms of the physician controlling the gate for access to medical care. Now, however, many other professionals and non-professionals also perform this function. From the patient perspective, gatekeeping is one of the most frustrating elements of managed care, for it is perceived as restricting, delaying, or even preventing what may very well be appropriate care . The patient decides that he or she needs to see a physician but must still pass through several gates in order to do so. First, the patient must get through the pre-recorded telephone message (gate 1), the operator (gate 2), the triage nurse (gate 3), and the physician's nurse (gate 4), before seeing the doctor (gatekeeper and helper). Patients are to visit the physician when they first experience some anomaly or possible symptoms of illness, to determine their medical status, the seriousness of an illness, and ultimately whether the patient needs treatment. In retrospect, a high percentage of such visits have been medically unnecessary, meaning the primary care physician's services weren't necessary and the patient's problem could likely have been handled by another less costly healthcare professional such as a nurse, nurse practitioner, or physician assistant. In the past, we knew that many primary care visits were to get assurance that the patient was all right when he or she experienced some anomaly. However, such conclusions can only be reached in retrospect in many cases. Now, however, battlefield-developed triage tactics have come to characterize managed care. In the battlefield environment, fewer physicians and nurses are available to provide care in that setting. Other personnel make medical decisions that under normal circumstances would not be acceptable.

While managed care is not intentionally designed to be a battleground, it is assuming some of those dimensions. The amplification and extension of gatekeeping is a subtle (or not so subtle) example of this. Gatekeeping is perceived as an obstacle or impediment to access rather than an opportunity for coordinating care. Administrative personnel who in the past primarily handled making appointments are now controlling access to physicians as well as to nurses. While these triage mechanisms are often effective, they may generate problems as well. In fact, one of the 10 largest legal verdicts in the US last year dealt with nurse gatekeeping.[1] Since MCOs pride themselves on contracting with top-notch physicians who are excellent at identifying and understanding the natural history of

---

[1] *Adams v. Kaiser Permanente Foundation of Georgia*, 1996.

diseases, having non-medical personnel serve in a gatekeeping capacity is troubling.

NEGATIVE GATEKEEPING

It is the "negative gatekeeper" who prevents, impedes, delays, or blocks the patient from receiving appropriate care in a timely fashion. In fairness, the physician is not the only gatekeeper. Organizational and administrative elements often cause the gate to open slowly even when access has been approved or suggested by the primary care physician (PCP). Administrative factors that affect access include an overcrowded appointment calendar, specialists who are available only one day a week or some other limited time, or medical services that require patients to travel inconvenient distances. If the physician opens and closes the gate to determine who gets into his or her office, the keeper of the keys to the gate itself presents a more serious problem. The insurance risk that capitated physicians bear severely exacerbates this problem.

Administrative delay in seeing the physician is becoming a much more serious matter than in the past. The greatest problem of the HMO approval process is the need for informed people at the other end of the phone whose goal should be to properly identify problems and suggest appropriate interventions to meet the patient's needs based on medical necessity. Their goal should not be to discourage or unreasonably delay access. We need healthcare professionals (both clinical and administrative) to act in our best interests when we put ourselves, our trust and our confidence in their hands. This kind of trust is one that many in managed care need to re-earn.

THE PHYSICIAN GATEKEEPER

The physician gatekeeper, on the other hand, is there to determine medical appropriateness and can open the gate and direct the patient to emergency services, hospitalization, specialty services, pharmaceuticals, and durable medical equipment. The physician's gatekeeping role is a facilitative one. On the lower level, the administrative gatekeeping function that controls access to the physician is a bureaucratic and often frustrating one. Physician gatekeeping, on the other hand, can have a much more positive dimension than other forms of healthcare gatekeeping. Care should be integrated not fragmented, for in theory physician gatekeeping means that someone is putting the pieces together and coordinating or integrating care. This can be a vast improvement over fee-for-service delivery models where there was little incentive to refer, with incentives to keep the patient as long as possible in order to maximize reimbursement. Similarly, the coordination and continuity of care in fee-for-service is often absent.

ETHICAL DILEMMAS POSED BY GATEKEEPING

A serious problem with gatekeeping hinges on two basic concerns. One is that if the gate will not open or is blocked, will the physician gatekeeper (who has the dual and conflicting role of protecting the plan's assets and also caring for the patient) be compromised? Will the physician be motivated primarily to act in the patient's best interests, or rather out of economic interests external to the patient? Another concern is the armamentarium of gatekeepers through which one must negotiate to reach the physician in the first place. The thicket of administrative gatekeepers through which the enrollee, member, insured life, or patient has to venture is unnecessarily cumbersome, frustrating, and often inappropriate.

The physician gatekeeper stands at the gate to regulate access and availability while determining medical appropriateness. The payor is concerned not with "appropriate" care but only with "care," that is "medically necessary." In this model, the physician can coordinate appropriate services and advocate for the patient by protecting the patient from both overtreatment and undertreatment.

Most discussions of gatekeeping unfortunately focus on the negative interpretation rather than on positive ones. Gatekeeping is a concept often viewed negatively by patients and caregivers alike. It is seen as an impediment to access and availability, a hindrance that must be overcome. The physician or nurse who acts as the gatekeeper may appear to be merely an agent of the payor or plan and not an advocate for the patient. Historically, however, the gatekeeper has been an empowering agent, someone who gets the right thing done at the right time and who has an obvious and dramatic role in reducing inappropriate medical costs while putting no one at disadvantage. The objective of such a gatekeeper is not to ration care by making access difficult or discouraging the patient but rather to assist the patient by ensuring that appropriate services/benefits are delivered.

HEALTHCARE LIABILITY, REFERRALS, AND MANAGED CARE

Besides the more obvious financial incentives to reduce referrals, referrals have other ambiguous connotations depending on how they are initiated.

For example, a contract may specify that as long as referrals are made within the provider network, there is "no cost" to the referring physician. As a result, there is an incentive to refer, because it costs the referring physician nothing; the physician may be able to obtain better diagnostic information for the patient as well as better insulate against potential liability, while reducing his or her workload and increasing patient satisfaction.

One of the unspoken problems caregivers and patients alike face surrounds "negligent referral," a referral to a physician that a caregiver would not otherwise choose. However, because the physician is on the plan's approved panel, and there are no other in-plan options, the referral is made. If the referring physician finds the specialist on the panel to be unresponsive or inappropriate for meeting their patient's needs, what must be done? What if the plan does not have other specialists available? For the patient it is quite difficult and takes a great deal of time to get permission to go "out of plan" to find another specialist and still get the HMO to pay for the services. Referrals have created many ethical problems due to the way in which financial incentives arise that make a physician reluctant to refer. This raises an interesting blend of physician duty, plan loyalty to its members, and informed consent. In May 1996 the American Medical Association issued a report called "Health Care Liability and Managed care: New Data and Its Implications."[2] Among other concerns, much discussion was directed to the obscure limitation in ERISA that says that damages are limited to the cost of the service that should have been performed. ERISA was basically a provision to insure continuity of healthcare plans that operated across state lines without forcing them to conform to each individual state's insurance regulations. The importance of this topic and its implications for MCO liability as well as tort reform will be discussed in greater detail in Chapter 6.

GAG CLAUSES AND INFORMED CONSENT

While their incidence decreased dramatically, gag clauses or gag rules are one of the most ethically insidious vehicles to compromise quality information and medical standards, one with which the AMA dealt expeditiously and effectively. The gag clause is an extrapolation of a gag order typically issued by the courts indicating that one neither discuss nor disclose any information pertaining to a pending case, either indirectly or

---

[2] *Health Care Liability and Managed Care: New Data and Its Implications,* American Medical Association, Chicago, May 1996, p. 2.

directly. An individual who does discuss a pending case will be held in contempt of the court. A gag rule in managed care is an obstacle or an impediment to informing a patient about a particular treatment option or alternative that is not offered in the particular health plan. A physician who violates the gag order can accordingly be admonished or dismissed by the plan. The gag rule undermines and impedes the ability of a physician to do what he or she is obligated to do ethically, legally, and professionally. Basically, a gag rule attempts to gag the physician; that is, it prevents him or her from informing the patient about a treatment that is not specifically covered by the healthcare plan's benefit package. A gag rule violates the fundamental duty of informed consent, which among other considerations mandates that the doctor inform the patient of reasonable alternatives to address his or her condition or complaint. Whether or not the patient avails himself of treatment within or without this plan, that patient has a right to know and the caregiver has a duty to inform the patient about reasonable options. A gag rule is intrinsically unethical in that it thwarts the physician's duty and disables the patient. This is contrary to ethical and medical standards.

Informed consent requires the physician to inform the patient regarding probable risks, probable outcomes and benefits, alternatives that are available, and what the implications are of failure to accept the treatment or procedure. Gag rules attempt to minimize this duty (which of course they do not) by limiting the information concerning what is acceptable and what alternatives exist to the options covered in the plan. There are also mandates that require the physician to inform the patient of any financial incentives which might influence his decision or ability or willingness to treat. Violation of a gag rule can result in a physician being deselected from a managed healthcare plan. Fortunately, the popularity of using these vehicles for non-disclosure is rapidly decreasing.

BEYOND GATEKEEPING: ISSUES OF SPECIAL CONCERN TO PHYSICIANS

Physicians are being forced into some historically unprecedented circumstances. Payment for their services is dwindling, their autonomy has been assaulted and further threatened, and the MCO or delivery system is monitoring their practice patterns and how much they spend. They are "incentivized" not to treat and the physician-patient relationship is constrained and severely jeopardized. In spite of these changes, medicine will survive and physicians will become active agents in change rather than being victimized by change. They will become active participants in the process of shaping the direction of healthcare delivery once they step out of their passive role and begin to show a better understanding of the issues at stake. Already the knowledge base of physicians regarding negotiating contractual relationships with MCOs has increased dramatically, supported by performance data and by the assistance of MSOs, who act as agents for the physician practice as well. (A more detailed discussion of MSOs can be found in Chapter 4 on contracting.)

CHALLENGES TO PROVIDING ROUTINE CARE

Patients are often unaware of what to do when they feel they are not getting appropriate care, or when they are unhappy with their primary care physician or specialist to whom they have been referred, or when they feel they are being unreasonably delayed or impeded from getting care they need. There are formal mechanisms as well as medical management policies and procedures that provide guidance for challenging delays in access or for going outside of plan when need is not being met. The average person, or for that matter the plan's medical director, may not know that the quality assurance component of the healthcare organization can provide them with assistance. Most MCOs have an office manager in their care and service provider organizations (formerly called an ombudsman) who can help in such circumstances.

Generally the lines of authority within most managed care organizations are:

1. Office manager
2. Quality assurance representative
3. Medical director

Patients who avail themselves of these resources can often find assistance in getting problems resolved or at least having them reviewed by the right person with sufficient authority to address and solve them.

RATIONING

One development that has dramatic ethical implications for healthcare is rationing, which one author refers to as "the R word."[3] This concept lies at

---

[3] Havighurst C. "Prospective Self-denial: Can Consumers Contract Today to Accept Health Rationing Tomorrow?" *University of Pennsylvania Law Review,* 1992;140:1755-1808.

the very heart of debate about what kinds of healthcare we should pay for, but it is such a volatile issue that few have the courage to raise it in an honest and forthright manner. Since we do not yet have a coherent way of deciding what we can afford or are willing to pay for on a national basis, we rely on idiosyncratic plans and on the marketplace to shape the future direction of healthcare. Yet, at the same time, issues involving waste, medical futility, the costs of practicing defensive medicine, ineffective treatment modalities, exotic therapies, and reducing financial risks through lifetime caps are all topics being discussed with increasing frequency. Unfortunately, they are discussed in a fragmentary rather than a comprehensive way. Our society's unwillingness or failure to address this topic results in continuing confusion about rationing, despite the fact that care is generally rationed anyway, whether through nonreimbursement, restrictions on access or availability, gatekeeping, delays, or waiting lists.

Rationing is either done covertly, which is more common, or overtly. The goal of rationing is to logically and equitably distribute something— to cut up the pie. Each person should have his or her own piece of the pie (ration), sufficient to fulfill certain agreed upon expectations. The concept of unnecessary care arises when a person has already received his or her ration or for some reason is an inappropriate recipient of care. Of course, there is no need to consume one's portion of the pie if one is not hungry, particularly if the portion will be there if and when it is needed.

The topic of rationing has been repeatedly avoided in the American healthcare debate, while at the same time appropriateness is unquestionably tied to what is reimbursable. The failure to address this topic sensibly has resulted in a tourniquet approach to access to services and a failure to provide the American people with a dependable and consistent healthcare package coupled with sense of security and reliability. As a result, prioritizing and allocating finite resources still remains at a primitive stage of development in our current healthcare system.

There have also been attempts to publicly develop ways to allocate resources and set forth criteria determining what is appropriate and what is only marginally beneficial. The Oregon plan is an excellent example of this.

THE OREGON PLAN

The first statewide attempt to address rationing issues was the Oregon plan, which attempted to provide a much greater breadth of coverage for those in need than most traditional state Medicaid programs. The concept behind the Oregon plan was to extend coverage to those in need by openly discussing and prioritizing the allocation of resources to meet the needs of a wider spectrum of people. The goal was to reduce the use of marginally beneficial services and ensure the use of effective ones. What is interesting about the Oregon plan is that allocation issues were addressed in a public forum and were not left to be decided through chance.

Factors such as efficacy, benefit to the individual, benefit to society, and the like, are integrated into the Oregon plan. It appears that there is minimal quibbling about whether a person will get services so long as the person's condition is listed as covered. The plan is intended to give greater access to a greater number of people rather than provide only emergency services for a select few and a wide range of services for others who are Medicaid-eligible. This approach tries to offer equity for a large group of citizens and is a laudable attempt at fairness and access.[4]

FINANCIAL INCENTIVES TO LIMIT CARE FOR HMOS AND INDEPENDENT PRACTICE ASSOCIATIONS (IPAS)

In June 1990, the AMA Council on Ethical and Judicial Affairs issued a report titled "Financial Incentives to Limit Care: Financial Implications for HMOs and IPAs"[5] which described the financial incentives that managed care plans offer physicians to limit their provision of care. The report focused on the often-precarious role of the physician being forced to decide between allegiance to his or her patients and allegiance to those who finance the his or her livelihood. There are obvious conflicts that arise between providing timely and appropriate care to patients and placating those who either finance a plan or have the power to deselect a physician. Economic profiling often causes great discomfort to the physician who may need more time to make a decision or run additional tests, while external constraints demand that he "be certain quickly." Another major concern in the report is the use of various financial incentives that promote cost awareness among managed care physicians, particularly when such inducements result in inappropriate reductions in the delivery of timely and appropriate medical

---

[4] For additional information, see Garlands, Michael J. "Rationing in Public," from *Rationing America's Medical Care: The Oregon Plan and Beyond*, Strosberg Brookings Dialogues on Public Policy, 1995.

[5] *Financial Incentives to Limit Care: Financial Implications for HMOs and IPAs*, Code of Medical Ethics, Reports of the AMA Council on Ethical and Judicial Affairs, Chicago, IL, June 1990, p. 130–135.

care. This may adversely affect clinical outcomes and impose pressures on physicians to make premature diagnoses which can result in error and danger to the patient. The report underscores the importance of the patient, and explains that the patient's welfare always must be the primary concern of physicians. It speaks to the importance of full disclosure of "all relevant financial inducements and contractual restrictions that affect the delivery of healthcare to patients." The Council also treats issues of patient safety and welfare and discusses a number of potential conflicts of interest faced by physicians practicing in the managed care setting. The Council in no way ignores the significance of cost as a factor in decision making but permits it only to the extent that such cost/benefit determinations are part and parcel of their routine professional responsibility in treating patients. Yet the rationing of resources that results in the denial of a procedure that clearly benefits the patient is inconsistent with the physicians's professional duty.

Informed consent requires physicians to disclose all reasonable treatment alternatives, regardless of cost, as well as probable outcomes, in no way limited to whether such alternatives are covered or not by the healthcare plan. This is extremely important. For example, if a particular pharmaceutical was not provided but could be of great benefit to the patient, the patient needs to know that he or she could attempt to go through the quality assurance department (QA) to access it, or pay out of his or her own pocket. The Council warns against incentives that exploit the physician and insists that incentives should be based on quality rather than on quantity.

DESELECTION ISSUES

Perhaps the greatest fear physicians in managed care arrangements experience is the potential of deselection. The fear is more real than at any time in the past, for physicians are being judged on a variety of factors that have been peripheral or unimportant to them in the past, such as how many patients they see how quickly, how effective they are when they do see them, their rate or frequency of referral, and other aspects of economic profiling. The fear is that physicians will be dropped or de-selected from the plan. Many contracts now have terms and conditions that include provisions that a physician can be terminated or de-selected without cause. In such cases the health plan is not obligated to issue warnings or assure due process, regardless of what the real reasons might be. Interestingly enough, while care is directed towards aggregates, deselection is aimed solely at individuals. When it is in the organization's best interests to make money they treat the aggregate; when it is in their interest to save money, they refocus towards the individual. The challenge for physicians is to stay employed but not to do so at the expense of compromising their patients.

LEGAL REMEDIES AND DESELECTION

The best legal remedy is to appeal to established policies and procedures to determine whether a plan is conforming to its own rules and regulations governing deselection or whether these are ambiguous or nonexistent. Initiating your own discovery process is an important step whether or not legal counsel is involved in establishing a foundation for appeal, and is a worthy endeavor in pursuing a remedy to deselection.

Creating systems as well as policies and procedures to reduce problems and fears associated with deselection can be effectively achieved in a manner that is palatable to the practitioner as well as the healthcare plan. Deselection cannot be based on something that is capricious or whimsical, as *Harper v. Healthsource of New Hampshire, Inc.* has affirmed. It must be based on reasonable measurement criteria. Deselection issues should be enumerated in medical management policies and procedures, including associated appeal processes and due process requirements.

ADVICE REGARDING DESELECTION

The tenor and tone of a policy is an important factor in how a policy is received and perceived. The AMA model of managed care agreement speaks to this dimension in the following excerpt:

> Words matter. Nowhere is that truism more accurate than in the arena of business relationships and the laws that govern them. In medicine, provisions in the agreement that runs between a managed care company and a physician glossed over at the time of signing suddenly spring to life in new and often dangerous ways when a controversy arises that requires interpretation, clarification and resolution. Physicians, as well as their attorneys, too often discover that important issues not negotiated or discussed prior to signing are the very issues that the unread or unnegotiated contract both addresses and interprets in a manner disadvantageous to the interests of physicians and their patients. . . . Today the deteriorating relationship between physicians and managed care organizations which is reflected in the many managed care agreements that make material terms—such as the services to be provided and the compensation to be

paid wholly illusory, and add into the relationship extraneous, punitive provisions that are both unwise and unnecessary.[6]

The chief failing among many managed care contracts is their very ambiguity. Good agreements lead to the creation of well-thought-out medical management policies and procedures, which can facilitate important processes and resolve or even preclude conflict, while providing guidance, clarification, and consistency. Such policies should regulate the criteria and processes used in any deselection action and establish:

- Clear definition of the criteria being used in deselection determinations.
- Clear processes by which all avenues and options are exhausted before a decision to deselect is made
- Fair and equitable processes and criteria for appeals of deselection decisions that identify and outline the pathway of the appeals process
- The role of the medical director in resolving conflicts and appeals attendant to deselection
- The identity of the final arbiter in the determination of a pending deselection decision
- Clear criteria in terms of standards and credentials regarding who is eligible to be admitted to the plan's provider panel
- Performance measurement criteria and quality assessment criteria to determine and define eligibility for renewal to the provider panel
- Reasonable time-specific appointments to the panel rather than open-ended and ambiguous contracts
- A specific range of clinical and economic practice and performance criteria and responsibilities to be expected of the physician
- Physician involvement in the creation of deselection criteria and process

CONCLUSION

The issues discussed in this chapter were intended to highlight not only gatekeeping but also other concerns physicians face, such as deselection based on economic profiling, gag rules, and incentives to limit care. The intent here was less to expose these issues than to offer guidance on how to deal with these issues proactively and to develop policies and procedures so they can be managed more effectively. For example, gag clauses would never have achieved the momentum they reached even in the short run if

---

[6] American Medical Association Model Managed Care Agreement, Part I, Introduction, p. 1.

physicians and legal counsel had been more aggressive about finding out what such clauses entailed and why they were inappropriate. It is also important to discuss issues such as gatekeeping that are perceived differently depending on one's perspective. If the health plan sees the physician gatekeeper as a positive element, coordinating and regulating access and availability, and the enrollee sees it as a hindrance, something that delays access to the physician, this should be highlighted and discussed. If we can appreciate the perspective of others and learn not only from our successes but also from our shortcomings, we can be better at what we do.

CASE STUDIES

CASE 1

A seven-year-old girl with a history of juvenile arthritis is experiencing significant relief from her symptoms from daily pool therapy. In fact, this therapy is the only treatment that has proven to be effective in alleviating her symptoms. Unfortunately, the child lives in a very remote rural area and the nearest pool facility is located over fifty miles from their home. Her parents are unable to invest the time to drive the distance every day for her therapy because they would lose their jobs. If they went after work, the pool would be closed by the time they arrived. They also cannot afford the cost of the pool membership or the cost of gas associated with the travel, and their automobile is not very dependable.

A case manager involved in this particular case was quick to realize that therapy compliance was an important and integral part of helping this child to achieve a dramatically improved quality of life. The case manager approached the girl's physician, trying to find a creative solution to meet the child's needs and do so within reasonable financial limits. She asked the physician, "putting all the typical insurance questions aside, is there any treatment that would help this child improve?" The physician responded rapidly, almost jokingly, "Sure. Get her a pool." The case manager explored the costs of a pool and the cost of daily home therapy visits. She spoke with the family about accepting responsibility for pool maintainance and presented a plan to the payor. The payor agreed to the plan to buy a pool for the patient, because the cost of home care (excluding the pool) was 80 dollars less than outpatient treatment. With therapy compliance, the patient made significant improvement, is attending school regularly, and has not been hospitalized for eight months.

Discussion Questions

- What are the ethical issues here?
- Does the case manager have a responsibility to be as creative as this case depicts?

- How can providers be informed of the flexibility available in care options to provide care when cost savings are clear?

CASE 2

A 20-year-old student is living away from home on a college campus but is covered under her parents health insurance plan. She has a history of cystic fibrosis and has been frequently hospitalized for intravenous antibiotic and respiratory therapy. A new FDA-approved durable medical device has just come on the market that can help her reduce airway constriction and break up many of the clogged secretions she has. This equipment is not covered by her parent's plan but could represent significant cost savings over other forms of treatment. The physician responsible for her care would like to offer her this alternative.

Discussion Questions

- How should this be handled?
- Does the fact that the student is out of town at college make any difference in terms of her needs being met?
- How should the physician approach the payor with this proposal?
- Is this a quality assurance issue?
- Is it an ethical issue?

4

C H A P T E R

Ethical Issues in Managed Care Contracting, Negotiating, and Partnering

INTRODUCTION

This chapter will discuss ethical issues associated with entering into managed care contracts and partnering from both the payor and provider perspectives. By exploring partnering reluctance, key objectives to be considered in negotiating a contract, and the importance of having outcomes data available before coming to the table, the reader will gain a clearer perspective on how to evaluate of these issues. A discussion of management service organizations and their potential role in this process will be explored in terms of outcomes and performance information, practice profiling, benchmarking and providing the statistical base to show a financial as well as a clinical profile. The chapter will address special kinds of partnering such as point-of-service partnering and specialty capitation. It will also explore positive and negative dimensions of partnering. Special topics involving the contract negotiation process aimed at reducing or sharing financial risk such as carve-outs, withholds, provisional outliers, and shared accountability will be discussed. Case studies to illustrate some of the dilemmas which arise in the partnering, contracting, and negotiating areas will be included, each followed by discussion questions related to material presented in this chapter.

PARTNERING

One of the major issues of physician concern that arises in discussions of managed care involves clinicians' ambivalence about entering into relationships with managed care partners. They are uncertain about how to enter into a partnership, how to do so for mutual benefit, how not to be put at unfair disadvantage, and how to protect against legal or financial risk. Increasingly, physicians and other providers are collecting data on outcomes and using them to negotiate an acceptable partnering relationship. This chapter will also discuss the use of carve-outs, provisional outliers, and management service organizations (MSOs) as vehicles to assist in this process, which allows both the provider and the payor to customize contracts, relationships, and ways to deal with risk sharing.

When involved in partnering, the disposition or the posture that one assumes is of utmost importance. If we approach partnering with fixed vision and limited interests in integrating and appreciating the view of the other, little will be achieved. A partnering relationship involves recognition of the other's autonomy and the need for some leeway where common ground can be established and used as a starting point for developing a mutually advantageous relationship. This can provide the impetus for reaching a common vision and shared decision making. A good process will include and prioritize highly desirable as considerations guiding threads in weaving together a contract where all parties are happy with and benefit from the relationship.

In the past, partnering was viewed as a positive development in which two or more parties merged together to offer something better than any party could offer alone. Partnership was an example of the whole being greater than the sum of its parts. Partnering, however, also is perceived negatively by some when it becomes an excuse to become more intimately involved and knowledgeable about the partner. The goal is not mutual benefit but to learn more about the other so as to be better positioned to put him or her at disadvantage. This is not the rule, but rather an important exception that must be guarded against.

PARTNERING WITH SHARKS

Small organizations that partner with larger organizations often fear being asked to do things in a way that compromises them as well as those whom they serve. Large is by no means bad, but a large bully can be a terror. If a prenuptial is necessary because you don't trust the partner, you should probably rethink partnering. When the larger partner has too big a market share for you to ignore, then you need to rely on appealing to professional standards or medical management policies and procedures so that clinical care is not compromised. There is even recent activity in New Jersey for physicians to try to become unionized, for if indeed they are "employees," they should be able to collectively bargain for the standards they require.

Mature partnerships, like any mature relationship, need to allow differing views to be tolerated and vulnerability to be exposed without fear of recrimination or reprisal. With increased pressure to contain costs, there is a good deal of gaming present on both payor and provider sides. The stakeholders who influence how contracts are negotiated include healthcare and business professionals and nonprofessionals from diverse backgrounds, perspectives, and allegiances. There is a great deal of discussion regarding the caregiver caught in the middle, the physician caught in the middle, and certainly the patient caught in the middle. The payor and the employer are often in this situation as well. The big question is how to we get from the middle to where we would like and can reasonably expect to be. New concerns about where to turn, where to appeal, whistle blowing, and unfair business practices are among these concerns, as are concerns of gaming the system, misuse, overtreatment, undertreatment, error, and waste.

MANAGEMENT SERVICES ORGANIZATIONS

One vehicle receiving a great deal of attention is the management service organization (MSO). It is spoken of as either a medical service organization or a management service organization. The MSO is a non-medical entity that may be established within a physician practiceor farmed out to a discrete entity that has no specific relationship other than providing certain services to a given medical practice. The MSO is a "service bureau, providing basic practice support services to member physicians. These services include such activities as billing and collection, administrative support in certain areas, electronic data interchange (such as electronic billing) and other services . . . MSOs can further incorporate functions such as quality management, utilization management, provider relations, member services and even claims processing. This form of MSO is usually constructed as a unique business entity."[1]

---

[1] Kongstvedt, Peter R. *The Managed Health Care Handbook,* 3rd edition, Gaithersburg, MD: Aspen Publishers, Inc., 1996, p. 57.

The MSO can fulfill a number of functions, including monitoring and overseeing data collection. It can collect data on outcome measurements of the practice. It can perform benchmarking functions, construct comparisons and baselines to track practice utilization rates, measure effectiveness in terms of success and complication ratios with a wide range of procedures, and provide the statistical base to show a financial as well a clinical profile. It can identify areas of success and well as areas of improvement. It offers several advantages to the physician practice, such as information about how a given practice compares with other physician practices that an MCO is negotiating with. Physician practices rarely have such data at their disposal. The outcome figures can be used as bargaining tools to achieve higher capitation rates when a physician practice can show that its ability to handle certain cases is greater than other practices. Rates can then be negotiated on the theory that even if your practice is paid a certain increment beyond the previously proposed agreed-upon amount more per member per month, the MCO would still profit more from using the more efficient practice. Having access to the outcomes data of others allows providers to assess their negotiating strength and better determine their worth to the negotiating partner. Such data can increase the willingness and confidence of all partners to negotiate on a fair and equitable basis.

The MSO can also identify practice patterns of other providers in the community and enable the practice to expand and become a more attractive service unit for the large payor. Information on malpractice experience can be a positive negotiating tool as well. The collection and identification of this data can be quite time-consuming. The MSO can also collect data of practice patterns, "best practices," outcomes studies and benchmarking. This, coupled with knowledge of what a fair capitation rate should be for a given specialty, can set the stage for success in conducting fair and open negotiations. Such partnering is unlike those shaky arrangements to work together that are infused with distrust, uncertainty, and a suspicion that the partnership will likely not last. The most successful arrangements and ventures will be those that strive towards mutually beneficial goals. The MSO is an entity to provide the information and foundation to better achieve this; it can collect and organize appropriate data regarding clinical outcomes and practice data, and offer viable solutions that can enhance the negotiation process.

MSOs can work to minimize some of those strategies that are perceived to compromise patient welfare. "Prior authorization procedures can be cumbersome for physicians, prescription caps can be unduly restrictive for patients with chronic conditions, and excessive co-payments can block access to optimal treatment. . . . In addition, personal financial incentives have been used to encourage physicians to switch patients to different drugs, pitting the interests of patients against the economic interests of their healthcare providers . . . Some managed care plans have used techniques to encourage switches to a different drug without ensuring adequate disclosure of the benefits and risks of the different drug to the patient."[2] The MSO can protect against such practices through developing appropriate guidelines and safeguards. This empowers the practice to better negotiate an arrangement that is financially attractive with sufficient flexibility in terms of care. The MSO can serve as a bargaining unit to flesh out issues and insure protections that minimize exposure to problems of health and risk, and in so doing create a healthier foundation for partnering.

POINT OF SERVICE (POS) AND PARTNERING

HMOs and MCOs realize that a major impediment to increasing market share and building a strong provider network has been the reticence of those who have exclusively used fee-for-service settings to relinquish their freedom to choose non-participating providers. Both consumers and providers fear they would be kept from using a facility or provider they felt had special resources, skills or expertise to treat an illness or perform a procedure that the HMO would not pay for. A potential solution to this is the point-of-service (POS) plan, or open access, where HMO enrollees or members "decide whether to use HMO benefits or indemnity style benefits for each case. In other words the member is allowed to make a coverage choice at the POS when medical care is needed. The indemnity coverage available under POS options from HMOs typically incorporates high deductibles and coinsurance to encourage members to use HMO services instead of out-of-plan services."[3] The availability of a POS option can be an effective bargaining tool with an otherwise reluctant provider with whom an HMO would like to partner.

NEW PRESSURES IN PHYSICIAN PRACTICES

In part of a report dealing with ethical tensions generated by cost-containment strategies and techniques associated with managed care, the

---

[2] *Managed Care Cost Containment Involving Prescription Drugs.* Report of the Council on Ethical and Judicial Affairs; CEJA Report 2-A-95 1995, pp. 1–2.

[3] Kongstvedt, *Handbook,* p. 37.

AMA's Council on Ethical and Judicial Affairs deals with situations in which the physician is forced into a position in which he or she is "unduly compromised." "Excessive pressure may be imposed on physicians to preserve resources for other patients and to withhold too much care from individual patients they are treating."As a result, recommendations were made regarding constraints and limitations that should be placed on financial incentives commonly offered by managed care plans. The concern of the AMA council is that such efforts be designed in ways that do not compromise patient welfare or safety or undermine the integrity of the physician-patient relationship. It is important therefore to minimize problems in the negotiation stage and to create a matrix that allows the caregiver sufficient flexibility but also includes the expectation of certain outcomes and appropriate efficiency to meet the needs of the payor. Partnering involves a movement of each side towards the middle without compromising integrity or professional standards. When the results include minimizing overtreatment as well as undertreatment, the goals have merit.

Many of the better health care plans are as concerned about undertreatment as much as they are with overtreatment. They believe their charge is to do the right thing, which means guarding against overutilization as well as underutilization. Managed care organizations that base their physician profiling only on overutilization have a skewed view that focuses more cost than on quality. Quality and costs have to be considered simultaneously to develop sensible and equitable ways to allocate resources.

THE SPIRIT OF PARTNERING: POSITIVE AND NEGATIVE DIMENSIONS

Part of the difficulty in addressing the cost/quality tension or gap comes from the diverse perspectives of key players. Payors, for example, often have their own agenda and in many ways operate in both a manner and an environment that is dramatically different from the clinical forum. If making money by doing the right thing is the goal, there are greater disincentives to do the wrong thing, even it if it may be for the right reasons.

If the caregiver feels that the health plan is unreasonable and forces him or her to go through hoops, the clinician will quickly learn how to package appeals, treatment, or care plans and grievances to achieve the desired result. If physicians feel unduly disadvantaged, they will be more likely to seek loopholes in the system or "game" the system than if they perceive themselves as active partners or agents in a process of improvement and change. Unethical practices on the part of the plan will generate unethical behavior on the part of those with whom the plan interacts.

The disposition one takes towards working with another and the reason one chooses to become a partner should be identified up front as soon as possible to determine whether the fit will be an appropriate one. This involves good communication skills as well as serious up front negotiating with the various parties to identify and select partners who share the same vision for creating a relationship. Educating the partner about common goals as well as creating formal means to resolve conflicts is a critical factor in working together. "All too often, providers are simply given a procedure manual and a metaphorical kiss on the cheek."[4] Partnering should be both an initial and a continuing invitation to work together and share ideas while working towards common goals.

A contract should be a celebration rather than a concession! Good contracting should address needs while minimizing the fear or discomfort of the parties involved. Good medical management guidelines and a mission of the organization are critical ingredients in partnering. Clinicians need some commitment from the partner, whether in the form of a mission statement they ascribe and adhere to, or through policies and procedures they support. Ethical and patient advocacy considerations should be woven into the very fabric of daily practice and the commitment of both caregivers and the broader organization. Refusing to compromise clinical standards, having realistic and effective mechanisms for internal conflict resolution, and integrating patients' wishes into the decision making should be included as well. Clear guidelines on such areas as the relationships that an organization has with other organizations should be discussed and negotiated. Corporate or system-wide mission statements and principles provide direction as well, particularly when they are grounded in integrity, truth, and accountability. Policies are an excellent means of integrating promises made to patients with clinical and organizational commitments. They protect caregivers from liability by providing guidance and ensuring consistency, and serve as support when there is a crisis or challenge.

CARVE-OUTS

Carve-outs mean different things in different contexts, and often constitute critical factors in the negotiating and contracting process. From the

---

[4] Kongsvedt, Peter R., *Essentials of Managed Health Care*, Gaithersburg, MD: Aspen Publishers, Inc., 1995, p. 287.

managed care plan side, a carve-out is defined as a mechanism to separately purchase services that are customarily part of an inclusive managed care package. Carve-outs are most often negotiated for services or procedures that are not controlled by discretionary utilization. For example, an HMO may carve out the optical care benefit and identify an outside or specialty vendor to supply the service.

Carve-outs can also be used to reduce physicians' financial exposure of certain types of procedures, interventions, or treatments. In contract negotiations a carve-out might be a mechanism for addressing adverse cost concerns on the part of the physician or physician group who may want to identify procedures that put them at great financial risk and make the contract less attractive. The physician may, for example, want to cover a wide range of routine procedures but carve out procedures that involve costly surgical and hospitalization interventions. This mechanism can be an important vehicle for negotiation. Physician practices need to become adept at deciding what to carve out based on data that they collect or that they contract with others to collect. Making decisions based on accurate collected information rather than on what you suspect to be true is important for all parties involved in the negotiation process.

PROVISIONAL OUTLIERS

Another way to reduce financial exposure is through agreement on how to deal with cost outliers. Outliers are any standard deviations from the center of a bell curve. They may refer to a physician or patient utilization pattern or any dramatic deviation from the norm or expected range. Provisional outliers are a statistical or mathematical way of arriving at an agreed-upon degree of risk. The parties to a contract settle on what they determine will be the likelihood of patient utilization, and further determine that if patient utilization exceeds a certain amount or if a particular type of high cost procedures arise, costs and financial risks will be shared by both parties. For example, the payor might assume half or all of the costs, depending on the contract provisions. This allows for flexibility in reducing financial exposure for the physician but allows for greater oversight and progressive follow-up on the part of the health plan.

THE CAPITATION LEARNING CURVE

Having some mechanism in place to reduce financial uncertainty and potential disadvantages or advantages for providers while they are on early parts of the learning curve might minimize undertreatment. Perhaps as part of the contract there can be different mechanisms for cost/risk sharing or for a withhold, for example, a time period in which physicians are not pennalized during their learning how to deal with capitation, that is, until they get comfortable working in a capitated setting. This could be a very seductive inducement to capitation and a clear step towards achieving common goals.

CONCLUSION

Managed care contracting, negotiating and partnering are important emerging concerns in the development of healthcare delivery. Too often, partnering has been seen as a soft spot or area of vulnerability when MCOs and physicians were not on equal footing. With the advent of MSOs and using carve-outs to determine degree of participation and degree of risk, a common ground easier to achieve. A partnership should include recognition of the each partner's autonomy and also some leeway where common ground can be established and used as a starting point. With these ingredients in place, a common vision and mission can be shared. As noted above, policies and procedures that are clear about appeals to coverage decisions, second opinions and the like need to be discussed openly, and common goals must be discussed and integrated into the partnership. Leaders of the health plan and physicians should actively engage in this process. In this way, the whole should become greater than the sum of its parts.

CASE STUDIES

CASE 1

A physician has been de-selected by a managed care company (Company A) from one of the mature managed care markets that has an outstanding reputation for quality. The company has followed all due process procedures and has been working closely with the QA and UR professionals in the plan, who concur with the de-selection. The de-selected physician goes to work at Company B. Company A and B merge and now the de-selected physician is part of the new entity, Company AB. The contract negotiating provisions did not address cases like this and there is no is no re-credentialing process in place for the new management entity. Neither are there clear policies and procedures to address this concern. The newly formed plan's medical director was the impetus in the physician being de-selected in the first place for what he believed was substandard practice.

Discussion Questions

- What should be done?
- Who should do what and why?
- Should the de-selected physician retain privileges in the company AB
- What role can UR and QA play in resolving this circumstance?
- What is the primary ethical dilemma here?

CASE 2

An ophthalmology practice is considering partnering with a large managed care organization. The managed care organization is aware that this practice is not too sophisticated about managed care contracting. The practice has little in the way of performance or outcome data about itself. The MCO has offered the practice capitation rates that the practice needs to determine if they "make sense." One of the opthamology partners is aware of a database that contains relevant information about capitation rates for a wide range of specialties across the country. He pays a small fee for the information, which he believes will help the practice make a more informed decision. It is learned from the new data that the MCOs out-of-date capitation rates bear little resemblance to current capitation rates in their market. Despite this suspect business practice, the payor has such a large portion of the community marketshare that the team still considers working with it if the rates are adjusted to reflect the current market conditions.

Discussion Questions

- Is this an organization the physicians should avoid?
- Is gaming an ethical issue? Why or why not?
- Are there any ethical principles, which come into play in any partnering process? Which ones? Why?
- Does the MCO have an ethical obligation to present fair and accurate information to the potential partner?
- Are guidelines needed to regulate transactions among partners. Why or why not?

5

Managing Information and Communications Technologies: Ethical Concerns

INTRODUCTION

This chapter addresses present and future concerns posed by recent improvements in data collection technologies. Included are discussions of confidentiality, security of information, archiving, and problems associated with the replication of errors. (A more detailed discussion of error will follow in Chapters 6 and 8, and privacy and confidentiality are addressed in Chapter 13.) Ethical issues involving information and economic profiling will be introduced. Attention will be directed to the seductiveness of technology, the cost of technology, and the technology of cost. Some practical examples of issues that arise in daily practice will be included in the texts, as will case examples, following some concluding remarks.

ETHICAL DIMENSIONS OF INFORMATION AND COMMUNICATION TECHNOLOGIES

Information and communication technologies pose critical challenges for all in healthcare, particularly when we examine the roles they play as new technologies enter the marketplace. The focus on the cost of technology

and the technology of cost presents ambiguous clinical and ethical implications. These are particularly interesting because information technologies often serve both sides of the cost-quality equation.

DATA WAREHOUSING

Information collection is at an all time high both in the management of
healthcare systems and the provision of patient care. Data is often confused with information. When we speak of data we refer to something like
a crossword puzzle. The puzzle pieces are dumped onto the table and then
we begin to see how it might fit together, how they might be aggregated.
Data warehousing is "the systematic process of transferring data from several diversified sources into a structured, centralized electronic storage
and retrieval system . . . that can later be transformed into meaningful information" to support and facilitate more informed decision making.[1] The
goal of the collection of this data is to transform it into useful information
that can enhance quality and manage healthcare expenditures. The attempt
to integrate functions and define the most appropriate alternative is a good
example of what is meant by a consequentionalist ethic, where an array of
alternatives is assessed and a choice of the best alternative is the goal of
that process. Data warehousing can help determine effectiveness, appropriateness and patient safety.

CONFIDENTIALITY AND PRIVACY: BEYOND ENCRYPTION
AND FIREWALLS

Information technologies are not without their downsides, however, and
one that prominently raises its head is the concern with privacy and confidentiality. Providing appropriate safeguards and protections to ensure
continuity of care and protect patient wishes are the carrot at the end of
the stick. The subtleties and complexities surrounding access to and confidentiality of information can be overwhelming. For example, how do we
protect sensitive information? We know that we can create a wide range
sophisticated encryption codes to limit and all but deny access except for
certain users. Yet despite the best laid plans, human dereliction or error
can ruin the recipe.

---

[1] Littman, Steve. "Data Warehousing in the Managed Care Organization," *Managed Care Medicine*,
    1995, July/Aug., p. 24.

One case to illustrate this arose in the normal day-to-day operations of a medical school, although it could just as easily have happened at a hospital or any healthcare institution. It involved a physician who had accessed a patient database that was highly protected. Only a select few non-physicians in the organization could access this encrypted database. The physician was busily making his entries into the computerized patient record, when his beeper sounded. He left the live terminal and went to the phone to return his call.

Since he was already in the computer, his access code had been used and all safeguards and sophisticated protections had been bypassed. Anyone who now came across the computer in the physician's absence would have complete access. Any changes or modifications made to the patient record would show as being made by the physician who initially accessed those records. There would be no way to distinguish his entries from those made by any unauthorized person.

The possibilities that emanate from this example are almost too numerous to imagine: Patient data could be modified and transmitted to the insurer to have a procedure covered that should not have been; information could be deleted or sabotaged by someone who did not like the physician, or a letter could be written justifying a patient's eligibility for worker's comp eligibility that the physician would otherwise be unwilling to write. As an aside, a camera could be placed at the computer or remotely to guard against this problem to some extent.

There are also issues involving scanning, reporting and confidentiality. The best way to preserve confidentiality is to create systems that reduce error and inappropriate access. The concerns that many have about downloading and transmitting information to the payor, for example the federal government requirements for nursing homes and OASIS for home care, can be color coded or otherwise designated so that sensitive information can be protected from being scanned and transmitted.

ARCHIVING

Archiving is another interesting element in the domain of the patient's medical record. The very fact that modifications can be made to a patient's medical record without adequate archiving or having some way of identifying and confirming what changes were made and who made them raises some interesting concerns about the need for additional safeguards in this area. A potential safeguard, for example, would be going back and checking the archiving process in a manner similar to the word processing programs that allow one to go back several earlier steps while still working in a program. Archiving information to record what was modified, by whom, when, and for what reason can be an important tool for quality assurance, and can provide protection for both the patient and the institution. Otherwise, the patient could be at risk of having many things done to him or her without knowing why. It is not only a data management problem; it has to do with the disposition one assumes when dealing with the information in the first place. This example illustrates some of the privacy concerns with information technologies in terms of who has access and why. Patients put themselves in the hands of caregivers and share intimate personal information. Patients need to know that their medical history is privileged information and they need to know the conditions under which that information is shared. This is an obligation. We must establish clear guidelines and guard against misuse of information.

The computer as a communication device is a pervasive one, and whether it empowers or threatens you depends on whether you have the ability to gain information about what you need to know, or whether someone else is gaining information about you that you may not know or want to share.

Electronic medical records are a logical extension of the computer's use in healthcare contexts. An excellent example of an integrated electronic medical record is illustrated in the "Digital Doc" section of *Postgraduate Medicine*. It discusses a large hospital system that has mainframe-based billing and scheduling are connected to their satellite facilities. It features integrated computerized laboratories, pharmacy, diagnostic imaging, and office and dictation systems. The hospital's goal is to have a "single view clinical workstation for all the computerized systems . . . with all their patient information at their fingertips whenever they need it."[2] The system is interactive, configurable and accessible even from home by modem. Toward the end of the article, the author raises the issue of access and includes caveats concerning privacy and security.

ELECTRONIC MEDICAL RECORDS AND ERRORS

Confidentiality and security are the most obvious problems with electronic medical records. Identifying and correcting errors is less conspicuous, yet

---

[2] Potts, Jerry, M.D., "The Best Medical Record System," *Postgraduate Medicine* Vol (101) 3, 1997, March, p. 31.

poses a significant ethical challenge to protect the interests of the patient. Electronic records have potentially superb protective measures and provide consistency and continuity of information, but there are also some concerns. One of the most serious involves correcting errors, particularly when an error has been replicated as it is transferred from place to place. How does the patient or provider know who has the erroneous information, and how can it be identified and corrected? Another concern has to do with information shared with third parties whose interests may compete with the interests of the patient. How do you protect the patient from the possibility of insurers or employers obtaining patient information to which they should not have access? How do you control information that is accessed by "anonymous parties" via modem? How do you avoid putting the patient at the disadvantage that arises from the very process of care and clinical decision making? Medical assessment and differential diagnoses made while physicians investigate clinical suspicions and run various tests is information that can be downloaded, accessed and interpreted prematurely by third parties. The dynamic nature of medicine creates potential risks by the very process of documenting and logging in diagnostic and prognostic information. Confidentiality to third party payors for billing purposes is also a major concern. The Health Care Access and Cost Commission has instituted new safeguards for patient confidentiality in this domain. Their database has a "subgroup of data [that is] submitted to insurance companies for billing purposes. The patient identifier is encrypted by the insurance carrier. . . . Data regulations have been recently changed to remove the exact date of birth and race variable,"and the Commission has decided to reencrypt the identifier submitted by the carrier."[3]

For example, let us assume that in the process of diagnosis a physician conducts tests on a patient to rule out or confirm the presence of AIDS. While the physician suspected AIDS, the tests results were negative and the patient was not confirmed as having AIDS. However, the same clinical profile and data remain on the chart. How can we still ensure some kind of integrity to prevent a physician's clinical suspicions from being retransmitted or shared with the insurer and still provide the insurer with information it might otherwise legitimately need? What kinds of safeguards can we establish that protect the patient from such information being shared? Again, the fact that error can be replicated electronically in a shared integrated network creates the

---

[3] Wilson, Donald E. M.D. *More on Computer-Based Patient Records.* Letter to the Editor, New England Journal of Medicine 335:(12) 1996, September 19, p. 899.

potential for serious problems. Ensuring that all the information is accurate is another problem.

INFORMATION AND ECONOMIC PROFILING OF PHYSICIANS

Economic profiling and collecting massive amounts of information put physician privacy in jeopardy as well. In the past, physician profiling was limited to peer review, morbidity and mortality conferences, and quality assurance, and focused on physician competence. Profiling conducted now revolves around whether physicians are as cost efficient as their competitors and whether or not they exceeded the capitation rate on the basis of what kind of insured lives and patient profiles they treat. One of the problems with physician profiling is that it does not account well for those physicians who treat high-risk, high-cost patients such as AIDS patients or low birthweight micropreemies.

NETWORKS, BUSINESS, AND PRIVILEGED INFORMATION

Information is important in creating organized delivery systems and establishing effective networks. Interestingly, when we talk about confidentiality, we talk about business and profit and the need for the payor to obtain information. On the other hand, we really talk very little about consent and permission to allow private information to be shared with others. We talk little about consent or permission or the right to determine what should be done with one's own body. Similarly, we often only give lip service to the concerns of keeping information confidential and protected from third parties. Again, managed care plans' focus on aggregates causes potential problems for confidentiality. The individual is not the operant model for decision making. However, when we talk about confidentiality, we deal only with the individual's (not a group or aggregate's) right of privacy. Privacy is not a right assigned to aggregates; it is a right assigned to individuals. Consent is a permission that allows us in healthcare to do through clinical interventions or sharing information what would not otherwise be allowed in the absence of that permission. Yet, in various information technology contexts, the requirement of consent evaporates and patients can lose control over that information. Still, this in no way reduces their right to have that information remain confidential.

LIMITING DISCLOSURE: THE RIGHT NOT TO KNOW

Patients should be able to exercise some kind of control over their medical record in terms of preventing access to certain information, particularly information regarding disabilities, predisposition to a genetic disease, or medical conditions that they do not wish to disclose to outside parties.

The problem is deciding how patient databases should be managed and who should manage them. What safeguards must be established to protect patients from confidential information being used to exploit their disabilities or medical conditions?

Disclosure should be based on the need to know. We should use modern information technology to benefit the patient rather than to put the patient at risk or at undue disadvantage.

INFORMATION "HAVES" AND "HAVE NOTS"

Beyond the more obvious ethical questions of confidentiality—protecting against unwarranted access and the misuse of information—lie more subtle issues, such as limiting access to information. There is an increasing trend to publish journals, reports, and government publications electronically which will only be available only through computerized access. The changes are motivated in the name of cost savings but will likely enhance access for some and exclude others. Disparities between information haves and have-nots are based on who has the technological sophistication and permission to access the information in question. The public may be denied access because of proprietary databases, which specify who may use them, or because of licensing agreements. There are some mixed messages that are sent here, for on the one hand we want to encourage the consumer to become more actively involved in his or her healthcare, and on the other, he or she may be denied access.

MANAGEMENT AND MEASUREMENT SYSTEMS: LIMITATIONS

As already noted, managed care is demanding more information about what is effective and what is not. Practice parameters, clinical pathways, practice guidelines, and diverse performance measurement systems and tools all claim to offer answers to troublesome issues that are often laden with uncertainty. There is a risk that these techniques will be accepted prematurely in a frenzy to create clearly defined outcomes as rapidly as possible. Part of this fear is stimulated by medical specialty organizations themselves, fearing that if they don't create guidelines and parameters someone less informed and knowledgeable than they will. Its motivation is reactionary not scientific. Many of these types of tracking, assessment, and measurement guidelines are in their infancy. We must be careful not to act too quickly. It is important not to put excessive trust in these new tools before they are proved worthy of it.

THE SEDUCTIVENESS OF TECHNOLOGY

Technology can be seductive; it can give us more control over our lives and enhance our freedom. However, it can also be used to manipulate our lives and reduce our freedom. It presents opportunity as well as a danger. New technologies often create new problems, yet technology is often blamed rather than the people who create and misuse it. This is troublesome, for technology enables innovation, unless it is used to distance us from constructive processes. For example, the array of phone prompts through which one must navigate in some telephone networks is an example of disempowerment and frustration rather than enhanced access. On the other hand, when information and communication technologies become handmaidens of medicine and are used to improve care or to provide better information, they becomes exciting and important assets. For example, the electronic medical information card can be a wonderful mechanism, but it creates questions about who can or should have access to the information it provides. Are there regulatory or statutory protections that can prevent the patient from becoming a casualty of information collection and financial efficiency? How do we set limits and provide information sufficient to allow the payors to make decisions?

INFORMATION, TELEMEDICINE, AND LIABILITY

The advent of another information-rich technology, telemedicine, may help address this concern to the extent that providers can better evaluate, diagnose, and know when to refer. This source of information and data collection is not computer-based, although CPUs are involved, meaning data are gleaned and shared through electronic means. Telemedicine can provide real-time access to vital medical information.

The use of communication technologies to monitor patients will enable better communication between patient and caregiver from locations other than the clinical setting, or from one clinical setting to another. This constitutes an important supplement for patient care and adds a sense of security for those patients who do not have the luxury of twenty-four hour in-home support. It can also be an effective vehicle for forming support groups with other patients (particularly those who receive home care), developing a more expanded sense of community, and creating a network for those who suffer from similar ailments. It can provide an opportunity for benefitting from the experience others have in coping with similar illnesses, and facilitates mutual support among patients. It also offers an important sense of worth to a person that is home-bound and can help minimize uncertainty and fear. Even though one may be restricted to the home or physically immobilized, one can still help others rather than be helpless.

Telemedicine can serve as a valuable resource for family caregivers who may be uncertain about wound healing or pain control, and who may require additional information and guidance. If someone can focus a videocamera on the wound site, a clinician at a remote location can communicate additional instructions to the family caregivers while they are transmitting. Perhaps the most serious ethical issues in this domain deal with cost issues, specifically if telemedicine and telecare become a substitute rather than a supplement to hands-on care. Other cost concerns pivot on the willingness of a first or third party payor to provide or reimburse for needed audio-visual equipment in the home.

Telemedicine, including telecare in a wide variety of clinical settings, can increase access to healthcare. It can enhance healthcare providers' diagnostic capabilities by helping them to identify or rule out possible causes of illness. It can also aid them in supervising the provision of healthcare services to patients. For example, health professionals can use the phone to talk over case-related issues with family members ministering to the needs of a loved one in the home. They can also help create a support network between the patient and other patients. Telemedicine saves time and money, and thus it can help fill in the gaps in care caused by tighter and tighter cost constraints.

Perhaps the most serious ethical issue in this domain, however, is ensuring that telemedicine remains a *supplement to* and not a *substitute for* hands-on care provided by trained professionals. One potential problem is patient noncompliance. The caregiver has to trust that the patient is availing himself or herself of the information provided by phone, fax machine, or computer terminal. The patient may have faulty equipment that prevents proper communication, may have a medical condition that interferes with his or her capacity to understand what is being transmitted, or may be simply unwilling to follow the doctor's orders. If the caregiver does not see the patient occasionally, the consequences of these obstacles to compliance may remain hidden.

In addition, there are legal and ethical issues surrounding confidentiality, quality assurance, fraud and abuse, recordkeeping, and licensure that need to be addressed by anyone who engages in this form of care provision. Telemedicine allows caregivers to "treat" patients across state lines, which can also create various problems that need to be addressed.

RELATED ETHICAL CONCERNS ABOUT TELEMEDICINE

Other cost concerns pivot on the willingness of a first- or third-party payor to provide or reimburse for needed audio-visual equipment in the home. Ownership, sale, fair market value, and fraud and abuse issues must also be addressed. Other ethical issues associated with telemedicine include questions of who manages the information concerning the remote patient.

Telemedicine has enormous potential for training and education, and it can easily be integrated into the caregiving process. Legal issues surrounding recordkeeping and confidentiality must be considered, but these generally will present little difficulty.

Economic profiling and doctor privacy is in jeopardy as well. In the past profiling was limited pretty much to peer review M and M and QA, that is, profiling on the basis of competence. Now, however, profiling has assumed other dimensions with money making and putting money at risk being the utmost and primary concerns.

CONCLUSION

This chapter has identified some of the potential ethical issues associated with new and emerging information technologies. Issues dealing with privacy and confidentiality, archiving, telemedicine, profiling and related issues have been highlighted as food for continuing thought. As electronic transfer of data and the electronic medical record become realities, these issues will likely become more important. The goal is to anticipate issues before they arise rather than applying tourniquets after the fact.

CASE STUDY

An error has been made in an electronic medical record to which many other parties have immediate access through the network. The error was overlooked for several weeks. The error has since been corrected, yet paperwork reflecting the erroneous information may have already been generated.

Discussion Questions

- What responsibility does the healthcare organization have to follow up and correct mistakes made from the input of erroneous information?
- Should the patient be informed of the potential problems that may be forthcoming?
- Who is responsible for correcting the errors and for their sequelae?

6

Legal Frameworks, Liability, and the Regulation of Managed Care

INTRODUCTION

This chapter will explore legal foundations of pivotal issues that arise in managed care contexts. It will also identify and define many key legal and ethical concepts. In addressing access to care and availability of services controversies, changing trends in liability, legislative and regulatory initiatives, and remedies, the stage will be set for discussing more specific issues that arise later in the chapter, including key concepts and terms related to legal and ethical issues such as privacy, self determination, duty, and consent. The chapter will then identify and address the most influential legal actions in managed care. It will discuss changes in liability trends and conflicts between clinical judgment and cost containment. It will further examine gag rules and hold-harmless clauses. Joint Commission standards integrating leadership and ethics to better meet legal and ethical challenges will be addressed and complemented by a discussion on the HCLA coalition and AMA initiatives for tort reform. Other legal regulatory issues involving ERISA and antitrust regulations will be followed by a discussion of the cost of liability actions and defensive medicine practices. This will complement some of our earlier discussions on contracting (Chapter 4) and the cost/quality interface

(Chapter 2). This chapter will also set the stage for later chapters on advance directives (Chapter 14) and end-of-life issues (Chapter 12).

OVERVIEW

Growing controversy involving access and availability and the balance of cost and quality, supplemented by a growing demand for high quality and effective care, has intensified the need to understand, anticipate and address a wide spectrum of ethical and legal issues in managed care. Among the emerging legal issues associated with managed care initiatives, many involve a shift in the type of legal actions and initiatives and the shift in focus from malfeasance and nonfeasance to failure to refer or failure to diagnose. A study in 1994 from the Medical Underwriters of California, for example, showed that failure to diagnose cases have increased dramatically since 1990. The study showed that 19 percent of all indemnity involved failure or delay in diagnosis, while by 1994 "these cases comprised 43 percent of the total and accounted for 40 percent of all 1994 indemnity."[1] Outpatient settings dominated the 1994 list of cases involving injury to patients. Another interesting issue involves the fact that settlements and arbitration are much more common now than in the recent past. This method of malpractice claim resolution has been largely confined to Kaiser Permanente, which because of the confidential nature of these arbitration proceedings, is not known by the general public. Cases involving gatekeeping issues are also on the rise, with plaintiffs seeking damages for injuries associated with unreasonable delay and lack of follow-up, while cases involving failure to inform are on the decline. There is a growing array of legal responses to insurance coverage decisions. In fact, more than 400 legislative or regulatory initiatives to control various aspects of managed care were considered in 1995, and 1000s were considered in 1997. When people perceive something to be ethically wrong, they respond that "there ought to be a law." Four of the top ten largest verdicts in the entire US were "managed care cases" involving millions of dollars in awards. There has been increased settlement behavior of cases as well as significant amounts of arbitration, keeping many of these cases out of the courts.[2] Challenges to ERISA and a wide range of other kinds of regulatory and legislative efforts to "control" managed care have been spawned in many states.

---

[1] 1994 California Medical Malpractice Large Loss Trend Study from HCLA website
http://www.wp.com/hcla/castudy.htm (10/11/96).

[2] Tillinghast Study: *Tort Cost Trends: An International Perspective,* from HCLA website
http.//www.wp.com.hcla (11/17/95 Tillinghast-Towers-Perrin).

Staffing issues, including the unavailability of services due to lack of staff to advocate on behalf of the patient, played a central role in some of these verdicts. The largest malpractice award in 1996 involved staffing and rapid access to emergency services. Two of the other largest verdicts last year dealt with gatekeeping and with errors involving lower-cost, inexperienced personnel providing care that required additional training or oversight.

The best way to characterize current liability issues is to say that there is a lot of flux and uncertainty regarding questions of who is ultimately accountable to the patient. That question is changing as rapidly as delivery systems are changing, and becomes more urgently in need of an answer as the number of legal actions against healthcare providers and organizations continues to rise.

Weird things are beginning to happen to claims with increase in enrollments (and consequently, power) of large managed care organizations. Some of the specialties being affected are those that one would not have imagined would have increased exposure. One of these is psychiatry. Psychiatrists in many managed care organizations have had their traditional medical roles dramatically transformed. They are often relegated the task of prescribing drugs because lower level, less medically and clinically astute, and less expensive therapists are providing care. As a result, in a discipline where the ability to observe subtle changes has always been a cornerstone of care and treatment, the increasing distance between the psychiatrist and the patient puts the psychiatrist in the uncomfortable position of being unable to closely monitor appropriate care and dosages.

The field of anesthesiology is experiencing claims in outpatient settings that have not been seen for years. This may be due in part to cost savings associated with purchasing less expensive, less reliable and less current technologies and equipment that are being sold in secondary markets. The problem of error in healthcare is assuming new dimensions. It has become very rare in certain specialties to see certain kinds of errors because of so many safety mechanisms in place; however, when error does happen, it takes a unique trajectory.

LEGAL AND ETHICAL CONCEPTS
Privacy and Self-Determination

The right of privacy is rooted in common law. The privacy right developed out of the concept of trespass, in the context of property, like many common law concepts. It was only extended to deal with persons as an afterthought, for matters of person were generally of less import to the courts than were matters of property. Trespass to persons became transformed into battery, which means little more than unpermitted touching, or an unpermitted violation of a person's privacy. Battery was construed as an insult to that invisible sphere that surrounds each person and is legally protected from intrusions by others.

Privacy is often discussed in healthcare contexts, not so much as a protection but as an overarching right that encompasses such specific examples as the right of self-determination, including the right to refuse treatment, and the right to die as well.

A right is something to which someone is entitled. Normally, it cannot be easily taken away, as a privilege can. A privilege generally has conditions attached to it, conditions that must be met if the privilege is to remain in force. The only way a right can be challenged or undermined is when it conflicts with another right, which it may be balanced against and indeed which may override it. The process of weighing conflicting rights against each other is directed toward arriving at a resolution to what might otherwise be an irremediable problem. Each right is still viewed as legitimate, but one is seen as stronger than the other.

The concept of autonomy, in philosophical contexts, corresponds to the concept of self-determination used in legal contexts. In case law, it was argued as early as 1914, in the Schloendorff[3] case, which said that any individual of sound mind has the right to determine what shall be done to his own body. The concept of self-determination expanded over time to encompass the larger sphere of privacy, including not only bodily privacy but also psychological privacy. According to the concept of autonomy, a person should be free to do as he or she wishes.

One of the first steps in addressing ethical issues is to ensure consistency in the way similar topics are characterized and assessed. This includes assessing policies within a given facility or plan to ensure consistency, continuity, and coherence. It is also important that the policies be congruent with the facility's or health care plan's mission. By evaluating the policies to see whether they meet these conditions, the facility's/plan's staff can reduce administrative frustration and devise clearer mechanisms to prevent and resolve conflicts. Before taking on this task, the staff should be familiar with important ingredients in decision-making and key concepts and criteria for addressing ethical issues.

---

[3] *Schloendorf v. Society of NY Hospitals* 211 N.Y. 125, 105 N.E. 92 (1914).

As mentioned above, rights are adversarial in nature. They are essentially entitlements and are associated with sanctions or penalties levied against those who do not honor them. Not acting in accordance with rights can lead to serious consequences, including claims for financial damages.

People have a private sense of self that partially determines their values, wishes, and choices, and it is they who should decide what is done to them medically. If a patient is not capable of deciding this, a surrogate or substitute decision-maker should act for the patient and tell caregivers what the patient said or would likely have decided were the patient able to do so. Significant problems may arise in such cases, especially when the patient's wishes are unclear or unknown. Determining decisional capacity becomes an important factor in honoring patient intent and identifying what is best for the patient.

CONSENT AND DETERMINING DECISIONAL CAPACITY

In order to make decisions, the patient must be able to understand and appreciate the significance of the information being communicated. Many attorneys who have little experience working with healthcare facilities and little clinical exposure or sensitivity will assert that determining decisional capacity or competence is a legal matter and that persons are considered competent unless legally demonstrated in a court of law to be otherwise. In fact, the clinical determination of decisional capacity is an important part of the clinical enterprise and is a prerequisite for ensuring patient self-determination. It is appropriate to replace the word "competence" with "decisional capacity," for while a patient may not be competent in every sense (e.g., may be unable to handle financial affairs) he or she may still be able to appreciate the significance of a specific medical decision. The important question is whether the patient can understand the significance of a specific medical decision now, not yesterday or tomorrow.

FLUCTUATING CAPACITY

Patients whose capacity fluctuates can make binding decisions when they have or possess decisional capacity. Requiring a legal determination of capacity by a court for a patient with fluctuating capacity seems to be unduly burdensome and impractical. Imagine a scenario where a patient with fluctuating capacity must be reviewed by a court to determine his capacity. He would not necessarily be judged incapacitated, but his thinking is not always dependable and clear. Suppose he wakes up clearheaded and at that point has the capacity to make a medical decision, but loses his capacity while being transported to the court. Later he regains his capacity but loses it again on the way back to the court. The patient might have to be transported back and forth repeatedly before the timing finally is right. In a case of fluctuating capacity, having a court determine decisional capacity is unnecessarily cumbersome and a wasteful use of dollars at a time when resources are limited.

Sometimes there are medical conditions that decrease a patient's capacity. The loss of potential for participating in ongoing decision making will be exacerbated if the patient becomes debilitated or sick as a result of going back and forth to a courthouse. This is a major reason why a clinical determination of capacity to make decisions is often acceptable in a wide range of circumstances. There are cases where a patient has a guardian, but, in the estimation of a caregiver, still has the capacity to make medical decisions. In such circumstances, clear and explicit documentation is critical.

The role of the caregiver is also critical, because the caregiver must balance paternalism against autonomy. The caregiver is not vulnerable like the patient and possesses superior knowledge of the patient's condition and what it implies. Given this discrepancy in power, the caregiver has the opportunity to hinder or disable the patient. The flip side of consent is always the integrity of the caregiver and the caregiver's willingness to honor the patient's wishes. The caregiver should support and encourage self-determination on the part of the patient. When the patient consents to a procedure, the consent is an ingredient of the ongoing process of integrating the patient into the decision-making enterprise.

THE MAJOR CASES: LEGAL ISSUES AND MEDIA PERCEPTIONS

As noted earlier, in the past malpractice cases involved failure to perform or properly perform a procedure. Cases now focus on failure to diagnose or to failure to refer. Breast cancer and mammography are the most rapidly growing areas of legal exposure, followed by colorectal cancer. The public perception is that if the test was performed, you should not get the disease. When people fear they will get less, they demand more! Part of the problem is that with all the changes occurring in healthcare, with new agents and new players and new settings, the legal underpinnings for healthcare delivery have become a complicated maze that must be more carefully negotiated than in the past. Despite the changes, there has been an extreme increase in large medical malpractice awards, which "dominated the top ten verdicts of 1995. [They] allowed for half of the ten largest awards to individual plaintiffs, which ranged from $40 million to $98.3 million. Three of these cases involved brain injuries to babies."[4]

Wickline v. State of California[5]

The most frequently cited case associated with managed care did not occur in a managed care context but arose early in the history of prospective reimbursement. It was not decided until almost 10 years after the case was brought. *Wickline v. State of California* was decided in 1986, and was the first test of a payor's liability. *Wickline* involved a woman who suffered postoperative complications pursuant to a thrombectomy, a relatively uncomplicated surgical procedure. Her attending physician contacted Medi-Cal (as Medicaid is known in California) to request approval for an eight-day extension in order to observe her more carefully and monitor her progress, however, a Medi-Cal reviewer instead authorized only four days. She subsequently developed gangrene, which led to her leg being amputated. A cause of action ensued against Medi-Cal for "negligently influencing a physician judgment" and the lower court found in favor of Mrs. Wickline.

The lower court decision was reversed by The California Court of Appeals on the grounds that the doctor has a duty to reasonably exhaust an appeals process and the doctor is not and should not be exonerated from having such a duty. The court however did dismiss consideration of the role of the payor lightly. The court pronounced that payors "can be held legally accountable when medically inappropriate decisions result from defects in cost containment mechanisms." The court warned that "the physician who complies without protest to the limitations imposed by a third-party payor, when the physicians medical judgment dictates otherwise, cannot avoid his ultimate responsibility for the patient's care."[6]

Wilson v. Blue Cross of California[7]

While not cited as often as *Wickline,* this case has received a great deal of attention. *Wilson v. Blue Cross of California* involved a young man who

---

[4] Lawyers Weekly USA (LWUSA) Section B, Jan. 15, 1996, p. 1.
[5] *Wickline v. State of California* 192 Cal. App. 3d. 1630, 228 Cal Rptr. 661 (Cal.App 2 Dist. 1986).
[6] Rice, Berkeley: "Look Who's on The Malpractice Hot Seat Now," *Medical Economics* 73(15), Aug. 12, 1996, p. 198.
[7] *Wilson v. Blue Cross of California,* 222 Cal. App. 3d. 660, 271 Cal. Rptr. 876 (Cal. App 21d. Dist. 1990) from *Medical Economics* 73(15) Aug. 12, 1996, p. 198.

was suffering from severe depression. The attending physician's treatment plan consisted of four weeks of inpatient care, but only ten days were authorized by the health plan's utilization review company. The physician did not formally appeal the utilization reviewer's decision, and the patient was discharged immediately after the tenth day of treatment. Within three weeks after discharge, the patient committed suicide. Both the UR company and Blue Cross attempted to argue that the case should be dismissed on the grounds that "the denial of extended inpatient care was a payment decision not a treatment decision."[8] An insurance company cannot be dismissed from a case simply by arguing that the treating physician has the sole liability. "If the payment decision was a 'substantial factor' in Wilson's death, the court concluded, the insurer and the UR company could be found negligent and thus 'at least partially liable' in a wrongful death claim."[9]

Fox v. HealthNet[10]

This case involved a 38-year-old woman, Nelene Fox, who suffered from metastatic breast cancer. After exhausting a course of standard doses of chemotherapy, her approved HMO oncologist told her she needed an autologous bone marrow transplant to hopefully arrest her disease and save her life. Fox was told that she was a good candidate for such a procedure. What followed was alarming and unfortunate, because Nelene's treatment was both a covered benefit and determined to be medically necessary by her oncologist. Despite that, coverage was later denied on the grounds that such a procedure was investigational or experimental, and that it was not routine conventional therapy. The transcript from one of the important depositions in this case described the change of heart on the part of her physician who was convinced by "a very persuasive individual able to change physicians' behavior in a way that helps the company's bottom line." These events resulted into an egregious case of bad faith denial of care. It was not a question of efficacy; it was a question of fiscal arrogance. It involved the question of how a physician's bonus pivoted on how many treatments were denied, creating incentives not to treat instead of incentives for treating well and providing quality care. The longer the delay, the

---

[8] Rice, p. 198.
[9] Rice, p. 199.
[10] *Fox v. Health Net*, Riverside Superior Court No. 219692 (Cal. Super. Ct. Dec. 23, 1994).

easier it would be to demonstrate that this costly treatment modality was not going to be effective. Despite testimony to the contrary, no clear causal relationship was demonstrated between the existence of an unused fund with millions of dollars set aside to pay for transplants for plan patients, and Christmas bonuses of a similar amount shared by the top four executives in the plan. This situation still seemed to have some impact on the jury, as did the fact that the local medical group wanted to fundraise to help Nelene Fox, but they were dissuaded or discouraged from doing so because of the plan's concern about publicity that might bring attention to this case. Perhaps the most egregious example of fiscal arrogance we have seen in any of these cases appears in the case of Fox, in light of the influence and attitude of shareholders and the allusions to Wall Street so common to this segment of healthcare payment and investing. When Mark Hiepler, Nelene Fox's brother and the attorney who argued the case, questioned one of the main shareholders of HealthNet who referred to his "rulebook," Mr. Hiepler asked what rules the shareholder played by. The shareholder responded, "the golden rule." When Hiepler, a clergyman's son, asked this shareholder what he believed the golden rule to be, the response was alarming: "Them that's got the gold, make the rules." In the actual trial setting the shareholder, when reminded of this statement in his deposition, clarified that that was not his rule; it was the company's rule![11] There were lots of victims of the system in this case. When Mark Hiepler approached the jury for damages he did not ask for a specific amount but rather asked for enough to send a message that could be heard by this multibillion dollar company and others who might be influenced by this decision. It was the largest verdict dealing with managed care in history and rendered a jury verdict of $89.3 million. The actual amount settled for, though substantial, is not available because of a confidentiality clause as part of this award. It did, however, have the effect of telling this organization as well as others that such breaches will not be tolerated.

Ching v. Gaines[12]

The *Ching* case, another of the cases Mark Hiepler argued, involved a 34-year-old woman who thought she was getting the right care from her

---

[11] I am indebted to Mark Hiepler for sharing this important information and helping the reader get beyond the headlines to a human dimension and the intricacies of these important cases.

[12] *Ching v. Gaines*, Superior Court of Ventura County, California, CIV 137656.

physician. She presented with a treatable but undiagnosed colon cancer, but because of repeated delays and failure to take an appropriate history (her father had colon cancer), her cancer progressed. It perforated the bowel, and her condition went from 80% to 20% curable; she died tragically. She had initially presented with severe abdominal pain and rectal bleeding to a new group with whom she had been a member for two weeks, and who received $29.00 per month for her care as part of a capitated contract. Her repeated unsuccessful attempts to have her primary complaint addressed were exacerbated by the disregard of a nurse's note that the patient had rectal bleeding, and inadequate history and examination. During a subsequent examination, her doctor identified a mass but failed to make an appropriate referral to identify the nature of the mass in question.

The patient's symptoms continued but she was unable to contact her physician, despite several attempts to do so. She was also denied access to emergency services. Meanwhile, while the utilization review committee was evaluating the request for referral and coverage, the Chings approached the primary care physician in hopes of expediting the referral and insisted that the doctor act promptly. The referral was made only after Dave Ching, Joyce's husband, stood between the door and her six feet-six inch physician and demanded that something be done for her. A referral was made and a gastroenterologist performed a biopsy, which confirmed that Mrs. Ching had colon cancer, which was subsequently resected. They trusted the doctor until it was too late. *Ching v. Gaines* was among the top ten verdicts of that year and one of the largest verdicts for Medical Malpractice in the History of Ventura County, CA (in excess of $3 million).

DeMeurers v. HealthNet[13]

This case, also argued by Mark Heipler, was the largest arbitration verdict for denial of healthcare in US history ($1.4 million). As in the *Fox* case, Christy DeMeurers was denied coverage for a costly autologous bone marrow transplant her oncologist had recommended. She was told there was a short window of opportunity for her to potentially benefit from this procedure, and because she knew that this HMO didn't like to pay for these procedures even though they were covered, she began her own fundraising immediately and requested that Mr. Hiepler assist her. Her doctor

[13] *DeMeurers v. Health Net*, Riverside Superior Court; Calif. #239338.

admitted that he didn't know she was in an HMO. At that time her physician, a well-known university based oncologist, recommended that she act quickly. Seven days later, after being influenced by the HMO, he took the opposite position. Her doctor testified that had he known she was an HMO patient he would never have advised her of all the possible treatments and could never account for the disparity between how one week he advocated for her treatment and seven days later advocated against treatment. Interestingly enough, the arbitration panel said that "to the public, the HMO holds itself out as an alternative to insurance coverage. The HMO makes the same promise to pay for covered services and the public buys these plans for the same purpose it buys health insurance—peace of mind in time of illness or emergency." Her HMO's rationale was that her treatment was experimental/investigational and therefore would not qualify for payment.

An arbitration panel concluded that the treatment in question was not experimental and should have been approved. The language used in the final arbitration verdict surrounding this concern is quite interesting. They defined investigative procedures as those "that are mainly limited to laboratory and/or animal research and are not recognized as standards of care in the organized medical community." They further stated that HDC/BMT was not "experimental" as it was not mainly limited to laboratory or animal research.[14] Investigative procedures were defined by the panel as those "that have progressed to limited use of humans, but which are not widely accepted as proven or effective by the medical community." The panel found this term to be ambiguous particularly in respect to proven and effective as well as what was meant by "the organized medical community." The panel concluded that there was tortious interference with the doctor-patient relationship, an outrageous violation of this relationship that should shock the conscience of our society. The arbitration stated "HMO actions designed or intended to interfere with an existing doctor-patient relationship constitute extreme and outrageous behavior exceeding all bounds usually tolerated in a civilized society. It is conduct undertaken with reckless disregard of the probability of causing severe emotional distress."[15] People need care in these circumstances, not lawyers, and since these cases Heipler has helped over 140 patients receive treatment they were denied with only five having to pursue litigation!

---

[14] Case #72-193-01004 24 in the matter of the arbitration between Alan DeMeurers and HealthNet, p. 2–4.
[15] Taken from lecture on Nov. 7, 1997 by Mark Hiepler at ABQAURP meetings in New Orleans.

Adams et al. v. Kaiser Foundation Health Plan of Georgia[16]

The *Adams et al. v. Kaiser Foundation Health Plan of Georgia* case involved a six-month-old infant who was febrile. The baby's mother took him to the HMO PCP pediatrician, who examined the infant and confirmed that he had a 102 temperature and advised her that babies can run temperatures up to 105 without much worry. He prescribed Tylenol and sent the child home. That evening the baby's temperature rose to 104 and he appeared rather listless and was moaning, and later "limp and not moving."[17] The mother had to negotiate several levels of gatekeepers to get appropriate care for her child. She dialed the HMO operator, who turned the phone over to the nurse, to whom the mother described the infant's symptoms: that he was "limp and not moving, and moaning." The nurse contacted the pediatrician and told the mother to try to reduce the child's fever by immersing him in cold water. The mother never actually spoke directly with the physician but only the nurse who occupied an uneasy advocate/gatekeeper/bureaucratic role. Fortunately, the physician decided that it was appropriate to send the infant to the emergency department. The nurse instructed the mother to take the baby to Scottish Rite, their preferred provider hospital, located 42 miles from their home, which had a reputation as being the best pediatric facility in Atlanta.

The plaintiffs' attorney argued that because Kaiser received a 15 percent discount from the distant hospital, money, not quality of care was the root of the decision to send the baby there. He said that this prevented the baby from receiving prompt medical attention, thereby causing his symptoms to escalate.

> The family passed several other hospitals on the way to Scottish Rite; any of those hospitals could have provided the critical care that the baby needed, and any of them could have prevented what happened next. . . .
> The baby suffered cardio-pulmonary arrest in the car. During the ill-fated drive the family saw highway signs identifying a hospital at the next exit; the Emergency department there successfully resuscitated the boy and sent him in an ambulance to Scottish rite. However the baby had gone at least three minutes with low blood pressure, artificial circulation and the blood in his hands and legs had clotted. Gangrene set in and a few days later, 6 month old, James Adams III, had both hands and both legs amputated.[18]

---

[16] *Adams et al v. Kaiser Foundation Health Plan of Georgia,* Case #93 -VS- 7985-E (2-2-95) Fulton County Court, Atlanta) Lawyers Weekly USA 96LWUSA87 Section B11, Jan. 15, 1996, p. 1.

[17] Rice, p. 199.

[18] *Top Ten Verdicts of 1995.* 96 LWUSA 87. 116, Jan. 15, 1996, p. B21.

The child suffered from meningococcemia. In most cases of meningococcemmia the patient will recover fully "but in a rare 5-10 percent, complications set in [because of circulatory problems and endotoxin release] that result in limb loss or death."[19] Five million dollars were awarded in damages to the parents and $40 million to the amputee son. This case involved significant delays that can cause pain, injury, or even death. The case involves limited access to care because of gatekeeping and delayed and inappropriate triage. In this case the real gatekeeper was the nurse, not the physician. She told the doctor what she thought was pertinent and did not tell him that the child was panting and moaning. Thus, the physician, not knowing of the true emergency nature of the situation, told the nurse to send the baby to the emergency room at the distant PPO which was too remote, given this emergency. When there is an emergency in the hospital, one uses the stairs instead of the elevator. Why, when HMO patients suffer an emergency, should they travel out of their way to receive care? The triage criteria of emergent, urgent and non-emergent care still apply, and decisions should be based on such criteria. When this case was argued, a map of the city of Atlanta was introduced to the court to show all the facilities that were passed in order to get to Scottish Rite.

McClellan v. Long Beach Community Hospital[20]

The *McClellan v. Long Beach Community Hospital* case involved a hospital PPO who had a contract with the patient's HMO to perform post-Cesarean vaginal births (VBACs). Mrs. McClellan experienced a uterine rupture, the most common and likely complication of such a patient, particularly one with a previous midline incision. The nurses "failure to recognize the most common risk of that procedure, a ruptured uterus, cost her baby ten minutes of oxygen that would have made the difference between a normal life and life of a spastic quadriplegic."[21] This is a specialized type of service. In this case all the nurses on duty that night in labor/delivery were young and had relatively little experience about vaginal births after C-sections. There were four nurses on duty who collectively had six years of obstetrical

---

[19] *Top Ten Verdicts of 1995.* 96 LWUSA 87, p. B11.
[20] *Top Ten Verdicts of 1995.* 96 LWUSA 81, p. B5 Los Angeles Superior Appeal pending Mar. 17, 1996.
[21] *Top Ten Verdicts of 1995, McClellan v. Long Beach Community Hospital,* Los Angeles Superior Court Mar. 17 Appeal pending 96 LWUSA 81 (B5).

nursing experience among them. The lawyer for the McClellans argued that the hospital "made a conscious decision to save money by having less experienced nurses on duty"[22] which he argued was a "breach of duty." The neonate was severely injured and a verdict of $98.5 million was returned.

FEAR OF LEGAL LIABILITY

One of the easiest ways to strike fear into the hearts of most healthcare professionals is to threaten to sue them. As exemplified by the cases discussed earlier in the chapter, frequent multimillion dollar jury verdicts remind healthcare professionals that errors and missteps can be incredibly costly. The ethical concern over whether an action is right or wrong is dwarfed by the concern that the time, emotional energy, and expense involved in defending against a lawsuit, not to mention the adverse publicity, will simply be overwhelming. Usually, however, the publicity obscures the facts. Healthcare professionals are often exonerated in court, and in some cases reverse suits against careless plaintiffs for abusing the legal system or suing frivolously have paid off. Still, the perceived risk of legal liability can clearly drive a cautious healthcare provider to practice inappropriately.

Only in a perfect world could a claim be made that every law insures right action. Laws are imperfectly written to correct imperfectly perceived situations. As a result, what would appear to the mythical "reasonable person" to be proper is often in fact illegal. So what does ethics have to do with protecting against legal liability? It is generally acknowledged that if the party to a lawsuit can demonstrate he or she pursued an ethically based approach, he or she is likely either to succeed in litigation or to minimize his or her liability. The ability to frame ethical and legal issues and to use ethical principles to justify an action can be critical to success.

The ethical pressures listed above would be difficult enough to deal with in a cooperative society. Add to these the real or perceived exposure of healthcare providers to legal liability, and the situation becomes even more explosive. Part of this is due to the fact that many fears of legal liability are based on a misunderstanding of the legal concepts involved in duty, negligence, and injury. An understanding of these concepts not only reduces fear but also permits the planning of protective clinical and organizational measures. Clearly, informed legal counsel is critical, as are

---

[22] *Top Ten Verdicts of 1995,* 96 LWUSA 95, p. B19.

informed clinicians. Likewise, decisions based on a thorough prior examination of the relevant issues will usually be respected by a court reviewing provider actions months or years later. If the provider response to a crisis is carried out in accordance with carefully crafted policies that reflect the mission, vision, and values of the organization, much legal protection will be afforded.

In the current healthcare arena, emphasis is shifting from the way in which liability was construed in the past: that is, with a primary focus on whether procedures were performed properly or improperly or whether they should have been performed at all. As already noted, the new focus is on failures to diagnose and to refer. In most cases, however, the concern with legal liability arises more from misperception than from reality. Later chapters in this book will include recommendations on how to insulate oneself against legal liability. The recommendations pertain to, among other topics, ethics committees and clinical ethics rounds (Chapter 10), informed consent (Chapter 6), patient advocacy (Chapter 8), documentation, and especially, the development of policies and procedures (Chapter 13).

NEGLIGENCE AND MALPRACTICE

This section offers a short excursion into the concepts of negligence and malpractice. *Malpractice* means bad practice. Since it is perceived that people have a right to good practice and its results, when they get bad practice and the accompanying bad results, they may choose to seek compensation for the loss or injuries they suffered.

In any negligence claim, someone is alleged to have failed to provide something—good practice. Most negligence in healthcare also involves consent, specifically informed consent. A patient consents to a procedure but the expected results do not occur. The field of tort law deals extensively with questions of duty and negligence. Negligence includes everything from leaving a surgical instrument in a patient to performing the wrong procedure, doing surgery on the wrong patient, or allowing a serious complication to occur because of lack of follow-up, or failure to make a timely and appropriate referral.

The following framework can often be helpful in assessing potential liability. There are four components that must be present if an allegation that negligence occurred is to be worthy:

1. *A duty owed.* Did someone have a responsibility to do a certain thing in a certain way? If not, there was no duty; if so, there was a duty.

2. *A breach of duty.* If it has been established that there was an affirmative duty, the question arises whether there was a failure to fulfill or act in accordance with that duty. Even if there was an affirmative duty, as long as there was no breach of that duty, negligence cannot be demonstrated.

3. *An injury.* The patient must have suffered an injury or related damage as a result of the breach of the duty owed.

4. *A proximate cause.* Proximate means very near, and a proximate cause is an event or action directly causally related to the injury that occurred. If the caregivers' breach of duty (failure to perform or act in a certain way) was causally related to the patient's injury, there is a high likelihood that a legal action could successfully be brought.

In cases involving strict liability, one might not have to show fault but only show that something occurred. Sometimes the principle of *res ipsa loquitur* (the thing speaks for itself) comes into play. For example, if a surgical sponge were left inside an individual, that sponge, strange as it may sound, speaks for itself; it would not be there unless someone involved in the surgery had left it there. The patient had no control over the placement of the sponge. If a medical device or pharmaceutical, after being offered to a patient with the assurance that the product is safe, is later discovered to cause injury or death, strict liability can be demonstrated solely by the fact that the product was used and the patient has an injury (examples are the recent challenges against the tobacco industry).

ON CONSENT

One of the pivotal legal issues providers face when dealing with access, gag rules, and other legal concerns involves consent, or the permission that allows us to do what in the absence of consent would not otherwise be acceptable. People have the right to determine what shall be done with their own bodies if they possess the capacity to appreciate the significance of their decisions. In the absence of capacity, someone can act in their stead. This may be a designated surrogate or can be determined from a list outlining the priority of who decides for the patient when the patient lacks the capacity to decide for him or herself. In situations of fluctuating capacity, attempts to reverse the processes that prevent capacity should be adequately undertaken before a surrogate steps in to make decisions for the patient.

CONTINUITY OF CONSENT

Continuity of consent has been made more complicated by the advent of managed care contracts, prospective reimbursement systems, and creative financing mechanisms. A patient's wishes, documented during treatment in other healthcare settings, and the office records of the patient's primary care provider should be integrated into current and future decision making as a way of ensuring patient autonomy. In the case of continuity of consent, the goal is not only to identify patients' wishes from what they say and what can be gleaned from surrogates and family members, but also to establish a database containing information about their wishes. Often, during an extended hospital stay, important information about decision making, the patient's wishes, and family dynamics is generated, information that could be extremely helpful for future decision making in other settings. It is important that there be knowledge of and access to this information. It is a serious omission, for example, to omit information about the wishes of a long-term care resident who enters the hospital with an acute problem. The hospital should be supplied with pertinent information about the patient and the wishes and concerns that he or she voiced while in the long-term care facility. The transfer of such information helps ensure that the patient's wishes are honored, provides appropriate guidance, and increases the caregivers' comfort and confidence that they are doing the right thing.

The legal test in such circumstances is whether one exercised reasonable care. Showing that an extra effort was made to identify and act in accordance with the patient's wishes can often serve as low-cost legal protection. Caregivers can better serve patients by ensuring that their decisions do not fall through the cracks when they are transferred from one healthcare setting to another. The increased flow of patients through the healthcare system has created added pressure to identify and communicate patient wishes.

CONFLICTS BETWEEN CLINICAL JUDGMENT AND COST CONTAINMENT

Conflicts between clinical judgment and cost containment are not always resolved easily and are potentially irreconcilable. Providers can only be expected to give so much uncompensated care before they no longer have the resources to give any more,nor can they ignore those whom they serve.

This problem is being exacerbated by foreigners in dire need of medical care crossing our borders and receiving uncompensated services. This is a problem that has to be addressed with both delicacy and fairness. So how can the dilemma be resolved? Having a firm ethical foundation for determining the point at which the provider can no longer be expected to deliver free care will provide a significant defense against legal and ethical challenges. Certainly, it is better than refusing to address the problem, particularly when it may seriously threaten the continued health and viability of a healthcare facility or organization.

THE COST OF LIABILITY AND DEFENSIVE MEDICINE

There is a clear trend toward increased claims frequency for physicians involved in managed care. A study published in November 1995 states that "liability costs have been rising at 10–12 percent per annum since 1990, and while there are not many cases one can cite, it is not because legal actions are not being brought—only that most are being settled. According to a recent study conducted by Tillinghast-Towers-Perrin, medical malpractice costs have increased nearly 50 percent in the five years since 1990. Claims payments, legal defense costs and other expenses related to medical malpractice liability rose to $12.69 billion in 1994, up from $8.54 billion in 1990 based on an internal Tillinghast database of state by state medical malpractice costs. Overall tort costs moved from $129.93 billion in 1990 to $151.54 billion in 1994, rendering the U.S. tort system 'by far the most expensive in the industrialized world' . . . 2.2 percent of the gross domestic product."[23] The study found that malpractice costs have increased 48.6 percent since 1990, as compared with a figure of 16.6 percent in overall tort costs.[24]

The Tillinghast study did not include "costs attributed to unnecessary defensive medicine practiced to avoid lawsuits. These defensive medicine costs have been separately estimated by Lewin-VHI and equaled an additional $12 billion dollars in 1994. Product liability costs have been estimated by manufacturers to be more than $10 billion per year."[25] The

---

[23] *Medical Malpractice Costs Jump Nearly 50 Percent in Five Years,* HCLA, Washington D.C., Oct. 10, 1996, p. 1, http://www.wp.com/hcla/tilling.htm (Tillinghast-Towers-Perrin 1995).

[24] *Medical Malpractice Award Median Returns to Decade-High Level,* HCLA, Oct. 10, 1996, http://www.wp.com/hcla/1215.htm.

[25] *Medical Malpractice Costs,* p. 1.

costs of defensive medicine are not easily defined, for they include not only conscious practices but also those acquired through medical training. "Defensive medical practices can be classified as positive and negative. Positive defensive medicine involves tests and treatments that would not have been provided if the threat of being sued was not present. For example, physicians may order more tests or procedures, take more time to explain risks or treatment options, and spend more time maintaining patient records than they would if there were no threat of malpractice suits. Negative defensive medicine involves not performing services because of risk of malpractice actions. For example, physicians may restrict the scope of their practices to low-risk patients or procedures. While positive defensive medicine drives up the cost of healthcare, negative defensive medicine reduces its availability."[26] The cost of diagnostic tests and procedures that "are motivated primarily by the fear of litigation and the perceived need to build a medical record that documents a healthcare professional's judgement" is staggering—Lewin VHI (now the Lewin Group) estimates the combined costs of physicians' and hospitals' defensive practices to be $25 billion in 1991 (based on a very conservative definition of defensive medicine).[27] In an April 1994 study, the Hudson Institute's Competitive Center reported that liability premiums and defensive medicine contributed $450 per patient admitted to a large urban hospital in Indiana—an average of 5.3 percent of the patient's healthcare costs.[28]

Many argue that the United States has the most cumbersome and inefficient injury compensation system of any comparable developed nation. Everyone bears the brunt and burden of these costs. According to the aforenoted RAND Corporation study, only 43 percent of all the costs associated with compensating those who have been injured by medical malpractice is actually received by the patient, with almost 60 cents of every dollar being exhausted on a combination of attorneys' and administrative fees. The direct costs of liability insurance exceeds $10 billion dollars a year, and when this is coupled with both direct and indirect defensive medicine costs, the figure exceeds $35 billion annually.

Physicians are sued more than any other segment of society. Practicing physicians have almost a 40 percent chance of being sued sometime in their career. If their practices include any kind of surgery,

---

[26] HCLA, *Malpractice Award Median,* Oct. 10, 1996, p. 9.
[27] HCLA, *Medical Malpractice Costs,* p. 1.
[28] HCLA, Malpractice Award Median, Oct. 10, 1996, p. 11.

their odds increase to over 50 percent. The average obstetrician sustains three claims during his or her career. Defensive medicine—tests and procedures motivated primarily by the desire to avoid a lawsuit—is the result. Lewin-VHI estimated that defensive medicine contributed up to $25 billion in health care costs in 1991.[29]

The legal system also stimulates over-utilization of health care services in personal injury cases where medical malpractice is not even an issue, such as automobile accident litigation and "slip and fall" cases among others. Because medical treatment expenses are an element of the damages, plaintiffs and their attorneys have strong incentives to obtain as much medical care as possible. In an April 1995 report, the RAND Corporation estimated that motor vehicle accident litigation alone may have generated $13–18 billion in excessive medical claims in 1992.[30]

LIABILITY ISSUES ASSOCIATED WITH INTEGRATING COST AND QUALITY

As we attempt to integrate cost and quality considerations, these concerns may become blurred or may become exclusionary. These are, however, important considerations. Co-mingling clinical with business concerns may present situations that are difficult to sort out. Will there be comparative liability and a determination that the fault was 20 percent business and 80 percent clinical? Can business data infused into the clinical realm compromise the insulation that acting in accordance with clinical standards might otherwise afford, or might it very well be seen as corrupting that insulation? Mechanisms for determining how to address this question need to be explored.

There is a trend towards going beyond the deep pockets of physicians to the deeper pockets of the healthcare systems and managed care organizations. People appreciate doctors and what doctors do much more than they appreciate systems If the defendant in a lawsuit is a system, particularly an impersonal one, there is little fear of harming someone who takes care of you and in whose hands you put your life, health and trust. The system may be perceived as no more than an obstacle to be overcome. To put this concern in perspective, overall tort costs in

---

[29] *The Impact of Liability on the Cost of Health Care Services,* HCLA 10/10/96, p. 1, referring to "Estimating the Costs of Defensive Medicine," Lewin-VHI March 1994, by Robert Rubin and Daniel N. Mendelsohn, M.P.P.

[30] HCLA, *Impact of Liability,* p. 2.

1994 were $151.54 billion accounting for 2.2 percent of the gross domestic product. Medical malpractice costs have increased 48.6 percent since 1990.[31]

As new technologies arise, challenges will arise as well. Already several claims have been filed in the field of telemedicine. There are no verdicts yet.

HOLD-HARMLESS CLAUSES

Hold-harmless and indemnification issues continue to plague physicians. As payors get bigger and control huge segments of the markets, not aligning with these large payors can be economically very costly for physicians. Physicians may feel forced to negotiate terms that they would not really want, feel they must accept because they "need the business." Hold-harmless clauses may be very specific. When, however, they involve the communication of a coverage decision, this can be perceived as a business decision rather than a medical one. People may be led to believe that their conventional malpractice insurance will cover actions based on the failure to treat or the communication of a decision not to cover. While at this time most general liability policies would cover such decisions, it is important that physicians purchase broad coverage to insulate them from individual exposure to these emerging risks spawned not by medicine but by business. There are some interesting considerations having to do with conventional medical malpractice insurance. Medical malpractice insurance is designed to provide coverage for clinical practice, not for business decisions. There will either need to be expanded coverage or at least an awareness of the difference between clinical and business decisions.

REMEDIES FOR LIABILITY: TRENDS IN RISK MANAGEMENT

New trends in how we should deal with regulating and coordinating actions dealing with liability are emerging. The enterprise liability theory has been percolating since it was first discussed in President Clinton's initial healthcare reform package. The discussion arose in the context of healthcare collectives. In Clinton's original plan, he believed that this mechanism could be used effectively to reduce broad liability exposure

---

[31] HCLA, *Medical Malpractice Costs Jump Nearly 50% in Five Years* http://www.wp.com.hcla/tillin.htm Nov. 17, 1995.

for the physician by making the healthcare purchasing cooperatives responsible for risk as well as for quality considerations. This was perceived as a rational response both in terms of the cost of defending against a lawsuit and its coordination, particularly because multiple plaintiffs often are named from the same organization and because continuity can be better established by a broader entity than it can by virtue of discrete individuals.

THE EMPLOYEE RETIREMENT INCOME SECURITY ACT (ERISA)

ERISA was to encourage employers to establish health plans but not to overload them with regulatory requirements.[32] This act took five years to pass. Among the aforestated issues, it was designed to provide consistency and continuity of insurance benefits across state lines and not to force health plans to conform to each state insurance department's regulations when operating in broader geographical contexts. ERISA was spawned in the context of a balancing act much like managed care; it attempted to encourage employers to develop health insurance benefits and plans for its employees and at the same time attempted to insulate them from state taxes and having to conform to each state's insurance regulations. ERISA was primarily designed to deal with pensions, not insurance. Yet ERISA is being used as a bar to recovery for broad liability concerns and used as a limitation to damages for which a managed care organization is responsible. This "preemption clause" is perhaps the most contested area of the ERISA act and of managed care liability issues. Recovery for damages under ERISA is specifically limited not to exceed the cost of the benefit that should have been provided (e.g., the 91,000 bone marrow transplant). The suit can be aimed only at the denial of benefits. There is also pressure from the plaintiff's bar to allow for punitive damages, but MCOs have successfully used ERISA as a bar to further recovery and have interpreted the limitation quite strictly. This has been a hotbed of political debate and we may see the insurance elements of ERISA being separated from the pension components. The National Association of Insurance Commissioners has been at the forefront of dealing with this question and is generating interest in both the Department of Labor as well as in Congress.

---

[32] I appreciate the insights of Barbara Ryland with Michaels, Wishner, and Bonner in Washington DC from our discussions on the current state of ERISA, Mar. 23, 1997.

As noted above, ERISA was created to facilitate administration of healthcare benefits by companies across any state without requiring that each individual state insurance regulations be satisfied. ERISA "shields self funded employer health plans from state rules. ERISA covers nearly three quarters of all people who get health insurance through an employer."[33] Its intention was indeed to facilitate administration, not to deny benefits for recovery for damages or injuries. ERISA does, however, contain a clause that states that recovery is limited to the value of the benefit denied. This obscure limitation for recovery for damages has made ERISA a constant battleground for change.

MCOs have firmly advocated that no changes be made in the wording of ERISA, and the plaintiffs' bar is arguing that without change in the managed care area involving ERISA, broad reaching tort reform is highly unlikely. There are many assaults on ERISA and powerful and repeated attempts to chip away at it. The American Trial Lawyers Association (ATLA) is pressuring Congress to amend ERISA so that patients can receive fair compensation. Controversies involving ERISA can be expected to escalate in the future. In fact, at the time of the writing of this book, Secretary of Labor Robert Reich, who is responsible for the administration of ERISA, indicated that the Clinton Administration is considering several proposals to address the inequities of ERISA when compared to other types of recovery for damages. Reich recently was quoted as saying "If the courts won't do it, the Congress will."[34] The recent Healthcare Portability and Accountability Act has also brought the ERISA preemption into the foreground of concern.

CHIPPING AWAY AT THE ERISA PREEMPTION: RECENT LEGAL BACKLASH

An interesting case was filed in late February 1997 before the U.S. Court of Appeals in the Eighth District[35] that dealt with a type of case that many have anticipated for some time. This case involved a man who was forty years old and complained of chest pains. His gatekeeper doctor was

---

[33] Azevedo, D.: "Will the States Get Tough with HMOs?" *Medical Economics* 73(16), Aug. 26, 1996, p. 178.

[34] "Clinton Administration Considers Narrowing the Scope of ERISA," Alexandria: *Health Plan Business Advisor,* Jan. 9, 1997, p. 2.

[35] *Shea v. Medica* No 95-4029MN United States Court of Appeals for the Eighth District 1997 U.S. App. LEXIS 3378, Filed Feb. 26, 1997.

unwilling to refer him to a cardiologist because he said that the patient was "too young and did not have enough symptoms to justify a visit to a cardiologist."[36] A few months later the patient died from heart failure. Mr. Shea (the patient) was insured through his employer in an HMO. Mr. Shea had chosen his doctor from the HMO's authorized panel of licensed physicians. The court transcript alluded to the fact that "unknown to Mr. Shea, Medica's (the HMO's) contracts with its preferred doctors created financial incentives that were designed to minimize referrals. Specifically, the primary care doctors were rewarded for not making referrals to specialists, and were docked a portion of their fees if they made too many."[37] (This is an example of a withhold.) The patient's wife indicated that had they known that the physician was motivated by financial interests rather than the patient's best interests they would have sought a cardiologist on their own. However, they trusted and relied on the physician's judgment.

Initially, Mrs. Shea brought a wrongful death claim in a Minnesota state court, alleging fraudulent nondisclosure and misrepresentation. The case was moved to federal court based on the contention that ERISA preempted the state tort claims act.

Mrs. Shea amended her complaint to assert that Medica violated their fiduciary duties under ERISA in its clandestine efforts to reduce coverage referrals.

The court of appeals acknowledged that ERISA often supercedes state laws and preempts legal action. However the allegation was that the plan "wrongfully failed to disclose a major limitation in the benefit package." The court ruled that in most cases the intent of ERISA is to ensure the nationally affirmed administration of employees' benefit plans."[38]

The case then went to federal court, with the plaintiff arguing that ERISA authorizes certain plan participants to assert a claim for breach of fiduciary duty. Mrs. Shea's contention was that if not for for Medica's failure to disclose the doctor's financial stake in discouraging covered referrals to specialist, Mr. Shea could still be alive. The court stated that ERISA should not be construed to permit the fiduciary to circumvent its ERISA imposed fiduciary duty in this manner.[39] The court stated that Congress invoked the law of common trusts to define the general scope of a fiduciary's responsibility, and the fiduciaries must comply with the common

---

[36] Shea Case, p. 3.
[37] Shea Case, p. 3.
[38] Shea Case, p. 4.
[39] Swinney, 46F 3d. At 518-19 (1996).

law duty of loyalty, which includes the obligation to deal fairly and honestly with all plan members. The duty to disclose material information is the core of the fiduciary's responsibility, animating the common law of trusts long before the enactment of ERISA.[40]

Although the district court had acknowledged the HMO's duty of loyalty, the court felt that "compensation arrangements between Medica and its doctors were not material facts requiring disclosure."[41] (Materiality refers to what amount of significance a reasonable person would attach to this information and is often used as a test to determine whether there was consent.) The U.S. Court of Appeals disagreed with this determination, arguing that from the patient's perspective knowing that there is a financial incentive which can influence a doctor's referral practices when a patient needs specialized care is certainly a material consideration.

The court continued by saying that "the patient must know whether the advice is influenced by self-serving financial considerations created by the health insurance provider . . . that they could earn a bonus by skimping on specialized care. [The court concluded that the patient] had the right to know Medica was offering financial incentives that could have colored his doctor's judgment about the urgency for a cardiac referral. Healthcare decisions involve matters of life and death, and an ERISA fiduciary has a duty to speak out if he knows that silence might be harmful. Indeed in this case the danger to the plan's participant was created by the fiduciary itself."[42] The failure to disclose financial arrangements is a breach of ERISA's fiduciary duties.

This discussion of fiduciary duty focuses more on the notion of ethics than in law (in this case the law of trusts). This case brings many of the caveats and concerns discussed in the text into focus, including financial incentives to physicians (Chapters 2 and 3), informed consent (Chapter 6) and gatekeeping (Chapter 3).

A COALITION AIMED AT TORT REFORM AND QUALITY

The Health Care Liability Alliance (HCLA) is a coalition of 40 major national healthcare organizations and insurers representing physicians, hospital blood banks, liability insurers, health device manufacturers, healthcare insurers, business producers of medicine, and the biotechnological

---

[40] *Eddy v. Colonial Life Insurance of AM*, 287 App. D.C. 76, 919F.2d. 747,750 (D.C. Cir 1990).
[41] Shea Case, p. 5.
[42] Shea Case, p. 4.

industry. The Alliance promotes patient safety and injury prevention programs. It proposes that state healthcare licensing fees should be used to promote patient safety, including disciplining healthcare professionals, implementing quality assurance programs, producing public information on the comparative quality of health plans, and encouraging volunteer services in medically underserved areas. HCLA, in partnership with outside groups, is undertaking a consumer education program with the goal of liability tort reform. It serves as a barometer and information brokerage center to track trends in malpractice liability reform.[43]

The Alliance's major goals to implement liability reforms on a nationwide level include but are not limited to the following:

- Placing a $250,000 ceiling on noneconomic damages
- Holding each defendant responsible only for the portion of noneconomic damages attributable to their own acts or omissions
- Applying liability reform provisions to all potential defendants in clams arising from healthcare-related injuries
- Limiting the amount of attorney contingency fees
- Halting double recovery
- Paying awards for future expenses and losses over time. (Future expenses for losses over $50,000 should be paid periodically over time.) This reform also insures that money is there when needed.
- Providing for a uniform statute of limitations
- Encouraging alternative dispute resolution methods
- Reforming punitive damages

GROWTH IN LIABILITY CONCERNS

Healthcare lawsuits are increasing dramatically, and are accompanied by an increase in million-dollar malpractice verdicts (which of course fuels the desire to bring more lawsuits). Insurers are offering new products to better meet the need for affordable coverage through general liability policies. A recent study in California examined the experience of malpractice awards in 1994 and showed more settlements, higher awards for severe

---

[43] I appreciate the support of Ann Marie Higham of the Health Care Liability Alliance for providing this helpful information on this important resource, and for her continuing assistance over the course of writing this book.

injuries, outpatient settings dominating the location of injuries, and more allegations of failure to diagnose cases. The latter two factors are of special interest. The study, performed by the Medical Underwriters of California, found that "more than one-third of the cases (36 percent) . . . accounted for more than one-third of total indemnity."[44] The study also found that most of the increase was attributed to treatment provided at "urgent care centers, large multi-specialty clinics, and staff model HMOs."[45] A study of the malpractice experience in Ohio[46] demonstrates other trends in malpractice and identifies "million dollar closed claims" involving mishaps in:

- surgical service (29%)
- labor-delivery (19%)
- patient room (14%)
- emergency room (17%)

This study also showed that the leading causes of injury associated with the million dollar closed claims were:

- diagnostic error/delayed treatment (37%)
- labor-delivery mishaps (21%)
- anesthesia events (16%)
- surgical mishaps (14%)

The study goes on to say that 75 percent of the million dollar cause of action came from inpatients and that 84 percent of the million dollar claims involved "physicians as the principal participants," but the four categories of healthcare professionals most often cited in the Ohio experience were surgeons, nurses, emergency physicians and obstetricians. The study also showed that the million dollar claimants were "more likely to be Medicaid patients and less likely to be Medicare patients."[47]

---

[44] Naupauer, Ron, VP, Medical Underwriters of California: *The Large Loss Trend Study, A Report of the Medical Underwriters of California.* Oakland California, 1994 (courtesy of Health Care Liability Alliance website http://www.wp.com/hcla/summer2.htm, p. 1).

[45] Naupauer, p. 1.

[46] Sites, Richard L. J.D. M.S. and Rizzo, J.: "Medical malpractice closed claims in Ohio: Are teaching hospitals and student physicians at greater risk?" *Iatrogenics* 1(3-4):127 July-Dec. 1991 and from *The Journal of Healthcare Risk Management,* Summer 1994, 14:(3) Columbus OH from HCLA website http://www.wp.com/hcla/summer.htm.

[47] Courtesy of Health Care Liability Alliance, *Years of Million-Dollar Malpractice Claims in Ohio* http://www.wp.com/hcla/summer2.htm, p. 6.

TORT REFORM AND MANAGED CARE

Healthcare liability requires action and reform at the federal level, but the greatest impediment today is posed by managed care itself, for managed care has been effectively hiding behind ERISA in terms of its malpractice exposure.

Since MCOs are increasingly being targeted by plaintiffs, the shield provided by ERISA may not hold for long. The increasing trend of employed physicians will accelerate this development because under the doctrine of *respondeat superior,* or vicarious liability, the law holds that employers are responsible for their employees' negligent acts. The large verdicts indicate that these shields are already breaking down.[48]

The AMA has "resisted the overtures of the organized bar, who have attempted to enlist AMA support in targeting managed care organizations."[49]

> In February 1996 the House Judiciary Committee held hearings that were notable in that the managed care industry was targeted as **the** central problem by anti-tort reform witnesses. The consumer witness was the daughter of an alleged victim of poor care at Kaiser Permanente. Mark Hiepler, an attorney who is also the brother of the plaintiff in the Fox v. Healthnet case, pleaded with the committee to preserve maximum sanctions available against "corporations practicing the business of medicine." Phil Corboy, former president of the Association of Trial Lawyers of America, was relatively physician-friendly but adamantly opposed any system that established incentives to reduce needed care, as he contends that managed care industry does. . . . The plaintiffs bar is now practically advertising for cases against managed care organizations, attracted no doubt by these organizations' exceedingly deep pockets. Neither managed care organizations nor employers' groups have been actively engaged in advocating liability reform, relying instead on ERISA to shield them from state tort law remedies and on "hold-harmless" indemnification clauses inserted in their contracts with health care providers.[50]

Another emerging trend dealing with malpractice and risk is called "channeling." Channeling is occurring with increased frequency in vertically integrated HMOs. The concept of channeling involves one insurer

---

[48] AMA memorandum, *"Health Care Liability and Managed Care: New Data and Its Implications,* May 1996, p. 2.

[49] AMA memorandum, p. 2.

[50] AMA memorandum, p. 3.

being in control of financing risk. An umbrella policy buys insurance for the system or hospital. In such a scenario there is no financial risk for the individual physician, as this is taken care of up front by the system or organization for the company or group. Additional insurance can be purchased by the individual physician at discounted rates from the hospital or healthcare system. The creation of an insurance umbrella to streamline coverage and increase risk management is perceived as an attractive option by many.

The American Law Institute, which outlines the future of the common law, sets forth recommendations to shape the future. They believe that it makes more sense to hold the hospital responsible. Because there are often multiple defendants named in lawsuits, it is better for the institution to fiscally coordinate the defense.

REGULATORY ISSUES

A *New England Journal of Medicine* article reports that "in 1996 alone 1000 pieces of legislation attempting to regulate or weaken HMOs were introduced in state legislatures, and 56 laws were passed in 35 states. The [anti-managed care] backlash movement brings together patients who complain of services denied and physicians who are suffering the loss of autonomy and income."[51] There is direct access to care legislation in six states where patients can refer themselves directly to certain medical specialties such as gynecology and infectious diseases. Thirteen states have passed laws that require HMOs to pay for visits to the emergency department on the basis of 'a prudent layperson" definition of emergency"[52] which is less restrictive than definitions used by HMOs. "Drive through deliveries" have generated the strongest backlash.

ANTITRUST AND RELATED REGULATORY CONCERNS

"Provider networks are growing more popular among doctors and among officials at the Federal Trade Commission. The provider-controlled network clearly was the area of health-care antitrust enforcement that drew the most attention last year . . . and will probably be the area that draws

---

[51] Bodenheimer, Thomas: "The HMO Backlash—Righteous or Reactionary," *New England Journal of Medicine,* 335:(21), 1996, Nov. 21, p. 1601.
[52] Bodenheimer, p. 1601.

the most attention this year."[53] Antitrust issues are regulated by the Federal Trade Commission. Two of the most visible and important areas of anti-trust as related to provider networks are "whether the network is going to be able to exercise market power—that is, whether it will be so strong that it'll be able to raise prices . . . (and) whether the way the network establishes its reimbursement presents some type of per se unlawful price fixing."[54] To be able to insulate oneself from these charges or allegations one can do various things. The network "can either put the physicians who own and control the network at financial risk through capitation or fee-for-service with a withhold, or it can set up the network so that it offers a 'new product producing substantial efficiencies.' The first strategy will allow to network to be evaluated by what's called the rule of reason, a more liberal, and from the networks perspective, more desirable way to measure its potential to unduly influence market prices."[55] Unfortunately it is unclear how this will be measured and a great deal of ambiguity exists concerning the definition of a "new product producing substantial efficiencies."[56]

THE JOINT COMMISSION ETHICS AND LEADERSHIP STANDARDS

The Joint Commission for the Accreditation of Health Care Organizations (JCAHO) has had clinical ethics standards for years. These standards require healthcare providers to establish mechanisms to deal with clinical issues and maintain a high level of quality. The Joint Commission has expanded its standards to many initiatives dealing with ethical issues and to integrate ethical issues in its Rights and Responsibilities Standards with other standards such as leadership (LD), treatment (TX) and performance improvement (PI). There have been dramatic changes in the marketplace for such standards, and the Joint Commission, like other accreditation bodies, has responded with the creation of many new products, through both standards and educational opportunities. Some of the newest areas that address ethical issues are the Network Standards, the Managed Behavioral Health Care Standards, and the PPO standards. All of these as well as others address both clinical and organizational ethics. Whether the

---

[53] Pretzer, Michael: "Why You Should Have Been at the Health Lawyers Convention," *Medical Economics,* August 26, 1996, p. 168.
[54] Pretzer, p. 168.
[55] Pretzer, p. 168.
[56] Pretzer, p. 168.

focus is PPOs, networks, or delivery systems, the importance of ethics to these standards is prominent. The intent of these standards is to encourage providers to address issues of access to and availability of services, resource allocation, and interorganizational referral and payment systems. They also address concerns of mission, vision, and values. That they have been added on is a reflection of the reality of managed care and the shrinking public tolerance for rising healthcare costs. Their addition is also a response to legislative initiatives to reduce inappropriate utilization of healthcare resources, such as the anti-referral laws sponsored by U.S. Representative Stark. By causing providers to deal with the ethical implications of inappropriate referral and utilization pressures, the Joint Commission hopes to reduce the need for further legislative and regulatory restrictions in this area.

An example indicative of the Joint Commission's efforts follows: The Rights, Responsibilities and Ethics Overview dealing with networks is an effort to blend clinical and business concerns. The Rights, Responsibilities and Ethics Section reads as follows:

Overview

"The goal of the rights, responsibilities and ethics function is to help improve member outcomes by respecting each member's rights and conducting business relationships with members and the public in an ethical manner . . . A healthcare network's behavior towards its members and its business practices significantly affect the members' experience of and response to care. Thus access, treatment, respect and conduct affect member's rights."[57] The standards, which address a wide range of ethical concerns, are as follows:

RI.1 The network develops and implements a code of ethical business and professional behavior for its activities and those of its components.

RI. 1.1 The network's code of ethical business and professional behavior protects the integrity of clinical decision-making, regardless of how the network compensates or shares financial risk

---

[57] *1997 Comprehensive Accreditation Manual for Healthcare Networks,* Oakbrook Terrace IL, Joint Commission for the Accreditation of Healthcare Organizations, p. 65 (with permission from John Laing, Ph.D, Director of Corporate Relations, and Larry Hipp, M.D., VP for Managed Care JCAHO).

with its leaders, managers, clinical staff and licensed independent practitioners.

RI.2 The network requires its components and practitioners to involve members in all aspects of treatment, care, and service.

RI. 2.1. The network provides for the family to facilitate care or treatment decisions when the member is unable to do so.

RI .2.2 The network provides for member involvement in resolving disagreements in care or treatment decisions.

RI. 2.3 The network provides for member involvement in decisions to withhold resuscitative services.

RI. 2.4 The network provides for member involvement in decisions to forgo or withdraw life-sustaining treatment.

RI. 2.5 The network provides for member involvement in decisions to participate in investigational studies or clinical trials.

RI. 3. The network protects the confidentiality of patient information.

RI. 3.1 The network communicates with members.

RI. 3.2 The network protects member privacy and security.

RI. 4 The network provides for the receipt and resolution of complaints and grievances from members.

RI. 5 Members are informed of their responsibility for providing necessary information to facilitate effective treatment and for cooperating with health care providers.

RI. 5.1 Members are informed about any potential consequences of not complying with a recommended treatment.[58]

The Joint Commission is a leader in identifying ways to enhance as well as to measure healthcare quality. It is a private body that accredits various types of healthcare providers according to standards it developed. It also provides educational and consulting support. Several years ago, the federal government determined that accreditation by the Joint Commission was equivalent to the federal certification that a hospital or nursing home complies with in order to meet Medicare conditions of participation. As already noted, standards addressing diverse facets of the healthcare continuum now fall within the purview of the Joint Commission. Networks, PPOs, Home Health and Hospice, Ambulatory

---

[58] Joint Commission, pp. 66–67.

Care, Hospitals, Behavioral Health Care, Managed Behavioral Health Care, Long Term Care and Long Term Care Pharmacy exemplified the breadth of this organization and its initiatives.

Once accredited by the Joint Commission, a provider may be deemed in compliance with Medicare standards for up to three years and can use the interim period to improve patient care rather than frenetically prepare for its next Medicare survey. Even for providers who are not Joint Commission accredited and have no intention of becoming so accredited, Joint Commission standards are important because they are often used as models for federal and other third party regulatory and payment standards, though NCQA may be a more accurate model for managed care.

MEDICARE AND MEDICAID FRAUD AND ABUSE

In 1977, the Medicare and Medicaid acts were amended to prohibit any type of payment or consideration for referrals of Medicare and Medicaid beneficiaries. In its simplest form, the law is easy to understand. It is illegal to pay or provide consideration to anyone as a lure for referral of patients for healthcare services covered by Medicare or Medicaid. Unfortunately, interpretation of the law has become much more complex. The issue of consideration has expanded from the simple payment of money to include any type of benefit provided at less than full market value. For example, a pharmacy may provide a computer terminal to a hospital or nursing home so it can electronically order drugs and medicine for patients, or a medical equipment supplier may provide training to facility staff designed to ensure they know when to order and how to use supplies. In both cases, the benefits have traditionally been provided to the healthcare providers free of charge. Such practices have been curtailed or discontinued because of court decisions that have held that if any part of the intent of providing a benefit is to encourage referrals, the entire transaction is poisoned.

The ethical and legal problem is to be able to determine which relationships inappropriately taint a healthcare provider's clinical judgment. Because of the almost unlimited variations on this theme, a provider who blithely ignores referral issues runs a substantial risk of severe penalties, including, very likely, exclusion from any participation in the Medicare or Medicaid programs for a minimum of five years. This is a penalty that would bankrupt most providers. Showing that a relationship in which some benefit is provided at less than full market value is ethically correct and justified by the healthcare mission of the provider can be critical to defending against a fraud or abuse charge successfully.[59]

NEW INITIATIVES IN HEALTH CARE FRAUD AND ABUSE

The topic of fraud and abuse in healthcare has been receiving a great deal of attention, primarily because of the dramatic increase in the federal government's interest in this area. Healthcare fraud and abuse are believed to cost up to $100 billion per year. In fact, the U.S. General Accounting Office estimates fraud and abuse costs in healthcare to be as much as one tenth of the trillion dollars spent each year on healthcare.[60]

Stronger enforcement provisions to give teeth to enforcement of fraud and abuse statutes, coupled with funding to identify violations are spearheading such initiatives as part of "Operation Restore Trust." The sanctions are quite severe. A violation can result in up to ten years' imprisonment as well as large fines. If the "violation results in serious bodily injury, the term of imprisonment increases to twenty years; if it leads to death the term is life in prison."[61]

The promise of recapturing large sums of money that have been fraudulently acquired, coupled with treble damages has stimulated the government to invest substantial financial and personnel resources to attack these issues. The concerns, while laudable and appropriate, may have unintended consequences, including more litigation and "the entanglement of the innocent in the intricacies of the government's new and very broad punishment tools."[62] This new plan is administered through the Attorney General and the secretary of HHS.

To induce compliance, there is a beneficiary incentive program designed to encourage Medicare beneficiaries to report suspected fraud and abuse. Financial incentives are offered to those whose reporting results in the federal government receiving monies obtained by fraudulent means for amounts as little as $100.

---

[59] Adapted with permission from Robbins, Dennis, *Ethical and Legal Issues in Home Health and Long Term Care: Challenges and Solutions,* Gaithersburg, MD: Aspen Publishers, Inc., 1996, p. 29.

[60] Colleen M. Faddick, *Annals of Health Law* Vol. 6 1997. Chicago: Loyola University of Chicago School of Law, Institute for Health Law, in cooperation with the National Health Lawyers Association.

[61] Faddick, p. 93.

[62] Faddick, p. 28.

These new initiatives also mandate that any entity that receives Medicare or Medicaid funding establish a corporate compliance program that requires a "comprehensive and systematic method for identifying and addressing areas of risk, auditing and measuring the plan's effectiveness, solving problems as they arise enforcing the plan, reporting violations and swiftly disciplining violators."[63] Such compliance plans can preclude or significantly reduce legal exposure and hopefully discourage fraud and abuse.

REFERRALS AND FRAUD AND ABUSE

The way in which we approach fraud and abuse is changing as well and is facing unprecedented challenges. It is being argued that the failure to refer to the best in the community may invite liability. If a physician makes a referral to a restricted panel and the physician knows or believes that the panel members are not the best in the community, this may potentially be perceived as fraud and abuse.

Regulatory challenges can only be successfully dealt with by a thorough understanding of the legal and ethical ramifications of appropriate delivery of healthcare services. The issues are often framed in terms of legal liability, but because of the inexact and changing nature of the laws dealing with end-of-life decisions, provider relationships, and other legal issues, virtually every such legal issue involves ethical precepts.

CONCLUSION

This chapter has focused on a wide range of legal and regulatory issues that arise in healthcare, with particular focus on managed care. By examining legal foundations of the concepts we employ as well as gaining understanding of the major legal cases that impact managed care, we gain greater sensitivity and awareness of the impact such concepts and cases have. It also allows us to examine ethical and legal issues in a specific context. Knowing what a key legal decision implies arms the reader with knowledge, guidance and caveats that the reader would not otherwise possess. Discussions of hold-harmless clauses, consent, and related issues enable the reader to better understand the intricacies of some of these legal issues.

---

[63] Faddick, p. 98.

CASE STUDY

Mr. Davis had several serious complications after having a surgical procedure performed. It is later learned that a major part of his injury was due to medical equipment failure. The risk manager of the plan wants to contact the patient's family members to inform them that their investigation has yielded information that the error that arose could likely have been avoided had newer, more sensitive equipment had been used, but that the outpatient surgical center had purchased used equipment on the secondary market to save the cost of new equipment.

Discussion Questions

- Is the risk manager obligated to inform the patient? Who, if anyone, is obligated to inform the patient?

- What if the plan had a "gag rule" to preclude employees or physicians with whom it has contracted from providing information that could result in significant financial exposure for the plan?

- Which cases discussed in the chapter would offer some direction in this case?

- What role might the Joint Commission Leadership Standards play in this scenario?

7

CHAPTER

Advocacy in Managed Care

INTRODUCTION

The chapter on advocacy is distinctive because prior to the rapid expansion of managed care, this subject received minimal attention in healthcare contexts. The chapter begins by defining advocacy and a wide range of advocacy initiatives. Different varieties of advocacy based on a variety of settings, providers, and associations including physicians, payors, medical and other healthcare associations, and case managers will be discussed. Discussions of state-based advocacy, consumer advocacy and protection, and best practices advocacy will also be included. The chapter will also describe advocacy coalitions and initiatives related to access to pharmaceuticals, specifically addressing medication access and availability, as well as related issues of therapeutic interchange, therapeutic substitution, formularies, medication errors, and discharge criteria.

WHAT IS ADVOCACY AND WHY IS IT SO IMPORTANT IN MANAGED CARE?

Advocacy comes from the Latin word *advocare,* meaning to stand in someone's place and speak for that person. In the past, the notion of advocacy implied a kind of paternalism in which patients were assumed to be incapable of speaking for themselves and others would speak on their behalf. Lawyers are often called advocates because they stand in for clients and argue on their behalf. It is common for lawyers to tell a client "Don't say anything without talking with me first." The concept is that the advocate can better articulate a position or argument than the person for whom he or she is advocating. From this legal perspective, advocacy involved replacing the person for whom an advocate was speaking rather than supplementing or clarifying what the person had said. The increasing complexity of healthcare has created an unparalleled need for caregivers as well as facilitators from the payor side to become advocates for their patients.

As used currently, however, the concept of advocacy differs greatly from the paternalism that prevailed in the past. Once the difference is understood, advocacy will be perceived as more empowering for the patient than it was in the past. Whether one is a physician, physician's assistant, nurse, nurse practitioner, dietitian, social worker, or other health professional, patient advocacy is an essential component of the care process, especially when appropriate care is in jeopardy of being replaced with inferior and less costly care and access to services is becoming increasingly more difficult. The need for caregivers to be advocates for those whom they serve has increased rather than decreased. Standing in a patient's shoes and arguing in favor of availability of services or negotiating with payors is an emerging challenge. The objective is not to substitute one's judgments or choices for the patient's but rather to argue for or even demand appropriate treatment.

In the past, the language of advocacy was used most often by members of the nursing profession whose role was to intercede on behalf of the patient when the physician was unclear or mistaken about the patient's wishes. In the past, the nurse's role was really that of facilitator, helper, or interpreter; while the nurse did attempt to act in the patients' stead, the goal was not to supplant or replace but only to serve as a complement to buttress the patient's wishes or concerns that may have otherwise been overlooked or ignored.

Unfortunately, clinicians may find that advocating for those they serve is not only increasingly important but is even a necessary precondition of providing care. This is especially true when the best treatment for a patient is more costly than other standard treatments. The clinician needs to anticipate challenges by claims reviewers and claims managers and be prepared to explain why care is needed, why this case is a deviation from the norm, or why this is a special health and risk issue. The goal is not to get what the patient wants at all costs but instead to protect the patient's interests so that timely and appropriate care is provided.

PHYSICIAN-BASED ADVOCACY

In our rapidly growing managed healthcare environments, advocacy has become a buzzword. National healthcare trade associations such as the AMA are acutely aware that the physician's traditional role as primary care provider is being challenged, as can be seen in a wide range of memoranda, documents, reports, and policies. One of the most recent is the "Health Plan Data Initiative." One of the topics it tackles is physicians' duty and allegiance to their patients versus the pressure to make their primary allegiance to the managed care plan. The AMA and other medical and healthcare organizations are encouraging patient advocacy and safety and the physician's special qualifications to act as an advocate as a way of protecting both the patients' and physicians' interests. Physician advocacy is most appropriate in terms of identifying and enhancing what is best for patients and protecting them. Pressures for increased profit jeopardize the range and extent of services provided. Advocacy will be an increasingly important ingredient in the care process affecting all types of caregivers.

CASE MANAGEMENT: A MODEL FOR ADVOCACY AND PARTNERING

Case managers are being increasingly used to identify appropriate care, meeting unmet needs, and trying to reduce or contain costs in the process. Many employers believe case management to be the most effective means of achieving the goals of assuring quality and controlling cost. Case management has seen a shift from dealing with episodic interventions to more continuity-related issues. Case managers often utilize an "internal and external dynamic" where case managers from different settings (e.g., payor and plan) work together to best identify appropriate needs and to ensure that they are met. This excellent model is also a model for patient and payor advocacy in which each party's goals are synchronized and all involved work together towards common goals of getting patients' needs met.

However, the case manager is not without constraints, for many times case managers are unfairly perceived as cost-containers who intrude on and try to diminish or compromise needed care rather than to better ensure quality care. Such unfair caricatures will evaporate as the efforts of case management become more familiar to the public at large. In many cases, case managers have indicated that third parties, often attorneys assumed to be "protecting the patient" from the intrusion of case managers, actually impede or undermine services for the patient.[1]

The failure to identify the possibilities for working together can force us into rigid roles and functions. Meeting the challenge of working together is a goal in itself, for only in such a relationship can we achieve positive outcomes and some sense of efficiency. An initiative on assessing and improving outcomes related to case management is currently underway. This will yield important information on the value of case management in a variety of case-specific settings.

PAYOR-BASED ADVOCACY

The case manager working for the insurer, who ensures that patients obtain whatever medical care they require, is often the last bastion of protection for the patient. Case managers have a unique position and role in terms of balancing the needs of the insurer and the patient. In being placed "in the middle," they can serve as positive models to observe how cost efficiency can be effectively and appropriately blended with patient care. With the right intervention and coordination at the right time and with appropriate continuity, care can be provided that improves the patient's condition and saves money. The case manager from the HMO and the case manager from the provider side are superb examples of how caregivers and insurers can work together. There is already interaction that must take place on a routine basis between these two positions, referred to as the internal and external case managers. Strengthening and amplifying this dynamic can help meet patient needs and control costs and achieve goals efficiently.

Payor-based advocacy can assume other forms as well. For example, case managers can be used to coordinate care for those who demonstrate heavy utilization in service. In coordinating their care they can better serve the patient, direct care to more appropriate channels and save money in the process. Such interventions serve all parties well.

---

[1] These issues were discussed extensively at the Case Management Society of America Annual Conference in Orlando, FL, in September 1996 and the MCMC conference in Nashville in November 1997, with additional follow-up with Jeanne Boling, Executive Director, CMSA; Cynthia Armstrong, current President of CMSA; Nancy Skinner, President-elect, and Marilyn Severson, Immediate Past President, CMSA.

TRADE ASSOCIATIONS AS ADVOCACY FORUMS

On a broader plane, organizations such as the American Association of Health Plans (AAHP) and the National Center for Quality Assurance (NCQA) are working diligently to improve the image of managed care organizations, as well as to maintain their high standards as an advocacy forum. These organizations can redirect misplaced energies and create appropriate architectures into which all shareholders can more comfortably and safely fit. The mission statement of the AAHP, which includes many examples of patient advocacy from the plan side which if adhered to would reduce many of the bad faith and breach of trust actions we are seeing and take positive steps to reaffirm patient confidence, follows:

OUR PHILOSOPHY OF CARE

- WE REPRESENT a philosophy of healthcare that emphasizes active partnerships between patients and their physicians. WE BELIEVE that comprehensive healthcare is best provided by a network of healthcare professionals who are willing to be held accountable for the quality of their services and the satisfaction of their patients. WE ARE COMMITTED to high standards of quality and professional ethics, and to the principle that patients come first.

- We believe that PATIENTS SHOULD HAVE THE RIGHT CARE AT THE RIGHT TIME IN THE RIGHT SETTING. This includes comprehensive care for acute and chronic illnesses as well as preventative care in the hospital and the doctor's office and at home.

- We believe that ALL HEALTH CARE PROFESSIONALS SHOULD BE HELD ACCOUNTABLE FOR THE QUALITY OF THE SERVICES THEY PROVIDE AND FOR THE SATISFACTION OF THEIR PATIENTS.

- We believe that PATIENTS SHOULD HAVE THE CHOICE WITHIN THE HEALTH PLANS OF PHYSICIANS WHO MEET HIGH STANDARDS OF PROFESSIONAL TRAINING AND EXPERIENCE and that informed choice and the freedom to change physicians are essential to building active partnerships between patients and doctors.

- We believe that HEALTH CARE DECISIONS SHOULD BE THE SHARED RESPONSIBILITY OF PATIENTS, THEIR FAMILIES AND HEALTH CARE PROFESSIONALS, and we encourage physicians to share information with patients on their health status, medical conditions and treatment options.
- We believe that CONSUMERS HAVE THE RIGHT TO INFORMATION ABOUT HEALTH PLANS AND HOW THEY WORK.
- We believe that WORKING WITH PEOPLE TO KEEP THEM HEALTHY IS AS IMPORTANT AS MAKING THEM WELL. We value prevention as a key component of comprehensive care—reducing the risk of illness and helping to treat small problems before they become more severe.
- We believe that ACCESS TO AFFORDABLE COMPREHENSIVE CARE GIVES CONSUMERS THE VALUE THEY EXPECT AND CONTRIBUTES TO THE PEACE OF MIND THAT IS ESSENTIAL TO GOOD HEALTH.[2]

This statement is a welcome and laudable effort. What could be added to their philosophy of care is the importance of the initial partnership between the employer and the insurer and the need to create appropriate infrastructures and benefits to effectively meet the needs of those whom they serve. Despite that concern, the statement is an honest and forthright expression of what managed healthcare should achieve; those who act in accordance with it will more readily gain the public's and providers' trust and support.

"BEST PRACTICES" ADVOCACY

Medical directors in MCOs are barraged by physicians suggesting better ways of performing a given procedure and best practices that should be considered for adoption and payment by the plan because they can better meet need and reduce risk. It is important to have well-grounded medical management criteria to integrate best practices. As we learn more and learn from the experience of performance improvement and benchmark-

---

[2] American Association of Health Plans 1996.

ing, the need to identify and integrate best practices will be even more pronounced.

ADVOCACY AS EMPOWERMENT

As a result of the challenges of working in a managed care environment, advocacy is playing a greater and more empowering role in patient care than even in the past. The notion of advocacy as excessive paternalism has been replaced by the emergence of caregivers advocating on their patient's behalf for greater access to medical care and availability of services and negotiating with insurers to ensure that patients' needs are met. Clinicians are learning that advocating for their patients is not only an increasingly important part of patient care, but one that is becoming a necessary condition for timely and appropriate access to such care. This is particularly true when the provision of costly medical services is delayed or denied. Advocacy also comes into play when a caregiver can anticipate challenges by an insurer/plan/reviewer and takes steps to protect the patient from and inform him or her of such circumstances and alternatives the physician or patient might pursue or exhaust.

The word professional is derived from the Latin word *profiteri,* meaning "to avow publicly." A healthcare professional professes to be able to offer medical knowledge and assistance to those who are sick or injured who are accordingly especially vulnerable and at risk. Healthcare professionals deal with people who are vulnerable in that they are unsure of their health status or the seriousness of their malady, or are not knowledgeable about appropriate treatments as they might like. On the other hand, healthcare professionals are in a position of greater power. They can either use this power wisely or abuse it. Caregivers have the authority to decide whether patients have decisional capacity, and thus can grant or deny patients the right to make choices about their care. The autonomy of the patient is tempered by the integrity of the caregiver to either empower or disable the patient. Being able to control patient access to needed services is a further indication of the healthcare professionals' controlled power, hence the patients' need for their caregivers' integrity to supersede their concern for profit is even more pronounced. What keeps most caregivers from misusing this power is professional integrity and accountability as well as an understanding of their specific legal and ethical responsibilities to their patients.

ADVOCACY AND PUBLIC POLICY: REGULATORY INITIATIVES

Advocacy can express itself not only on the caregiver level but also on the policy level, where proposals to constrain, regulate, or control managed care currently abound. "Whether they're aimed at physician gag clauses, consumer grievance procedures, provider network rules or maternity length of stay, the proposals share a common assumption: The market isn't capable of producing responsible health plans itself, so government had better help it along."[3] How exactly HMO oversight and monitoring is to be achieved is unclear. Often, states are using their departments of insurance and departments of health to accomplish these tasks, but the points of origin are more expansive. State governments, which are responsible for regulating many aspects of MCO operation, are unsure how to approach these problems but want to do so. Many states are either in the process of developing or considering guidelines via rules, regulation, or statute, to address managed care issues such as access, quality, consumer grievance, and both physician and patient de-selection. Many states currently use the medical audit as a way of monitoring or evaluating healthcare organizations. For example, such medical audits can evaluate MCO policies and procedures regarding quality assurance, utilization review, peer review, grievance and patient satisfaction issues and related concerns. Audits will usually be performed by existing staff, however some states may require independent organizations such as the Joint Commission or National Committee on Quality Assurance to perform such audits.

STATE-BASED CONSUMER PROTECTION ADVOCACY

Several state-based initiatives related to patient advocacy are increasingly present in the popular media. This has been further fueled by discussions of drive-through deliveries, early discharge criteria, and related issues. Some states have extended the authority of their agencies to address emerging issues like this. One of the leaders in addressing HMO-related concerns is the California Department of Corporations, which has an 800 number to permit easy access to consumers lodging complaints about HMOs. "Some 4,000 calls per month have been flooding the switchboard."[4] The hotline is used primarily for patients to report problems, but

---

[3] Azevedo, D., "Will the States Get Tough with HMOs? Anti Managed Care Proposals Pile up Nationwide," *Medical Economics* 73(16): 1996, Aug. 26, p. 178.
[4] Azevedo, p. 183.

it does have the potential of being a point of reference for quality, consumer satisfaction criteria, and medical survey results. California has recently levied a $500,000 penalty against an HMO based on knowledge gained from this resource.

Oregon regulators levied a $20,000 fine on PacifiCare of Oregon for "improper denial of emergency department claims," contending that "the HMO had established a pattern of denying claims without prior investigation, and then reversing a large percentage of denials that were challenged."[5]

Another tactic that is being scrutinized involves false billing. This is an insidious kind of abuse, because people don't routinely challenge their medical bills, or may believe they have to pay something that they really should not have to pay. The tactic of trying to get the enrollee to "double pay" for already covered costs hurts the less educated, the weak, and the impaired more than anyone else. Similarly, many procedures that would be considered routine or important prophylactic procedures that would have been encouraged outside of managed care settings lay dormant as a benefit unless specifically requested by the patient. This practice saves money but is not in the best interest of the patient in the short or long run.

A COALITION FOR ADVOCACY

The Health Care Liability Alliance (HCLA) is a "national advocacy coalition that supports effective federal liability health reform to enhance the fairness, timeliness, and cost-effectiveness of the civil justice system in resolving healthcare injury disputes."[6] The alliance promotes patient safety, educates the public and elected officials about the need for comprehensive, effective healthcare liability reform, and coordinates HCLA members' lobbying on liability issues.

CONFLICTS BETWEEN PATIENT DECISIONS, CAREGIVERS' PREFERRED COURSE OF TREATMENT, AND MEDICAL ASSOCIATION ADVOCACY POLICIES

Several national and state organizations have developed policy statements and/or corporate or system-wide mission statements and principles that provide direction for patient advocacy. Such polices integrate the obliga-

---

[5] Azevedo, p. 184.
[6] HCLA Mission and Goals, p. 1.

tions of caregivers towards their patients and clinical and organizational commitments to fulfill them. Problems arise when the commitments are ambiguous, not followed, or misinterpreted, and many policy statements try to provide tools for challenging decisions that may not be in the patient's best interests. To address such circumstances, there are some tools for clarification as well as for challenges to such decisions. Perhaps one of the best guidelines for addressing issues in this area comes from the AMA.

THE AMA MANAGED CARE GUIDELINES[7]

The AMA Council on Ethical and Judicial Affairs has created some guidelines to deal both with the Wickline case and other legal responses to insurance coverage decisions. These selected guidelines promote advocacy and safety for patients and assist doctors in practicing practice sensible and appropriate medicine. The guidelines state:

1. The duty of patient advocacy is a fundamental element of the physician patient relationship that should not be altered by the system of healthcare in which physicians practice. Physicians must continue to place the interests of their patients first.

2. When managed care plans place restrictions on the care that physicians in the plan may provide to their patients, the following principles should be followed
   (a) Any broad allocation guidelines that restrict care or choices—which go beyond the cost benefit judgments made by physicians as part of their broad professional responsibilities—should be established at a policymaking level so that individual physicians are not asked to engage in ad hoc bedside rationing.
      i. Regardless of any allocation guidelines or gatekeeper directives, physicians must advocate for any care they believe will materially benefit their patients.
      ii. Physicians should be given an active role in contributing their expertise to any allocation process and should advocate for guidelines that are sensitive to differences among patients. Managed care plans should create structures similar to hospital medical staffs that allow

---

[7] Council on Ethical and Judicial Affairs, "Ethical Issues in Managed Care", *JAMA* 273: (4), Jan. 25, 1995, pp. 334–335.

physicians to have meaningful input into the plan's development of allocation guidelines. Guidelines for allocating health care should be reviewed on a regular basis and updated to reflect advances in medical knowledge and changes in relative costs.

iii. Adequate appellate mechanisms for both patients and physicians should be in place to address disputes regarding medically necessary care. In some circumstances, physicians have an obligation to initiate appeals on behalf of their patients. Cases may arise in which a health plan has an allocation guideline that is generally fair but in particular circumstances results in unfair denials of care, i.e., denials of care that in the physician's judgment would materially benefit the patient. In such cases the physician's duty as patient advocate requires that the physician challenge the denial and argue for the provision of treatment in the specific case. Cases may also arise in which a health plan has an allocation guideline that is generally unfair in its operation. In such cases the physician's duty as patient advocate requires that the physician challenge the denial and argue for the provision of treatment in the given case. Cases may arise in which a health plan has an allocation guideline that is generally unfair in its operation. In such cases the physician's duty as patient advocate requires not only a challenge to any denials of treatment but also advocacy on the health plan's policymaking level to seek an elimination or modification of the guideline. Physicians should assist patients to seek appropriate care outside of the plan when the physician believes the care is in the patient's best interests.

iv. Managed care plans must adhere to the requirement of informed consent that patients be given full disclosure of material information. Full disclosure requires that managed care plans inform potential subscribers of limitations or restrictions on the benefit package when they are considering entering the plan.

(f) Physicians should also continue to promote full disclosure to patients enrolled in managed care organizations. The

physician's obligation to disclose treatment alternatives is not altered by any limitations in the coverage provided by the patient's managed care plan. Full disclosure includes informing patients of all their treatment options, even those that may not be covered under the terms of the managed care plan. Full disclosure includes informing patients of all their treatment options, even those which may not be covered under the terms of the managed care plan. Patients may then determine whether an appeal is appropriate or whether they wish to seek care outside of the plan for treatment alternatives that are not covered.

(g) Physicians should not participate in any plan that encourages or requires care at below minimum professional standards

   i. When physicians are employed or reimbursed by managed care plans that offer financial incentives to limit care, serious potential conflicts are created between the physician's personal financial interests and the needs of their patients. Efforts to contain health care costs should not place patient welfare at risk. Thus financial incentives are permissible only if they promote the cost effective delivery of care and not the withholding of medically necessary care. (a) Any incentives to limit care must be disclosed fully by plan administrators on enrollment and at least annually thereafter. (b) Limits should be placed on the magnitude of fee withholds, bonuses and other financial incentives to limit care. Calculating incentive payments according to the performance of a sizable group of physicians rather than on an individual basis should be encouraged.

   ii. . . . c. Health plans or other groups should develop financial incentives based on quality of care. Such incentives should complement financial incentives based on the quantity of services used.

   iii. Patients have individual responsibility to be aware of the benefits and limitations of their health care coverage. Patients should exercise their autonomy by public participation in the formation of benefit packages and by prudent selection of health care coverage that best suits their needs.

THE NATIONAL PATIENT SAFETY FOUNDATION AT THE AMA

The National Patient Safety Foundation is a newly formed foundation whose goals are to ensure quality improvement through educational and public awareness regarding reducing and preventing errors in healthcare and to promote patient safety. Designed as a clearinghouse for identifying best practices and best products as well as for information and research, the primary goal of the foundation is to promote patient safety. Some of the first focused research projects the NPSF will pursue will be aimed at identifying and reducing pediatric risk, monitoring medication compliance, and reducing medication error (which is the largest source of error in healthcare), and a variety of risk factors associated with older persons.

AMA ADVOCACY POLICY REGARDING FORMULARY ISSUES

Another AMA patient advocacy initiative addressed problems that result from the use of drug formularies. The problem has less to do with the issue of substituting a generic pharmaceutical for a trademarked brand than removing an effective pharmaceutical from the formulary simply because it is too costly as determined by the plan.

Formularies, which are limited lists of approved pharmaceuticals, are the most prevalent means of containing drug costs and are used by most managed care plans and a large number of employers. In a formulary system, if a physician prescribes a drug that is not on the formulary list, the plan ordinarily will not cover the cost of the drug. The needs of specific patients may be ignored in this framework, since approved drugs are selected on the basis of average patient outcome, not individual effectiveness. Patients also may not be duly informed of formulary implications, either in advance of enrolling in the plan or on a prescription to prescription basis. There is also the potential for physicians to sacrifice optimal therapeutic treatment for the benefits of cost containment, and in so doing fail to appropriately account for variation.

RECOMMENDATIONS ABOUT FORMULARIES

An AMA report stressed the ethical tension generated by managed care cost strategies regarding formularies, and provided some advocacy guidelines. The report "compels physicians to advocate for formulary decisions that reflect the needs of the individual patient rather than just the needs of the average patient. Mechanisms to request formulary additions should be

established. Incentives for physicians to comply with formulary requirements should be limited. In addition, incentives should be calculated according to group practices rather than based on the record of the individual physician . . . Managed care plans should fully inform patients
about methods used to contain prescription drugs in the course of enrollment . . . Doctors are obliged to tell their patients when they are not
receiving a drug of significant benefit because it is too expensive or not
covered by the plan. Research in determining the impact of drug cost containment on patient well being should be pursued."[8]

"Other managed care strategies threaten patient welfare as well.
Prior authorization procedures can be cumbersome for physicians, prescription caps can be unduly restrictive for patients with chronic conditions, and excessive co-payments can block access to optimal treatment
. . . In addition, personal financial incentives have been used to encourage
physicians to switch patients to different drugs, pitting the interests of patients against the economic interests of their healthcare providers.
Managed care plans have also used techniques to encourage switches to a
different drug without ensuring adequate disclosure of the benefits and
risks of the different drug to the patient."[9]

The AMA has also become involved in advocacy initiatives dealing
with formulary issues. Among other recommendations, the AMA board of
trustees recommended that the formulary system must:

- Have the concurrence of the organized medical staff
- Openly provide detailed methods and criteria for the selection
  and objective evaluation of all available pharmaceuticals
- Have policies for the development, maintenance, approval and
  dissemination of the drug formulary and for continuous and
  comprehensive review of formulary drugs
- Provide protocols for the procurement, storage, distribution and
  safe use of formulary and non-formulary drug products
- Provide active surveillance mechanisms to regularly monitor
  both compliance with these standards and clinical outcomes
  where substitution has occurred, and to intercede when
  indicated;

---

[8] *Drug Formularies and Therapeutic Interchange* American Medical Association, Chicago IL, 1995
(Intro to CEJA 2-A-95 Report), p. 1.
[9] *Managed Care Cost Containment Involving Prescription Drugs,* American Medical Association
Council on Ethical and Judicial Affairs, (CEJA Report 2-A-95), Chicago 1995, pp. 1–2.

- Have enough qualified medical staff, pharmacists and other professionals to carry out these activities; and

- Provide a mechanism that allows the prescriber to override the system when necessary for an individual patient without inappropriate administrative burden[10]

Physicians must advocate for formulary decisions involving needs of the individual patient, rather than just the needs of aggregates or the average patient.

ADVOCACY RELATED TO DISCHARGE CRITERIA AND STANDARDS

The AMA Council on Scientific Affairs has been addressing the need to establish criteria for patient discharge. In its *Evidenced-Based Principles of Discharge and Discharge Criteria (CSA Report 4-A-96)*[11] the Council discusses discharge criteria currently in force not only to deal with premature discharge but also to "lay a foundation for a more comprehensive, coordinated, patient-centered approach to the provision of medical care across healthcare settings."[12] The Council on Scientific Affairs recommended that various policies surrounding discharge and discharge criteria be adopted. The first three provisions of this recommendation are:

1. The AMA defines discharge criteria as organized, evidenced-based guidelines that protect patients' interests in the discharge process by following the principle that the needs of patients must be matched to settings with the ability to meet those needs.

2. The AMA calls on physicians, specialty societies, insurers and other involved parties to join in developing, promoting and using evidence-based criteria . . . that are flexible to meet advances in medical and surgical therapies and adapt to regional and local variations in healthcare settings and services.

3. The AMA encourages incorporation of discharge criteria into practice parameters, clinical guidelines and critical pathways that involve hospitalization.

---

[10] Board of Trustees Report: *Drug Formularies and Therapeutic Interchange Recommendations Adopted at the AMA House of Delegates Interim Meeting* 1993 (Policy 125.991)1-93-45, pp. 4 and 5.

[11] I am indebted to Joanne Schwartzberg, M.D., Director of Geriatric Health and staff member of the Council of Scientific Affairs of the American Medical Association, for bringing this important initiative to my attention.

[12] Council on Scientific Affairs Report 4-A-96 American Medical Association, Chicago, IL, 1996, p. 8.

4. The AMA promotes the local development, adoption and implementation of discharge criteria

5. The AMA promotes training in the use of discharge criteria to assist in planning for patient care at all levels of medical education. Use of discharge criteria will improve understanding of the pathophysiology of disease processes, the continuum of care and therapeutic interventions, the use of healthcare resources and alternative sites of care, the importance of patient education, safety, outcomes measurements and collaboration with allied healthcare professionals.

6. The AMA encourages research in the following areas: clinical outcomes after care in different healthcare settings; the utilization of different care settings; the actual costs of care from onset of illness to recovery; and reliable and valid ways of assessing the discharge needs of patients. The report is more extensive that what has been shown however the following chart is a good representation of the discharge process.[13]

Figure 7–1 on page 145 is an excellent graphic representation of the discharge process the AMA council envisions.

These AMA initiatives set the stage for safe and appropriate medical discharge criteria. These criteria will be helpful in assessing what is an appropriate stay based on outcomes and experience. In this way, drive-through deliveries and rapid discharge that seems unsafe and unfounded will have a more dependable foundation which will enhance efficiency as well as good patient outcomes.

CONCLUSION

Advocacy will play an increasingly important role in managed care. Doing the right thing for the right reason has a positive ring to it. The dilemmas arise when we are not quite sure what the right thing is. These questions (what's to be covered, what's not to be covered, what's investigational and questions of spurious efficacy) are always where the greater uncertainty will exist, which will generate both danger and lawsuits. In the interim, if our common goals are to help the patient get what the patient needs, whether that comes from the plan side or the payor side is irrelevant. What is relevant is that we have good policies and procedures in

---

[13] Council on Scientific Affairs Report—Discharge, p. 2.

Discharge process

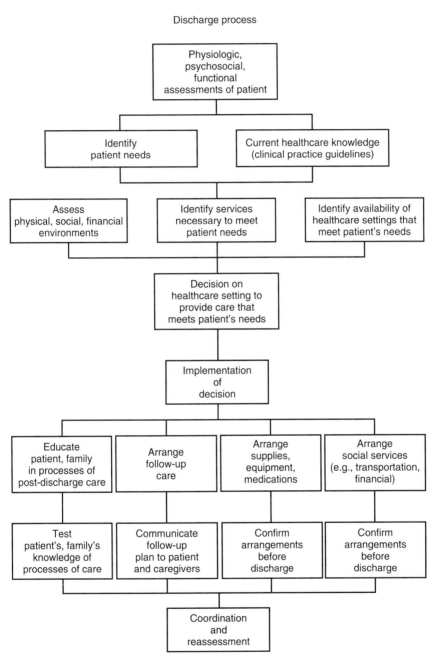

FIGURE 7–1. From CSA Rep 4-A-96, p. 12.

place to provide guidance and that we know where to turn for advice or support when a controversy or dilemma arises. Advocacy that creates the foundation for appropriate safeguards and protections will be good for the industry. As our measurements, clinical pathways, and outcomes information become more readily available, we can reduce some of this controversy and develop clearer and more dependable standards. Until that occurs, advocacy will continue to have a major impact on the delivery of and access to care.

CASE STUDIES

CASE 1

Mr. Jones required surgical intervention on repeated occasions due to a rare fungal infection of his chest. He became ventilator-dependent following his final surgical episode. Because he had sought treatment in a center of excellence in another state, transfer to an alternative environment was delayed while the treatment team and family sought to identify an acceptable facility closer to their home. Mr. Jones was later transformed to a ventilator facility near his home but "weaning attempts" were unsuccessful. Because of the intensity of his care and the associated costs of therapy he was beginning to approach his lifetime coverage cap of $1,000,000.

His family was not eligible for public funding and the facility social worker could find no other funding sources.

Discussion Questions

- What should be done with Mr. Jones? Who should advocate for him?
- How can the family find other funding sources or resources? What about catastrophic insurance?
- What responsibility does his family have?
- Can the facility discharge him to his death?

CASE 2

A medical practice known for its innovativeness and its high-quality services gets a large percentage of its business from managed care. The managed care plan has been rather slow to respond to innovations even when they are less costly and more effective. An HMO patient requires a procedure performed. One of the surgeons in the provider panel has been using a new technique for her patients that is safer, less traumatic to the tissue, faster, and more effective. The new technique also creates less morbidity and is less costly to perform. The surgeon has indicated that this falls within the plans "best practices" commitment that is consistent with the medical management policies and procedures of the plan. However, the patient's HMO will not authorize the new procedure.

Discussion Questions

- What responsibility does the surgeon have to advocate for the patient?
- What is the problem, if any, with using the new technique?
- What responsibility does the administrative director of the practice have?
- What role might the patient or his surrogate play in this matter?
- What role, if any, might the courts play in this matter?
- What legal issues are involved?

CASE 3

A brain injured patient has been identified for active case management to assist with his care plans and to help identify appropriate resources, including durable medical equipment, to assist him. He needs a particular type of wheelchair and, at this stage, aggressive physical therapy. He also has some emotional needs that are not being met. Some of the delays on having his needs met are based on the plan being hesitant to incur the long term costs of physical therapy.

Discussion Questions

- Does the case manager have an advocacy responsibility to help the patient get needed service? Should the case manager be familiar with all aspects of the benefit package or the master contract?
- What is the role of the case manager in disseminating information regarding benefits outside the plan and advocate for coverage of those services for a particular individual?
- What happens when the case manager finds something is covered but the plan is unwilling to provide it?
- Could there be litigation based on promise of payment?
- What if a necessary component of the continuing care plan is not a covered benefit?
- Does the case manager have a duty to explore alternative funding sources or identify costs to the patient?
- What should be done if a necessary component of the treatment plan is missing? Should the case manager advise the physician and/or patient of the omission?

CASE 4

A case manager has requested a service for a patient who does not quite meet the eligibility criteria for that service. She has learned that creative writing is one means of getting care for borderline patients, those not quite sick enough to be approved for services by the insurer. This tactic and others like it have become standard practice, and the case manager feels justified in using them because she is convinced they help her ensure that her patients get the care they need.

Discussion Questions

- Is anything wrong with her actions?
- To whom does she have a responsibility?
- Should lying be a precondition of care?
- How does this fit in with the mission or organizational ethics guidelines of the agency or company?

8

C H A P T E R

Clarifying and Applying Ethics[1]

INTRODUCTION

Chapter 8 will discuss the process of applying ethics, providing the reader with examples of ethical theory while addressing misconceptions of what ethics is and how it can be used to solve problems. Ethics is thought by many to be an interesting intellectual exercise that offers few, if any, solutions to complex problems. Many believe that ethics can be reduced to mere opinion. Unfortunately this misperception undermines the ability to look to ethics as an effective problem-solving tool. This chapter will show how a combination of ethical theory and proven practical strategies for addressing ethical issues can provide direction and assistance in clarifying and solving problems. First, some key concepts from the field of both ethics and law, including rights, wishes, self-determination, capacity, and consent will be introduced. This will be followed by discussions of knowledge and ethics, providing the reader with

---

[1] The material in this chapter is adapted with permission from *Ethical and Legal Issues in Home Health and Long Term Care: Challenges and Solutions,* by Dennis A. Robbins, Gaithersburg, MD: Aspen Publishers, Inc., 1996, pp. 42–48. This information also appeared in *Home Health Management and Practice* 10(1), Dec. 1997, in the article "Developing Tools for Addressing Ethical Issues," pp. 41–53.

both a historical and methodological resource to problem definition and problem solving skills. Among the techniques discussed will be defining the problem, framing the issue, and justifying the position you take. (This process will be discussed in much greater detail in Chapter 9.)

THE PROCESS OF APPLYING ETHICS, MORALS, AND ETHICAL THEORY

There is frequent confusion about what ethics really is. Ethics is thought to include any difficult question that is not easily squeezed into some etiologic framework or established procedure or protocol. Dealing with ethical questions can be disturbing and often frustrating. Many are of the opinion that dealing with ethics requires little more than to raise a question and show how truly difficult it is. Having done this, one can then either ignore it or cite its complexity as an excuse for not addressing it. Articulating or raising a question is not equivalent to addressing it. If one really wants to address ethical questions seriously, there must be some rationale for constructing and evaluating principles and then justifying the rationale used. This involves examining the principles carefully, weighing alternatives, and deciding what principles most appropriately address the issue at hand.

Ethics is a field of study that deals with concepts and principles surrounding what is right and wrong and how we justify our assertions and judgments about what we determine to be right and wrong. Ethics and morals are frequently viewed as exactly equivalent, but this is inaccurate, for ethics deals with principles of right and wrong and justifications of ethical judgments, whereas morals deal more with how we apply these principles and judgments in our daily lives. Morals are closely tied to sentiments, that is, how we "feel" about something, while ethics is aligned more closely with principles and reason.

Historically, the distinction between ethics and morals can be traced back to the seventeenth century, when the opposing theories of rationalism and empiricism were competing for supremacy. Rationalism is a theory of knowledge that asserts we gain knowledge primarily through reason, while empiricism asserts that we gain knowledge primarily through the senses. Ethics and its principles are more closely associated with the rationalist tradition, and morals more with sentiments (how we feel about something and why we feel the way we do). It is important to recognize this distinction. In this book, the focus is primarily on principles and concepts and the way in which we justify them. In other words, the focus is on ethics.

ETHICS AND BIOETHICS: CLARIFYING AMBIGUITIES

Some speak of *bioethics* and *medical* or *healthcare ethics* as being synonymous. The term *bioethics* was coined in the late 1970s when the field of medical ethics was gaining prominence in this country just as new concerns in research and scientific development were entering the realm of public discourse. One of the most interesting emerging issues in science and ethics at that time concerned recombinant DNA research and the possibility that some aberrant viral strain would be let loose. Simultaneously, medical ethics was expanding as a field in response to the Quinlan decision. This case involved a young woman, Karen Ann Quinlan, who had stopped breathing and was brought to an emergency department and placed on mechanical ventilatory supports to try to reverse her condition. The New Jersey Supreme Court was asked to decide the question of whether or not life-prolonging medical procedures should be withdrawn when the prognosis became hopeless. The case was influential not only because of the legal and ethical ramifications involved, and the role medical technology had in the decision-making process, but also because the central question involved what was to constitute the most appropriate forum for making such decisions. Bioethics was generated as a more expansive definition that attempted to accommodate both the ethical and the biomedical and behavioral research issues; hence the term "bioethics" was coined.

Some critics of medical ethics in the United States have claimed that death-related issues are given a central, almost exclusive place, ignoring other equally if not more important issues that affect larger populations. In fact, such critics have renamed bioethics as "biodeathics." This focus has plagued the field and is unfortunate, because the breadth of ethical issues is extensive; looking only at the fringes of life and not at other ethical issues is an error this text will not make. The range of topics, after all, includes fundamental concepts of trust, integrity, and accountability; professional issues as well as issues concerning transfer and admission; continuity of consent and care; access and availability; challenges posed by managed care; challenges to the doctor-patient relationship; unexamined opinions regarding how changes in the provision of care affect the caregivers' view of patients; self-determination; telemedicine; confidentiality; and others.

CONSEQUENTIONALISM AND NONCONSEQUENTIONALISM

Many feel overwhelmed by the intricacies of ethical theories and ultimately believe that ethics boils down to little more than individual opinion. Such people make little distinction between examined opinions that have been carefully tested, and unexamined opinions. To minimize the feeling of being overwhelmed, it is essential to understand the difference between consequentionalism and nonconsequentionalism. (If you serve or will serve on an ethics committee or merely want to sharpen your own skills for clarifying and resolving issues, knowing the difference will enhance your confidence and comfort.) It will allow you to be clearer about how people justify their opinions and to what type of justification they appeal.

A brief and broad-brushed overview of ethical theory is instructive here. Consequentionalism and nonconsequentionalism are broad categories that encompass many different ethical theories. Consequentionalism asserts that the rightness or wrongness of a given course of action or choice is determined primarily, if not exclusively, by its consequences or ends. A person using a consequentionalist theory will attempt to assess an array of possible results of different courses of action. Then, based on the probability of the different options, the person will identify the best course of action. Also, testing provisional theories and judging them in the light of possible counterexamples is a way of determining the most appropriate alternative.

Nonconsequentionalism holds that the consequences of an action are not the deciding factor, but that something other than the consequences (often a principle) dictates or determines whether the action is right or wrong. Most people believe, for example, we have a "duty" to keep our promises, to tell the truth, not to harm others, not to kill, and so forth. This duty does not mean, for example, that we should tell the truth when it is convenient to do so and lie when it is not. It entails we should tell the truth whether it is convenient or not.

The nonconsequentionalist, Immanuel Kant, argued that if we do not tell the truth or keep our promises, people will learn that they cannot depend on what we say. He raised the question of what would happen if everybody made promises without intending to keep them. He pointed out that promising would lose its meaning. After all, what good are promises if people always break them? Our duties do not pivot on the results or ends but on the principle of promise itself. One must rely on the integrity and accountability of the person making the promise.

In healthcare contexts, the notion of duty, a nonconsequentionalist notion, plays an important role. There is a point beyond which caregivers will not be pushed or will not bend. They take their duties seriously, and external considerations will not be allowed to undermine those duties, yet increasing pressures and submission to other challenges have called this reliability into question. Yet nonconsequentionalism is not an absolutely rigid doctrine. Sometimes it is necessary to weigh and balance conflicting principles in order to resolve an issue. For example, it may be necessary to lie in order to avoid breaking a promise or hurting another person.

ETHICAL PLURALISM

Consequentionalism and nonconsequentionalism may seem to be irreconcilable, and either approach by itself may seem inadequate given the complexity of many healthcare decisions. In fact, most people do not embrace one approach to the exclusion of the other; they adopt a sort of ethical pluralism. I have often referred to this as a "gourmet ethics" where one takes a little of this or a little of that and develops a position accordingly. The goal of healthcare professionals is to achieve certain desired results. On the other hand, their principles are important to them. They act in certain ways because they believe it is their duty to do so, it is part and parcel of what it means to be a doctor or nurse or other healthcare professional. They feel obligated to be truthful and trustworthy and responsible to their patients no matter what the consequences. The overriding principle not to harm and to benefit the patient, for example, guides healthcare professionals in every set of circumstances. The circumstances affect how the principle is to be applied, but do not fundamentally change the principle.

In other words, heathcare professionals are ethical cherry pickers. They reap the best they can find as well as compare a given situation with similar situations in the past, which some refer to as casuistry.

UNDERSTANDING KEY ETHICAL AND LEGAL CONCEPTS

It is important for caregivers to understand key concepts that arise repeatedly in ethical contexts in healthcare in order to gain insight and comfort and to develop better evaluative and decision-making skills. Becoming familiar with ethical, administrative, systemic, and legal concepts increases the ability to address issues in a more proactive and comprehensive fashion.

Occasionally, ethical and legal issues so closely overlap they are almost indistinguishable. A process of uncovering the similarities between
the issues while defining their distinctiveness can be important.
Sometimes the same term is used differently, or different terms are used
identically, by different professions. For example, an ethicist may speak
of *autonomy* or *self-determination* and an attorney may speak of *privacy*.
An attorney may assert that the right to privacy encompasses the right to
determine what should be done with one's own body (which sounds
much like the self-determination of which the ethicist speaks). While the
ethicist, when questioned about self-determination, may begin talking
about the right to privacy. And, of course, the clinician may speak of values and the right to decide. All are dealing with the same issue yet speaking of it equivocally.

RIGHTS AND WISHES

The notion of rights deserves some attention, primarily because it is assigned such great importance by so many. Ethicists generally view rights
as good things. Rights have great weight or authority and, like privileges,
cannot be easily overridden or ignored. Rights are always adversarial, for
the assertion of a right always entails a demand that others have a corre-
sponding duty to act (or refrain from acting) a certain way and may be
subject to sanctions or penalties if they fail in their duty.

When clinicians talk about honoring rights, they really mean identifying the wishes, values, preferences, and directives of patients and acting
in accordance with them. It seems that talk of wishes and choices rather
than talking about rights is more in keeping with the non-adversarial clinical setting. Certainly, as a last resort, rights always can be invoked.

Of course, it is possible to argue that rights is the traditional term
used in policy statements, such as The American Hospital Association Bill
of Rights and the JCAHO Rights, Responsibilities and Ethics Standards,
and because of this, we should stick with this kind of language. One response is that tradition is not always a good guide, and that we should develop enforceable "rights."

When the Patient Self-Determination Act first came into effect,
many healthcare facilities and agencies responded by informing people of
their rights in accordance with their federally dictated obligations rather
than assuring them that their wishes would be acknowledged and sup-

ported. Yet complying with the spirit of the act is what is most important, not talking about rights and obligations. Setting a more positive tone by telling patients that their wishes will play an important role in shaping their care creates a more comfortable environment for them. Focusing on identifying and honoring wishes and values can transform what might otherwise be perceived as an unwanted and annoying compliance provision into a vehicle which increases patient comfort and also is a positive marketing and community relations tool.

People put themselves in our hands and in our trust. We should honor their wishes (so long as they fall within a reasonable realm of medical standards and the ethical integrity of our professions) and serve them well. *Rights,* on the other hand, are invoked and are accordingly adversarial. If we start off in an adversarial mode, we create adversaries. We break into different sides—into different camps. We create distance and begin to raise the legal spectre. If instead we speak of patients' wishes or desires and try to integrate them into our decision-making process and use such wishes as a guide to our decision making, we do not provoke the same discomfort and conflict as with the adversarial posture and language of rights.

INFORMED CONSENT AND KNOWLEDGE

Having a foundation of knowledge upon which to build is essential for resolving the ethical issues we confront. To see this, consider the concept of informed consent. Informed consent is consent that has been given voluntarily by someone who is demonstrably knowledgeable about the risks entailed by the consent (e.g., the probable risks of a specific procedure the person has agreed to undergo, the probable outcomes, reasonable alternatives available, and what the implications are of refusing to avail oneself of the treatment option).

Informed consent is sometimes treated as an ethical issue and sometimes as a legal issue, but, in fact, it is both. There are ethical and legal reasons for ensuring that when someone agrees to a medical procedure or treatment, the person understands what is at stake and is not simply nodding his or her head to be amenable. Another way of looking at it is that the person must be informed of and have the capacity to understand the risks (and benefits) if consent is truly to occur. Knowledge and decision making necessarily go hand in hand. (The topic of consent receives a thorough review in Chapter 6.)

KNOWLEDGE AND ETHICS

The idea that ethics and knowledge are closely, if not inextricably, linked is well rooted in the Western tradition. The ancient Greeks believed that knowledge and ethics were necessary for understanding how to address an ethical issue. How could one possibly make reliable decisions in the absence of pertinent information?

The Greeks distinguished different levels or stages of knowledge. The first and most primitive way of knowing is that of unexamined opinion, which the Greeks called *doxa.* This often involves the uncritical adoption of information and the uncritical acceptance of opinion as truth or knowledge. At this level, all opinions are considered to be of equal merit, everyone is entitled to his or her own opinion, and there is no court of appeal. Blind faith, strict adherence without examination, is standard procedure.

Phronesis, the next level, is basically examined opinion. At the level of phronesis, people think through and improve their opinions. They try to achieve a richer understanding of what they have previously believed. Phronesis does not involve the same degree of certainty as scientific knowledge (i.e., knowledge that has been rigorously examined), but it is a step in the right direction. *Episteme* is richer and more refined knowledge. Superior to doxa or phronesis, it is attained when we develop theories and carefully examine our preconceptions and past judgments using the best of our critical assessment and evaluative tools. It involves testing our provisional solutions and hypotheses and arriving at reasoned and well-founded judgments. The highest form of knowledge for the Greeks was *sophia,* or wisdom, or knowing how things fit together in the larger scheme of things. The Greeks believed that few if any could achieve sophia in this life. (Unfortunately, sophia is the form of knowledge we have least of and the type of knowledge that would seem necessary to understand and effectively coordinate our healthcare system and establish its priorities based not on knee-jerk responses but on important overriding principles of trust, integrity, and accountability.)

It is important to recognize that remaining on the level of opinion, especially unexamined opinion, is unsatisfactory. Addressing issues in a way that accounts for their complexity requires going well beyond prejudice, hearsay, innuendo, and misperception. By focusing on important root issues, we can evaluate what we are investigating or attempting to understand and then proceed to higher levels of knowledge. Although we may never exceed the level of *phronesis* in our determinations, at least we will not allow ourselves to be comfortably and uncritically entrenched at the level of *doxa*.

MAKING SURE WE'RE TALKING ABOUT THE SAME THING

Long-winded and heated debates all too frequently end up with the parties involved thinking they disagreed, and after some discussion, discovering that really didn't disagree. By the same token, they may have assumed they agreed, and found in fact out that they disagreed after all. So often this realization results from a lack of clarification about what they are talking about. People quite often think they know what they think, but when they begin thinking more about it, they find they need to refine their position or to think more about what they should think about a given state of affairs. In other words, it helps to be talking about the same thing and making the same interpretations as a starting point. Even such emotionally and ethically neutral terms as "risk," for example, have dramatic implications when a person doing risk assessment looks at past patterns, while the person who requested the risk assessment assumes "risk" to mean the inherent risk in a given population, or another perceives risk to be associated with cost. Terms such as quality, responsibility, and fairness require that we understand what is being said and why if we hope to find common ground. It is also important to define the components of an argument or an issue so we can treat it fairly and comprehensively.

ESTABLISHING A FRAMEWORK FOR USING ETHICS TO ENHANCE DECISION MAKING

Establishing a framework for decision making is an important step in dealing with ethical issues. It involves framing an issue, determining the position one will take in addressing the issue, and then testing that provisional decision in light of counterexamples through a kind of imaginative variation. Through this process we can justify the position we take and determine its validity.

FRAMING THE ISSUE

An important step in developing an ethical framework for dealing with an ethical issue is framing the issue. Framing the issue involves making an initial decision as to what the ethical issue, controversy, or dilemma actually is. It also involves deciding what the components of the issue are and how to set up the topics to be discussed. It can greatly facilitate later steps by ensuring the issue is given a clear, workable formulation.

The importance of framing an issue is well illustrated through examining the abortion issue. Although not a burning issue in managed care, it does acutely illustrate how people can dig in their heels and dogmatically hold their ground where resolution of the issue is elusive. For example, if one person takes the position that abortion is murder and another takes the position that the choice to have an abortion should not be fettered with restrictions, the likelihood of any resolution (or even agreement on the way to present the issue) is small. Facile formulations of a complex issue preclude better understanding or resolution of the issue. Framing the abortion issue as a question of *life versus choice* will obstruct any move toward agreement. Framing it as a question of *life versus privacy* (i.e., the right to privacy, which arguably includes the right to determine what shall be done with one's own body) may lead to success. In the latter case, whether life begins prior to conception, at conception, at viability, or at any other stage of pregnancy, is irrelevant. The beginning of life is a consideration that would come into play, not in the framing of the issue, but in the process of addressing it and trying to achieve a consensus.

Framing an issue, especially an emotionally-charged issue, provides a more dependable starting point for dealing with it. When an issue is well formulated, the opposing sides, even if they do not revise their views, will at least have a better understanding of what their own views are, as well as the views they disagree with. In short, they will at the least be arguing about the same issue. If an opponent is unwilling to play the "framing game" it may be best to avoid further debate so as to minimize frustration. Without this important step, people tend to talk at cross-purposes or discuss different, perhaps dramatically different, issues.

For example, people speak of early discharge in delivery room settings as an "ethical issue." Although there may be ethical issues associated with early discharge and the accountability, motivation, and standards associated with such a determination, early discharge is not itself an ethical issue. Some of the concerns at stake have to be examined before we can frame this issue in a way that will allow us to proceed along a clear path. Cost containment, offering the best possible care, limited resources, for example, initially come to mind. Perhaps the crux of the issue should be viewed as a conflict between cost containment and offering the best possible care. This formulation, however, seems wrong because the "best possible care" would supersede, if not preclude, considerations of cost. Maybe "best possible" should be changed to "high-quality" or even "appropriate" care. Also, are we are really talking about "cost containment"? Maybe we are really talking about "cost control" or "cost reduction." Framing the issue as *"balancing the delivery of appropriate care against wishes to reduce costs"* is more realistic and offers more hope that a mutual understanding, if not a consensus, can be achieved.

Those vested with the responsibility of addressing ethical issues in delivery system, network, PPO, any care or service provider organization, or other types of healthcare facilities or agencies, or those who serve as members of an ethics committee, should try to provide caregivers and employees with the skills and knowledge they need to figure out what they should do. The goal is not to resolve controversies at all costs but to offer a forum for airing controversies, focusing on the issues at stake, increasing understanding of the issues and their implications, and helping all involved arrive at sensible decisions.

JUSTIFYING YOUR POSITION

Once someone has made a provisional decision, the way in which he or she justifies the decision becomes an interesting process in itself. In teaching ethics, I have found that one of the most difficult things for the students of ethics to understand is what justifying a position means. The best way to determine whether a provisional decision is valid is to test its weakest components. The old adage that a chain is only as strong as its weakest link applies here.

In challenging a provisional decision, we examine whether its weaknesses are too great for us to live with the decision. If they are, we need to go back to work and find a superior one. We imaginatively construct circumstances or counterexamples that others might use to challenge our decision. By examining what might occur, we can arrive at a richer understanding of any complex problem and hopefully arrive at a good decision.

Justifying a decision is perhaps more important in ethics than many other fields because it is the primary and most dependable way of testing the decision and refining it. While a clinical decision might be shown to be wrong if its medical consequences turn out to be harmful, an ethical decision is not allowed this kind of test. It is shown to be a good or bad decision through the imaginative exploration of an array of consequences and alternatives.

The process of justifying an ethical decision also allows others to discuss, disagree with, challenge, or support the decision on the basis of knowledge. If the person justifying the decision claims to be motivated by a sense of obligation to do no harm, others involved in the decision will at least understand where the person is coming from. This creates an opportunity for refining, reformulating, and collaborating on the decision to achieve better results, a process which itself might be helpful in evaluating the validity of the decision.

A similar process is operant in law. The result in a legal case will always pivot on a certain principle, rule, or interpretation. Perhaps a major difference between ethics and law is that law generally defines the outcome in advance. A lawyer will decide what outcome to pursue and will start from the outcome and work backwards, looking for the principle or rule that will support the desired outcome. In ethics, we start with the rules and principles and work toward an outcome—a defensible decision.

RIGHT AND WRONG ANSWERS

It is difficult if not impossible to "do ethics" if one lacks the appropriate information upon which to base decisions. The process of refining a provisional decision involves determining what information we need to make a better decision. As we test or weigh the decision, we look for its strengths and weaknesses and thereby uncover what needs clarification or improvement. By assessing a wide range of options and alternatives, we can arrive at a better decision, perhaps even the best.

Those who assert that there are no right or wrong answers miss the boat. Even those who assert that "it's all relative" must identify *what* is relative and why, and justify their position. (As an aside, saying that "it's all relative" makes a universal assertion that there can be no universal assertions, because everything is relative.) An unexamined decision will always be inferior to one that undergoes refinement and upgrading. A refined decision is much more likely to resolve the issue being addressed. If an ethics committee or some other formal body or designated individual is undertaking the refinement process, it is important for the members to remember that their primary goal, contrary to common opinion, is not to smooth over any conflict but to define the process of making a good decision (which hopefully, but not necessarily, will also settle any conflict).

CONCLUSION

Ethics is mistakenly thought by many to be an interesting intellectual exercise, but little more. Many believe ethics can be reduced to mere opinion. This chapter has shown how techniques for addressing ethical issues can assist us in gaining understanding of these issues, and can assist in problem solving as well. Learning how to frame issues, and how to support and justify the position one takes, are important tools in this process. Having some understanding of the historical framework and the relationship between knowledge and ethics can also be a helpful resource in enhancing our skills in defining and addressing ethical issues in healthcare.

CASE STUDIES

CASE 1

Mr. and Mrs. B. are a bright, financially successful middle-aged couple. Mrs. B. is terminally ill with a severe metastatic disease. She is in the hospital, but she makes a point of keeping well groomed. She wears a beautiful robe and always has her makeup on. One day a nurse walks into the room and sees that she has not put on her makeup, her mouth is wide open, and she is staring aimlessly at the ceiling. It looks like the end is near. It is extremely hard on Mr. B. to see his wife in such a situation. One of the nurses who has been intimately involved in the case takes the husband aside and encourages him to go home and get some sleep. She assures him that he will be called if anything changes in his wife's condition. This nurse, after she leaves at the end of her shift, is away from the hospital for three days attending an out-of-town conference.

When the nurse returns, a colleague smilingly tells her to go see Mrs. B. "How is she?" asks the nurse. The reply is, "See for yourself." "Why the grin?" the nurse asks. "Well, the patient thinks you are having an affair with her husband," her colleague replies. The nurse is devastated, for she thought Mrs. B. trusted her. How could she have gotten this bizarre and totally wrong idea?

The nurse walks to the room and finds Mrs. B., last seen depressed and seemingly in the throes of death, now animated and smiling. When asked where she has been, the nurse responds by saying, "I've been out of town at a conference." "Indeed," Mrs. B. replies with a grin.

The nurse feels terrible but in her judgment the patient is happy and she decides not to raise the topic of the rumor. She leaves the room without saying anything about it, and later develops a plan to deal with the situation. Before she can act, however, she learns Mrs. B. has suddenly died. At an opportune moment she approaches the husband and tells him she is extremely sorry for the misunderstanding. Mr. B. says, "Don't be. My wife was happy believing that I was being taken care of in that way. Our sexual relationship was a very important component of our marriage. Thank goodness you didn't tell her it wasn't true."

Discussion Questions

- Is truth telling a good thing in itself?
- Is it okay to avoid the truth when it causes discomfort or pain?
- What role do the consequences of an act play in determining whether it is right?
- What role does professional responsibility play in this scenario?
- What are the major ethical issues in this case?

CASE 2

Mr. J. has been hospitalized for several months and desperately wants to go home and be with his family. His wife joins him in pleading with the physician to do everything the physician can to release her loving husband from the hospital, but the physician is not having a great deal of success getting Mr. J.'s pain under control.

A new morphine pump is able to finally provide more or less constant pain relief. When Mrs. J. learns her husband will get his wish and be able to return home, she smiles lovingly at her husband. What is totally unexpected is her reaction after she leaves the room with the physician. When she is out of sight of her husband, she tells the physician firmly that if her husband is sent home, she'll go crazy. There is no way she wants him home.

Discussion questions

- Should the physician inform the patient of this event?
- What are the central ethical issues that the physician must confront as a result of the wife's response to the news?
- What responsibility, if any, does the physician have to the patient's wife?
- What responsibility does he have to the hospital?

CASE 3

A physician orders physical therapy for an adolescent with long bone fractures. The physical therapist knows that providing this modality to the patient will stimulate bone growth significantly—to such an extent, in fact, that one leg will become longer than the other. The physician does not realize the danger. The physical therapist, who has been only recently licensed, is uncomfortable challenging the prescription of a senior member of the medical staff. She provides the therapy but never turns the machine on. She also tears up the bill.

Discussion Questions

- Do her actions solve the problem? Why or why not?
- What are the ethical issues in this case?
- How can such issues best be addressed?

9
CHAPTER

Applying a Model for Decision Making

INTRODUCTION

This chapter offers the reader a decision-making model to address multi-faceted ethical issues. It offers a step-by-step process to define the issue, assess alternatives, and make provisional decisions, which are then tested, revised, and upgraded so that a resolution, or at the very least, a better decision upon which to base future decisions, can be made. In order to demonstrate how to apply the model, a case example will be used. The case example is an interesting managed care provider, payor, and patient safety example that illustrates how this model can be applied in step-by-step fashion. It involves a combination of several topics discussed in previous or subsequent chapters, including:

- Best practices (Chapters 7 and 10)
- Conflict resolution (Chapter 3, 4, and10)
- Consent (Chapters 6 and 13)
- Coverage denial (Chapters 3, 7, and 10)
- Experimental/investigational procedures (Chapter 1)
- Fraud and abuse (Chapter 6)
- Legal cases (Chapter 6)

- Key ethical and legal concepts (Chapters 1, 6, and 8)
- Medical management policies and procedures (Chapter 10)

A DECISION-MAKING MODEL

Many of the ethical problems that arise in managed healthcare or in any healthcare delivery system are multifaceted and require more sophisticated treatment than a facile application of personal values or beliefs. In the spirit of evidence-based decision making, the following model will be offered, applied, and illustrated by a case example. Such problems are seldom neatly packaged; instead, they are complicated by an array of legal, policy, economic, or systemic considerations. Thus, in order to focus on central issues, some process of organizing and isolating these issues is required.

The model described here, the Robbins Model for Decision Making and Isolating and Defining Ethical Issues,[1] is an organized format for assisting with complex decision making. Since problems have various degrees of complexity, the format is designed to be easily simplified or upgraded to adjust for individual circumstances. Although the model is not a cookbook of answers, it will serve as a framework for identifying and understanding issues and making decisions, and it will suggest possible decision options. Figure 9–1 is a flowchart outlining the basic steps of the model. The case example will demonstrate, step by step, how the model works.

The case example illustrates the conflict that arises when a physician recommends a procedure that is medically appropriate yet not reimbursable under existing insurance coverage.

CASE ILLUSTRATION

Mr. Jones is referred to an ear, nose, and throat specialist for a consultation about a surgical procedure required to correct a severe snoring problem. The surgeon and his colleagues in his university-based practice have been using a laser technique called UPP (uvulopalatopharyngoplasty), a new procedure used to correct severe snoring problems. In the past, a uvulectomy was the standard procedure

---

[1] This model originally appeared in *Grief, Dying and Bereavement: Clinical Interventions for Caregivers* by Therese Rando, Research Press, Champaign, Illinois. It was further modified in *Ethical and Legal Issues in Home Health and Long Term Care* by Dennis Robbins, Gaithersburg, MD: Aspen Publishers, Inc., 1996, pp. 63–71. Also from *Health Management and Practice*, 10(1), Dec. 1997: Developing tools for addressing ethical issues, pp. 45–50.

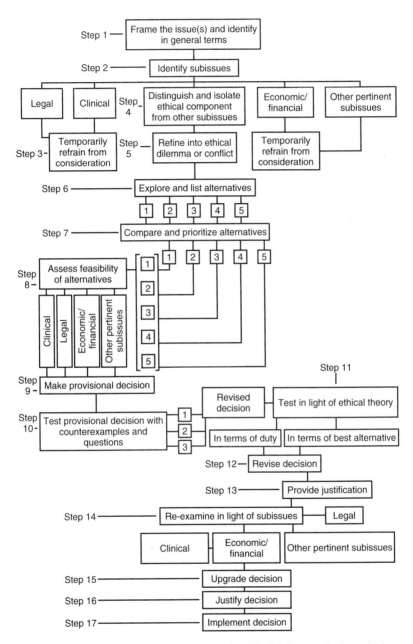

FIGURE 9–1. Flowchart of Decision-Making Model © Dennis A. Robbins. Adapted from The Robbins Model in T. Rando, ed., *Grief, Dying and Bereavement: Clinical Interventions for Caregivers.* Research Press, Champaign, Illinois.

performed to correct such a problem. The medical standards of care, however, have changed. The new UPP laser procedure results in less trauma to tissues, and actually cauterizes the vessels as the procedure is performed, minimizing risk, complications, and bleeding. The new procedure requires less healing time, is less costly, and less invasive. The surgeon recommends the UPP procedure as the best way of treating Mr. Jones' problem.

Mr. Jones's health care plan, however, does not reimburse the specialists for the newer procedure, even though it is less costly and safer. When the plan negotiated its contract with the specialist panel several months ago the newer procedure was not then the conventional and routine treatment it is now. The uvulectomy is the only covered procedure available to Mr. Jones. No provisions in the contract anticipated such a circumstance and the medical management policies and procedures, unfortunately, do not address this kind of circumstance. The physician wants to do the right thing and his primary obligation is to his patient. He could perform the new laser procedure and bill for the old one to "help out the patient" (which constitutes fraud and abuse and could compromise his livelihood significantly by virtue of fines and jeopardy of removal from the Medicare program (Mr. Jones is a managed Medicare patient) as well as de-selection from the HMO. He could perform the inferior procedure because it will be paid for and, in so doing, will receive the compensation agreed upon in his contract for such procedures. If a complication arose, however, the patient could allege that his care was compromised by other than sound medical judgment. The surgeon knows that deviating from what he thinks is most appropriate for the patient for financial reasons will hardly constitute a viable defense in a lawsuit. He could also initiate an appeals process with the HMO and its quality assurance department in order to obtain approval for conducting the laser procedure.

Ultimately, he needs to know what to do, what alternatives to pursue, and how to justify the path he decides to take. The model is applied as described below:

APPLYING THE MODEL

Step 1. Identify and frame the central ethical issues in general terms. The central ethical issues to be faced in this dilemma can be stated in such questions as these: What obligations do caregivers have to provide appropriate care? How far must a physician go in ensuring such care? What is their responsibility to do so? What constitutes an appropriate appeal and what can be done to safeguard the patient's interests and the interests of medical propriety? What resources exist to assist in decision making? How does payment weigh against clinical propriety? Some discussion among the decision makers on what rights or issues are at stake must occur before proceeding to the next step.

Step 2. Identify the subissues. (These are often confused with the central ethical issues.) This minimizes confounding factors and provides early identification of other pertinent issues.

There are legal, clinical, and financial subissues involved in this example. Legal issues include the patient's right to determine what shall be done to his own body, the physician's duty and perception of potential liability, and the delivery system and the specific care and service provider organization's liability. The clinical issue involves what is feasible and appropriate from the medical perspective, based on standard medical practice and working within established guidelines and relationships. The financial issues involve the physician's ability to conduct a cheaper but more effective procedure and be reimbursed for this choice and whether he will risk losing payment by doing the right thing medically but the uncertain thing contractually.

Step 3. Temporarily refrain from considering or weighing all subissues and focus on the central ethical issues. Since in this case the financial and clinical issues have such dramatic impact, they need to be discussed more extensively at a later stage.

Step 4. Distinguish and isolate the ethical component from other subissue components. The legal and ethical issues are often confused and must be separated. Special care must be taken not to confound other pertinent subissues such as administrative, cost, or systemic issues with ethical issues. However, in this case, cost is indeed an important component of the ethical issue. In an era of more efficient resource allocation and reduction of unnecessary or inappropriate spending, caregivers have an affirmative ethical duty to do the right thing clinically, as well as financially, so long as the latter does not compromise or inappropriately ignore clinical appropriateness. The ethical issues to be entertained in this case might include the following: (1) the right to practice safe and appropriate medicine, based on current medical standards (the physician's right); (2) the desire not to have medicine dictated by pre-established guidelines that tie or impede skilled hands and put the patient at greater risk; (3) the right of self-determination, or the right for the patient not to have his wishes compromised by external considerations; (4) the physician's duty to the patient; (5) the conflicts surrounding medical propriety and insulation from liability due to contractual (not medically-based) constraints; (6) the responsibility of the health plan as well as the physician's contractual responsibilities, and (7) the question of clarifying patient intent when financial considerations are involved.

The central ethical conflicts here involve the physician's professional obligation to do the right thing vs. the inflexibility of the payor in
this particular circumstance. The patient is caught in the middle. This case
also deals with the patient's rights and wishes, as well as the rights of the
provider not to be placed in a compromising situation. The conflict is
whether the physician either should follow what he/or she perceives as the
most appropriate course of treatment or act contrary to his/or her clinical
judgment, that is, not be motivated because he/or she is being financially
rewarded to do something inferior. The dilemma can also be characterized
as a conflict between duty, providing the best care for one's patient, and
taking the least restrictive course (performing the inferior but reimbursable procedure).

*Step 5. Refine the ethical component by transforming it into an eth-
ical dilemma.* State it as a conflict between at least two alternatives, each
of which has its merits.

The central ethical conflict here is a cost-quality conflict. The dilemma
can also be characterized as a conflict between doing one's best to serve the
patients needs, and taking the least restrictive course by succumbing to reimbursement restrictions without regard for quality or best practices.

*Step 6. Explore and list alternatives for resolution of the ethical
dilemma in order to develop a provisional decision.*

For purposes of examination, three possible alternatives for the
physician are suggested. 1: Motivated by duty, provide the best possible
care and inform the plan why you deviated from the "old (yet reimbursable) way"; 2: Lie to the plan about what medical procedures are performed and perform the newer, safer procedure, while billing for the older
procedure; 3: Ask the plan partner to handle this case as a reasonable exception, and immediately initiate the process to upgrade your contractual
agreement with the payor for the benefit of future patients.

Step 7. Compare, prioritize, or grade alternatives. This step can be
adjusted as the complexity of problems increases. In grading alternatives,
consider conflicts between subissue components to further clarify each
component. Also, at this stage some alternatives can be discarded and others can be revised or added. Assume in this case that the physician has fulfilled his appeals duty and performs the inferior treatment after informing
the patient of all treatment options, including the choice between the
newer (non-reimbursable) and the older (reimbursable) one. The option
would be for the physician to perform the newer, safer, less traumatic, less
costly, laser procedure, thereby insulating himself from liability. He could

examine what documentation and other internal processes might be undertaken to insulate him from future problems, while still honoring the wishes of his patient and acting in accordance with prevailing medical standards.

In this case the most appropriate alternative may not be obvious. The physician's duty to the patient is important, yet so is the individual right to be appropriately informed and to choose on the basis of that information. There may be a still better alternative at this point; he or they might choose to consult with an ethics committee or some formal conflict resolution mechanism at the facility to adjudicate the conflict. For purposes of simplification, however, assume that the decision maker adopts the third option.

Step 8. Assess the feasibility of the alternatives.

Since in this case, option 3 is our choice, it will be unnecessary to assess the feasibility of each alternative. In other circumstances, however, it may be appropriate to do so. Assessing feasibility includes focusing on clinical, legal, financial, and other pertinent components. For instance, is an action consistent with legal standards or hospital or network policy or by-laws? When the goal is better quality, and that goal can achieved for lower cost than an inferior procedure, what should impede us from performing the better procedure? The financial aspect is a major component in this particular example.

Step 9. Make a provisional decision on the basis of the assessment of earlier steps. This is a summarizing process. Now an upgraded decision can be made incorporating the clinical, legal, financial, and policy perspectives. In this case, the provisional decision will likely be that the physician should act in the best interest of his patient. When a challenge or controversy exists, all activities and options to address and resolve that controversy should be charted accordingly. This upgraded provisional decision allows for providing the most appropriate care for the patient, but at the same time includes a mechanism to minimize or insulate against potential liability by taking pains to best meet patient needs.

Step 10. Test the provisional decision by constructing counterexamples. The purpose is to refine or upgrade the provisional decision. If the provisional decision does not withstand the challenges the counterexamples pose, it may be necessary to return to earlier steps.

The following counterexamples and questions might be applied in this context: (1) Is it right for a physician to use an institution's resources and exhaust additional financial resources for the sole purpose of following outdated insuror provisions? (2) Does the introduction of nonmedical issues compromise medical care? (3) What if the literature suggests that there are several documented snoring recurrence problems after a UPP? (4) Should the physician exhaust the appeals process and then take the matter to court? Applying these questions and counter-examples may result in further modification and revision of the decision.

Step 11. *Test the upgraded decision in light of different ethical theories.* For example, consider the decision from the perspective of a non-consequentionalist theory where the focus is, for example, on duty, and a consequentionalist theory where focus is on identifying the best alternative to achieve the best results. This is not a demonstration of how ethics can justify a given stance. The purpose is to understand what two or more ethical approaches might offer as potential solutions. This step can also be used to apply a given ethical posture that a particular institution has already adopted as part of its policy.

Assume that only two ethical theories will be used to test the provisional decision: a non-consequentionalist theory and a consequentionalist one. The non-consequentionalist theory requires testing the decision in terms of duty or professional responsibility. The consequentionalist approach tests the decision in terms of identifying the best alternative from a range of options. In this example, duty brings up the question of why a patient comes to a physician in the first place. The answer is that the patient puts himself in the hands of the physician to receive the most appropriate care and assumes that the physician will do whatever is in the patient's best interests and not compromise care because of external considerations, and will honor the patient's wishes so long as the patient's wishes are consistent with the professional ethics. To act in opposition to the patient's wishes or consent, or to do what is medically inappropriate, is a violation of duty. Being motivated by something other than what is medically appropriate or best for the patient is a major concern as well.

The physician also has a duty to be aware of the institution's and plan's potential malpractice liability and to take steps to minimize it. This is particularly the case when risk issues and care issues overlap. This may involve contacting the hospital's risk manager or an attorney to find out how to fulfill his duty regarding appeals to the HMO plan, how to document the patient chart to insulate against potential liability and defuse future conflict, as well as using internal and external conflict resolution techniques. However, the previously mentioned duty of providing the best care (or at least medically appropriate care) to the patient overrides this duty.

To examine the decision from the consequentionalist perspective, those making the decision would try to imaginatively construct and list viable options other than the provisional one and to determine whether, in fact, the provisional decision is the best alternative. The results of the assessment of both ethical theories would then be considered and the decision revised accordingly. In this situation it will be assumed that it will not be necessary to revise the decision significantly.

Step 12. Make a revised decision as a result of the previous step.

Step 13. Provide justification for the decision. Explain why one option was chosen over another and why it is an acceptable decision.

The decision would be justified by showing that it has been tested against counterexamples and has held up to scrutiny from the perspectives of different ethical theories with minimal modification which has further strengthened it.

Step 14. Reexamine the decision in terms of subissues. Consider each subissue component separately, then all components jointly. Since cost efficiency, safety and the business relationships are such important considerations, they should be explored in greater detail here to establish guidelines for avoiding problems in the future. In this case, modifications are not necessary. This is a refinement that addresses the subtleties of a particular case.

Step 15. Upgrade the decision. This redefines or revises the provisional decision to include the results of considering the subissues. If there had been modifications in Step 14, the decision would have been revised here; since there were none in this example, this step can be omitted.

Step 16. Provide justification for the decision, this time including the subissues. Some of these may be so significant that they modify the earlier decision radically. Test with theory and produce counter-examples.

In this case the justification in Step 13 will suffice, since Steps 14 and 15 did not modify 13. If they had, a justification of the revised decision would have been attempted, using theory and counter-examples.

Step 17. Apply and implement the decision in the clinical context.

CONCLUSION

Application of this model can be a helpful aid in assisting the user in becoming more adept at addressing a wide range of ethical issues. It can be used as a tool as well as an educational resource for developing problem-solving skills and techniques. It is obviously neither necessary to use a complicated model to approach every issue, nor desirable to face a complex ethical issue and not know where to start. This model not only offers guidance on where to start but provides a systematic step-by-step process to reduce uncertainty and help the caregiver make better decisions. After using this model, which at first may appear quite complex, one may find that the way in which one makes decisions will be more formalized, and that this process can be integrated into your daily process of critically assessing a variety of choices and options.

Tools for Conflict Resolution: Ethics Audits, Guidelines, Medical Management Policies and Procedures, Ethics Committees and Ethics Rounds[1]

INTRODUCTION

Chapter 10 will focus on tools for resolving conflict as well as policies and procedures for both preventing and addressing conflict. It will also introduce the reader to useful ways to approach ethical concerns through ethics audits, ethics committees, and clinical and administrative ethics rounds. The starting point of this chapter, the ethics audit, is primarily an

---

[1] Discussion of the ethics audits, clinical ethics rounds and some of the material of conflict resolution were drawn with permission from material published in *Ethical and Legal Issues in Home Health and Long Term Care: Challenges and Solutions,* by Dennis Robbins, Gaithersburg, MD: Aspen Publishers, Inc., 1996, pp. 137–139, 153, 156–60.

assessment tool. Clinical ethics rounds are a helpful resource to identify and solve problems rapidly and efficiently.

Several types of policies and procedures are included dealing with the preclusion and resolution of conflict. General conflict resolution policies, appeals of utilization decisions, medical management decisions, traditional hospital-based committees, payor-based committees, and LTC and home healthcare committees will be examined in detail. The chapter will also discuss how to form an ethics committee, the role and scope of the committee, educating the committee, and the relationship between the committee and ethics rounds. This chapter will try to expand the realm of possibilities of how we can more effectively deal with problem solving and conflict resolution.

ESTABLISHING A BASELINE AND DIRECTION THROUGH AN ETHICS AUDIT

In order to create or upgrade an ethics program, it is important to assess organizational strengths and weaknesses. This includes investigating the organization's history, identifying past cases or situations that could serve as a basis for education, and uncovering any impediments to establishing or refining such a program. It is also important to identify past successes and to institute policies that will create an appropriate environment for addressing ethical concerns.

One of the first steps is to perform an "ethics audit" to determine whether policies are consistent across departments or care and service provider organizations and congruent with partners so "we are all coming from the same place." Using existing internal mechanisms such as QA to explore consistencies and inconsistencies between the various constituent organizations and plan partners is an important component in the ethics audit process since it is not uncommon for intra-institutional departments to have contradictory ways of dealing with the same issues. For example, disparities may exist between DNR policies and procedures from department to department; a DNR order might be honored in most departments but might be ignored or temporarily suspended without patient permission during palliative surgery. When people use a policy in an inconsistent fashion, it invalidates the policy and reduces its effectiveness. A policy is intended to provide consistency and direction, and any deviation from the policy must be explained and documented. Policies should better assure continuity of action in accordance with patient's wishes across the continuum.

Also having transfer policies to ensure continuity of consent and of care is important, as is having a conflict resolution policy. It should also include guidance for appeals of caregivers, foundations for proactive partnering and ways of blending organizational with clinical ethics.

CLINICAL ETHICS ROUNDS

If, on the clinical level, a healthcare facility is unwilling, or for some reason unable to create an ethics committee, clinical ethics rounds may serve as a helpful vehicle to address ethical issues. It can also be an excellent teaching resource as well as a valuable addition to an extant working ethics committee. Ethics rounds can offer a more natural forum for open discussion in the clinical setting than an ethics committee, which is more public in nature and accordingly more visible. Active and ongoing participation in ethics rounds allows clinicians to become better informed, and better educated, and allows them to master problems and issues that otherwise may appear to be overwhelming.

Unit- or facility-based ethics rounds have many advantages over an ethics committee as a means of dealing with controversy in a timely fashion. Departmental ethics rounds should be offered regularly, ideally weekly, but at least monthly, with interim ad hoc meetings as required. Attendance is not obligatory, and care providers need not attend every meeting to keep up with issues and solutions, for the content of such rounds is informally transmitted quickly and easily.

Whereas an ethics committee, or any committee for that matter, has the luxury of being able to carefully sort through alternatives, ethics rounds can be a valuable asset to the clinician who must make a decision immediately. Having other individuals involved in thinking about a difficult issue can be very helpful. The clinician can accept the assistance of peers without losing face and without having to make his or her confusion or indecisiveness known to a large number of people. Furthermore, all of those on the rounds gain insights and critical skills that each caregiver is able to bring to a decision-making process.

Ethics rounds may be integrated into regular clinical rounds or they may occur as a separate educational tool. In the latter case, rounds often last approximately one to one and a half hours and occur at least twice a month, with ad hoc meetings as requested. High-tech settings and critical care services often require more frequent meetings.

Ethics rounds may consist of a roundtable discussion in an informal setting where medical and nursing staff can float in and out as their schedules permit, or they can be a component of patient care or even case management rounds. Specific presentations may be scheduled to clarify a certain issue endemic to the type of the decision being contemplated or to explicate certain facets of decision making. There is almost always informal discussion after each session, and when indicated, chart notations are made concerning suggestions or modifications in care plans resulting from the session.

THE BENEFITS OF ETHICS ROUNDS

The problems that arise in this kind of situation can be minimized if other caregivers are provided the chance to discuss them and try to arrive at reasonable solutions, which is exactly what ethics rounds are intended to do.

If the ethics committee has developed and adopted a clear policy or for that matter medical management policies and procedures that address this and related issues, caregivers will have better guidance and better insulation against potential legal liability as well as ways to better assure care for the patient. The policy might indicate that the stated wishes of a patient will not be allowed to be thwarted, undermined, or compromised by any third parties, including family members. It might also define what steps should be taken to resolve a conflict of this type. Such a policy would help the physician honor the patient's wishes and ensure patient autonomy.

Of course, ethics rounds might also help. Other caregivers might suggest to the physician that he take the following steps: (1) chart the disparity between what the competent patient wants and what the family members want; (2) request a family conference and chart the results (via the department of social work); and (3) request that pastoral care be called in and chart their involvement. In taking these steps, the physician will increase his protection if he chooses (as he should) to honor and support the wishes of the patient. If he wants to do this but is still uneasy, he could ask for a consultation to determine whether the patient is competent to make a medical decision. Regardless of whether guidance comes from an ethics committee or ethics rounds, it will help in dealing with ongoing problems and avoiding mistakes.

Again, suppose an attending physician is reluctant to perform a given task (such as the writing of a DNR order). What would likely happen if a colleague brought this problem to the attention of the ethics committee? Her ability to work with the attending could well become compromised and the seeds of future interprofessional conflict might be planted. Yet the attending's continued reluctance is causing problems for the patient's family and the hospital staff. Now suppose the ethics committee has developed good policies on consent, DNR orders, and withholding or withdrawing of other life-prolonging medical procedures.

Further, suppose that the issue of the attending's reluctance is raised for discussion during ethics rounds. The administrator or medical director would then be able to intervene without interloping, because all he or she would be doing is bringing the already-established hospital policy to the attention of the physician and giving fair warning that failure to act in accordance with the policy could create potential problems, including a charge of malpractice.

A similar scenario could arise in a circumstance where a specific intervention is needed and covered by a managed care plan but a physician has been warned that he is out of range in terms of his overutilization, and may jeopardize his entire withhold of 20 percent if he does not reverse his process of overuse and inefficiency. Department rounds can bring this to the fore and offer some way of meeting the patient's needs without compromising the physician for doing the right thing. It may also serve as a proactive foundation for insulating physicians who make appropriate medical decisions, regardless of the cost.

Departmental ethics rounds offer a means for discussing and addressing recurring issues fruitfully. They should not serve as a mechanism for pursuing business as usual or for evading troublesome problems and issues. In fact, ethics rounds tend to force issues to the fore. They provide an opportunity to talk formally about problems that are causing mere grumbling and can make explicit what has been to date only implicit.

CLINICAL ETHICS ROUNDS AND THE ETHICS COMMITTEE

The relationship between ethics rounds and the ethics committee is important to understand. Obviously, the better equipped the rounds members are to address controversies and dilemmas, and the better they know the institution's, network's, or PPO's policies, the more effective they will be in ensuring the policies are adopted and followed. The rounds can help the ethics committee identify the need for policy development by bringing recurrent problems to its attention. Since the rounds are usually open only to care team members, some mechanism for getting information to the other services may be needed. However, they need not be limited to clinicians.

One strategy is to include a representative from legal services on the rounds to provide a legal perspective. Having an in-house lawyer and a risk manager present will be of value when developing institutional policies, since they will better understand clinical issues and appreciate the dynamics of providing medical services. By bringing together clinicians and lawyers in a context where they can educate each other and learn to work together, ethics rounds can increase the likelihood that institutional policies and problem solving will be more effective and more practical.

Ethics rounds also offer a forum for clarifying and addressing guidelines. If the facility/plan has adopted guidelines but situations arise that do not seem to be covered by the guidelines, the hospital attorney, after learning about the problem from attending the rounds, can bring any problems to the attention of the appropriate person and make suggestions for modifications.

It is currently an open question whether ethics committee discussions must be recorded and whether the minutes are discoverable or covered by the umbrella of peer review. In many cases, some of the proceedings of an ethics committee may indeed be discoverable, depending on what information is requested and why. Some may argue that if the ethics committee proceedings are part of the quality assurance process, then they are not discoverable, particularly when there is a peer review component. Clinical discussions during ethics rounds, however, need not be documented and minutes need not be taken. Minutes are never taken for clinical discussions or rounds, so this is no deviance from accepted policy, nor could it be perceived as an attempt to hide information.

DEVELOPING POLICIES AND ADJUDICATING CONFLICT

There is another critical function that ethics rounds can perform: assisting in the development of policies in areas where distinctive or novel issues arise in a given setting or unit. For example, in many hospitals a high percentage of ICU beds are filled with nursing home residents, some of whom are in persistent vegetative states. As a consequence, patients who could benefit from treatment in an ICU are denied a bed.

Suppose a hospital ethics committee wishes to address this issue, which was brought to its attention by participants in the ICU ethics rounds. Since the ethics rounds participants are used to working together to define and resolve problems, they would be exceptionally well qualified to play a major role in developing a policy regarding the use of ICU beds for patients with long-term acute care needs.

Other issues arise from the "trampoline effect," the repeated transfer of patients from the hospital to the nursing home and back again. For example, how do caregivers ensure that a patient's wishes will be honored when he or she is transferred from one facility to another? The patient's chart does not accompany the patient, and a mere discharge summary that says the patient is a DNR might not be adequate. This continuity of care issue is an example of the issues that ethics rounds can help to address.

Ethics rounds offer an informal environment for identifying or talking about ethical issues. They can enhance the effectiveness of a given service and the ethics committee as well. Having an ethics committee is not a prerequisite for holding ethics rounds, but such a committee, unlike ethics rounds, can develop policies that will help caregivers resolve recurrent, avoidable problems.

EVALUATING CONFLICT RESOLUTION TECHNIQUES

There are many different ways to address conflict. One important rule is to avoid jumping to the last step first; that is, going to court and seeking a legal solution. The best way to address conflict is to have polices and procedures in place that ensure consistency on how to address and resolve conflict. Generally, such policies will indicate that the first attempt at conflict resolution should be undertaken between the patient (or surrogate) and the caregiver. Identifying impediments to resolving issues and controversies, clearing up misconceptions, and identifying other blockages to decision making are often fruitful tactics. If they are insufficient, there are other intrainstitutional resources to call upon to stimulate the resolution process.

In-house conflict resolution mechanisms are generally preferable to external mechanisms. At times, however, it helps to bring in an outsider. The usual internal tools for resolving conflict are (interdisciplinary) patient care conferences, pastoral care conferences, and family conferences with the social work department.

Evaluating an existing procedure for resolving conflict (or creating one) is another step in an ethics audit. A conflict resolution policy should define how conflict should be addressed, by whom, and under what circumstances. In the past, guidelines such as those outlined below were sufficient to address most of the conflicts that arose.

GENERAL CLINICAL CONFLICT RESOLUTION GUIDELINES

The following guidelines should be used in case of conflict on the health-care institutional level whether it involves caregivers, family members, the patient, or the patient's surrogate:

1. Conflict is ideally resolved through opportunities for informal but enhanced communication between the parties.
2. Involvement of a third party, such as a supervisor, an administrator, or a risk manager, can increase the likelihood of a resolution.
3. If a conflict arises between the patient (or surrogate) and representatives of the facility, the following should be considered:
   - A pastoral care conference might be initiated. Pastoral care staff can help in addressing problems of denial, unresolved grief, religious perceptions and misperceptions, and impediments to decision making.
   - Involving a social worker in family conferences can be beneficial. Often, decision making is impeded by concern or frustration on the part of family members who may be worried that they will not be able to meet the patient's needs at home.
   - Both social workers and pastoral care staff can assist with the conflict resolution process. Which to use first depends on the circumstances and the availability of personnel. Both can enlist other individuals in the agency, facility, or health plan to assist in decision making as well as offer the family the option of convening the ethics committee. It is not uncommon for social workers and pastoral care staff to be on ethics committees and to be able to identify the resources needed for a timely resolution of conflict.
4. *Ethics rounds and consultations can assist in bedside problem solving.* The ethics committee should be a forum for identifying problems, resolving current issues, or precluding future conflict. It can also help create educational opportunities for staff and surrogate decision makers and interpret policies and procedures for anyone who is unclear about them. (These will be discussed in greater depth later in this chapter.)
5. As a patient, try working out the problem with the office manager of the plan, who may be able to help adjudicate the

conflict or perhaps involve the medical director in the conflict resolution process. From the caregiver side, approach the medical director to help resolve the conflict if unable to work out the problem directly with the caregiver involved in the conflict.

6. If the conflict involves a quality assurance issue, contact the quality assurance department.

7. Involve the benefit manager of the employer to help adjudicate the conflict. This is a helpful intervention that is often overlooked.

8. Consulting the legal counsel is sometimes an important step in the conflict resolution process. The legal counsel can identify or clarify policy provisions, highlight ambiguities and inconsistencies, and suggest future directions. Also, if reasonable attempts to address a conflict using internal processes fail, the legal counsel can evaluate whether the probate system or another external mechanism might be appropriate. Note that consulting the legal counsel, except for clarification of a policy issue, is generally not one of the early steps in the conflict resolution process.

CONFLICT RESOLUTION IN MANAGED CARE: GUIDELINES FOR APPEALS OF UTILIZATION MANAGEMENT DECISIONS[2]

Conflict resolution policies focused on clinical environments may not be sufficient to deal with the more complex issues and tradeoffs that caregivers face in managed care environments. The diverse professionals and non-professionals associated with managed healthcare delivery will have greater need for creative ways of addressing issues on the cost-quality interface. The following provisions are adapted from the *Managed Health Care Handbook* and are an excellent example of how appeals of utilization management decisions should be undertaken by the physician. These can be modified to serve other healthcare professionals as well. For example, they can be easily adapted to assist pharmacists in dealing with formulary issues and challenges, therapeutic interchange and substitution, and drug sensitivities and individual variation. They can be helpful for case managers as well. Selected provisions and guidelines appear as follows:

---

[2] Adapted with permission from Kongstvedt, Peter: *The Managed Health Care Handbook,* 3rd edition. Gaithersburg, MD: Aspen Publishers, Inc., 1996, p. 186.

- Providers must advise the MCO of their medical judgment. The physician needs to be aware of each plan's utilization review process and to advise the plan of his or her medical judgment in clear terms. If a disagreement arises, the physician may need to support the validity of the clinical recommendations with documentation of the medical necessity. This could include diagnostic test results, and providing an opinion as to the possible adverse outcomes [should the request be denied] might also be helpful.

- Develop a "fast track" second opinion program. Providers need to support the development of a system that can quickly render a second opinion in case of disagreement surrounding clinical judgment. Ideally, the second opinion should be rendered by a healthcare professional whose skill and training are commensurate with those of the provider whose judgment is being questioned.

- The patient should be informed of any issues that are being disputed relative to the physician's recommended treatment plan and the MCO's coverage decision. Alternative approaches and the potential cost and outcome of those approaches should be discussed with the patient. Also, the patient should be informed that, if the plan continues to deny coverage, the patient may be responsible for payment. The patient should continue to be informed throughout the appeal process.

- Exhaust the appeals process. In the event that the treating physician firmly believes that the MCO has made an incorrect decision, then the best defense in the case of treatment denials is staunch patient advocacy. The physician should request to speak to the medical director in charge of the utilization decision and explain the rationale behind the intended treatment. If a plan continues to deny coverage for a service that the physician feels is necessary, the process that allows for a second opinion fails to support treatment, and the physician continues to believe that the denial of coverage is an error, then the decision should be appealed aggressively. All avenues of appeal should be exhausted. If unsuccessful the physician should inform the patient of treatment options without regard to coverage.

RECOMMENDATIONS FOR REDUCING CONFLICT AND LIABILITY EXPOSURE IN MEDICAL MANAGEMENT DETERMINATIONS[3]

Plans should take steps to resolve and hopefully preclude conflict dealing with medical management activities and to minimize their liability

---

[3] Kongstvedt, *Handbook*, pp. 939–942.

exposure related to these activities. They should also provide guidance, clarification, and consistency.

■ Plans should incorporate specific definitions (e.g., of medical necessity emergency services, experimental or investigational procedures, and custodial care) and specifically explain any exclusions or limitations . . . to avoid ambiguity concerning what services are covered by their certificates.

■ Ensure that marketing brochures accurately describe the benefits, exclusions, and limitations of the certificate to avoid conflicts between these documents.

■ Make a reasonable effort to ensure that any medical management issues are thoroughly investigated before the organization makes an adverse benefit determination . . . [As an example,] it may be advisable to develop a checklist of the type of information that should be obtained in order to document that the plan has fully and fairly evaluated the circumstance of each case before an adverse determination is made . . . and generally to follow established policies and procedures before making an adverse determination.

■ Ensure that the plan's medical policies are consistent with generally accepted standards of medical practice.

■ Implement a provider appeal procedure similar to that used to resolve member grievances. That procedure should permit providers to request a hearing before an impartial and appropriately qualified physician hearing officer to present and explain their arguments concerning a disputed medical management determination. That procedure should also provide for an expedited review if the attending physician reasonably believes that an adverse determination may preclude a member from receiving urgently needed services. The ability to identify and resolve disputes quickly, or at least to demonstrate that the plan fully and fairly considered relevant information before making an adverse determination, should significantly reduce the plan's liability exposure, particularly in bad faith or negligence actions.

■ Obtain current technology assessments concerning the status of new, experimental, or investigational procedures. Such assessments should help demonstrate that the plan acted in good faith and exercised reasonable care when making decisions concerning the coverage of those procedures.

■ Provider bonuses should consider performance measures, such as member satisfaction, compliance with applicable administrative standards and satisfying quality of care requirements, in addition to the provider's utilization experience. This will limit any incentive to deny necessary care to members. The plan should also ensure that members have the right to appeal any provider's decision to deny or limit access to covered services directly to the plan.

■ Implement quality assurance programs to evaluate members' access to services, any apparent underutilization of services, and patient complaints. This will help prove that the plan has exercised reasonable care in reviewing the quality of services provided to members.

Do not delegate medical management responsibilities to another entity . . . unless that entity's medical management programs are comparable with the plan's programs. The plan should retain the right to audit that entity's activities to ensure that it exercises reasonable care when performing delegated management activities. The provider entity should also be required to refer all complaints to the plan so that it can promptly address any problems related to that entity's performance of its delegated duties.

THE ETHICS COMMITTEE IN MANAGED CARE

The ethics committee in managed care can address a wide variety of issues and determine how care is delivered, how appeals are handled, and what image the organization displays to the general community. Ethics committees can handle grievances and appeals as well as identify policies and procedures to preclude or address recurring problems, providing another level of protection for both the organization and the patient.

There is increased pressure to create formal mechanisms for conflict resolution and policy development in healthcare facilities. Ethics committees can be helpful in dealing with ethical issues and resolving conflicts of various sorts. They can also be used to mend the seams of the delivery system to better ensure continuity of care as well as responsiveness to patient wishes. Questions about their value, role, and scope, however, need to be answered fully. Existing committees can easily become stagnant and purposeless and need revitalization.

Establishing an ethics committee, an institutional forum for addressing a wide range of ethical issues, is not always an easy task. Like many innovative mechanisms for addressing controversy, an ethics committee may be feared as potentially too influential, and its role may be reduced from problem solving to identification of and education about ethical issues. Many committees were actually set up primarily for educational purposes. Considerations when establishing an ethics committee include:

- the type of committee and its membership
- the role, scope, and charge of the committee
- the use of consultants, clinical ethical tools, and clinical ethics rounds

The greatest opposition to ethics committees from the clinical side stems from concerns that these committees will question or interfere with caregiver decision-making autonomy. One option for dealing with ethical issues, clinical ethics rounds, can provide an opportunity to address ongoing ethical issues for patients and staff as they occur. (This will be discussed in greater detail later in this chapter). An ethics committee also can perform an ethics audit of decision-making guidelines to evaluate strengths and weaknesses as well as identify and respond to unmet needs in the organization.

From the plan side, the forum for dealing with ethical issues has been QA. Having a mechanism that can serve as a resource or complement to QA has some distinct advantages for the MCO. Active participation and a displayed sensitivity towards a fair assessment and treatment of clinical ethical issues can be a positive step towards continuity of care, a means of achieving common goals with the partner.

A HISTORICAL PERSPECTIVE ON ETHICS COMMITTEES

Historically, ethics committees were created, not to solve systemic institutional problems, but to solve a specific problem in an acute care setting. Over time, however, they began to be used for addressing a wide range of medical and administrative issues. Few have arisen in long-term care facilities, where there is less support and medical guidance than exists in a hospital, and where end-of-life issues are often more subtle.

The first use of an ethics committee to resolve an end-of-life issue occurred in *Quinlan*. The court made use of a medical prognosis committee, one composed of physicians who speculated as to the prognosis based on their clinical findings. This medical prognosis committee was widely misinterpreted to be an ethics committee that could appropriately address a wide range of difficult legal and ethical questions. The use in *Quinlan* of a medical prognosis committee, despite or perhaps because of the misunderstanding of its nature, fueled the desire of many practitioners to institute an ethics forum. On the other hand, many physicians, fearing that their clinical decisions might be questioned, did not want such a forum. Other vehicles for physician oversight, such as quality assurance and risk management committees, were also viewed negatively by many in the medical community. As a result, the ethics committees that were created were reluctant to encroach on clinicians' turf and thus remained relatively ineffective. Physicians tend to perceive advisory committees as unwelcome intruders and as a source of additional stress in an already nerve-wracking situation.

New pressures have created a need to re-evaluate the scope and mission of ethics committees. Although resolving clinical and administrative conflict became a fruitful role for many committees, current conflicts have expanded far beyond the intrainstitutional bickering of the past. Healthcare reform and the drive toward managed care have admitted patients, courts, insurers, and even politicians into the wrestling ring. Systemic issues, including questions regarding what services can be provided to whom and when, have grown in importance. It is these issues that present an opportunity for ethics committees to expand their role, not only in hospitals, where discussion of these issues is relatively mature, but also in long-term care facilities and home health agencies, which are relatively inexperienced in dealing with the constraints imposed by managed care.

ETHICS COMMITTEES AND ADVOCACY

The traditional role ethics committees have played in education and policy development is often complemented by their expanding role as advocates for healthcare providers when external constraints compromise the delivery of care or services to patients. Patient advocacy, of course, has become a byword of healthcare reform. Both the AMA and the American Hospital Association (AHA), for example, place a greater emphasis on advocacy than in the past. The role of advocate for patients and providers is somewhat different than the role assumed by prototypical ethics committees. (See Chapter 8 for a more complete discussion of patient advocacy.)

NON–HOSPITAL-BASED ETHICS COMMITTEES

Many highly trained clinical specialists spend an inordinate amount of time getting administrative approval to treat from third-party payors. Meanwhile, long-term and home care providers, who have less credibility than physicians, often find the approval process almost unfathomable. The role of oversight by government agencies exacerbates the challenge and may create regulatory disincentives that do not exist in the hospital. For example, although most hospitals are required to provide staffing appropriate to the needs of the patient, long-term care regulations will usually specify the number of hours each day and even the times during the day that various levels of care must be provided. Procedures and services that are discretionary in a hospital, such as evening snacks for patients, are required in a long-term care facility. Thus, long-term care facilities lack the flexibility to plan effective and efficient healthcare for their residents in a managed care atmosphere.

In addition, long-term care facilities are perceived as "warehouses" for the elderly, and the health professionals who work in them are often viewed as more concerned about making money than about providing care. The reality that government reimbursement is limited but government service demands are vast is hardly ever mentioned in the public debate on healthcare. Thus having a forum, such as an ethics committee, to increase their credibility is becoming a necessity for many long-term care providers. They need opportunities for input and negotiation to combat the pressure from managed care organizations to compromise care.

For example, managed care organizations may mandate that physicians in long-term care be board-certified geriatricians. This would exclude many physicians currently working in long-term care facilities and might put them out of business. The facilities, on the other hand, may be unable to attract and pay for board-certified specialists to oversee the care provided to their residents, and may themselves be forced to close.

LONG-TERM CARE AND HOME HEALTHCARE ETHICS COMMITTEES

It is difficult to obtain accurate and up-to-date information on ethics committees in long-term and home care delivery environments, but it is clear that, unlike the crisis management model found in many hospitals, they have a more expansive role as a forum for developing policies that affect the daily lives of residents and patients. At the same time, although facilities and agencies are encouraged to address ethical issues by the Omnibus Budget Reconciliation Act of 1991, there may be sufficient financial disincentives to impede or even undermine the process. For example, reimbursement for both home care and long-term care is currently based primarily on the costs incurred by the provider. In order to increase reimbursement, the provider must provide more care. Thus, it is not in the provider's best interest to cease providing care by not resuscitating a patient. Likewise, the mandate to implement a process of advance directives for residents and clients is unfunded. The costs in terms of time, effort, forms, and recordkeeping are not reimbursed by the government and therefore detract from an often-slim bottom line. There must be positive incentives for ethics issues to be fully and properly explored in long-term and home care settings. Perhaps the recognition that increasingly verdicts are being rendered against providers for the failure to honor advance directives will help correct this.

A RESPONSE TO MANAGED CARE FROM CARE AND SERVICE PROVIDER ORGANIZATIONS

The emergence of the ethics committee in long-term care is a creative response to managed care and other external pressures. It can enable the clinical process to run more smoothly and at the same time it can develop systemic safeguards. The ability to frame issues in a way that encourages mutual understanding across institutional and community boundaries nurtures respect, which in turn leads to greater commonality of purpose. Similarly, home health providers are increasingly faced with the task of providing a certain level of care and at the same time are constrained by managed care contracts as well as by Medicare/Medicaid provisions to provide that care at minimum cost. Since home health providers do not have the same supports as exist in many other healthcare settings and have to make decisions and exercise judgment on their own, they experience constraints and tradeoffs more acutely than many other caregivers. Often caught between a rock and a hard place, they need to develop a framework for addressing cost issues while creating formal mechanisms to prevent patient care from being compromised.

PAYOR-BASED ETHICS COMMITTEES

Leadership can be integrated with ethics to better ensure that the mission values and vision of the MCO leaders can translate into practice within all facets of the organization. The leaders of the MCO need a way to inculcate their vision, mission and values into some forum that markets their commitment to quality, best practices, and the like. Having a payor-based committee can be quite attractive in achieving this. Its role would be one less of problem solving than of assuring that its care and service provider organizations and licensed individual practitioners acted in accordance with the mission, values, and vision of central operations and that the payor's actions be grounded in integrity, reliability, and trust. Its role would be to evaluate the need for policies and procedures that ensure their mission and goals and that set the tone for the rest of their organization and its employees. Many managed care organizations have been contemplating or creating their own ethics committees There is even some discussion that NCQA may include an ethics component in their oversight programs, as does the Joint Commission. Such a committee would focus less on consultation than on policy review, development, and refinement.

SOME ADVANTAGES OF ETHICS COMMITTEES

The fact that ethics committees are usually interdisciplinary testifies to the importance of diversity of perspective in handling a wide range of complex problems. For example, people often say they have an ethical problem they want to address when what they really mean is that they are concerned with legal liability. They disguise legal questions as ethical ones. This covering of one's backside has been and will probably continue to be a significant motivating factor in bringing issues to the attention of an ethics committee, since this forum is more accessible and less threatening than the hospital legal counsel or an outside attorney.

An initial step in appealing to an ethics committee is to identify why a given concern is brought to the attention of the committee and to sort out the legal, ethical, and administrative components. This serves several purposes: (1) It minimizes the scattergun approach to problem solving (the wider the spread, the greater chance of being on target); (2) It allows the committee to define precisely the issues at hand; (3) It can break down a complex problem into simpler components; and (4) It allows the committee to identify any misperceptions that exist.

What is discussed in the committee must be kept confidential. Talking in the elevator or the hallway about a case that is currently being considered is inappropriate. This is particularly true where sensitive concerns are voiced in the committee that would not have been voiced in a less protected setting. Whether the problem at hand is primarily legal or ethical in nature, it must be addressed. The doctor and patient still must make a decision together. If the patient's wishes are unknown or unclear and there are no advance directives and no appropriate surrogate, the physician will have to act in the best interests of the patient.

Ethics committee discussions create an opportunity for enriched understanding and allow caregivers to deal with difficult problems more effectively than in the past. They also can increase the comfort level of those involved in a decision-making situation and allow them to hold in abeyance their own moral preconceptions and prejudices and look at issues in a clearer way and without feeling threatened.

RESPONSIBILITIES OF ETHICS COMMITTEE MEMBERS

Ethics committees have often been labeled as "advisory," which means their function is to encourage the physicians through education to "do the right thing." There was an assumption that rational solutions to ethical dilemmas would somehow float to the top and magically display themselves so clearly that physicians could not help but do what was right. Another assumption was that ethics committees, by deliberating on ethical issues, would become so adept at solving problems that they could deal with the very complex problems beginning to arise in high-technology medicine.

To play their proper role, ethics committee members must:

- Gain some sense of what ethics is all about
- Understand the role, scope, and charge of the committee
- Identify the strengths and weaknesses of the committee
- Master problem identification, problem solving, and conflict resolution techniques
- Know how to test and refine provisional decisions or recommendations
- Recognize that there will not necessarily be clearly defined right and wrong answers but that the problem-solving process itself can be helpful and illuminating
- Learn how to clarify important components of a problem and explore an array of solutions to identify the most appropriate one
- Recognize that getting together to talk about a problem and merely feeling better as a result is not a sufficient response to the problem
- Understand the ethical and legal issues that often arise in case discussion and policy development

EDUCATING COMMITTEE MEMBERS

An ethics committee must be provided with certain "tools of the trade." Members need to be familiar with key ethical and legal principles and how to define issues, test provisional decisions, and offer advice. They need up-to-date materials and other resources. Developing a small library of books or articles is a sensible way of increasing members' knowledge and skills.

Although models can be used for developing policies, going through the process of development themselves is important for committee members so they understand why the specific language was employed. Understanding this will help them perform their advisory role and reduce the chance of conflict. For example, if the committee chooses not to use the words "heroic measures" and replaces them with something more appropriate, the reason behind the choice is important, particularly when a caregiver approaches the committee for advice and uses "heroic measures" to define the issue. The committee should be able to explain that heroism implies sacrificing oneself or putting oneself in danger for a noble cause and that therefore "heroic measures" is inappropriate for referring to procedures that do no more than prolong the dying process. Being supplied with that insight might be extremely helpful to the staff member who has come to the committee for advice.

EDUCATING OTHER STAFF MEMBERS AND THE COMMUNITY

If staff do not understand why a policy was created or changed or framed in the way it was, they likely will not take ownership of it, and the development of the policy will be little more than an interesting intellectual exercise on the part of the committee. The staff must receive in-service training on policies and procedures if they are to have a positive effect.

Occasionally an interesting case arises, a recurrent or even an unusual problem is identified, or a new regulation is put into place. These are appropriate teaching moments, and the ethics committee should use them as part of the process of educating staff about ethical issues and problem solving.

Developing brochures, informing patients of options and resources available to them, and developing community education programs using outside consultants or committee members are all tasks that an ethics committee should perform or at least be actively involved with. The marketing resources of the MCO can be a valuable asset in this process.

COMMITTEE COMPOSITION AND MEMBERSHIP

As a general rule, an institutional ethics committee should have at least 7 members but no more than 10, although many variations involving substantially more or less than those suggested have been effective. Obviously, the structure and membership of a particular committee will depend on what resources are available, whether the organization is part of an integrated delivery system or PPO, whether it is a home health agency, long-term care facility, or some other kind of non-acute care facility or agency.

The makeup of the committee will largely be determined by the assigned role, scope, and charge of the committee. For example, is the committee intended to play an educational, advisory, or decision-making role? Is it going to be a facility-based, shared or network model, or a community-based committee?

Typical ethics committee members include the following:

- Director of nursing
- Medical director
- Leader or head of the care or service provider organization
- Director of social work
- Director of pastoral care
- Representatives from managed care and/or management company organizations
- Director of quality assurance of the MCO
- Representatives from other community care providers (e.g., long-term care facilities and home health agencies)
- Representatives from referring institutions (e.g., hospitals and clinics)
- Other appropriate healthcare professionals

CASE CONSULTATIONS

When a patient's case is being considered, people with whom the patient has established a strong relationship, including those from previous stays at other facilities, should be considered for inclusion or at least contacted to obtain pertinent information. Also, people with special talents in the organization or system can be integrated into the decision-making process.

Insurance and risk management personnel are often appropriate advisors, and their participation can serve as an opportunity for committee members to learn how to address similar problems in the future.

Depending on the content of the case, other parties may be invited to attend special sessions. If, for example, the case concerns admission and transfer policies, representatives from the appropriate departments should be present.

People who face ethical and legal issues regularly or have experience dealing with such issues and are interested in serving on the ethics committee should be considered for membership. In smaller or rural facilities without a legal counsel, risk management and quality assurance personnel or a local attorney with interest in medical ethics would offer an important perspective on many issues likely to arise.

If the committee is to be primarily a policy-making group, there will be leaders and few if any doers (lots of chiefs, but few if any indians). However, if clinical advising is part of the committee's charge, those responsible for care at the bedside must be included. Department heads may have clinical responsibilities, but they do not have the same perspective as staff nurses, for example, who must occasionally make on-the-spot decisions in the middle of the night.

The committee, whether or not its main job is developing and upgrading policies, will still have a responsibility to educate physicians, nurses, and other caregivers and support them when they are faced with difficult decisions.

CONCLUSION

This chapter has offered a range of options for reducing conflict as well as developing policies and procedures that provide guidance and consistency in resolving controversies and conflict. It is hoped that this discussion has helped breathe new life to your ethics committee or suggested new directions you might take. For those who are contemplating establishing an ethics committee there are helpful suggestions concerning what approach you might take in forming a committee. This chapter also has discussed the importance of putting general conflict resolution policies in place and of integrating components into policies where conflict might routinely arise. Finally the chapter has attempted to offer a range of options rather than only one way to deal with the resolution of conflict.

CASE STUDIES

CASE 1

A patient has coverage for an autologous bone marrow transplant in another state and has recently been transferred by her company to another state. She is still a member of the HMO she signed up with earlier in the year. The new HMO, which is part of her network, refuses to provide coverage for the service.

Discussion Questions

- How can the conflict be addressed in a timely fashion?
- What obligation does the physician have?
- What obligations does the plan have?
- What might the plan's medical director do to intervene?
- What rights and recourse does the patient have?
- How should the physician proceed with challenges to coverage?
- How should the patient proceed with challenges to coverage?

CASE 2

You are particularly interested in reducing utilization of resources on patients for whom you can do little more than prolong the dying process. On repeated occasions you have heard doctors stop by a patients room and say "We need to talk about code status. If your heart stops, do want us to start it back up? Or we need to know if you want us to do everything." You know that this manner of communication is ambiguous and doesn't really inform the patient of what is involved and why. At the same time, going in to talk with the patient and saying "I can come in and crack your ribs, and cause you great discomfort to no avail—do you want me to do it?" directs the answer in quite another direction. Your real concern is that options which are medically viable or medically appropriate might not be offered to the patient in the first place. Instead the patient should be told what reasonable management and attempts to keep him comfortable and pain free should be initiated.

Discussion Questions

- Is this a managed care partner issue where involvement of the payor or plan is appropriate?
- Can a formal body like an ethics committee assist in such a matter?
- Do we ever "do everything?" What does that mean? Does it mean doing advanced CPR regardless of medical efficacy? Does it mean the surgeon

should be called in to transplant the kidneys as the patient is dying from multisystem failure?

- What can ensure better management of such cases in the future?

CASE 3

A managed care partner has a huge impact on a given healthcare market yet its standards for quality are less than acceptable by the majority of clinicians in the community. One of the physician panel members is threatened with de-selection if his performance standards, specifically the unit cost per patient, do not change. This surgeon performs high risk procedures that no one else will undertake and he has a wonderful success rate. If he continues performing the procedure in question he will be de-selected from the MCO and lose a significant part of his income. He wishes to appeal to the managed care partner that he provides services and care not available elsewhere and that his outcomes are superb given the high risk level of this procedure.

Discussion Questions

- How can the aforementioned advice on de-selection help resolve this matter?
- What vehicles exist to protect the physician from being de-selected?
- How can the medical director assist the physician?
- How can a middle ground be negotiated between the plan and the licensed practitioner?
- Who should be involved in this conflict resolution process?
- What impact might the managed care partner QA department have in this process?

CASE 4

When Mrs. C. entered a long-term care facility 10 years ago, she was aware that it would not perform certain procedures or honor certain wishes, and she agreed to its terms. Now, however, the condition has deteriorated dramatically and she has become much sicker and suffers sharp uncontrollable pain shooting into her limbs. She never envisioned spending the last days of her life in severe pain and she is adamant she does not want to be kept alive merely to suffer. She is becoming weak and, while she still has the capacity to make her wishes known, she clearly states that under no circumstances shall a feeding tube or even an IV be inserted to prolong her life. The facility says that it will not honor such a wish.

Discussion Questions

- What is the likely outcome of the dispute between Mrs. C. and the long-term care facility?

- Can patients give up the right to change their mind?

Suppose this facility originally had a policy of honoring patients end-of-life wishes but has recently been purchased by a religious-oriented healthcare network and now will not honor certain wishes. When Mrs. W. entered the facility, she was told she could request a DNR order and it would be respected. Now, at the end of life and in extreme pain, she is told the facility's new policy does not permit the staff to abide by her wish to be allowed to die.

- What responsibilities does the facility have?

- What rights does Mrs. W. have?

- What role might a community ethics committee play in such a scenario?

- What role might an institutional ethics committee play in such a scenario?

11
CHAPTER

Community-based
Ethics Committees¹

INTRODUCTION

This chapter is primarily an examination of the concept and implementation of the community-based ethics committee. It also examines notions of shared accountability, continuity of care and of consent, and shared vision. In addition, advice is included on how to form as well as who should serve on the community-based committee. A community-based ethics committee can address issues that fall within the healthcare continuum that are not the responsibility of individual institutions yet are not handled well within the broader community. A community-based committee can meet needs, identify future problems, and take steps to address those as well; it can serve as a voice of the community to address issues that individual facilities or organizations are unable to address on their own. The scope and role of these committees will be discussed here, as well as their potential impact in a changing healthcare environment.

---

¹ This chapter was adapted with permission from material taken from *Ethical and Legal Issues in Home Health and Long Term Care: Challenges and Solutions,* by Dennis A. Robbins, Gaithersburg, MD: Aspen Publishers, Inc., 1996, pp. 165–173.

A NEW MARKETING CONCEPT

Marketing has not usually been seen as a natural offshoot of an ethics program. This has led to many missed opportunities. Patients do not always know which is the "best place" for them to go for medical care. An important criterion in their choice of providers is that they feel comfortable with the policies of the facility and believe that the staff will work with them, listen to them, and respond to their fears and anxiety. In short, they are looking for a place they can trust. Knowing that a facility has an ethics committee to deal with thorny problems will give them a sense of security and added confidence that the facility will do the right thing. This marketing element is perhaps more important now than ever before in the history of our healthcare system.

There is a clear need for providers to protect their patients and challenge inappropriate constraints without jeopardizing their relationships with managed care partners. One mechanism for achieving this is a community-based ethics committee. Often, challenges to third-party payors are perceived negatively. Payors are inclined to view the providers as wanting to supply unlimited services, and accordingly, they respond to most challenges as if they were unreasonable. A central forum for decision making may very well have greater credibility than any individual caregiver.

A community-based ethics committee is intended to serve as a forum to meet many of the challenges associated with healthcare reform as well as respond to some of the pressures of managed care as patients travel across the healthcare continuum. A community-based committee can support continuity and consistency of care and consent across facility lines as well as deal with problems that require broader community integration and coordination than any one facility can provide. It should be part of an integrated community delivery and problem-solving system. It is a place where issues and problems can be addressed that individual facilities take neither ownership of nor responsibility for, but that may dramatically affect the community. These include a wide range of community-related issues covering the whole spectrum and continuum of healthcare. It also includes problems associated with terminally ill patients who have indicated that they do not want to avail themselves of advanced cardiopulmonary resuscitation techniques. A community-based ethics committee can address a wide range of community issues for which there is no other appropriate forum for identification and resolution.

Whereas an institutional ethics committee may serve as a forum for conflict resolution as well as an important resource for education and advice, a community-based ethics committee can be used to tackle system-related issues, which in many ways are more complicated than intrafacility or intraorganizational issues. It can prevent certain problems from arising by increasing consistency among different healthcare organizations and by shaping the way in which access, availability, and continuity issues are addressed. The committee can also be a base for outreach into the community. Accordingly involving community leaders is an essential strategy to acheive this function.

ETHICS AND THE COMMUNITY

Whatever issues are being considered by an ethics committee may also eventually be considered in the wider community. For example, even though patient confidentiality is of paramount importance, it must be considered in light of the need of care providers to share information to create a seamless delivery system. While protection of patient information is critical, the sharing of information actually enhances patient care by transmitting critical patient data from one healthcare setting to another. Community ideals can be influential and may help shape legislation and even national policy, but the day-to-day issues that make life better for those served in the community should be the main focus of committee discussions. Community concerns about resource allocation, access to care, and cost must be brought to the committee by community representatives, and the committee's (and facility's or plan's) responses should be publicized in return. Although managed care organizations and providers may sometimes be perceived as adversaries, it makes sense to have an appropriate managed care representative on a community-based ethics committee in order to minimize miscommunication and create commonality of purpose. Working together allows facility and nonfacility committee members to learn how to frame problems and issues so as to engender community understanding and acceptance. If there is a foundation of community support, there is a greater likelihood of shared initiatives, shared responsibility, and shared accountability.

Given the perception, right or wrong, that making money is a primary goal and patient care is secondary, and also the realization that the capitated physician essentially becomes the insuror and the caregiver (which creates unresolvable conflicts of interest), managed care already has two strikes against it. Thus, having some forum to increase its credibility, such as a community-based ethics committee, makes good sense, particularly for plans that possess a high degree of integrity and accountability. An ethics committee can also provide room for input and negotiation, which is a growing need, since pressures from managed care organizations are forcing clinicians and administrators to compromise the very thing they are expected to provide—quality care.

SHARING RISK, ACCOUNTABILITY, AND VISION

Managed care requires that provider organizations become partners in the attempt to supply high quality services within cost constraints. Shared risk, accountability, and ownership are essential if managed care is to succeed in the long term. A community-based ethics committee can assist in the functional integration of the members of a managed care network so that it indeed becomes an integrated network. The process may be time consuming at first, but the participants can anticipate and deal with issues that arise in an organized and coherent fashion, recommend modifications, and generally influence the way services are provided in the network.

If the committee is to serve as a voice for the community, its composition must reflect not only the mission of the various provider organizations but also the mandate to create a seamless delivery system. Case managers, social workers, patients, family members, acute care liaisons (physicians and nurses), clergy, and community leaders are appropriate members, as are informed healthcare attorneys with both administrative and clinical sensitivity. The rationale behind opening the ethics committee to the broader community is to enlist and encourage the community to understand the difficult healthcare issues routinely addressed by providers. Community representatives, by sharing responsibility and accountability in facing tough issues, will learn to respect the provider organizations and will be more inclined to act as their advocates in the community. Finally, having third-party payors participate in the ethics committee will create a tremendous opportunity to minimize misperceptions and bad blood while creating a true continuum of care.

A SCENARIO FOR THE COMMUNITY-BASED COMMITTEE TO ADDRESS

Imagine a patient suffering from severely labored breathing. The emergency medical technicians (EMTs) are called in to help the patient and if necessary take the patient to the emergency department. These personnel kick into high gear in the throes of an emergency, which is desirable so long as their interventions are consistent with the wishes of the patient. In this particular case, the family had asked the patient's physician to write a letter indicating the patient has a terminal condition and did not wish to avail herself of cardiopulmonary resuscitation. They produce this letter for the EMTs. The EMTs, however, are still uncomfortable, thinking they must do everything. On the one hand, they worry that if they fail to do everything they can, they may get sued or lose their licenses. On the other hand, they became EMTs in order to help people, not to override people's wishes. Is that letter enough to rely on? What if the family members are just overwhelmed by the circumstances and are not thinking clearly? What if the cause of the distress is a mucous plug and the act of intubation could free the plug and easily avert death? Also, why did the family members call for support in the first place if they did not really want it?

Furthermore, the emergency department may legitimately be reluctant to accept the letter as an expression of the patient's current wishes. The letter was written when the patient was a resident of a long-term care facility. She has since returned home, and the change in settings may have caused her to change her mind. On top of that, the emergency department may hold the view that long-term care facilities do not employ the same rigor and safeguards in writing DNR orders as does their hospital and that such a directive may be unreliable.

Developing ways to reasonably and safely respond to individual requests, ensure consistency across institutional lines, and reduce fears on the part of the families and first responders is an example of a worthy community goal. It is important to clarify obligations, protocols, policies, and procedures surrounding such issues, and an ethics committee composed of caregivers from various kinds of healthcare facilities can play a major role in such an endeavor.

ASSURING CONTINUITY ACROSS THE CONTINUUM

In situations such as the one described above, how can a community-based ethics committee identify the most appropriate way to address multiple needs without sacrificing the self-determination of patients or obstructing the professional duties of caregivers? In each case that comes before the committee, the committee's first step should be to examine:

- The wishes of the patient
- The directive from the physician to the first responders
- The perceptions and responsibilities of the first responders
- The roles and responsibilities of the emergency personnel
- The role and status of family members

Everyone wants to do the right thing. No one wants to err by doing too little or too much. The first responders, who are less likely to know the parties on the scene than family memebers or those who care for them, have legitimate concerns. In fact, all the people involved have legitimate concerns, and a community-based ethics committee can address those concerns and possibly arrive at a reasonable solution that takes into account everyone's needs and desires.

First responders to an emergency and emergency department personnel are often frustrated and confused when dealing with a family that called for help but at the same time wants to restrict help. Getting beyond their frustration is a necessary step in solving the problem. EMTs may perceive the family members as filled with denial or overwhelmed with grief, but the EMTs have a job to do. What is needed is a mechanism to ensure that patients' wishes are honored. One possible solution is a state-mandated "orange form" such as the one the state of Arizona uses. Each patient with a DNR order has a number that first responders can call to get the phone number of the appropriate hospital, home health agency, or long-term care facility, which can confirm the validity of the order.

Caregivers must deal more effectively with patient self-determination across the healthcare continuum. The healthcare delivery system will not become seamless magically. Caregivers need to repair the gaps by developing better ways of coordinating services across traditional boundary lines. In hospitals and nursing homes, when a new team begins its shift or changes its rotation, the transfer of critical patient information can be delayed or the information can even be lost. The problems of transmitting information from facility to facility are obviously more complex and require radical solutions. For example, shouldn't there be community or interfacility DNR or transfer orders? Implementing a community-wide policy on end-of-life issues would help prevent aberrations in the provision of services and coinfringement upon patient rights. This is the sort of policy that community-based ethics committees are intended to design and address.

BETTER ENSURING CONTINUITY OF PATIENT WISHES

The need to resolve issues such as the coordination and continuity of patient wishes across provider organizations is reason enough to develop a community-based ethics committee. For example, take again the case of a terminally ill patient who no longer requires the intensity of care provided in a hospital and has been transferred back into the home with appropriate home care supports. The family, with the assistance and guidance of home health nurses and aides, serves as the primary support system for the patient. The family was assured that should the patient become too difficult to manage, she could be sent to an appropriate healthcare delivery location, probably a long-term care facility. This presents no problem so far, if coordination and planning allow for such mobility. The problem arises when other service agencies in the community get involved in the case.

COMMUNITY-BASED ETHICS COMMITTEE MEMBERSHIP

There are many ethical issues that have a broad impact on the community, which the membership of a community-based ethics committee should reflect. It should include locally influential people who can speak for the community and act as reliable barometers of community concern. Enlisting community leaders increases the committee's effectiveness as well. The committee itself will then be viewed as speaking for the community, and it will be more effective in addressing common issues and topics of importance and seeing them with a broad vision rather than from the limited perspective of a particular institution.

Having a political leader on the committee, perhaps even the mayor or a representative from the mayor's office, can be very helpful, particularly when bond issues or changes in the system's architecture are required. Local clergy are appropriate choices for membership, not necessarily because of their advanced training in ethics (which many do not have) but because they are trusted by their congregants and are often intimately involved in many of the complex and difficult situations families and patients face. They are aware of the impediments, frustrations, fears, and anxieties that their congregants experience and can act as their advocates in committee deliberations.

An attorney who is sensitive to community issues and knowledgeable about health law would be a very valuable committee member. Cost is no deterrent, since community-based ethics committee members serve on a voluntary basis and without remuneration. Participation is perceived as a civic responsibility. It is important to find the right kind of attorney, one who will cooperate in the spirit of the committee and not impede deliberation and decision making, that is, one who will facilitate rather than undermine process.

Trustees or key members of major healthcare organizations in the community can identify impediments and supports. So can key representatives of special interest groups. The best members are those who know the mission and have leadership and decision-making authority in the organizations they are representing.

An ethics consultant or a person with advanced training in ethics can be a helpful resource for educating committee members as well as for developing tools for analyzing problems and identifying solutions. Ideally, the ethicist will have experience working with healthcare facilities and even more to the point managed care organizations. Knowing what has been effective, as well as some knowledge of the intricacies of the healthcare system, can save valuable time, resolve problems, and stimulate progress.

Those involved in liaison and triage functions and the movement of patients between institutions may be able to contribute important insights regarding issues related to these functions. Other possible committee members include EMTs, emergency department staff, risk management and quality assurance personnel, local businesspeople, representatives of insurance companies, and other payors.

The committee, however, should not be a Noah's ark, nor is there an exact recipe for determining its membership. If necessary, outside consultants and specialists can be used as resources, allowing regular members to be chosen based on their status in the community, their position in key organizations, and their talents.

A community-based ethics committee is not a viable substitute for an institutional ethics committee, as they have different roles. Certain members of an institutional committee, however, can and should serve on a community-based ethics committee. Generally, the community committee will deal with broader issues than the institutional committee. It would generally review not individual cases but types of anticipated or recurrent cases with broader community implications that could be effectively addressed through its intervention. The only time a community committee would get involved in an individual case would be if the central issue was a recurrent one that could not be resolved at the institutional level. In such cases, a family or patient might petition a community-based ethics committee as a resource, but the committee would have the final decision as to whether or not to accept the case.

An institution can deal with ethical issues in a variety of ways: through meetings of an ethics committee, for example, but also through discussions during case management rounds, teaching rounds, or even special ethics rounds. For a community, a community-based ethics committee is virtually the only vehicle for confronting community-wide ethical issues. In addition, it is a wonderful forum for networking and developing jointly sponsored educational programs, and it can be an excellent barometer of concern about the healthcare system.

COORDINATION AND NETWORKING

The problems and issues the community-based ethics committee will likely address may not be complex, but they will require the imagination and creative energy of people with vision and a good overview of the community. Years ago, I was involved with creating a hospice program in Cambridge, Massachusetts, as part of a Harvard Community Health Outreach initiative. When the key players got together, they realized they already had all the necessary resources to offer services needed in the community. It was merely a matter of knowing how to network among themselves and integrate existing healthcare, transportation, and volunteer services into a single package.

Although a community-based ethics committee is a superb resource for ethics-related networking, it is by no means the only resource. Liaisons with partners and sister (and brother) organizations and other sectors of the healthcare community can set the stage for addressing a wide range of issues, ethical issues included.

COMMUNITY-BASED ETHICS COMMITTEES AND ADVOCACY

A community-based ethics committee can become an advocate for the healthcare organizations represented on the committee as well as for the community. It can insulate the community from bad decision making and enhance its skills in dealing with issues that affect the community. It is a benevolent way to get people involved. A community network can create a community vision.

One way in which the community-based ethics committee works can be illustrated in a healthcare continuum example involving an emergency department and an LTC facility. If anyone blows the whistle on a long-term care facility, it is likely to be an emergency department. In the MCO context, when other MCOs as well as other care and service provider organization representatives in the community are involved, cross-community issues can be more easily addressed. One reason for different provider organizations to work together in an integrated multi-institutional setting is to develop a system for solving common problems and sharing of responsibilities and accountabilities. Inconsistencies in policy can occur between departments in the same hospital, but inconsistencies between the hospital and a long-term facility, even if they are part of the same network or delivery system, are a virtual certainty and are sure to be much more pronounced. Furthermore, if discussions and coordination of effort between the hospital emergency room and the long-term care facility have not occurred, advance directives and DNR orders may be viewed as spurious and not as an indication of the wishes of a patient who presents to the emergency department.

As mentioned above, a community-based ethics committee can also function as a marketing tool, creating an image of sharing rather than secrecy. In addition, provider organizations who are represented on the committee are seen as proactive leaders rather than as only responding to allegations of malpractice.

Long-term care facilities have an image problem which a community-based ethics committee can help to remedy. Home health agencies do not have the same problem. Their special need, because of the independence associated with home healthcare, is to make sure their policies and procedures are known by other types of provider organizations. Thus, a community-based ethics committee is a "natural" for home health, since it is a wonderful mechanism for identifying and creating links to the community and addressing continuity of care and continuity of consent concerns. It is equally natural for managed care if seamless delivery is a key to its success, particularly when it involves the managed care organization's own care and service provider organizations or its practitioner panels.

CONCLUSION

The community-based ethics committee attempts to address an unmet need in healthcare. While terms like "seamless delivery," "continuum," and "integrated delivery" abound, there are many topics that arise among institutions or within a broader community for which no one has responsibility and where no clear vehicle to ameliorate or address them is available. The community-based ethics committee is meant to meet this need. The EMT example that was discussed in the chapter has been solved in some states and communities, but for the most part it continues to be a problem. Dealing with problems like those, that affect a community rather than impacting a specific institution, are the fodder of the community ethics committee. The community ethics committee can enhance the continuum of care, or in some cases, create it.

CASE STUDY

A 46-year-old man is hospitalized with amyotrophic lateral sclerosis. He requires ventilatory support to increase his vital capacity but is reluctant to go on a ventilator. He says he does not want to become prisoner to a machine. He has clearly indicated that he didn't want to become "another Karen Ann Quinlan." His physician tells him that if he does not go on the ventilator he will surely die. The physician also assures him that if the patient determines enough is enough or the physician feels there is no benefit, there will be no problem removing the ventilator. The physician has checked with the hospital legal counsel, who agrees with the physician's position. The patient reluctantly allows the physician to intubate him and put him on the ventilator on the strict condition that he be taken off when he decides he wants to be taken off.

Several months later, after being discharged home, the patient is still receiving ventilatory support but is in a much more deteriorative state. He feels that the burden now outweighs the benefits, and he decides to exercise his right to have the ventilator withdrawn. The physician calls the hospital legal counsel, who advises her that since the patient is no longer in the hospital, the promise made to him could not be honored with the hospital's blessing. The attorney admits to being uncertain about the physician's and hospital's liability outside of the hospital setting.

Discussion Questions

- On whom should the patient rely for help in this situation?
- Who is responsible for the patient?
- What is the ethical thing to do and why?
- What role might a community-based ethics committee play?
- What responsibility does the physician who provided him assurances have?

12

Managed Care and End-of-Life Decision Making: Tracing the Legal Legacy[1]

This chapter will examine the legal foundations of self determination and end-of-life decision making. While this topic is often not identified as a "managed care" issue, it should be. This is a fertile area for the challenge of reducing costs and increasing member satisfaction. In fact, it is a strong challenge to managed care to do what traditional medicine has done so poorly. For many years, patient wishes have been thwarted and medically ineffective processes have been imposed on dying patients. Even when prognosis appears to be hopeless and further interventions futile, many continue to exhaust resources. A primary goal of managed care is to discourage ineffective interventions and to attain a high level of patient satisfaction. This domain is an unmet challenge!

A recent article in the *Lancet,* in fact, speaks to the managed care driven concept of evidence-based decision making in this arena. In a recent study from Seattle involving the examination of 865 bone marrow

---

[1] Material in this chapter was adapted with permission from Dennis A. Robbins, *Ethical and Legal Issues in Home Health and Long Term Care: Challenges and Solutions,* Gaithersburg, MD: Aspen Publishers, Inc., 1996, pp. 75–78.

transplant patients, researchers defined criteria with which they can so re-
liably predict the certainty of death that the presence and confirmation of
these risk factors in a patient justifies a sufficiently futile condition as to
merit the withdrawal of life support. The researchers' goal was to identify
dependable predictors. Evidenced-based factors included such combinations of complications as lung injury coupled with either a specific level
of hemodynamic instability, and hepatic failure." The researchers calculated that of 398 of the 865 patients who developed one of these combinations, none survived . . . Of the 476 patients who developed two complications in any combinations, only one survived."[2] The study attempts
to demonstrate that dependable predictions as to outcomes could be determined by the fourth day of ventilator support, and that on the average,
risk factors developed six ventilator days and nine hospital days before
death. If life support had been withdrawn on the first day that two of
the three risk factors were met, and if death followed swiftly, more than
7300 hospital days and 4800 ventilator days could have been avoided for
the 812 patients who died.[3]

Even in light of these factors a fiduciary element of trust must be cultivated. The ethicist Arthur Caplan notes that "the greater the trust between the physician and the patient . . . the more willing patients will be
to refrain from pursuing long odds to achieve bad ends."[4] Yet data can help
direct reasonable patients and physicians toward the right decisions. This
chapter will include a detailed analysis of pivotal legal cases and key ethical and legal concepts dealing with end-of-life decision making. It will
include a detailed discussion of determining decisional capacity, fluctuating capacity, surrogate and substitute decision making, and guardianship.
After exploring the common law background and historical progression of
these cases, it is hoped that the reader will have a strong sense of the issues and trends in this area.

THE HIGH END COST OF HEALTH CARE AND THE HIGH COST OF END-OF-LIFE CARE

One area of improvement where financial and clinical goals can mesh is
end-of-life care, particularly the resources exhausted on last-ditch efforts

---

[2] McCarthy Michael, "Evidence-based guidelines for withdrawing life support," *Lancet* 348:(9034)
    Oct. 19, 1996, p. 1087.
[3] McCarthy, p. 1087.
[4] McCarthy, p. 1087.

aimed not at appropriate symptom control when cure or reversibility or even temporary respite is highly unlikely, but rather when the perception exists that "everything must still be done." The care of patients in the end stages of ongoing deteriorative or degenerative diseases demands more scrutiny than we have offered in the past and more creative solutions than we have been generated. The American Medical Association has addressed this problem as well in discussing care of marginal value:

> While the expenditures on care of marginal value and futile care before death have not been estimated with precision, almost every physician can recount experiences in which such care was provided . . . Pressures and incentives to carry treatment to excessive lengths are systemic flaws . . . and the most effective way to deal with them is through transformation of the system. The basic solution is to remove distortions in the system that prevent alignment of costs and benefits in the decision making of patients, physicians, and the institutions in which medicine is practiced.[5]

For this reason extensive discussion of both the legal legacy surrounding end-of-life decision making as well as advance directives will be included in latter parts of this text. It is no accident that the Patient Self Determination Act was introduced by Senator John Danforth during the time that *Cruzan* was pending before the U.S. Court. This senator from Missouri did not want any other family to have to suffer the tragedy and roadblocks the Cruzans suffered. It was part of the Omnibus Budget Reconciliation Act of 1991 by HCFA, the primary healthcare financing entity in the United States. Their motivation of "self-determination" was "reducing costly outliers." In other words, patient protection and cost containment were partners in this process. This is an example of how appropriateness and quality can be melded with cost. If we can save money by doing what people want done anyway, we can better assure their self-determination and validate their wishes while saving money. Unfortunately the literature suggests that identification of advance directives and their implementation is extremely low. This is a ripe area for collaboration. Giving those working to contain and control costs tools in this area tools with which to work— including both an understanding of the legal legacy in this domain and an understanding of the importance of advance directives in reducing costs and reducing patient vulnerability—is an important initiative. Also included in this chapter is a policy for withholding and withdrawing life-

---

[5] *Transforming Medicare and Other Budget Proposals,* June 22, 1995, Chicago IL: American Medical Association Section I, p. 2.

prolonging medical procedures that has been tested and refined in many settings and reviewed by clinicians and health attorneys as well to serve as a helpful resource in this domain.

The amount of money exhausted at in the last several weeks of life is enormous. It is clearly excessively costly when it involves last-ditch procedures that are inconsistent with patients' wishes. Yet, many of the interventions performed in such contexts are aimed at reducing morbidity, pain, and suffering, and with the hope that something can be reversed or delayed. This area is increasingly complicated by the fact that these decisions pivot more heavily on medical experience and medical judgment, that is the art of medicine, that the science of clear and accurate prognosticating. The standard to which the physician may hold himself and the reason for dragging his or his feet in such matters may very well depend on the fact that the art deals with probability and uncertainty and the science with theory and certainty. Perhaps physicians need to abandon the quest for certainty in this domain and recapture the task of reducing uncertainty to a manageable level while still making well-founded medical judgments.

The role of the caregiver also is critical, because the caregiver must balance paternalism and autonomy. The caregiver is not vulnerable like the patient and possesses superior understanding of the patient's condition. Given this discrepancy in power, the caregiver has the opportunity to hinder or disable the patient. The flip-side of consent is always the integrity of the caregiver and the caregiver's willingness to honor patient wishes. What the caregiver should do is support and encourage self-determination on the part of the patient. When the patient consents to a procedure, the consent is an ingredient of the ongoing process of integrating the patient into the decision-making enterprise.

ETHICS AND POLICY DEVELOPMENT

End-of-life issues are becoming a hotbed for political, legal and financial debate. In the past, providers often avoided dealing proactively with ethical issues. An oft-cited study funded by the Robert Wood Johnson Foundation and reported by the American Medical Association (in JAMA) as well as *The New York Times*[6] found wide gaps between what terminally ill patients wanted and what they got.

---

[6] Open Society Institute, *Project on Death in America*, PDIA Newsletter. March, 1996; 1:1–8.

Forty-nine percent of the patients who wanted to avoid cardiopulmonary resuscitation did not have DNR orders. The patients who did often had DNR orders written in the last two days; as a result half of these patients spent their last eight days either comatose or receiving mechanical ventilation in an intensive care unit. The second phase of study proved even more discouraging. Testing a system that was designed to help patients avoid unwanted life-prolonging treatments by fostering better communication between patients and their doctors, the study found no change in ordering or the number of days that dying patients spent in undesirable states. Researchers involved in the study told *The New York Times* that every facet of medical culture, from the training of physicians to reimbursement systems encourages over-reliance on high-tech treatment and causes physicians to ignore patients' wishes. Most of us will die of an illness that will not be labeled as dying until the last couple of days at best.[7]

Patients who were terminally ill or in the late stages of a degenerative disease, where interventions were likely only to prolong the dying process, were avoided because of unwarranted fears about legal liability. Much of the negativity surrounding end-of-life decision making can be defused if the necessary time and energy is taken to develop policies in advance of a crisis. Administrative policies can provide guidance for addressing ethical issues and also insulation against legal liability. They can increase the comfort level of caregivers and minimize discontinuity and mistakes, thereby reducing risk of a lawsuit. Such policies should include:

- A clear statement of the commitment of the healthcare organization to honor the wishes of patients
- Guidance for clinical staff regarding documentation procedures for conflict resolution
- Safeguards regarding patients' capacity to make medical decisions, and
- Mechanisms to ensure continuity of patient consent

Well-thought-out policies create a framework for risk management activities. Investing energy in formulating policies is easily justified, and ultimately the energy required is less than the energy consumed in dealing with the uncertainties that exist in the absence of policies.

Policies should diminish recurrent problems so caregivers and administrators can deal with issues proactively rather than waiting until they get out of hand. While institutional settings vary, policies should offer

---

[7] PDIA, p. 5.

guidance to clinicians and clarify the commitment of the administration to the community. Making policies available to patients can facilitate decision making and will show that the organization cares about patient input and honoring patient's wishes. Good policies support patients in making mature and informed decisions.

In the past, providers have not had good policies to provide direction to allow them to deal proactively with end-of-life issues involving terminally ill patients. Much of their reluctance arose from unwarranted fears of legal liability. The aforenoted study—which showed that of those who have advance directives, only 49 percent will have their requests honored, and 80 percent of that same 49 percent will only have their wishes honored within the last 8 days of their lives—shows that less than 10 percent of those who have advance directives can expect to have their wishes honored. (This study will be described in greater detail later in this chapter.)

The issues that have received the most attention include medical futility, the high cost of end-of-life care and the right to decide. Futility suggests that we can do nothing to help the patient in terms of reversing the course of the disease. For such cases, then, why should we exhaust our financial resources? Coupled with this is the fact that people want more control over these end-of-life decisions. It is no accident that Dr. Jack Kevorkian has gained popularity. While many are unsure of his agenda, they celebrate his cause as a means to regain control over their destinies.

THE RIGHT TO PRIVACY

The United States Supreme Court has clearly affirmed that every competent adult has the right to control and determine what happens to his or her body. This right is almost completely unfettered and only gives way in rare circumstances when the state has an overriding interest in seeing medical treatment carried out or specific interventions performed, such as a blood transfusion for a parent with minor children. Barring those rare instances where the state's right outweighs the individual's interest, any treatment offered to a competent adult individual may be legally refused. This is true despite the wishes of any third parties, be they family, friends, physicians, and even guardians.

There was a long-standing tradition in medicine that physicians must do everything medically possible to keep the patient alive. The transformation from "doing everything possible" to doing what is "appropriate" is a transition that still meets with a great deal of resistance. In recent years, the issue of allowing or even helping the patient to die has been opened up to vigorous debate and has resulted in some fairly dramatic legal changes in various parts of the country. At present, Do Not Resuscitate (DNR) orders are commonplace, as are orders to withhold or withdraw a wide range of other life-prolonging medical procedures, including medically and or artificially or technologically supplied respiration, nutrition, hydration, and blood. Courts have upheld the right of patients to refuse life-sustaining treatment in over 150 cases including two Supreme Court decisions, and the U.S. Supreme Court has indicated that a right to refuse life-sustaining treatment can be found in the U.S. Constitution.

The advance of life-saving technologies has also contributed to the increased attention to medical decisions that lead to the death of patients. Medicine now has the capacity to intervene and forestall death for almost any case. There has also been an attempt to legislate morality in this domain through legal decisions, most of which have attempted to shift decision making back to the clinical forum, where it should have occurred in the first place. Twenty years have passed since the *Quinlan* case was argued and a decision was reached, and confusion still exists about what the decision means. Therefore, a short excursion into patient intent and the issues of privacy and consent is in order.

Patients who possess the capacity to make medical decisions and understand and appreciate the implications of those decisions, as an extension of their right of privacy, can grant or deny permission for any medical intervention. Expressed in another way, the patient must consent to allow persons to perform procedures which, in the absence of consent, would not otherwise be permitted or tolerated. In fact, from a legal perspective, consent confers a legal privilege on healthcare professionals to perform in a way that, in the absence of consent, would constitute a battery, which is simply the unpermitted touching of one person by another.

Thus, competent persons have the constitutional right to consent to or to reject treatment or advice. Incompetent persons in a sense also have this right, although consent to or rejection of treatment in their case is determined through surrogacy, appointment of a guardian or advance directive. Involvement of a surrogate decision maker creates more complications than when the patient is competent (has the mental capacity to understand and appreciate what is being articulated as well as the whys and wherefores) or has signed or otherwise articulated an advance directive, but the rights of all patients must be respected.

CONSENT AND DETERMINING DECISIONAL CAPACITY

The clinical determination of decisional capacity is an important part of the clinical enterprise and is a prerequisite for ensuring patient self-determination. It is appropriate to replace the word competence with decisional capacity, for while a patient may not be competent in the broad sense (e.g., may be unable to handle financial affairs) he or she may still possess the ability to appreciate the significance of a specific medical decision. In fact, the question at issue is whether the patient can understand and appreciate the significance of a specific medical decision now, not yesterday or tomorrow.

There are still many questions about how we determine decisional capacity. The definition of decisional capacity varies from state to state, but there is an emerging consensus. So long as an individual has the capacity to understand the consequences of accepting or refusing medical treatment, that individual is competent for the purpose of making medical decisions. This level of competency is now generally referred to as decisional capacity, and it is usually determined by the attending physician. In some states, agreement by a second physician who has personally examined the individual is also required.

Psychologists and psychiatrists frequently ask what can be done to dissuade attending physicians from sending them patients to determine whether the patients are competent when the issue is whether they currently have the *capacity to make a specific medical decision.* If physicians asked that question instead of whether the patient is competent, which is more complicated and difficult to answer, they would more often get the kind of answer they really require. (In fairness to referring physicians, psychologists and psychiatrists have a responsibility to contact physicians for further clarification, a responsibility they do not always carry out.)

FLUCTUATING CAPACITY

Patients whose capacity is fluctuating can make binding decisions during periods when they are in a state of decisional capacity. Requiring a legal determination of capacity by a court for a patient with fluctuating capacity seems to be unduly burdensome and impractical. Imagine a scenario in which a patient with fluctuating capacity must be reviewed by a court to determine his capacity. He would not necessarily be judged incapacitated but his thinking is not always dependable and clear. Suppose he wakes up clearheaded and at that point has the capacity to make a medical decision but loses his capacity while being transported to the court. Later he regains his capacity but loses it again on the way back to the court. The patient might have to be transported back and forth repeatedly before the timing finally is right. In cases of fluctuating capacity, having a court determine decisional capacity is unnecessarily cumbersome and a wasteful use of dollars at a time of limited resources.

Sometimes there are medical conditions that increase a patient's incapacity. The loss of potential for participating in ongoing decision making will be exacerbated if the patient becomes debilitated or sick as a result of going back and forth to a courthouse. This is a major reason why a clinical determination of capacity to make decisions is often acceptable in a wide range of circumstances. There are cases in which a patient has a guardian but, in the estimation of a caregiver, has the capacity to make medical decisions. In such circumstances, clear and explicit documentation is critical.

GUARDIANSHIP

This concept of decisional capacity has had an impact on many legal paradigms, especially when applied to guardianship. When patients are unable to speak for themselves, others may exercise judgment in their stead and on their behalf. Substitute decision-makers try to make the same choices that the patients would have made had they been competent. If there is no substitute decision-maker and the physician knows the patient's wishes, he or she can act on the basis of that knowledge. In the absence of such knowledge, guardianship issues arise.

The basic legal remedy employed when an individual can no longer take care of himself or herself is guardianship. Previously, a guardian of either person or estate was appointed for an individual who was determined by a court proceeding to be "incompetent." Competency was defined as the ability to make or communicate decisions about one's person or estate. The guardianship procedure is set up under the various state probate codes dealing with the passing of property at death and continues to be biased toward the issue of determining heirship.

A guardian can be appointed, however, after only a cursory review of the individual's true mental status. A physician is nominally appointed to determine competency and issues a one- or two-sentence summary report to a judge who never sees the individual whose competency is questioned. In most cases, the individual's capacity to make personal decisions on a daily basis is not examined. The issue is simply too sensitive for most judges to deal with and so they ignore it. In fact, many people may be incapable of handling their financial affairs yet still have the capacity to indicate whether or not they want a limb amputated. Odd as it may seem, they have decisional capacity even though a court has determined that they need the protection of a guardian over their person or property due to their incapacity!

The definition of decisional capacity also does not clearly address the issue of minors. Traditionally, minors, usually defined as individuals under 18 or 21 years of age, have not been considered legally capable of making decisions for themselves. Emancipated minors, individuals who are at least 16 and are living independently, are exceptions to the rule. Clearly, however, children as young as 10 or 12 can understand the consequences of many medical decisions, and it can be anticipated that courts will therefore extend decisional capacity to minors.

Being placed under someone's guardianship is perhaps the most restrictive and oppressive thing that can happen to a person. It implies that the person has no capacity or authority to make *any* decisions. Of course, there are times when a guardian is needed to act in the best interests of someone who is incapacitated or in some context cannot make an informed and reliable decision. Therefore, many jurisdictions are engaged in developing more creative, less oppressive and less restrictive forms of guardianship that are oriented toward a specific area of capacity and are limited in some specific ways. A guardianship, for example, may be limited to a certain range of decisions (e.g., medical or financial decisions) and it may also be limited in time (e.g., only in force during a period of recuperation from an illness).

Guardians are required to try to choose the decisions their wards would have made or, if they lack the necessary information, to make decisions that are determined to be in the ward's best interests. This is an extension of the "substituted judgment" standard. A serious problem can arise when guardians are involved in end-of-life decision making. It is not unusual for banks or other financial institutions to act as guardians. Such institutions often become extremely uncomfortable when faced with end-of-life decision making, and they will often look to the family, which is fine. What isn't fine, however, is when they fail to fulfill their duty as guardians and prolong the process of dying because of their failure or omission to take those steps for which they are acutely responsible.

PATIENTS LACKING DECISIONAL CAPACITY

When a patient has indicated to caregivers what he or she wants or does not want, the caregivers' responsibility is to act in accordance with both the ethical standards of the healthcare profession and the wishes of the patient. If the patient becomes incapacitated, his or her wishes may potentially be undermined or challenged by the family's own desires. For example, the family may take the position that the mother has always been unrealistic in this domain (meaning they do not agree with her about this particular matter). The caregivers then are torn between honoring the wishes of the patient and carrying out the family's wishes (because it is the survivors who might sue). Their dilemma is not one of weighing battery against negligence (for failure to act) but of weighing the right of self-determination against the risk of litigation.

Ambiguity about who has the authority to make decisions for incapacitated patients whose wishes are unknown continues to cause clinicians significant discomfort. Dealing with patients who lack decisional capacity and have not indicated their wishes is particularly complex when the issue is whether treatment ought to be undertaken or withheld. The legal standards in this domain often have to be unbundled before they can be applied to a particular case. They are derived from several key legal decisions (which are discussed later in this chapter) as well as from standards promulgated by the President's Commission on Ethical Issues in Biomedicine and Biomedical and Behavioral Research and the American Medical Association's Council on Ethical and Judicial Affairs. (See Chapter 14 on Consent-Based Policies.)

THE COMMON LAW BACKGROUND: TRACING THE LEGAL LEGACY

Treating the right to refuse treatment as an extension of the right of privacy is not new. As early as 1914, Schloendorff[8] said that "every human being of adult years and sound mind has a right to determine what shall be done with his own body."

Since 1976, such major cases as *Quinlan, Saikewicz, Dinnerstein, Spring, and Eichner v. Dillon and Cruzan* have provided guidelines for making decisions on behalf of incompetent patients. They have assisted caregivers in deciding the significance of a prognosis of hopelessness *(Quinlan),* determining what incompetent persons would likely have

---

[8] *Schloendorff v. Society of New York Hospitals* 211 N.Y. 125, 105 N.E. 92 (1914).

decided for themselves *(Saikewicz),* charting do not resuscitate (DNR) orders in advance *(Dinnerstein),* and identifying whether there is a need to
approach the courts for prior approval *(Eichner v. Dillon).* These and other
cases are discussed here in detail.

LEGAL CASES INVOLVING THE WITHHOLDING/WITHDRAWING OF LIFE-PROLONGING MEDICAL PROCEDURES

In re Quinlan[9]

The first important case in this area was *In re Quinlan.* Karen Ann
Quinlan, a 21-year-old woman, stopped breathing for two 15-minute periods for reasons not clearly identified. She was taken to an emergency department, where she was resuscitated and put on a ventilator. The hope
was that temporary ventilatory support would start her on a return to normality. It was initially determined, however, that she was comatose and
later determined that she was in a persistent vegetative state (PVS).

This state is characterized by eyes opened unconsciousness and de-
struction of most of the cerebral cortex. Initial trauma to the brain may
cause the vegetative functions of the lower brain not to operate properly,
in which case technological supports, such as a ventilator, are needed.
Generally after three or four days, once swelling is reduced and the brain
stem regains homeostasis, vegetative functions resume. The goal of the
emergency department and of the hospital departments that treated Ms.
Quinlan subsequently was to return her to normality and reduce significant morbidity by prompt and efficient interventions.

Although Karen Quinlan was put on a ventilator to increase her vital
capacity and strength in hopes of reversing her plight, when it appeared
that the goal of reversibility was not likely, questions arose as to what
should then be done. For example, should she be kept on the ventilator if
it was only going to prolong the dying process?

Some have argued that most ethical issues in medicine are consequences of technology run rampant. They want to place the blame on technology and thus try to exonerate those who use it. Although it is true that
technology presents many challenges, it also creates exciting opportunities. It is our failure to address the ethical issues that is the problem, not
the technology.

---

[9] *In re Quinlan,* 70 N.J. 10, 355 A.2d 647 (1976).

Interestingly enough, our way of dealing with ethical issues in the United States reflect the Anglo-Saxon tradition of using the law to solve problems. When something is wrong, we say, "there ought to be a law" rather than "what can we do within the limits of ethical propriety?"

In the Quinlan case, the court attempted to solve the problem creatively. The court asked the doctors about the medical and ethical propriety of withdrawing mechanical ventilation. There was a question of whether the withdrawal of the ventilator would contravene the ethical standards and integrity of the medical profession.

The case was eventually decided by the New Jersey Supreme Court. The chief justice had the reputation of being an excellent problem solver. He had learned of an article about decision making and infant care review committees that suggested a committee forum was effective for addressing complex issues. He indicated that issues like the one in question could best be solved in the clinical arena, but that having some mechanism in place to assist in the decision-making process, such as an ethics committee, would be appropriate. An ethics committee had the advantage that it would disperse responsibility among the committee members (not a goal we often seek in clinical consultations). The chief justice warned against using the courts for decision making, which the chief justice felt would constitute a "gratuitous encroachment upon the medical profession."

The ethics committee in *Quinlan* was essentially a medical prognosis committee composed entirely of physicians whose goal was to determine medical prognosis and specifically in this case whether the patient could be returned to a "cognitive and sapient life." The Supreme Court of New Jersey indicated that "the duty to treat diminishes as the prognosis dims and when the prognosis is that of hopelessness there is no need to continue extraordinary treatment." Thus, the ventilator could be removed if there was no reasonable probability of improvement. It was also believed that as soon as the ventilator was removed she would surely die. Instead, Karen Ann Quinlan survived and remained in a persistent vegetative state for almost 10 years. (It was later discovered that the longest period someone had remained in a persistent vegetative state was 37 years, 111 days.)

At the time of the Quinlan case, little was known about persistent vegetative states. Quinlan's attorney, a friend with whom I have shared a podium on many occasions and who was recently embroiled in the Supreme Court controversy over physician-assisted suicide, once indicated to me that had he known what he knows now about the condition,

Quinlan would not have had to be in a nursing home in flexion for 10 years. A lot of agony and suffering could have been averted. Of course, we all have to do the best we can with the knowledge available at the time. It is pointless to flagellate ourselves for what is not yet known about the nature and natural history of all diseases or undiscovered techniques. Still we feel we should do more. It is a peril of the healthcare profession. Hopefully, the legacy of this young woman has saved and will continue to save others from the same plight.

In 1990 and 1991, almost 15 years after the Quinlan decision, I was part of a medical/goodwill expedition to the former Soviet Far East. I was asked to lecture on technology and ethics to approximately 400 Soviet healthcare professionals. The isolated region was ten time zones removed from Moscow, in fact it was closer to New York than to the largest medical centers of this country in Moscow and St. Petersburg. During the lecture, I was amazed to learn that everyone knew the intricacies of the Quinlan case, which obviously had reverberations across the globe.

One of the Russian physicians politely told me that the fundamental difference between the way we practice medicine in the United States and the way the Russians practice is quite dramatic. "In the United States, healthcare professionals use technology first and when that doesn't work, they use their heads: In Russia, we start by using our heads when that doesn't work, we try technology." Technology is their handmaiden, not their dictator. Technology cannot dictate appropriate medicine, for medicine is an art of caring, and of using our skills and heads to solve problems and better care for our patients. Technological tools can and should enhance but not replace our judgment. Interestingly, one strength of managed care is that it realizes that the physicians on the upward curve of knowing about the natural history of diseases, who possess superb diagnostic and prognostic skills, are those who can use their heads and will be the most sought after. The fear is to expect too much of generalists than their knowledge or experience commands.

Superintendent of Belchertown State School v. Saikewicz[10]

The next case that had dramatic and broad national impact was a Massachusetts case involving a 76-year-old man who was a public ward in a state mental health facility in Belchertown, Massachusetts. Saikewicz

---

[10] *Superintendent of Belchertown State School v. Saikewicz,* 370 N.E. 417 (1977).

had a mental age of 2 years and 10 months and an IQ of less than 50. He had been institutionalized for 53 years. He suffered from myeloblastic leukemia, and the only intervention that was thought to help him and offer any hope was chemotherapy. Since he did not possess the decisional capacity to give consent to this treatment and lacked the capacity to understand and appreciate the significance of the information he would need to make a responsible, informed and voluntary decision, the question was whether to administer it to him. Someone needed to act in his stead as a substitute decision maker to make a decision.

A guardian was appointed for purposes of the litigation. The Massachusetts Supreme Court suggested that the focus should be on the patient's wishes and because the patient lacked decisional capacity a substituted judgment standard would be used. Basically, this standard entails that decisions made for someone be consistent with "what this individual would likely have decided were he able to decide for himself." The court-appointed guardian was to determine what would be consistent with Saikewicz's views and what would be in his best interests. The guardian ad litem (appointed for the purpose of the litigation), believed that most people in similar circumstances would likely elect to undergo the therapy. The guardian, however, also had to consider what Saikewicz himself (the individual, not the aggregate) would likely have decided had he possessed decisional capacity. Given his inability to understand what was being done to him and why, instead of hope, Mr. Saikewicz would probably experience only fear and pain and might even perceive the treatment as punishment. Consequently, the guardian thought it would be inappropriate to administer the chemotherapy. The substituted judgment standard requires the surrogate decision maker to choose, not what most people would likely want or what the surrogate would want, but what this specific individual would likely have chosen.

This was a very sensitive and thoughtful decision. One year after *Saikewicz* had been decided, however, Chief Justice Liacos of the Massachusetts Supreme Court wrote up the case and took some rather creative liberties in the process. He, in fact, took aim at the New Jersey court that had decided *Quinlan.* That court had said that the courts should not routinely become involved in such matters, for their involvement would *"constitute a gratuitous encroachment upon the medical profession."* The response of Chief Justice Liacos was that *"rather than constituting a gratuitous encroachment, these cases require the dispassionate investigation of the court consistent with the spirit upon which this judicial branch of government was created.*" His opinion was criticized by many as an overstepping of proper bounds, an extreme example of legal imperialism. He seemingly went beyond the main issue and indicated that going to court was the best way to ensure that the wishes of incompetent patients were met. The reaction to his decision was enormous and he was flooded with letters loaded with frustration from clinicians and others.

In re Dinnerstein[11]

Within two months, another case, *In re Dinnerstein,* arose in Massachusetts that clarified *Saikewicz.* Shirley Dinnerstein suffered from late-stage Alzheimer's disease. Her physician asked that a DNR order be written in advance as an extension of the substituted judgment standard. This case was heard by a judge who was a hospital trustee.

    Dinnerstein was the first case in America to deal with the issue of writing a DNR order in advance. The decision supported this strategy as an extension of the substituted judgment standard outlined in *Quinlan* and *Saikewicz.* Unfortunately, many were confused as to what to do after Chief Justice Liacos, in *Saikewicz,* had indicated that it might be necessary to go to court to have decisions like this made. Instead of sensible DNR orders, a large array of codes was devised: Dr. no heart codes, code 250s, code 500s, designer codes (sky blue, light blue, etc.), gentleman codes, slow codes, and the like. Caregivers were also unclear about what DNR meant. DNR, which refers only to withholding cardiac and/or pulmonary resuscitation, was mistaken to encompass all kinds of other supports and treatment modalities, a confusion that still prevails.

In re Spring[12]

Not willing to leave well enough alone, the Massachusetts Supreme Court took another shot at resolving autonomy issues in its decision in *In re Spring.* Earle Spring, like Karen Ann Quinlan and Joseph Saikewicz, was incompetent. Mr. Spring stubbed his toe, which became infected and later necrotic. When he finally sought medical attention, he was put on a regimen of antibiotics and experienced renal failure. He then went on dialysis and perhaps developed dialysis dementia or aluminum toxicity (it was never clear which was the case). I had the chance to speak with the attending on this case and also worked with one of the court-appointed

---

[11] *In re Dinnerstein,* 6 Mass. App. 380 N.E. 2d 134 (1978).
[12] *In re Spring,* 380 Mass. 629, 405 N.E. 2d 115 (1980).

physicians, who said that the reason this case got to court was that the hospital learned the son was considering suing his (the son's) employer. Since the son "had lawyer contacts" the hospital decided it ought to "have this looked at more carefully." While this was being looked at more carefully, perhaps stimulated by the stress of her husband's plight, Spring's wife suffered a stroke, and she was in a long-term care rehabilitation facility while he was in the hospital. Meanwhile, his son was attempting to be appointed guardian so he could end the dialysis. The court wanted to retain control and a cumbersome legal process ensued.

The court set forth 13 different factors to be used in decision making. Interestingly enough, except for the patient's wishes, these were all medical criteria. The factors included what clinicians should consider in their assessment, such as risks, benefits, diagnosis, and prognosis. Exactly how these were to be integrated into decision algorithms and matrices was unclear, however, as was the question of what weights should be assigned to the 13 variables. Would the patient's wishes count a lot or a little? Five percent? Twenty-five percent? What about the prognosis? Rather than clarifying the issues, the *Spring* criteria exacerbated discomfort, confusion, and absurd delays. The *Spring* decision itself was less than expeditious. It came almost two years after Spring's death. An emergency in a hospital or nursing home calls for immediate action and rapid response. Comparatively the courts move at a snail's pace. Yet, incredible as it may sound, judges in Massachusetts were considering carrying beepers to be more readily available for assisting in medical decision making. This is not meant to suggest that the courts cannot be helpful and timely in dealing with emergency guardianship. However, there is no need for them to meddle in cases like Spring's in which family members are available and which should have been handled more effectively and less adversarily in the clinical forum. Clinicians also need to be more sensible in how they deal with decision-making responsibilities. The fact that the son knew some lawyers should not have made any difference, other than perhaps more careful documentation to assuage the physician's discomfort.

In re Eichner and *Eichner v. Dillon*[13]

The next important case was *In re Eichner* and its appeal, *Eichner v. Dillon.* Eichner was the surrogate decision maker for Brother Fox, an

---

[13] *In re Eichner,* 102 Misc. 2d 184, 423 N.Y. S. 2d 580 (N.Y. Sup. Dec. 6, 1979) and *Eichner v. Dillon,* 73 A.D. 2d 431, 426 N.Y.S. 2d 517 (N.Y.A.D. 2 Dept., Mar. 27, 1980), order modified by Storar, 52 N.Y. 2d 363, 420 N.E. 2d. 64, 438 N.Y.S. 2d 266 (N.Y., Mar. 31, 1981).

86-year-old religious cleric (who used to teach medical ethics). Fox was lifting a flower box on his roof when he suffered an inguinal hernia. He went to the hospital for routine hernia repair, but because of problems encountered during the surgery somewhat related to his advanced age he suffered an ischemic event that rendered him encephalopathic. Fox had both a biological and religious family, and together they agreed that Father Eichner, his religious superior, would act for him. Brother Fox, himself a teacher of medical ethics, had told his friend, Father Eichner, "If I wind up like Karen Ann Quinlan, pull the plug."[14] Eichner, as surrogate decision maker, attempted to have Fox's ventilator removed. However, Dennis Dillon, the district attorney of Suffolk County, New York, felt that the state had an obligation (state's interest) to protect life at all costs and mandated a five-point certification process that had to be undertaken to ensure the wishes of the incompetent. The process involved a mock adversarial legal proceeding, a court-appointed physician, and an ethics committee of three physicians, among other things. Eichner sought a more reasonable alternative and approached the New York State Court of Appeals which said "any reasonable indication of patient intent will suffice and that there was no need to approach the court to determine the propriety of these kinds of decisions." When someone is dealing with the loss of a loved one or a friend, we don't need to disenfranchise the patient nor to bludgeon his or her substitute decision makers with a mock adversarial process, particularly when the patient's wishes are so clear.

WITHHOLDING ARTIFICIAL NUTRITION AND HYDRATION

In re Conroy[15]

From 1983 to 1985 cases involving the withholding or withdrawing of artificial nutrition and hydration caused a great deal of discomfort and uncertainty. The first to bring the issue to national attention was a New Jersey case, *In re Conroy.* Claire Conroy, a woman in her eighties, had organic brain syndrome and a host of other medical problems, including artherosclerotic heart disease, hypertension, and diabetes. She eventually reached a point where she could not speak or even swallow sufficient amounts of nutrients to sustain herself, and a nasogastric feeding tube was

---

[14] Annas, G J.D. M.P.H. "The Promised End: Constitutional Aspects of Physician Assisted Suicide." *New England Journal of Medicine* 335: (9), Aug. 29, 1996, p. 684.

[15] *In re Conroy,* 98 N.J. 321, 486 A. 2d 1209 (1983).

inserted. She remained in a semifetal position and was unable to respond to verbal stimuli. In the opinion of her physician, she probably had no higher function or consciousness. Still, she was not brain dead, comatose, or in a persistent vegetative state. Her legal guardian argued that she would never have permitted the insertion of the nasogastric tube in the first place. The facility was concerned and sought guidance from the court, which agreed with the surrogate's decision. The state's ombudsman, however, intervened, saying that the failure to provide or the discontinuance of artificial nutrition and hydration would be construed as an act of homicide. Thus, this woman who had not seen a doctor in over 80 years now became prisoner to an unwanted technology she never requested.

Meanwhile, in California, a 55-year-old patient who underwent a simple ostomy repair suffered severe anoxic depression in the recovery room. The chain of events included short staffing, nurse-physician conflict, ignoring of legal counsel advice, and spurious data. The decision rendered in *Barber v. Superior Ct of California*[16] had a immense national impact and offered interesting guidance on how these kinds of situations should be handled. Had this case occurred today, it would have received front page coverage, since it arose in a prominent managed care organization, a target the media is fond of.

The court argued that each pulsation of a ventilator and each drip of an IV feeding tube is equivalent to a manually administered dose. The court said that a respirator is really no more than a mechanical ambu bag. An ambu bag works by repeatedly squeezing its contents out and then refilling. Similarly, an IV can be considered a substitute for a syringe. When someone depresses the plunger of a syringe, its contents are pushed out. During this process, the person is doing something–performing an act. After depletion, the person is not performing an act. If the person was to then insert a second syringe and push the plunger, that would be a separate act. Accordingly, while the IV is dripping, an act is being performed. In between the drips, nothing is being done.

The court said that between the drips and pulsations there was no act involved and thus the failure to continue respiration or IV feeding or hydration was an *omission* consistent with good medical care. It could just have easily said the opposite, which is what the New Jersey courts initially maintained. Yet in the end the New Jersey Supreme Court, in the *Conroy* decision, adopted the same logic of California, and many other states

---

[16] *Barber v. Superior Court,* 147 Cal. App. 3d 1006, 195 Cal. Rptr. 484 (Cal. Ct. App. 2d Dist. 1983).

followed suit. Later the ninth circuit court, building upon the logic of the U.S. Supreme Court in the *Cruzan* case was to indicate that they saw "little if any difference for constitutional or ethical purposes between providing medication with a double effect or a single effect . . . or between a doctor's pulling the plug on a respirator . . . and prescribing drugs which will permit a terminally ill patient to end [his or her] own life."[17]

Interestingly, the manner in which the *Barber* court determined that discontinuance of respiration or IV feeding or hydration was acceptable medical practice rather than homicide illustrates the incongruity between clinical and legal ways of establishing criteria for making decisions. This incongruity is reason enough to try to avoid going to court for a decision.

Cruzan v. Director, Missouri Department of Health[18]

Nancy Beth Cruzan was a "real person behind the headlines and head-notes"[19] who was involved in an automobile accident and like Karen Ann Quinlan suffered from lack of oxygen and was determined to be in a persistent vegetative state. A Missouri court affirmed her right which was upheld by the Missouri Supreme Court. Then a somewhat curious, national, politically inspired reargument arose and we saw the first case to deny the prerogatives of a loved one to act as an advocate for a family member's wishes. *Cruzan* was a dramatic deviation from the legal legacy surrounding end-of-life decision-making, which, prior to *Cruzan*, had been based on the right of privacy, specifically the right to determine what happens to one's own body. In *Cruzan*, the focus was on the right to liberty interest instead of the privacy right. The court also demanded a higher level of evidence than in previous cases. The standard shifted from "beyond a reasonable doubt," a "reasonable indication of patient intent," or "what the patient would likely have decided were he able to decide for himself or herself," to a "clear and convincing evidence" standard. For example, even though the testimony of her family and her roommate showed that Nancy Cruzan had clearly indicated her wishes not to be kept alive when the circumstances were futile or hopeless, the court wanted more convincing material. The case was filled with legal gymnastics, and many briefs were filed on the part of Cruzan by national healthcare organizations. Among

---

[17] Annas p. 683 (who cites *Compassion in Dying v. Washington* 79 F. 3d 790 (9th circuit 1996).
[18] *Cruzan v. Director, Missouri Dept. of Health,* 497 U.S. 261 (1990).
[19] This phrase is borrowed from Paul Armstrong J.D., legal counsel to Karen Quinlan and intimately involved in *Cruzan* and *Vacco v. Quill* and *Washington v. Gluckburg,* offering amicus briefs from major healthcare organizations such as AHA and AMA.

these was an excellent brief written on behalf of the American Hospital Association. It emphasized the historical right of the American family to make end-of-life decisions. Those who know the patient best should be given decision-making responsibility when that person is incapacitated from making decisions himself or herself. Despite the various legal gymnastics, the Cruzan case was important in its assertion of the fundamental right to make decisions at the end of life based on liberty rather than the broader role of privacy. It also clarified and affirmed the fact that artificial nutrition and hydration cases would not be dealt with differently than other forms of life prolonging medical treatment/procedures. Cruzan's shift from the privacy right to the liberty interest was to set the stage for the future discussions of physician-assisted suicide in the *Vacco v. Quill* and *Washington v. Glucksburg* cases.

In re Michael Martin[20]

A case filed in Michigan attempted to revive an effort to raise the level of proof required before a surrogate decision-maker, advocating on behalf of an incapacitated patient, could ask that life-prolonging medical procedures be discontinued. The Martin case involved a patient who was neither terminally ill nor in a persistent vegetative state. His wife had been appointed his guardian and conservator. In 1992, Michael Martin's wife requested that his artificially and technologically supplied nutrition be withdrawn. The hospital ethics committee determined that withdrawal was both ethically and medically appropriate, but that the hospital could not carry out the request without prior court approval. Mrs. Martin petitioned the court for the authorization to remove all nutritional support from her husband. Her husband's sister and mother filed an opposing petition.

Testimony given revealed that Michael Martin had indicated he would rather die than be dependent on someone for his care or be kept alive on a respirator. Even his sister testified that Michael had told her he did not want to be kept alive under those circumstances. The court determined that Michael Martin had not indicated "the exact circumstances" under which he would make such a choice. There were obviously strong dissenting opinions. This case is a vivid example of the importance of leaving well enough alone and proved to be a useless exercise of legal gymnastics that disenfranchised rather than supported patient self-determination. It is interesting how we withhold important care that

---

[20] *In re Michael Martin*, 538 N.W. 2d 399 (Mich. Aug. 1995).

could keep people healthy in non-urgent settings and err towards providing excessive and marginally beneficial care at the end of life when the prognosis is often poor and hope is futile. We should focus on symptom control and making the remaining days better rather than just longer. The U.S. Supreme Court has realized and affirmed this as well in the following cases.

PHYSICIAN-ASSISTED SUICIDE: *VACCO V. QUILL* AND *WASHINGTON V. GLUCKSBERG*[21]

The Quill case, recently argued before the U.S. Supreme Court, is the most recent example of end-of-life decision making cases and was decided in the summer of 1997. This case raised the question of having the physician assist in death and would potentially broaden one's right to choose.

Many who work in this area or who have been active in and following this field over the past 20 years have experienced a great deal of frustration. We had hoped for a national definition of death from the first Presidents Commission; that never occurred. We hoped that once there was a good ventilator case, and then a good artificial nutrition and hydration case, and then a durable power of attorney case, and a living will case, and a home healthcare case, and a long term care case . . . ad nauseam. After a legacy of 20 years, we have not made great strides. "The Quill case arose when four physicians and three patients in the ninth Circuit (one dying of AIDS, one of cancer, and another of emphysema) challenged a Washington law that prohibits aiding another person in committing suicide . . . In the second circuit, three physicians and three patients (two dying of AIDS and one of cancer) challenged New York laws that prohibit aiding another person in committing or attempting suicide." (All physicians felt they could not accede to patients wishes and requests "because of the laws against assisting suicide.")[22] Both of these cases raised the same issues: whether there is a constitutional right to have the assistance of a physician to commit suicide and whether there is any state's interest in the prohibition of that right being exercised. This creates new questions regarding physician advocacy for their patients and the physician's role. Many physicians feel that assisted suicide is inconsistent with the physician's caring role.

---

[21] *Dennis C. Vacco et al. v. Timothy E. Quill, M.D.* and *State of Washington v. Harry Glucksberg, M.D. et al.* on writs of Certiorari to the U.S. Courts of Appeals for the Second and Ninth districts, nos. 95-1858 and 96-110 (Brief amicus curiae of the American College of Legal Medicine).
[22] Annas, p. 687.

This case is particularly interesting for a variety of reasons, not the least of which is that none seemed to want to identify with Dr. Jack Kevorkian, who many feel spearheaded a movement towards patients being allowed to control their time of dying, insofar as that is possible. This movement had almost twenty years of momentum before Kevorkian jumped to the forefront. Some believe that his involvement may have actually impeded or delayed a decision being made.[23] The court was resigned to allow the states to address this issue individually.

The Supreme Court decision leaves decision making to the states in this regard but takes a positive tone to the role of healthcare professionals and in the process of decision making. Rather than allowing or disallowing, the court focused on the importance or reducing fear and uncertainty on the part of the patient and the importance or providing appropriate, effective and efficient palliative care.

SUMMARIZING THE LEGAL LEGACY

Figures 12–1 and 12–2 illustrate the legal legacy surrounding the end-of-life decision making. One refers to the cases and dates; the other refers to criteria that the cases set forth. The circle begins with *Quinlan*. In *Quinlan,* the fundamental criterion on which decisions should be based was medical prognosis, which was decided by an "ethics" committee. If the patient could not be returned to a cognitive and sapient state, then life supports could be removed. The ethics committee's sole role in *Quinlan* was to determine whether her medical prognosis was indeed hopeless. The court noted that the duty to treat diminishes as prognosis dims and when the prognosis is that of hopelessness, there is no need to continue extraordinary treatment. The court also felt that to become routinely involved in such matters would Constitute a gratuitous encroachment upon the medical profession.

The next slice of the pie is *Saikewicz,* in which the court argued that substituted judgment was the primary criterion for decision making. The substitute decision maker acts as if he or she were the person in whose behalf the decision is being made. The decision maker must take into account everything that has a bearing on the decision.

Next, *Dinnerstein* clarified the criterion of substituted judgment and established that a DNR order can be charted in advance. In *Spring,* the

---

[23] This insight was shared by Paul Armstrong, who filed an amicus brief on behalf of the AMA and New Jersey Physicians in *Vacco v. Quill* and *Washington v. Glucksberg.*

court set forth 13 criteria for decision making and attempted to redefine the court's role. However, clinicians remained unclear about what weights would be assigned to the various components.

This was followed by *in re Eichner.* Five criteria were established but then overridden by the New York Court of Appeals, which argued that it was unreasonable to demand such a cumbersome process be undertaken. Interestingly, when the *Eichner v. Dillon* decision was handed down (next slice of the pie), it was heralded as the best example of how these cases ought to be decided. Of course, it is critical to examine the criteria upon which decisions were made prior to Quinlan, for perhaps Eichner was not a giant step forward but only a return to more sensible ways of resolving end-of-life issues.

Most would argue that prior to 1976 (see Figure 12–1), such decisions were basically made jointly by the doctor and the patient on the basis of some reasonable indication of patient intent. In other words, it seems as if care providers ventured through a thicket of legal ambiguity from 1976 to 1981, with all the attendant agony and grief, only to end up with the same standards they began with. In fairness, caregivers do have a richer understanding of the criteria involved in decision making for incompetent patients, but the price was great. The standards for decision making, specifically for malpractice, did not change. The fundamental responsibility of the physician was and still is to act in accordance with the standards of the profession tempered by the wishes of the patient. During this period of legal clarification, the President's Commission on Ethical Issues in Biomedicine and Biomedical and Behavioral Research used insights gained from these cases to develop guidelines on decisions to forego life support. See, for example, its helpful publication *Deciding to Forego Life Supports,* especially the chapter "The Elements of Decision Making." And in 1986, the AMA gave further clarification on withholding or withdrawing life-prolonging medical procedures which was further refined in 1994.

Over 150 cases have provided direction and guidance and explored virtually every conceivable type of case in which questions could arise. Some have been helpful, some mean-spirited, and some politically motivated.

The feeding support cases of *Conroy* and *Barber* set the stage for *Cruzan,* which shifted focus from the right of privacy to that of a liberty interest and laid the foundation for *Vacco v. Quill* and *Glucksberg v. Washington.* As clear as these criteria seem, there has been a lot of confusion and many distinctions made that some still believe are overwhelming, as exemplified by Figure 12–2.

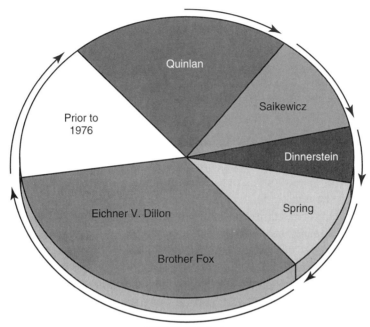

FIGURE 12–1

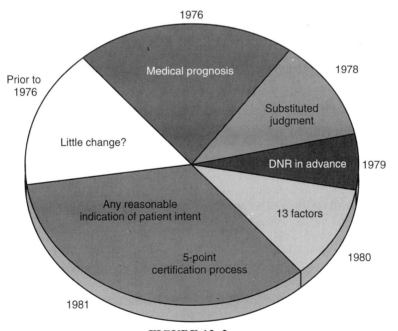

FIGURE 12–2

What managed care does in this area is a question that has been carefully evaded. Acting in accordance with patient's wishes near the end of life can yield a high degree of patient satisfaction and save financial resources. There are also great opportunities for abuse that create challenges for us to investigate in greater detail.

CONCLUSION

The legal legacy surrounding the protection of patient wishes near the end of life is tortuous. Court decisions range from overintrusive paternalism to benign neglect. The clear implication of this review is that patients' wishes regarding end-of-life issues need to be ascertained as early in the treatment process as possible (preferably even before treatment is necessary) and that when patient wishes are not ascertainable, a clear and effective mechanism must be in place to begin the process of determining and acting upon what the patient would have wanted. This process cannot be effectively carried out under the pressure of crisis; it must grow out of an understanding of the various roles that clinicians, the family, and as a last resort, the courts should play. A sound knowledge of the legal concepts and realistic clinical alternatives that underpin decision making in this area is critical. Only with such knowledge will caregivers be able to act with confidence in providing medical treatment while at the same time empowering and protecting, not disenfranchising, the patient.

CASE STUDIES

CASE 1

Mrs. B. is seriously ill. She has been successfully resuscitated three times in the past seven days. Prior to her admission to the hospital she was in a long-term care facility and had a chance to talk about her wishes regarding end-of-life issues. She has two sons, whom she characterizes as "screw-ups with potential." Her impending death, partly because she will no longer be there to help direct their lives along the right path, is devastating to her. When approached about a "do not resuscitate" order she says that she wants a no-code but she feels she needs to "have everything done" to show her sons that it is possible to fight to the end and wants to be coded.

Discussion Questions

- How does a discussion of medical futility affect her decision?
- Can or should clinical pathways or practice protocols and guidelines override the patient's wish?
- What could the caregivers do to help the patient help her sons so that she would not feel she had to undergo a course of futile treatment?
- What role should last wishes play in a case like this?
- Can the caregivers afford to honor the patient's wish?

CASE 2

Mr. S. is severely dehydrated but is very afraid of "being another Karen Ann Quinlan" and wants no procedure or technology that he perceives to be extraordinary, including use of an IV. His underlying medical condition is not terribly serious and he possesses decisional capacity. However, he doesn't really seem to understand the implications of his refusal. The situation then arises that the caregivers disagree and feel his decision is wrong. The nurse is aware that Mr. S. is extremely opinionated, and she believes he could not possibly understand the implications of his refusal of an IV. No sane person would make such a choice.

Discussion Questions

- What could the caregiver do in such a circumstance?
- Can the patient's wishes be honored?
- Is guardianship appropriate?
- What move, if anything, needs to be done?

CASE 3

Mr. B. has inoperable colorectal cancer. He is 89 years old and has lived at home with assistance for over 10 years. He has long complained of pain but the family and his caregivers have not always taken his complaints seriously. He is somewhat cranky and has always loved to make a fuss. The pain issue has been addressed many times and the response has usually been the same: Keep him on what he is already taking.

Mr. B's pain, however, has now become more pronounced, and his physician has prescribed a strong analgesic to relieve the pain, a morphine-based pill administered by mouth. The medication is given in small doses so as not to compromise his respiration. The physician tells the home health aide to administer one pill every six hours but to double the dosage if it does not work. After taking a single pill, Mr. B. goes to sleep, but when he awakens, he still complains of pain. The home health aide feels that a second pill might compromise his respiration and kill him and is very reluctant to give it to him. She calls into the agency for support, and a nurse comes to the scene and discovers that the patient is becoming septic.

Discussion Questions

- What should the aide do?
- What should the nurse do?
- Should prognosis play a significant role in determining whether to give the second dose?
- Does the patient's wish not to be in pain influence whether the second dose should be administered?
- What are the main ethical issues in this case?

13

CHAPTER

Consent-Based Policies and Procedures[1]

INTRODUCTION

This chapter will be dedicated almost exclusively to the examination of policies and procedures. It will address creating policies and procedures and the reason for their importance, and will include model policies that are founded in many of the principles of ethics and health law already treated in earlier chapters. The common ingredient and controlling principle in all of these policies is consent; it will be used as a vehicle for ensuring patient self-determination and the for legal permission of informed consent. The policies, which follow, were developed from over 20 years of working with a wide range of clinicians, health law firms and ethics committees. These policies can only be fully understood and appreciated with an adequate foundation in the principles underlying them, which the rest of the material in this book can provide. The policies that will be presented are called "integrated policies"; they address multiple concerns but are integrated with a guiding thread of consent. After a detailed discussion about

---

[1] These policies and procedures were developed with the assistance of many health care facilities and law firms around the country with whom I have worked. The Kentucky Hospital Association uses the Integrated Policy as their model policy, as do several other facilities around the nation. These policies were adapted from *Ethical and Legal Issues in Home Health and Long Term Care* by Dennis Robbins, Gaithersburg, MD: Aspen Publishers, Inc., 1996, pp. 111–132.

consent readers can read and use the policies as a model for developing their own variations. Please read the chapter with the realization that in order for a policy to be effective, the organization must take ownership in it. Even slight modifications to make it "yours" are extremely important.

One of the most distinctive aspects of the policy involves its section on withholding or withdrawing life prolonging medical procedures. It consists of two parts: part A, withholding cardiac and/or pulmonary resuscitation; and part B, withholding other life prolonging medical procedures. They should not be viewed independently, but rather as parts of an integrated whole.

POLICIES AND CONSENT

Many of the ethical issues we have already discussed involve the right of self-determination. When developing patient-related policies and procedures, consent must be the guiding thread that weaves individual components within the broader integrated policy. There also must be consistency in the way in which consent is addressed in all sectors of the healthcare continuum. In addition, the mission, vision and values of the managed care central operations as well as its care and service provider organizations and individual practitioners must maintain that consistency. As we have already discussed, policies can effectively create a foundation for ensuring that the patients' wishes are respected while at the same time insulating the organization and clinicians against potential legal liability.

Such policies must be created in accordance with clinically realistic provisions. Even financial aspects of the policy must be clinically sound. When hospital chief financial officers comply with provisions of the Joint Commission's IMSystem and HEDIS, they are weaving their reporting into a clinically sensitive framework which has implications for self-determination and consent.

In order to effectively integrate cost with quality, restrictions and changes in the way in which care is delivered must be explained to the patient. The Joint Commission, for example, in its network standards, is quite explicit about the duty to inform members in the healthcare plan of how to access services, how to get care outside of the delivery system, and other standards that affect autonomy and patient empowerment.

Having effective standards, reliable measurements for member satisfaction, and good policies in place, however, is not enough. Appropriate in-service education to familiarize staff, including physicians and in-house attorneys, with these standards, systems, and policies is critical. So too is the need to establish a common ground between payors and providers for dealing with sensitive issues and acting in accordance with the policies.

Developing a policy that ensures informed consent, not as acquiescence but as a reasonable indication of the patient's wishes, is a critical element in this process. It is better to develop policies before a later crisis arises than to develop them as a tourniquet to staunch the bleeding. It is important that the leaders of the central operations as well as its care and service provider organizations develop an overarching policy which integrates related policies into a single instrument for guidance. This avoids having to deal with a morass of divergent and often overlapping policies.

In addition to ensuring patient autonomy and allowing physicians to perform without excessive fear, an integrated policy can be an excellent marketing tool and provide a means of addressing costly outliers generated by physician discomfort and delays in decision making.

There are many reasons for the development of appropriate policies. For example, physicians and administrators assume that hospital attorneys will have clear answers to the questions that arise, but this is rarely the case. Many attorneys who work in healthcare settings are not trained in healthcare law and thus find they need on-the-job training. As a result, the advice offered is often excessively cautious. Accordingly, such attorneys are often perceived as "paid paranoids" operating in an unfamiliar milieu, and are often more comfortable handling the legal tasks involved in administration than providing guidance in the making of treatment decisions.

Most of the problems caregivers face arise less from the complexity of the issues than from a reluctance to make decisions and a tendency to dump decision-making responsibility on others. Attending physicians, for example, often avoid decision making by funneling it to the hospital legal counsel, the ethics committee, the medical director, risk managers, or pastoral care workers. These other professionals, although well intentioned, may act as enablers and infantilize physicians. It is, of course, important to distinguish this process of discomfort and infantilization from the process of making a proper referral.

CONSENT AS A DYNAMIC PROCESS

A wide range of ethical issues are encompassed by the general issue of consent, and many of these issues, while distinctive, are closely related to one another. For example, the question of whether to withhold or withdraw artificially or technologically supplied respiration, nutrition, and hydration should not be answered without knowledge and consideration of the patient's wishes.

It is important not only to understand what role patient wishes and informed consent play in the decision-making process but also to recognize that documenting this process is an important way to protect against legal liability. We are more effective at achieving this through acting in accordance with, rather than opposition to, patient wishes or those of a designated surrogate when the patient is unable to express himself or herself.

CONFUSION ABOUT CONSENT

Caregivers are often confused as to how they should deal with consent issues. In seminars across the nation, I have frequently asked participants to fill in the appropriate verb in the following sentence: "From the perspective of the caregiver, it is important to _____ consent." Consistently, the word *obtain* is offered as the first and often the only choice. At the same time, some will say that the sentence needs to be changed. "What good is consent," they ask, unless it is *"informed* consent"? It is not just permission that caregivers require but permission from someone who possesses the capacity to understand and appreciate the significance of what is being said.

In any case, the verb *obtain* betrays a misunderstanding about consent. It suggests consent is indeed something that can be obtained once and for all as if it were no more than a legal transaction or a discrete, static event. Instead, consent should be viewed as a dynamic and ongoing process. Patients come into a healthcare facility near death and leave quite healthy, or they come in reasonably healthy and leave in a worsened condition or dead. Decision making changes as the clinical course changes, so having anything other than a dynamic process makes little clinical or legal sense. Despite this, consent is frequently discussed as a form of contract that exists between the doctor and the patient as if it were a legal transaction, rather than a dynamic process. This seems odd, for one of the fundamental requisites of a contract is that the parties be on equal footing. It seems strange to think that clinicians, with their wealth of experience and knowledge, can be perceived as being on equal footing with their patients. In addition, patients generally get all their information about prognosis, risks, benefits, and alternatives from caregivers. Ultimately, patients just put themselves in caregivers' hands and require that they support them. Policies can strengthen caregivers' hands rather than make them shake with trepidation in the face of uncertainty. It is the spirit of the activity rather than the protocol that dictates the reasonableness of the activity, and policies should set forth the tone and spirit of caregivers' perceptions about consent and their duties to those whom they serve.

From an ethical perspective, the consent process should be aimed at allowing the patient to become actively involved in his or her care. Caregivers should thus transmit information in a way that is intelligible and useful to the patient. The ethical stance of supporting and caring for patients arises from a sense of professional duty and a sense of the duty owed to all other human beings, and is based on a willingness to help them in contexts where they would otherwise be overwhelmed. This facet is of particular importance in managed care organizations where many of the challenges and dissatisfaction with managed care involve members feeling that they weren't informed that a procedure would not be covered or that they could not use a given facility and so forth. Many of the frustrations members have are tied to claims that they didn't know or didn't agree to this or that. They often feel as passive recipients rather than active agents in the care. Consequently, they feel that their autonomy is being threatened. This can eventually transform them into adversaries, not partners. When adversarial postures are taken, legal remedies are suggested. The legal responsibility associated with consent concerns the nature, adequacy, and intelligibility of the information as well as the alternatives that are provided and the explanations of potential risks that are offered. How can someone consent to something without knowing the range of options available to him or her?

Defensive medicine has to some extent influenced caregivers to see law as primary and ethics as secondary. After all, although attention to ethics may give caregivers more professional satisfaction, ethical problems do not often keep them awake in quite the same way as potential lawsuits. That does not, however, provide license to treat patient wishes lightly.

CONSENT AND DUTY

Once caregivers realize the importance of informed consent, both as an important indicator of patient wishes in shaping their care and as an insulator against legal liability, they can better ensure that the wishes of patients are honored. From a legal perspective, the clearer it is that caregivers have fulfilled their duty to *cultivate* informed consent, the less exposure they will have to the risk of allegations of negligence. For example, acting in accordance with the wishes of the patients should be the foundation of policies regarding the withholding and withdrawing of life-prolonging medical procedures. A request for a do not resuscitate (DNR) order is merely an example of patient wish, in this case a wish not to be resuscitated should one go into cardiac arrest. These requests are not divorced from medical standards, for part of the duty physicians owe is to talk about the appropriateness of interventions and probable outcomes as well as the implications of refusing a recommended therapy or intervention.

Caregivers must protect patients from overtreatment as well as undertreatment. For example, suppose a patient is very sick and the prognosis is poor. The patient should be informed of what reasonable options exist. If she "wanted everything to be done" the caregiver would lay out what this might mean and try to get her to make a medically viable and reasonable choice. In other words, the caregiver needs to elevate the level of medical discourse to empower the patient to be better informed. He might respond to her wanting everything to be done by saying, "certainly we'll do everything that makes sense to keep you comfortable and we won't do things that do no more than cause you discomfort and prolong the dying process." Consent is a critical component of the twofold duty that clinicians owe to their patients: to act in accordance with the standards of the profession and to act in accordance with the patient's wishes. It is unusual for a malpractice suit to be brought that does not include an allegation that consent was either improper, insufficient, or absent. As already noted, caregivers often mistakenly view consent as something that must be obtained, a piece of paper or a form that, once completed, is put on the chart and not worried about once it has been obtained.

The model of "obtaining consent" is not consistent with the way medicine is practiced. Clinical care is dynamic; consent must be congruent with the clinical process, and so it must be dynamic as well. Perhaps a short etymological excursion into consent will help us shift our focus on consent as something we obtain to that of a dynamic process more congruent with clinical care. Consent comes from two Latin words: *con* meaning "with" or "together" and *sentire* meaning both "to know" and "to feel." Sentire thus has both cognitive and affective dimensions. Viewed in this way, consent requires continual transmission of information to the patient as circumstances change. The nature of this information as well as the manner in which it is shared play a very important role in the decision-making process. Information about the risks and benefits of a suggested treatment and available alternatives must be communicated to the patient. The information must be shared in a supportive and easily understandable way so that the patient (or surrogate decision-maker) is given continuing opportunities to be involved in the process. Rather than obtaining consent, caregivers should *nurture* or *cultivate* consent. They must make certain that their patients understand all important information and that the patients feel the caregivers are making an honest attempt to understand and appreciate their wishes and to act in accordance with them. This does not mean that caregivers have to share information in a neutral way but only that they have to provide appropriate information in a supportive milieu.

AN INTEGRATED CONSENT POLICY: AN OVERVIEW

An integrated policy dealing with broad consent as well as with withholding or withdrawing life-prolonging medical procedures should incorporate legal safeguards and ethical standards, conform to the constitutional rights of patients, and be clinically realistic. It must also be tailored to meet the needs of the particular institution.

The policy should offer guidance to clinicians and clarify the institution's commitment to the community it serves. The policy can serve as a marketing tool by showing that the institution or organization cares about patients and goes to some pains to ensure their wishes are honored.

It is important to set the tone of the policy by beginning on a positive note. The first sentence might read something like this: "Your wishes play an important part in shaping your care." This portrays the member or patient not merely as a partner in care but as the very focal point of care. It invites the member to become a partner while ensuring the mission of the MCO's central operations and constituent organizations and provider panels.

A definition section can be added to minimize ambiguity and offer consistency and guidance. Three sample definitions follow:

- *Informed consent.* The permission given to allow medical treatment(s) to be performed only after the patient has been reasonably informed or counseled regarding his or her condition, the nature and purpose of the proposed treatment or intervention, the probable risks associated with various options being considered, the prognosis, the expected probable outcomes, and the implications of foregoing treatment or a given procedure. Information should be provided in such a way that the patient (or surrogate) understands and appreciates the significance of the information provided so that the patient can make a valid and informed choice.

- *Surrogate.* Someone who acts in the patient's stead (substitutes in judgment for the patient) to determine what the patient would likely have decided were he or she able to decide for himself or herself.

- *Terminally ill.* A designation used to refer to those who suffer from end stages of disease and whose prognosis is extremely poor. In most cases, death is imminent or the patient suffers from an ongoing deteriorative or degenerative disease, and further interventions are viewed as only prolonging the dying process.

Since confusion abounds regarding "who decides?" the policy should include discussion of this issue. Although the body of the policy addresses consent for the patient who has the capacity to make decisions, clarification regarding surrogate or substitute decision making is necessary. Also, a DNR order does not entail withholding other life supports (e.g., artificial nutrition and hydration, antibiotics, blood, and antiseizure medications), but it does set the stage for discussing their withholding or withdrawal.

An integrated policy "integrates" clinical and administrative ethics, is an excellent risk management tool, and creates a more stable working environment. It is an alternative to the constellation of disjointed policies that cause problems of inconsistency in many healthcare institutions. In an integrated policy, each section builds upon and at the same time reinforces the other sections, giving the policy internal strength and coherence.

THE INTEGRATED POLICY

It is essential to ensure that the wishes of each patient be supported and respected. The initiation of many medical and nursing interventions requires that permission be given by the patient or a surrogate (often a spouse or family member). This permission is referred to as consent. In order for the patient to make an informed decision, the attending physician is responsible for informing the patient or surrogate (when the patient is unable to participate in decision making by virtue of disability or incapacity) about the patient's condition, the nature and purpose of proposed treatment(s), the probable risks, the likely prognosis, and expected probable outcomes. The imparting of the information should be accomplished in such a way that the patient understands and appreciates the significance of what is being discussed and explained. When and if the patient has been adequately informed, the patient's permission is referred to as informed consent.

Consent is a legal privilege that allows one to do what in the absence of that consent would not be acceptable. It is an extension of an individual's right to privacy (often expressed as the right of self-determination) and in healthcare encompasses the right to have one's wishes honored so long as those wishes are consistent with the ethical integrity of the medical profession. It is the patient (or a designated surrogate if the patient's wishes are unknown or unclear) who consents, and the patient's right of self-determination shall not be facilely compromised. Consent is not something one obtains, nor is it a static legal transaction; instead it is a process to be cultivated. Where decisional capacity fluctuates and it is unclear to the clinician whether the patient has the capacity to make a given decision, further assessment will be made. If the patient's medical condition interferes with his or her capacity to decide, then attempts will be made to correct the condition, if possible, to enable the patient to better participate in medical decision making.

Adults with the capacity to make medical decisions have the right to determine what shall be done with their own bodies and the patient shall not have wishes he or she expressed in advance (or his or her likely wishes as determined by a surrogate decision maker) thwarted or undermined.

If the patient, by virtue of disability or incapacity, is unable to express his or her wishes and there are no prior expressed wishes or advance directives, then another may serve as a surrogate for the patient and exercise "substituted judgment" on his or her behalf. The surrogate should attempt to determine what the patient's wishes were or what the patient would likely have decided were the patient able to decide for himself or herself.

Priority of Decision Makers

Safeguards should be established that ensure patient self-determination and provide opportunities for those wishes to be known. This is particularly important when family members disagree with the wishes of a competent patient. In such circumstances, the patient should be urged to identify someone to speak for him or her. The order of priority of decision makers is generally as follows: the durable medical agent, anyone specified by the patient, a legal guardian with specific authority to make medical decisions or decisions of person, the spouse, children of age, and parents.

Others may be sought to gain clarification or further indication of the patient's/resident's wishes (e.g., the patient's primary physician, clergy, and longstanding friends). If members of a specific class, such as children of age, disagree, some attempt to resolve the conflict consistent with the facility's conflict resolution policies should be made.

Advance directives, such as living wills, healthcare surrogate designations, or durable powers of attorney, should be evaluated for appropriateness as extenders of the self-determination of the patient and should be integrated into the decision-making process in accordance with the spirit with which these formal tools were drafted. Copies of advance directives should be documented and placed on the patient's chart. The chart should also identify agents or surrogates and how they can be reached and integrated into the decision-making process. (Advance directives, including living wills and durable powers of attorney are discussed at length in Chapter 14.)

Continuity of Consent

Patient wishes documented during former hospitalizations or treatment in other healthcare settings can guide future decision making. Information about expressed wishes should be integrated into the decision-making process and upgraded and re-evaluated as indicated. It is particularly important for minimizing uncertainty and confusion when a patient experiences an acute medical episode and initiating or withholding life-prolonging medical treatment may depend on the patient's prior directives. It can also serve as a safeguard of the patient's autonomy as he or she travels across the healthcare continuum.

Emergency Consent

When an emergency of sufficient magnitude warrants immediate action and the patient, by virtue of disability or incapacity, is unable to consent to appropriate treatment; his prior wishes are unknown and a designated surrogate is not available; and it is believed that the treatment will likely reverse an acutely reversible process, the treatment may be initiated. The goal in such circumstances is to stabilize the patient so that the immediate danger is removed. After the patient has been stabilized, his or her wishes regarding further treatment should be sought and honored in accordance with the spirit of the integrated informed consent policy. If the patient is unable to provide consent and a surrogate is not available, the nursing supervisor should be notified so he or she can institute procedures to locate the appropriate surrogate decision maker.

The primary duty of the physician is to act according to professional standards tempered by the wishes of the patient. During this period of legal clarification, the President's Commission on Ethical Issues in Biomedicine and Biomedical and Behavioral Research used insights gained from these cases to develop guidelines on decisions to forego life support. See for example its helpful publication *Deciding to Forego Life Supports,* especially the chapter "The Elements of Decision Making." And in 1986, the AMA gave further clarification on withholding or withdrawing life-prolonging medical procedures,[2] which was further refined in 1994 (see the following box).

---

[2] *Decisions Near the End of Life.* Chicago, American Medical Association Report 1991; 32(2).

OPINION OF THE AMA COUNCIL OF ETHICAL AND JUDICIAL AFFAIRS ON WITHHOLDING OR WITHDRAWING SUSTAINING MEDICAL TREATMENT*

The social commitment of the physician is to sustain life and relieve suffering. Where the performance of one duty conflicts with the other, the preferences of the patient should prevail. The principle of patient autonomy requires that physicians respect the decision to forego life-sustaining treatment of a patient who possesses decisionmaking capacity. Life-sustaining treatment is any treatment that serves to prolong life without reversing the underlying medical condition. Life-sustaining treatment may include, but is not limited to, mechanical ventilation, renal dialysis, chemotherapy, antibiotics, and artificial nutrition and hydration.

There is no ethical distinction between withdrawing and witholding life-sustaining treatment.

A competent, adult patient may, in advance, formulate and provide a valid consent to the withholding or withdrawal of life-support systems in the event that injury or illness renders that individual incompetent to make such a decision.

If the patient receiving life-sustaining treatment is incompetent, a surrogate decisionmaker should be identified. Without an advance directive that designates a proxy, the patient's family should become the surrogate decisionmaker. Family includes persons with whom the patient is closely associated. In the case when there is no person closely associated with the patient, but there are persons who both care about the patient and have sufficient relevant knowledge of the patient, such persons may be appropriate surrogates. Physicians should provide all relevant medical information and explain to surrogate decisionmakers that decisions regarding withholding or

Opinion of the AMA Council of Ethical and Judicial Affairs on Withholding and Withdrawing Sustaining Medical Treatment—Concluded

withdrawing life-sustaining treatment should be based on substituted judgment (what the patient would have decided) when there is evidence of the patient's preferences and values. In making a substituted judgment, decisionmakers may consider the patient's advance directive (if any); the patient's values about life and the way it should be lived; and the patient's attitudes towards sickness, suffering, medical procedures, and death. If there is not adequate evidence of the incompetent patient's preferences and values, the decision should be based on the best interests of the patient (what outcome would most likely promote the patient's well-being).

Though the surrogate's decision for the incompetent patient should almost always be accepted by the physician, there are four situations that may require either institutional or judicial review and/or intervention in the decision-making process: (1) there is no available family member willing to be the patient's surrogate decisionmaker, (2) there is a dispute among family members and there is no decisionmaker designated in an advance directive, (3) a health care provider believes that the family's decision is clearly not what the patient would have decided if competent, and (4) a health care provider believes that the decision is not a decision that could reasonably be judged to be in the patient's best interests. When there are disputes among family members or between family and health care providers, the use of ethics committees specifically designed to facilitate sound decisionmaking is recommended before resorting to the courts.

When a permanently unconscious patient was never competent or had not left any evidence of previous preferences or values, since there is no objective way to ascertain the best interests of the petient, the surrogate's decision should not be challenged as long as the decision is based on the decisionmaker's true concern for what would be best for the patient.

Physicians have an obligation to relieve pain and suffering and to promote the dignity and autonomy of dying patients in their care. This includes providing effective palliative treatment even though it may foreseeably hasten death.

Even if the patient is not terminally ill or permanently unconscious, it is not unethical to discontinue all means of life-sustaining medical treatment in accordance with a proper substituted judgment or best interests analysis.

---

* *Code of Medical Ethics Current Opinions, with Annotations,* 1994 edition, Chicago: American Medical Association, pp. 36–37.

Note: The AMA Council on Ethical and Judicial Affairs is the judicial authority of the AMA. The primary function of the council is to establish ethics policy and perform judicial review. This opinion is the latest version of the council's work in this area which was originally created in 1981.

Withholding/Withdrawing Life-Prolonging Procedures

The purpose of this section is to provide general guidance for the hospital and medical staff for withholding or withdrawing life-prolonging medical procedures. Adults with the capacity to make medical decisions have the right to actively participate in decision making. This right of self-determination includes treatment decisions as well as decisions to withhold or withdraw life-prolonging procedures.

The facility recognizes both the importance of maintaining patient self-determination and the importance of offering realistic and viable medical options. The physician should identify several factors when considering writing an order to withhold or withdraw life-prolonging medical procedures, including potential benefit, prognosis, morbidity, and the patient's expressed wishes regarding medical intervention and end-of-life decisions. The attending physician should participate in the decision-making process by making specific recommendations and defining reasonable alternatives based on viable medical options for the patient or acceptable surrogate.

These guidelines are intended to assist the physician, support the patient's self-determination, and reduce conflict; they neither exclude nor replace the exercise of the physician's clinical judgment, particularly in situations that arise unexpectedly and are potentially reversible. Such situations should be discussed with the patient in advance.

A. Withholding Cardiac and/or Pulmonary Resuscitation (WCPR)

1. A withhold cardiac and/or pulmonary resuscitation (WCPR) order refers specifically to withholding cardiac or pulmonary resuscitation. All other modalities for symptom control, such as those intended to reduce pain, prevent seizures, and provide comfort, should be implemented as needed.

2. A WCPR order may be considered when (a) there is a terminal condition with no reasonable hope for recovery; (b) the patient is in the late stages of an ongoing deteriorative disease; or (c) the patient has specifically expressed a wish, either directly or through an advance directive or an acceptable surrogate, not to be resuscitated.

3. Discussion of a WCPR order is preferably initiated by the attending physician (or his or her designate) or the patient. However, a surrogate decision maker or another clinician may initiate the discussion as well.

4. After the WCPR order has been written and properly documented in the medical record, resuscitative measures will not be initiated in the event of cardiac or pulmonary arrest.

5. The attending physician (or designate) is responsible for (a) discussing the WCPR order with the patient and, when appropriate, the family or an acceptable nonfamilial surrogate; (b) documenting ongoing discussions and decisions in the medical record; and (c) periodically assessing the WCPR order.

6. A WCPR order is not an endpoint but often sets the stage for a wide range of other decisions, including those involving the withholding or withdrawing of other life-prolonging medical procedures.

B. Withholding or Withdrawing Other Life-Prolonging Medical Procedures

1. Life-prolonging medical procedures include medication administration and artificially or technologically supplied respiration, nutrition, and hydration when such procedures serve only to prolong the dying process.

2. An order to withhold or withdraw life-prolonging medical procedures may be considered when (a) there is a terminal condition with no reasonable hope for recovery; (b) the patient is in the late stages of an ongoing deteriorative or degenerative disease; or (c) the patient has expressed a wish, either directly or through an advance directive or an acceptable surrogate, not to undergo such procedures.

3. Discussions of such an order should be initiated by the attending physician (or his or her designate), the patient, the family, or an acceptable nonfamilial surrogate.

4. Appropriate referrals should be made to confirm medical status and prognosis before a withhold/withdraw order is written by the attending physician.

5. The patient's physician is responsible for (a) discussing the withhold/withdraw order with the patient and, when appropriate, the family or an acceptable nonfamilial surrogate; (b) documenting ongoing discussions and decisions in the medical record; and (c) ongoing assessment of the withhold/withdraw order.

6. All other treatment modalities, such as those intended to reduce pain, prevent seizures, and provide comfort, should be implemented as needed.

C. Medically Futile Condition

1. If the attending physician determines that the patient's condition is terminal, and there is no hope of recovery, it follows that any attempted resuscitation or life support would be futile even if provided and would therefore be fundamentally inappropriate.

2. Ongoing discussion of the patient's condition is important as part of the anticipatory grief process if further intervention is determined to be medically inappropriate.

3. The patient's chart shall contain documentation of the basis for the determination of medical futility, the physician's written orders to withhold or withdraw resuscitation or life support, and documentation of attempts to notify family members.

Procedures: Medical Assessment and Documentation

A. Medical Assessment

1. A No Code or Withhold/Withdraw order should include a comprehensive assessment by the physician primarily responsible for the patient's care and be documented in the medical record. Reasonable efforts should be made to confirm medical status with appropriate referrals.

2. As in any other clinical decision, a No Code or Withhold/Withdraw order should be reevaluated periodically based on the medical status and specific circumstances of the patient.

B. Documentation

1. The No Code or Withhold/Withdraw order must be written and approved by the attending physician (or

his or her designate) on the physician's order sheet
and in the progress notes. This order must be signed and
dated.

2. Ongoing discussions with the patient, the family, or
an acceptable nonfamilial surrogate should be
documented in the progress notes (included should
be the date, time, and significant content of such
discussions). Any specific declarations made by the
patient directly or by the patient to the family or an
acceptable nonfamilial surrogate should be documented
in the medical record. Such information can help
ensure that the self-determination of the patient is
respected and resolve potential conflict.

3. There are special circumstances when a telephone order for
withholding cardiac or pulmonary resuscitation may be
appropriate. A telephone order for No Code must be
documented, dated, and signed by two clinicians.

4. There are circumstances in which a No Code or
Withhold/Withdraw order may be temporarily suspended
during a specific invasive procedure (e.g., palliative
surgery or a diagnostic procedure). Any proposed
changes (including a temporary suspension) in a
WCPR or Withhold/Withdraw order should be
discussed with the patient, the family, or an acceptable
nonfamilial surrogate and documented in the medical
record.

5. The patient or an authorized surrogate acting in the patient's
stead may request a change in a WCPR or Withhold/
Withdraw order at any time.

C. Conflict Resolution: The patient's wishes should be honored
provided that they are consistent with the ethical integrity
of the medical profession and the patient understands
and appreciates the significance of his or her wishes.
There may be circumstances, however, when the patient's
wishes are unknown or unclear or there is unresolved
conflict among surrogate decision makers. In such
circumstances, the formal conflict resolution mechanisms
of the organization should be enlisted to resolve any
conflict.

Related Provisions

1. When the patient is unable to make healthcare decisions and his or her wishes regarding specific decisions are unknown, then an acceptable surrogate may act on his or her behalf. In making any healthcare decision for the patient, the surrogate shall consider the recommendation of the attending physician, any evidence as to what the patient would have decided if the patient had decisional capacity, and what decision would be in the best interest of the patient.

2. Following is the general order of priority for surrogate healthcare decision makers: (1) a person with a valid medical durable power of attorney, (2) a legal guardian with authority for making medical decisions, (3) a validly designated healthcare surrogate, (4) the patient's spouse, (5) adult children of age, (6) either parent, or (7) adult brothers or sisters. Those who can provide a reasonable indication of the patient's views can offer helpful direction for decision-making purposes.

3. If, for reasons of conscience or of the patient's specific wishes, any caregiver cannot comply with a Withhold/Withdraw order, the caregiver must notify the appropriate department head or medical staff director of the refusal or inability to comply so that appropriate measures can be taken.

4. Advance directives, such as a living will, a medical durable power of attorney, or a patient-drafted directive, may be helpful guides for decision making and are usually considered to indicate patient intent. They can be critical in preventing or resolving conflict. (See Chapter 14.)

CONCLUSION

The integrated policy can be an extremely effective tool to minimize uncertainty and provide direction in many areas that in its absence might become very complicated. The strength of the policy, as the chapter has shown, is that it attempts to integrate clinical and administrative ethics. As indicated above, its provisions are strong and clear but it still requires additional work in the sense that if you choose to adopt this policy, you must tailor it to fit your organization or facility and make sure that it is properly inserviced. It will require the support of the leaders of your organization as well the clinical staff. Once those conditions have been fulfilled, a helpful vehicle to reduce uncertainty and support patients' wishes will be in place.

CASE STUDIES

CASE 1

Ms. D., a nurse and ethics committee member, has read extensively in the medical and nursing ethics literature that there is no ethical difference between withholding and withdrawing life-prolonging medical procedures. Yet she also knows by experience that when life-prolonging procedures are going to be withdrawn, special safeguards are instituted, documentation becomes more detailed, the ethics committee is always consulted, and each step in the process is subjected to extra scrutiny.

Discussion Questions

- Doesn't the extra care taken show that there is a difference between withholding life-prolonging treatment and withdrawing treatment that has already been put into place?
- If there is a difference, what implications would it have for patient care?
- What implications would it have for policy development?
- What implications does this have for caring for patients?

CASE 2

Mr. Z., after being in the hospital for 200 days, has become decisionally incapacitated. His physician says that the patient has never shared any information on his wishes regarding his medical treatment. The nurses on staff patently disagree, for they have identified numerous notations of remarks made by Mr. Z. about his wishes. They wonder if they should either highlight these notes or group them together in one inclusive progress note, with appropriate dates and times, in today's progress notes to encourage the physician to honor the patient's wishes.

Discussion Questions

- What guidance might the integrated consent policy play?
- Is this a risk management issue?
- Who is ultimately in charge of Mr. Z.'s care?
- Is this an advocacy issue? On whose part?

CASE 3

Mr. W. is admitted to a hospital emergency department because of a severe sore throat. The resident who takes the history overlooks some important information and fails to realize the seriousness of the symptoms. Appropriate tests are not performed and Mr. W.'s condition deteriorates dramatically.

Because of the incompetence of the resident and the unfortunate consequences of the misdiagnosis, Mr. W.'s family transfers him to another facility. His condition is evaluated and his family is told that he may be in a persistent vegetative state. Because this diagnosis has not been confirmed and Mr. W. may be experiencing pain, analgesics are prescribed and administered through a syringe.

Several days pass and Mr. W.'s condition does not seem to change. The family is coming to grips with the fact that he may never regain consciousness. One of the sons, more outspoken than the other children, asserts that Mr. W.'s time to die has come and requests that a lethal dose of some drug be administered. The staff refuse to consider this request seriously because it is perceived to be contrary to the ethics of the profession and illegal as well. The son who asked for the lethal dose becomes very sullen and even shows hostility toward the nurses when they enter Mr. W.'s room to check on him and give him the analgesic. Family members have even attempted to encourage the nurse to leave the syringe with its remaining contents behind. The family members are not mean-spirited but want to end Mr. W.'s life as he would have wanted. The nurses are concerned that the son might try to take events into his own hands and do something to end Mr. W.'s life.

Discussion Questions

- What provisions of the consent-based policy can help provide guidance in this circumstance?
- What should the nurses do in this situation?
- How might ethics rounds help in this scenario?
- What role might the ethics committee play?
- What are the main ethical issues at stake? The main legal issues?
- What is the physician's responsibility?

CASE 4

A patient is scheduled to have a liver transplant at a local network hospital. A review of UNOS data show that of the ten liver transplants performed at that facility during the past year, only four had a positive outcome. Another local non-network facility has outcome data the demonstrates positive outcomes in 28 of the 30 transplants performed at that facility.

Discussion Questions

- Does the case manager responsible for the case have a responsibility to inform the patient? the physician advisor? provider relations?

- What if the transplant surgeon has recently moved from hospital B to A. Is there an expectation that outcomes will improve?
- Do you say anything to anybody and if so what and why?
- Is this a case management concern or a quality concern?
- If the patent has a bad outcome at hospital B is the case manager legally liable?
- Would the failure to inform the patient be perceived as fraud?

CASE 5

Mrs. A. has been in a care facility for 18 years following a severe stroke. Her family had thought the stroke was just another episode of drunkenness and thus had delayed taking her to the hospital for some time. Mrs. A. is able to feed herself and talk but does not possess the capacity to make medical decisions. In fact, her son has been her guardian for over 15 years.

For financial reasons, the long-term care facility arranges for Mrs. A. to move to another nongovernment nursing home. Shortly after her transfer to the nursing home, she is rushed to the hospital with her trachea crammed with food. The emergency department clears the airway, but the medical resident evaluating her determines that she is probably in a persistent vegetative state. She is reddish colored and in flexion.

The medical resident informs her son that a persistent vegetative state is irreversible but fails to tell him that this is a complicated diagnosis that takes some time to establish with a reasonable degree of certainty. The son says that his mother would not have wanted her life prolonged and he states he wants no interventions. The medical resident asks if he could start an IV, and the son refuses to consent to this if the goal is only to extend the dying process. They agree together that no invasive procedures should be done. The patient's sodium level is close to 190 and her osmolality exceeds 400. The attending is mostly absent from the decision making, for she trusts the resident's judgment.

The resident informs the ethics consultant of what he is doing, because the consultant is involved in a study of persistent vegetative state patients. He tells the consultant that he is comfortable making such decisions and has had a good deal of experience with these kinds of cases. A dietitian becomes the source of greatest discomfort for the resident, for the dietitian feels that a decision to do nothing in such circumstances is wrong and contrary to her own practice and ethical guidelines. She urges someone to speak with the son and get his okay to initiate IV fluids to see if the patient's condition might change as a result of this minimally invasive intervention. After all, two weeks ago Mrs. A. had been sitting up and eating on her own.

The resident is encouraged by the ethics consultant to talk with the son. The resident tells the consultant to do it himself if he feels that strongly about it.

The son is approached by the consultant, who says he understands the son's fears that his mother's life might be unnecessarily prolonged. But he also says it is important that the son know he is doing the right thing and has exhausted all reasonable alternatives. He assures the son that the resident, the attending, and the ethics consultant know what his wishes regarding his mother are. The son agrees to a few days of hydration to see if his mother's condition will improve. A 1000D bag is hung, and within several hours Mrs. A. is verbal. After she is stable, she is discharged to her son's house. The home health nurse learns after some time that there is a great deal of guilt and unresolved grief on the part of all family members, who feel that had they taken their mother to the hospital more quickly she would never have been in this state.

Discussion Questions

- Should the aide or the nurse approach the family to talk about this issue?
- Should she inform the physician and set some mechanism in place to address it?
- Since she has a closer relationship with the family, should she deal with it directly?
- What are the primary ethical issues in this case?
- If the son had denied use of IV fluids, should a court order have been sought?
- What guidance does the policy offer in this situation?
- What duty, in terms of reversing hasty decisions, does the caregiver owe?

CASE 6

Mr. R. is an 86-year-old man who has never been quite the same after the loss of his wife several years ago. His daughters are in denial about his condition and about what he really wants. He is reluctant to talk about his wishes to the physician or nurse and is unwilling to even discuss the possibility of filling out an advance directive. Neither does he want to talk about the realities of his condition. He says he just wants a "tune up."

Mr. R. has a long history of diabetes, congestive heart failure, and heart disease, and is now experiencing kidney problems. His physician has made recommendations to one of the daughters regarding what should be done given his deteriorating condition and the likelihood of multisystem failures. The daughter explains to her father the realities of his condition, and although he becomes upset, he recognizes that decisions have to be made.

The physician is given the authority to write a DNR order for Mr. R. The nurse caring for him has very strong convictions about DNR orders, however, and she attempts to convince the patient to change his mind. This confuses him and he becomes depressed and angry with his physician. In fact, he says he wants another physician.

Discussion Questions

- If the nurse disagrees with the decision to write a DNR order and feels it is inappropriate for any reason, how should she try to effect a change?
- Who is responsible for an ethical decision of this sort?
- Would an ethics committee be helpful in resolving the case at hand? How might they resolve it without a clear policy? How about with a clear policy?
- What are the main ethical issues in this case?
- How might conflict resolution policies help in this instance?

14
CHAPTER

Advance Directives: Possibilities and Perils

INTRODUCTION

This chapter will incorporate the foundations of consent (discussed in Chapter 6), the discussion of advance directives as related to policies and procedures (Chapter 13), and discussions of consent, surrogacy and fluctuating capacity (Chapter 12), among others. The chapter will examine the strengths and weaknesses of various types of advance directives, including living wills, durable powers of attorney, and other instruments of expressing one's wishes in advance of the event. It will also discuss some of the problems associated with advance directives and their implementation, as well as lag time and the possible (if not probable) unwillingness of providers to honor directives. In addition, it will help the reader understand the strengths of these directives and know when drafting or articulating their own directives what caveats and concerns they will require.

ADVANCE DIRECTIVES[1]

Earlier discussions of consent, including the previous chapter on consent-based policies and procedures, mention advance directives as an extension

---

[1] The material included in this chapter was drawn and modified with permission from *Ethical and Legal Issues in Home Health and Long Term Care: Challenges and Solutions* by Dennis A. Robbins, Gaithersburg, MD: Aspen Publishers, Inc., 1996, pp. 95–108.

of the self-determination of the patient. An advance directive is exactly what it says it is. It is a *directive* (written or otherwise expressed) *in advance* indicating (and directing the physician to comply with) what one would or would not want done in certain circumstances. As already noted, one of the greatest frustrations and areas of dissatisfaction in managed care arises when members feel that they have no control of the destiny or their care, that "it is out of their hands." Advance directives are vehicles that, if honored, can ensure compliance with patients' wishes, empowerment at a time when they are most vulnerable, and in many cases reduce costs by providing guidance in advance or authorizing someone to speak for patients or members when, by virtue of disability or incapacity, they cannot express themselves.

Advance directives do not have to be written. They are often just verbal instructions given to physicians or other caregivers that are charted and honored. An advance directive may also be drawn from an earlier discussion or the significant content of one or more discussions with family members, clergy, or friends. The word *directive* comes from the first living will statute in the United States, the California Natural Death Act. A living will was called a "directive to physicians," and the act stated that the physicians *must* act in accordance with such a directive. Other states waffled on this issue and used the word *may* to relieve anxieties on the part of noncompliant physicians. California was not only the first state to take this step but also the first state to formally extend the durable power of attorney to be used for medical decision making.

LIVING WILLS

A plethora of living wills have entered the healthcare arena in the past several years. This is somewhat odd, because many states that have living will statutes have found them notoriously ineffective in ensuring that patient wishes be honored, and have typically adopted additional laws in a vain attempt to provide legislative certainty. A short investigation into these legislative efforts to clarify end-of-life decisions will demonstrate the difficulties that a legislative solution often poses.

A living will is a written declaration or directive to physicians in which the patient (declarant) affirms the wish not to be maintained by extraordinary measures if he or she is terminally ill, with death imminent. Imminence is defined in various ways across the nation. For example, the state of Maine offers the guideline "within a very short time," but within six months is the rule used in many other jurisdictions.

Theoretically, a living will tries to anticipate a healthcare crisis and to prescribe a decision ahead of time. Most living will acts require at least the following:

- The declarant (person drafting the will) must be found to be of *sound mind* when the living will is executed.
- The declarant must be (statutorily) *terminally ill* before the will takes effect.
- The declarant's *death must be imminent* when the will takes effect.
- *Extraordinary measures* will not be undertaken if they serve only to prolong life when the prognosis is hopeless. (Many state laws, oddly enough, exclude artificially supplied nutrition and hydration from the scope of extraordinary measures.)

Patients may create or customize their own living wills as well. If the patient has the foresight to execute a living will when competent and is able to affirm his or her intentions, the will can indeed be helpful. In the absence of the patient's later ability to interpret the declaration, however, clinicians and administrations may experience sufficient uncertainty about what the patient understood by the terms *imminent* and *extraordinary* that they refuse to honor the living will. Also, a patient may wish to refuse treatment even though he or she is not terminally ill and death is not imminent. A living will is often little or no help in these kinds of cases.

DURABLE POWERS OF ATTORNEY

In an effort to further support the patient's right to determine his or her medical care and assert his or her autonomy in advance of a medical crisis, most states have chosen to supplement the living will with the durable power of attorney for medical decision making.

Originally, the durable power of attorney was designed to address specific problems associated with wills and estates. It was quickly recognized, however, that it was an excellent mechanism to help patients, clinicians, and administrators deal with some of the thornier problems of medical decision making. A power of attorney has long been recognized as a valid way to appoint someone else (an "agent") to act in the place of the person making the power (the "principal"). However, in the recent past, a power of attorney made by a competent adult was no longer effective if the principal became incompetent. The only solution was to follow the often time-consuming, complex, and expensive procedure of asking a court to appoint a guardian. Since guardianship was unnecessarily cumbersome in life-threatening situations, an easier mechanism to ensure respect for the patient's wishes was needed. Through changes or sometimes just a reinterpretation in the law, a power of attorney was deemed to be "durable" (i.e., it would survive the disability or incapacity of the principal).

A durable power of attorney offers much more flexibility than a living will. The patient who has a durable agent does not have to be terminally ill and facing imminent death but only temporarily incapacitated in order for the agent to exercise judgment, and the instrument can be used to ensure patient wishes are honored for a variety of choices surrounding specific healthcare procedures and therapeutic options. In terms of acceptance in the healthcare community, durable powers of attorney are "already on the books" and most states have specifically extended them to medical decision making under the title of "durable power of attorney for healthcare." Also, a legislatively authorized durable power of attorney for healthcare makes medical decision making much less complex and uncertain and thereby reduces their discomfort.

Executing a durable power of attorney usually requires simply signing a document and (in some states) getting it notarized. No cumbersome guardianship proceedings need arise when the durable agent acts for the incapacitated principal. In most states, a durable power does not even have to follow a specific format, and durable powers executed in other states are generally considered valid.

It is important to recognize that durable powers of attorney are not right-to-die instruments. Rather, they are intended to ensure patient self-determination, and the outcome in a given instance could just as well be consent to treatment as refusal of treatment.

As already mentioned, a durable power of attorney survives the onset of incompetence. Appointing an agent under a durable power of attorney is a simple, inexpensive means of ensuring that the individual's wishes regarding choice of physician, use of intrusive procedures, and use of extraordinary life-prolonging measures are honored should the individual be unable to communicate them because of illness or incapacitation.

A subtle yet important concern arises here. The durable agent is not a stranger appointed by a court, nor a neutral or impartial spectator, but someone whom the patient, while competent, specifically designates to act for him or her in the event of an incapacitating illness or event. The appointment of someone whom the patient trusts is much more consistent with the clinical perspective than is the use of a neutral court-appointed decision maker. In clinical environments, caregivers seek those who can best represent the patient's wishes or intent. In other words, they seek out partiality and shun impartial involvement.

Mark Fowler, in a *Columbia Law Review* article, captures the advantages of a durable power of attorney:

> From the patient's viewpoint, an agent would help to assure that an incapacitated patient receives treatment in accordance with his own wishes. Also, the appointment of an agent, unlike a living will, is respected. The agent could ask questions, assess risks and costs, speak to friends and relatives of the patient, consider a variety of therapeutic options, ask the opinion of other physicians, evaluate the patient's condition and prospects for recovery, in short, engage in the same complex decision-making process that the patient would undertake if he were able. Thus, an agent extends the scope of the patient farther than a written directive by making decisions consistent with the patient's values in situations which he might not have specifically foreseen. Some basis for determining and documenting patient intent even in the absence of an appointed agent is important.[2]

It is increasingly important to document the patient's wishes on the chart. If the patient has a living will, it still serves as a reasonable indication of patient intent and should be attached to the chart.

An agent can not only voice and enforce the patient's treatment preferences but also has the advantage of extending the self determination of the patient. Unlike a living will, which may be ambiguous, an agent is someone who is not only legally empowered to make decisions but also is able to talk with caregivers and gain clarification of complicated issues. If the clinician is unsure about the patient's wishes and there are no surrogates that can be identified to indicate what a person may have specifically meant in his living will, the clinician can hardly assuage his uncertainty by talking to the living will document. A durable power of attorney will most of the time be a much better vehicle than anything that is written. Videotaping of patients articulating their wishes and choices can be helpful, but does not replace the agent who can deal with issues that were unanticipated or unexpected.

---

[2] Fowler, Mark: "Appointing an Agent to Make Treatment Choices," *Columbia Law Review* 84:(985) May, 1984, p. 1001.

The durable power of attorney is a wonderful mechanism for identifying patient wishes because we can always be surprised. For example, once a patient with serious head and neck cancer and a hopeless prognosis, while being videotaped for a teaching film on how to inform people they are dying, was asked, "do you want us to pound on your chest and stick a tube into you, and to have to go through a range of therapeutic furor?" He covered his tracheotomy site and responded, "Well, they did that to me before and it saved my life, sure!" Asking the wrong question can generate the wrong answer. It is not part of the caregiving role, however, to second-guess patients when they can tell us what they want. At the same time it is wrong to offer them clinically unrealistic options. If they are able to express themselves, let them state what they want; if they are unable to do so, consulting a durable agent is the best way to go.

ON SURROGACY AND SURROGACY LAWS

While the durable power of attorney has solved many problems, it is only effective if the agent is present. It is not uncommon for an elderly patient to appoint an agent the same age or older who doesn't survive them, or a relative who lives in another state or country. As a result, when a medical crisis arises, the agent may not be present or may have since become incompetent. And of course, many patients have not executed any advance directive, be it a living will or a durable power of attorney for healthcare. Consequently, many state legislatures have enacted surrogate decision-maker laws. These statutes provide that when an individual has been determined to lack decisional capacity, the attending physician will identify a surrogate decision maker.

PROBLEMS ASSOCIATED WITH ADVANCE DIRECTIVES

Patients do not have to be terminally ill to have their rights or wishes honored. Even patients who are terminally ill, however, may actually undermine their rights if they have executed an advance directive in certain states. In some cases, by executing a statutory living will or statutory-form healthcare surrogate designation, people may compromise their wishes more than if they had nothing. State-designed living will forms are often the result of political compromise. In the process of getting adopted they get watered down. They may compromise the patient who thinks he or she is getting something and may actually be giving something up that seemed innocuous at first glance, and it is unlikely that people signing the forms have read the statutes. Yet it is critical to know what restrictions such statutes impose. There are additional uncertainties as to what information must be collected, what must be asked of and told to patients, and how caregivers are to coordinate information regarding advance directives and pass it on from the hospital to the nursing home and from the nursing home to the hospice or home healthcare provider. Continuity of consent will likely become a major concern in the future.

Since these directives may potentially compromise the wishes of patients, caregivers must be aware of this and warn patients about any restrictions such directives may impose. This is not meant to suggest that all statutory forms are bad. In fact, some are excellent. The point is that caregivers need to evaluate these forms carefully to see if they say what the patients or surrogates think they say. If they do not, they will have to be amended.

Imagine a physician who is uncomfortable and not sure what to do in an end-of-life situation. She consults an attorney who is relatively inexperienced in dealing with such matters, and the attorney looks to the living will statute for guidance. The attorney tells the physician that the statute precludes the removal of artificial nutrition and hydration. What should the physician do? Hopefully, the physician will act on the basis of what the patient wants and will properly upgrade and amend the patient's wishes via the chart. In the past, all a patient had to do was to tell the physician or surrogate of any change of mind and this information would have been written in the chart. The fact that patients now take the extra step of preparing a written document should afford them a greater degree of self-determination, not compromise it.

When procedures that are inconsistent with the patient's wishes and only prolong the dying process are imposed upon the patient, this is wrong. When medication and predigested, premeasured, chemically created and prepared nutrition are injected into the patient through the nose or by means of a tube into the stomach against the wishes of the patient, this is wrong. Think of a patient who is in intractable pain and wants to die but whose life is being prolonged only because of a restriction in the living will statute. Feeding tubes should not have more rights than patients!

Caregivers can help avoid these situations by advising their patients about the limitations of these documents and by talking to them about their wishes. They can also inform their patients of the need to modify or replace these documents. In cases where a physician has developed a relationship with a patient over the years, the problems with living wills can be dealt with relatively easily. In healthcare settings where little might be known about patients presenting with medical conditions, having advance directives or identifying a spokesperson is more important.

The durable power of attorney for healthcare gives rise to few problems. It is not subject to the same restrictions as the other advance directive options. Well-designed documents can help to ensure patient wishes are honored, resolve interfamilial decision-making conflict, and provide clear direction to hospitals and physicians. A durable agent can both guard against and adjudicate conflict that arises in the clinical environment between family members who are split over what to do, and can inform clinicians what the patient would have wanted. If a durable agent has not been appointed, caregivers should go out of their way to determine patient intent and then document it on the chart. This provides excellent insulation against potential liability and retains decision-making authority within the institution. It is obviously much easier for clinicians to talk and reason with an agent than talk with a written declaration. As already noted, one problem that can occur is the unavailability of the appointed durable agent at the point he or she is finally needed. Another is that the agent may be only marginally competent or, for whatever reason, may not be acting in the best interests of the patient.

A WAY TO HIGHLIGHT THE IMPORTANCE OF ADVANCE DIRECTIVES

Sometimes having a brochure to inform the patient of the importance of having an advance directive and making that directive known can be helpful in assuring that patient wishes are known and acted upon. While many healthcare facilities are mandated by the Patient Self-Determination Act to ask if the patient has an advanced directive, encouraging the patient to enlist an advance directive is much less prominent. Many see "getting" the advance directive from the patient as just one more administrative encumbrance imposed from the outside rather than a opportunity to ensure patient wishes and reduce costs because of ambiguity and uncertainty. The brochure on pages 269-271 is an example of a helpful way to inform the patient about advance directives.

BROCHURE ON ADVANCE DIRECTIVES AND SURROGACY

YOUR WISHES ARE IMPORTANT IN SHAPING YOUR CARE

Making Health Care Decisions

We want to provide you with information and support regarding advance directives as you make healthcare decisions. An "advance directive" tells us what your wishes are regarding medical treatment if you become unable to tell us yourself. This brochure will help you to know what to discuss with your doctor and family, and explains your right to participate in making decisions. It also tells you how, under this hospital's policies and procedures, to continue to make decisions if you become unable to personally make them.

How Will Decisions Be Made If You Are Unable to Decide for Yourself?

An adult patient never loses the right to make treatment decisions when he becomes incapacitated. However, in circumstances where sickness or mental state interferes with your ability to make decisions, questions arise as to who can act for you and how this person knows or decides what to do. Under our policies, we first look for written answers from three sources: (1) an agent appointed through a *medical durable power of attorney* or *healthcare surrogate* designation (which is not as flexible as the durable power of attorney), that is, someone you have appointed in writing to act in your behalf; (2) *a living will,* that is, a document stating what you want or don't want done if you are terminally ill (and "terminally" is extremely narrowly defined); or (3) *legal guardianship.* Guardianship is often imposed rather than chosen. The guardian may not know what your wishes are or be able to honor or enforce them. It is better to choose someone you trust while you have the capacity to do so.

Unfortunately, not everyone has gone through the formalities of a written document, that is, a directive indicating in advance what your directions or wishes are or who you want as your spokesperson, or has a court-appointed guardian. When a patient has not provided the hospital with directions in writing, our policies have us consider information and viewpoints, including your past oral statements, that is, things you said to friends, family, or clergy, or other information provided by family or friends about your wishes, and any instructions from you, to get a reasonable indication of your wishes.

Brochure on Advance Directives and Surrogacy—Continued

Types of Advance Directives

A durable power of attorney, as well as the healthcare surrogate, allows you to name or designate an "agent" or "surrogate" who can make medical treatment decisions if you become unable to make them yourself. The healthcare surrogate is much more restrictive than the durable power of attorney and may not assure you wishes to the same degree. The durable power of attorney generally becomes effective when you no longer possess the capacity to participate in medical decision making. The durable power of attorney is much less restrictive than other advance directives and often is the best formal way to ensure your wishes. Not all advance directives require thay you consult an attorney, although you may do so if you wish.

How Will the Facility Know If You Have Any Advance Directives?

We will ask you when you are being admitted here whether you have designated in writing specific directions or a specific person by some form of advance directive regarding your medical care. If you have, we will file the documents that you give us in your medical record at the hospital, including the name, address, and telephone numbers of the person who you would like to make decisions for you in the event you are no longer able to make them for yourself.

How Can You Make an Advance Directive Through a Durable Power of Attorney for Healthcare, Designate a Healthcare Surrogate, or Create a Living Will?

Many advisors in the health care field believe that the durable power of attorney is an excellent way to have your wishes known because it allows you to appoint someone whom you trust to act and speak for you. The health care surrogate designation can also be helpful but is more restrictive than the durable power of attorney. If you wish to further explore this option, we will be glad to have a representative assist you.

Another written directive is the living will. Unlike a healthcare surrogate designation or medical durable power of attorney, a living will does not name anyone to make decisions for you and does not possess the flexibility of other advance directives. Instead, it lists or describes the kinds of medical treatments you wish to have or do not wish to have if you become terminally ill (it is often very restrictive in its definition of terminal illness).

Brochure on Advance Directives and Surrogacy—Concluded

Will Your Wishes Be Honored If You Have No Advance Directive?

There is no law that says you have to make an advance directive. Our policies recognize that many patients have had discussions about their wishes involving medical treatment options with their family, clergy, and close friends, even if they have not written them down. Most often this information is helpful and reliable enough for us to be able to honor your wishes.

How Can You Get More Information?

For additional information, you may contact the Social Services Office at ext. xxx to assist you with any other questions regarding advance directives or any other item covered in this brochure. This is part of our ongoing commitment to better serve you. If you want more detailed information about relevant state law, we recommend you consult your legal advisor.

COMPLIANCE WITH ADVANCE DIRECTIVES

In our discussion of the Robert Wood Johnson Foundation study, we saw a great disparity between terminally ill patients' wishes and the treatment they received. Again, of the patients who did not want to be resuscitated, 49 percent did not have DNR orders written. The remaining patients did not have DNR orders written until their last two remaining days of life, making over half of them spend their last eight days as either comatose on a ventilator in an intensive care unit. Their wishes, indicated in their advance directives, were all but ignored, and their self determination was thwarted. "Every facet of medical culture, from the training of doctors to reimbursement systems to cover over reliance on high-tech treatment, conspired to cause doctors to ignore patients wishes. Most of us will die of an illness that will not be labeled as dying until the last couple of days at best."[3]

LAG TIME BETWEEN THE IDENTIFICATION OF ADVANCE DIRECTIVES AND ORDERS TO COMPLY

Even when advance directives are identified and honored, there is often a lag between the identification of an advance directive and the actual

---

[3] Open Society Institute, Project on Death in America, PDIA Newsletter. March 1996; p. 5.

writing of orders consistent with it. In the case of an advance directive indicating the requirement of writing an order to withhold cardiac and pulmonary resuscitation, it is important that the person who is primarily responsible for the patient's care be advised that there is such an advance directive. Suppose an order is not yet written but the nurse is aware there is an advance directive and knows what it states. Should he or she honor the patient's wishes and refrain from resuscitation? As acuity increases, this and related problems will become more common, and healthcare policies will need to be altered to reflect the increase and its attendant problems.

TELEPHONE DNR ORDERS

A similar circumstance involves do not resuscitate (DNR) orders received over the phone. It is not uncommon for family members to take time before coming to terms with a DNR order. Imagine a brother and sister confronting the issue of whether to forego life-prolonging measures for their mother. They decide to tell the physician to write a DNR order but they cannot reach him immediately. In the meantime they tell the nurse responsible for their mother's nursing care about their decision. Before an order is written, the mother codes. This type of situation shows how important it is for caregivers to act on the basis of a reasonable indication of patient intent and develop appropriate policies and procedures.

POLICIES AND POLEMICS REGARDING ADVANCE DIRECTIVES

Occasionally, family members ask or demand that caregivers do something that is medically or ethically inappropriate. They do this not because they do not care about their loved one, but because they have been misled or misinformed. A tired staff physician may ask a patient's spouse, "Do you want us to do everything?" Doing everything is not a real option. Caregivers never do everything and they also never do absolutely nothing. Therefore, they must use language that is clinically appropriate rather than ask general questions that are inconsistent with medical standards.

Faced with uncertainty, caregivers feel they must do something, partly out of fear of legal liability. It is strange that they are often motivated by fear of legal liability and at the same time are unclear about how to insulate against legal liability. Even more, attorneys who counsel healthcare facilities and organizations are often ill-informed and have minimal training in health law. Many problems might be discovered to have simple solutions once healthcare professionals' legal duties are better understood.

Unfortunately, caregivers are not always entirely sure how to articulate or explain what their duty is. If they are unclear about their duty, they obviously will not be able to show they fulfilled it. When asked what their duty is, caregivers usually say it is to "do no harm." Although true, this is too general an answer. They must be able to explain in detail what constitutes appropriate medical care in the situation in question. Hopefully, as practice guidelines, practice parameters, and clinical pathways are created, some of the confusion in knowing what to do will be minimized.

CREATING SENSIBLE POLICIES

As mentioned, caregivers have a duty to act in accordance with the standards of the medical profession. The best way to demonstrate that they have fulfilled their duty is through ongoing documentation. They must also develop policies that give direction in end-of-life cases and provide education about standards and major legal decisions. Refining their communication skills will certainly help as well. They must be able, for example, to describe realistic medical alternatives to surrogate decision-makers. In many cases, patients and surrogates say they want everything to be done because caregivers ask the wrong questions in the wrong way at the wrong time. Patients and surrogates need adequate support and guidance.

It is often helpful to crystallize superior ways to approach a particular problem by creating a policy (See related discussion in Chapter 13). A policy on informed consent should ensure that consent is not mere acquiescence but reflects the patient's wishes. Ideally, the consent process should result in the patient's honest consent to clinically realistic treatments and alternatives. Learning from the mistakes and successes of others rather than having to remake the mistakes is the best strategy. Clinical education has to provide a better understanding of caregiver's legal obligations and the importance of documentation for demonstrating the fulfillment of these obligations. Effective and timely communication with patients and their families should be the rule rather than the exception. By honestly sharing medical realities, caregivers can help patients form reasonable desires and make sensible decisions.

By attempting extensive life-prolonging measures to avoid the risk of liability, caregivers will often exacerbate their problems. Practicing good medicine, providing good nursing care, making appropriate referrals, and demonstrating that the patient has given truly informed consent are the best protections.

Indeed, informed consent is one of the most important means available for dealing with end-of-life issues as well as insulating against potential legal liability.

DOCUMENTING CONTROVERSY

Caregivers often become more uncomfortable and often excessively paternalistic when their patients choose treatments or procedures other than what the caregivers believe is the best option. In fact, questions as to whether a patient has the capacity to make decisions most often arise when the patient disagrees with what the physician or other caregivers want to do.

The way in which caregivers document ethical problems that arise is of extreme importance, particularly when there is disagreement among parties, whether they are clinicians or family members. The best advice is to document controversy in an ongoing and dynamic way that is consistent with good clinical care.

Institutional conflict resolution procedures can be used to protect patients, caregivers, and the facility. In dealing with conflict, the clinician begins by talking with family members and documenting the significant content of the discussion. The clinician may then call in a social worker or someone from pastoral care. Whatever staff becomes involved should document their interventions. Creating a paper trail that records the patient's wishes and shows the family is of a different mind is a necessary part of the consent process. If a guardian is sought when the patient becomes incapacitated, notes of the discussions can be used to ensure that the patient's wishes are not compromised. If the clinicians caring for the patient are concerned that family members are likely to become adversarial, they may want to call another clinician in to confirm the decisional capacity of the patient as a further precautionary measure. This makes it harder for a guardian to argue that the patient did not know what he or she was doing or did not understand what his or her decision meant. Referrals can be used to confirm consent just as they are used to confirm a medical diagnosis. Referring the case to the ethics committee can also serve as an important protection for the patient.

MATTERS OF CONSCIENCE

Many medical and nursing practice acts and some advance directive legislation include room for matters of conscience. Caregivers have a right to self-determination just as as patients do, and thus they should not be forced to do what they feel is wrong or inconsistent with their religious or personal tenets. If indeed a matter of conscience creates a conflict between what the patient wants and what the caregiver is willing to do, the caregiver must inform the patient as well as identify a substitute caregiver.

Claiming that reluctance to treat a patient is a matter of conscience can be a convenient way to avoid dealing with issues that are difficult or uncomfortable. When initial concerns about caring for AIDS patients arose, it was amazing how many caregivers "had difficulty" dealing with such patients. Legitimate refusals to treat based on conscience should be respected, but sorting out the legitimacy of refusals is important.

At the institutional level, matters of conscience are more problematic. Although an institution is obligated to identify up front any procedures it is unwilling to perform, its refusal to perform procedures has to be consistent with the state law as well as the constitutional rights of patients. The right of patients to make decisions about their care includes the right to change their minds as they get older and sicker. Must a patient go elsewhere if he or she has lived in a long-term care facility for many years but now has decided to ask not to be resuscitated, a request that is inconsistent with the "conscience" of the facility or system? The answer to this question is unclear. Having a policy in place that clarifies how such changes of mind will be dealt with can be helpful. It shows at the very least that the actions are not arbitrary but rather in accordance with established policies.

CONCLUSION

Advance directives can be powerful extenders to a patient's decision making power when patients, by virtue of disability or incapacity, become unable to express themselves. Strengths and weaknesses of various advance directives were discussed as well as the caveats associated with statutory living wills or other advance directives. Often these are the result of political compromise and don't say what you might think they say or don't ensure what you might think they do. The reader has probably determined that the strongest vehicle for assuring patient wishes is the durable power of attorney. It allows someone the patient has designated to represent his or her interests. This person ideally either specifically knows what the patient wants, or knows well enough to guess what the patient likely would have wanted had he or she been able to decide for himself or herself. Many of the major difficulties with advance directives that arise in their implementation were discussed. Learning the value and relative strengths of these instruments as well as their limitations can reduce the uncertainty of what will happen to the patient by making clear not only what his or her options are but also how they can be best exercised.

CASE STUDIES

CASE 1

A patient has indicated he does not want to be resuscitated should he suffer cardiac or pulmonary arrest. One of the nurses has developed a close relationship with the patient and has talked with him about his wishes regarding DNR. She knows that the patient's physician has a reputation for overriding or ignoring the wishes of patients not to be resuscitated when they can no longer express themselves. The physician has strong religious convictions and believes it is always better to "err on the side of life."

Discussion Questions

- Should the nurse inform the patient or family members about the physician's reputation?
- If she does nothing, will she be guilty of legal or ethical negligence?
- How should the physician be dealt with?
- What role could a conflict resolution body (e.g., an ethics committee) play in helping to ensure the patient's autonomy?

CASE 2

After two friends had died within the past two years, Mrs. D. grew concerned that her wish not to be kept alive on artificial nutrition and hydration might not be honored. She appointed a close friend about the same age to be her durable agent. Many years previously, she had filled out a living will form. Eventually Mrs. D's condition deteriorated and she no longer possessed the capacity to voice her wishes. Her durable agent was sought to act in her stead but this person had already died and the living will had expired.

Discussion Questions

- On what basis should decisions be made?
- What effect on decision making and determining patient intent does an expired directive have?
- What might the caregiver do for direction?
- Should the facility's ethics committee be consulted? If so, what can it do?
- Suppose the living will had not expired but instead included a provision requiring that artificial nutrition and hydration not be withheld?

CASE 3

Mr. J., who has Alzheimer's disease, has drafted an advance directive saying that if he was to suffer an infection that might be reversible with antibiotics, he wishes to refuse the antibiotics. He does not want to deteriorate any more and believes that the septicemia that might result would be "an old man's friend."

Discussion Questions

- Should his wish be honored?
- If so, on what basis?
- If not, on what basis?
- Do you have to be terminally ill to exercise the right to refuse treatment?
- Can people with Alzheimer's still have the capacity to make medical decisions?

CASE 4

While driving to Florida, Mr. N is involved in a car accident in Georgia and is seriously injured. Attempts to treat her injuries have been somewhat successful but her condition remains critical and she may die. She has a living will from her home state of Kentucky that was found in her glove box.

Discussion Questions

- Should the facility honor the wishes expressed in her living will?
- Is the living will likely to be a sufficient indicator of what the patient would want to have done?
- How should the caregiver document the living will?
- Should an attempt to identify a surrogate or enlist other aids to decision making be undertaken?

C A S E   5

Mr. L. has indicated that he does not want to be resuscitated. Several years ago a close friend of his who had stopped breathing for 30 minutes was resuscitated by emergency medical technicians. Since then his friend has been in a persistent vegetative state. Mr. L. heard that the longest recorded case of someone in a persistent vegetative state was 37 years and 111 days, and he does not want to end up the same way. As a safeguard, he has drafted an advance directive saying he does not want to be intubated or to have chest compressions or pressors and the like under any circumstance. He has an acute apneac episode believed to be associated with a mucous plug.

Discussion Questions

- What should the nurse do?
- What role, if any, might the ethics committee play?
- What role might a patient care, pastoral care, or family conference play?
- How can Mr. L's caregivers address his concerns and give him the confidence to let them deal with acutely reversible events?
- What role could ethics rounds play?
- What implications does this have for avoiding "doing everything" and "doing nothing" discourse?

15
CHAPTER

Transforming Outcomes into Ethically and Socially Responsible Health Care Plans: An Unfinished Chapter

The intent of this chapter is not only to reflect upon the content of previous chapters, but also to use that knowledge as a catalyst to imagine and envision what a socially and ethically responsible healthcare plan should look like. The insights and suggestions offered here are intended to serve only as a glimpse in this endeavor and a humble beginning, for they are incomplete and by no means exhaustive.

This is a challenge that invites readers to construct their own ideas about a specific element or the entire model of what a socially and ethically responsible should be. Perhaps the reader's own healthcare plan offers a model or has deficiencies or assets that stimulate ideas for improvement that will help set the tone in this endeavor.

An important underlying motivation to create this text was developed from working with physicians, case managers, nurses and healthcare executives who seek a reliable framework for bridging the gap between fiscal integrity on the one hand, and clinical standards, patient confidence, professional duty, and standards on the other. It is intended to stimulate a dialogue that will enable us to blend financial with clinical concerns in such a way as to enhance rather than undermine the way we care for those whom we serve.

This book has identified a wide range of resources for addressing ethical and legal issues in diverse settings, developed new ethics-related policies and procedures, and identified materials that can be used to educate clinicians and other direct or ancillary healthcare professionals, patients, and families. It has addressed fundamental issues of trust, integrity, and accountability that set the tone for a wide range of ethical and legal issues that arise in managed care. It has offered guidance on how to use various vehicles for addressing ethical issues and challenges such as medical management policies and procedures, advocacy initiatives, ethics rounds, conflict resolution guidelines, and has introduced a wide range of materials that provide guidance on managed care challenges, formulary issues, and negotiating. It has also provided detailed information about ethics committees, has explored and traced the concept of patient autonomy and its implications for policy development, documentation, and risk management, and recommended ways to insulate against legal liability while better assuring that the wishes of the patient will be honored.

The book has attempted to take a different approach than many of the discussions of ethics that arise in managed care today. Most of the crusaders for ethical causes offer a diatribe against misplaced values or pontificate on sensationalistic accounts of what a given plan did or did not do in a certain circumstance. This book has attempted to offer a more balanced and broad approach to the field, to step beyond the individual circumstances and look at the bigger picture. Horror stories, unethical practices and unethical people neither started nor will end with managed care. However, we need to identify misplaced incentives and areas for substantial improvement to reduce their incidence. This in no way suggests that we should overlook, ignore or excuse these deviations from the expected norm, only that we must properly locate them in the context of a broader mission and use them to make a better healthcare delivery system.

Initially, the primary goal of this book was to equip healthcare professionals with information so that they could understand pitfalls and possibilities and thus be better able to negotiate with potential managed care partners. A more useful and lasting approach could only be achieved by identifying a common ground upon which bridges could be built that could span the apparent abyss created by cost and quality disparities. In achieving this, the book sought to integrate managed care with ethics in a manner that did not "homogenize the issues," yet was palatable to diverse audiences. Arming the stakeholders with better critical assessment and methodological tools coupled with a clearer understanding of key concepts and principles to help achieve goals was a recipe for empowerment, collaboration, and improvement.

In some areas, the text has been exhaustive in treating issues, and in other cases it has merely referred to an emerging concern, offering only a peek or glimpse at potential implications. The book was not designed as a panacea but instead has been a compendium of issues commonly associated with managed care aimed at relocating them into a more manageable matrix of related issues and offering some unifying concepts. While not a prescription for combating underlying causes, the treatment of issues intended to identify rather than to ignore the symptoms and offer options as to how such symptoms should be better managed.

The challenge to integrate managed care and ethics requires that we develop ways to transform challenges of the present into positive future outcomes. As the reader has learned from navigating through this book, there are a wide range of issues which have either been associated directly with managed care or with which managed care must contend. The challenge is to create a better, more efficient and safer system. This is now in the lap of managed care and many anticipate that the managed care industry can and will meet these challenges. There is a simultaneous call for accountability, often in the form of safeguards, to address and resolve the many ethical issues operant in various delivery systems and healthcare plans. Rules, guidelines, and standards must be followed to meet acceptable levels of expectation in quality, integrity, clinical appropriateness and leadership.

Many stakeholders are encouraged by the direction that healthcare is taking, particularly the focus of measurement criteria and outcome measures. While many of these efforts are just beginning, they offer the opportunity to identify what is most effective and in so doing enhance rather than diminish quality, giving us better information and better results that translate into better care and better health.

The challenge, as already noted, is to transform perceptions and eroding confidence on the part of the public into a recognition that improvement is in their best interests, and to honestly calculate what actually does or does not achieve that goal. For example, would not the public's response have been different to the attempt to reduce obstetric days for routine delivery by reducing in-patient days but adding a two-day home health nurse benefit followed by homemaker services to help new parents better integrate the new baby into their lives and routine. Rather than telling people they would lose something, perhaps it would have been better to show them they would get something better (which will actually cost less).

Managed care organizations must deal more effectively with change as well as with disgruntled patients, or those who feel that their care or lives will be jeopardized by change. The failure to accommodate and effectively address this need will likely result in managed healthcare being hyper-regulated and legislated to death. Long-term care offers a good analogy. Despite the fact that many LTC facilities offer very modern living environments in terms of ergonomics, lighting, comfort and safety, the perception of the industry is still negative. The manner in which they are micro-managed and micro-regulated is sufficient testimony. Managed care needs breathing space, not constraints, but it also needs a clear direction. The adage, "If you've seen one managed care organization, you've seen one" perhaps mandates that this needs to be changed; we need sufficient continuity and consistency so expectations can be based on something predictable. Part of this challenge lies in the process of assuring continuity and consistency without destroying innovation, and that whatever is accomplished must conform to the MCO's mission, vision, and values. Managed care is not fixed; it is fluid and can effectively respond to change to meet the challenges of today and tomorrow.

There are initiatives on the near horizon that will help managed care meet these challenges, including standards from the Joint Commission, NCQA and other accreditation and healthcare trade association bodies. For example, the integration of leadership, rights, responsibilities and treatment standards endorsed by the Joint Commission will hopefully be able to stimulate new directions and start a revolution in management styles and priorities. Also, more attention will to be paid to confidentiality than in the past, not only because of the advent of new information and communication, but also to safeguard patient confidences amidst a frenzy of data collection. This will require that MCOs be on their guard to protect the interests and confidentiality of their members and patients. There may be circumstances in which privileged information is requested, or even demanded, by interested parties that should be protected. This applies to healthcare plans, employers and insurers. Imagine, for example, a large company that wants to reduce its healthcare expenditures by identifying the top 5 or 10 percent of its utilizers of pharmacy benefits. A less than ethically-minded business leader might want to identify who these big spenders are and find a way to get them out of the company to reduce his costs. Physicians need to advocate for their patients even though this may be at odds with other things they wish to accomplish in their partnering with businesses. Businesses (including both employers and plans) must clarify their mission and leadership values to be consistent with their fiduciary role to their employees or members. The manner in which we exercise tradeoffs and balances, including how we justify that process, is the pivot upon which this concern turns. As employers become more actively involved in healthcare and learning how to create or select a good healthcare plan, and as they learn what they want in a plan, the potential for improvement and better meeting needs is exciting. While many argue that employers' desires to spend less on healthcare benefits has caused the very problems with which we now contend, employers nonetheless constitute a special ingredient in the process of facing the challenges of change, particularly if they become more informed consumers and purchasers of healthcare.

Obviously, not all that managed care does poses ethical challenges. Managed care has already stimulated dramatic change in the delivery of non-hospital services that can be delivered off site, often in the home. This is made clear by the explosion of subacute care and rethinking of continuity of care. Managed care has been creative in the area of manpower shifting, that is, that is using personnel in more cost-effective ways. When personnel who are less costly than the physician can meet a patient's needs effectively, then why not enlist their services and expertise, so long as care is not compromised? The use of different care providers is occurring much more in some fields than others. The ethical issues arise when less costly personnel work without sufficient expertise or supervision.

One of the advantages of personnel such as PAs and nurse practitioners is they can meet unmet need in rural and other medically underserved areas by providing not only primary care but also some kinds of specialty care as well. This is particularly the case for those PAs who have specialized training in surgery orthopedics and other surgical and medical specialties.

While there has been extensive discussion of the importance of performance measurement, we can anticipate a range of ethical questions to arise mostly related to the validity of the measurement instruments and the implications of reliance on data that we are not quite sure of at this early stage of development. Performance measurement, the evaluation of outcomes, and new benchmarking techniques allow us to take positive steps to reduce error and promote safety by improving systems and learning from industrial and engineering models such as those being examined by the Patient Safety Foundation at the AMA which was created in 1997. Other initiatives, such as the Harvard-Pilgrim Health Plan Project in Boston and the Case Management of America's outcomes assessment interests yield excellent models of integrating managed care and ethics.

The measurement of outcomes and effectiveness is calling a wide range of techniques and practices into question. One we can expect to hear about in the near future deals with formulary issues. We can expect increased discussion of restrictive formularies and will need to entertain such basic questions as whether formularies are indeed effective. Pharmacists have concerns about having reliable vendors to get them what they need when they need it. We will need to reexamine some of the fundamental assumptions associated with cost savings in managed care. A recent article referred to the fact that bed utilization in the cradle of managed care is five times that in California.[1] Heavy saturation of managed care in this market has created low competition. The low retention rates in HMOs also requires greater scrutiny to determine underlying causes.

Other ethical issues, which involve confidentiality and correcting errors that have been replicated to multiple parties electronically, are accompanied by other concerns that emanate from the risk management field. Benchmarking and defining audit trails are having a profound impact in hospitals and LTC and will soon expand across the rest of the continuum. However, increasing consumer knowledge of areas that in the past would likely not have been well-known raise some profound and interesting questions. If health care professionals once wondered "What if they really knew what went on here?" they should prepare for the fact that the public may soon be able to obtain previously inaccessible information. Some argue that benchmarking and performance reporting will initially increase liability perils at those facilities with high cost and high complication rates, because the public will be able know what in the past they never had access to. This is causing some uneasiness in the risk management community. However, benchmarking and quality improvement can and should help reduce long-term risk, particularly as we develop more sophisticated tools and techniques to accomplish this.

Better and more rapidly accessible information and new ingredients for making more informed decisions are things we can anticipate in the very near future. This should be an invitation to identify areas for im-

---

[1] Greene, Jan: *The Minneapolis Myth: Cracks in the Cradle of Managed Care.* Hospitals and Health Networks. February 5, 1997, p. 60.

provement and collaboration in order to identify risk areas and ways to address those risks in more timely fashion than in the past. If we are really concerned about quality, this is a step we must take. The future trends show an integration of liability-related issues more closely linked to outcomes and clinical efficiency. Through the identification of specific risks and having mechanisms in space for rapid correction of problems, we can improve outcomes and reduce injury and death.

The future offers some exciting problems to be solved and addressed in creative ways. Outcomes, fitness, evidence based medicine, and proactive plans that provide benefits such as access to fitness centers at no cost as well as transportation to and from such centers are examples. Self-help programs that empower people by giving them information, education and direction will continue to have an increasing impact on healthcare in the future. Our greatest challenges are in the present and the way in which we deal with them can create a future we can look forward to.

Novel programs require flexibility and novel approaches to problem solving, not rigidity. While there are issues that have to be addressed and problems that have to be worked out, putting the patient at risk or disadvantage because of excess rigidity is not to be tolerated and is certainly not a sensible way to practice. Rigidity will never be accepted as a reasonable clinical pathway or practice guideline. The times call for us to work together and use our expertise to help get appropriate care to the patient rather than to delay or preclude it.

A major challenge of the future will be to cultivate the trust of patients and members in the same way that favorite companies or favorite name-brand products have been able to do in the past. A major step in this direction will be to create ways in which people feel that the managed care organization is on their side. This challenge can be addressed only by admitting that there is a need to do this and addressing that need.

Last, but by no means least, there is a need to create a model of a socially and ethically responsible MCO. This would serve as the next step of applying what we have learned to make a better healthcare plan. To encourage the reader to apply the concepts and issues examined in this text and try to integrate them into contextual framework, imagining what a socially and ethically responsible MCO might look like, this exercise will build upon the wide range of issues and concepts that we have examined in earlier chapters.

Rather than focusing on deficiencies and assets, the advantage of a model is that it offers a picture of how something should or should not look. The reader or critic can then more easily evaluate what fits and what doesn't, and try to evaluate and balance the components against one another and rearrange, refocus and refine the picture. By offering a concrete model, one can criticize a certain facet and challenge or modify it to improve it, or offer something better, and in so doing have a basis that can serve as a positive guide for evaluation and improvement.

Supplied with a concrete model, the reader can agree or disagree with certain elements of the model and assess the interplay of the various components. For example, the reader might say, "I like the way that is described but I think the way it relates to other components of the model might be improved in the following way." On the other hand, the reader might be able to examine individual concepts in a broader context and better appreciate the interplay of various components displayed in the model.

One of the most revealing insights gained by examining ethical issues in managed healthcare settings is that ethical questions are generated less by specific concepts and processes than by the manner in which concepts are put into practice. Yet some concepts are more fundamental to the ethical integrity of an organization or healthcare plan and create the basic architecture that shapes or creates the context for how and where individual components are placed. These create the very foundation of the ethically and socially responsible healthcare plan or MCO, or for that matter any healthcare plan. For example, such notions as trust, integrity, and accountability are more fundamental concerns that will often create a context in which individual practices such gatekeeping or deselecting is performed in an ethical manner.

Trust is one of the most fundamental of these architectural ethical ingredients. One of the distinctive elements of healthcare is that patients often must trust other people in situations in which they may be in jeopardy of life and limb. Images of trust and protection are often juxtaposed against a charicterized managed care in which care must be negotiated and advocates brought to bear to ensure that the right thing is done at the right time for the right reason. A socially and ethically responsible healthcare plan would offer fair and equitable access efficiently, in a clinically justifiable manner.

The notion of trust is often expressed as a fiduciary relationship. It is characterized as one which demands that, within the context of a relationship, all parties involved can rely on one another to act on appropriate motivations rather than considerations external to or discordant with that trust. The *Shea v. Medica* case clearly demonstrates the consequences of eroded trust. Loyalty and trust require interdependence. One must be able to rely on a healthcare plan, their physician, or from the other side, even the patient, to do the right thing for the right reason. People need to rely on other institutions to do what they expect of them, and that means, at the very least, not compromising their well being or lives.

Trust manifests itself in relationships among partners as well. In a discussion of negative partnering we've seen how gaming and putting the other at a disadvantage create less optimal environments in which to share and grow together than those based on demonstrated and perceived mutual trust. Trust is necessary for a healthy and successful relationship. In fact, trust is the foundation upon which relationships are built.

Trust expresses itself in the relationship between the physician and a plan as well. For example, in the case of a physician appealing a reviewer's initial determination, if the reviewer at the plan perceives a given physician as always trying to get a little bit more than what he or she needs, the reviewer may become reluctant to believe the physician making the request for appeal. Similarly, if the physician anticipates that there will be resistance and that he or she will likely have to sacrifice days that he or she feels are necessary for the proper care of the patient, then the physician will request more than what is needed, anticipating that the initial request will be pared down by the plan's reviewer.

Trust, fairness, and working towards a common goal must be tempered by the realities of the internal gaming that so often occurs. Trust should not be compromised, and special pains should be taken to cultivate it. There should be a clear correspondence between what is promised by marketing and what is actually delivered. The healthcare goal should be to facilitate medically necessary care and promote health, as well as to reduce sickness rather than to unreasonably deny care in the hope that patients will become discouraged and give up. Trust is often tied to or at the very least buttressed by accountability. The shared accountability component should minimize gaming. Trust and accountability must be the firm foundation upon which a health plan is built.

Shared accountability traverses a broad area of the healthcare experience. Accountability is generally identified with honesty, loyalty and fairness. Accountability suggests being responsible for the consequences of one's actions. Examples can be found in the context of confidentiality, in partnering arrangements, or even in terms of meeting patients needs. Accountability is a more general term than access, gatekeeping, or denial of care. Accountability is a primary notion, setting the stage for how something should be done. Accountability regulates gatekeeping, denial, and other less basic categories. Accountability sets the stage for leadership, mission, vision, and the specific values of a healthcare plan or delivery system. Broader values such as trust, fairness and the like shape accountability, but accountability has an important place in shaping the values of a specific organization.

Accountability contains some interesting dynamics in terms of its derivation. One might argue that it should be internally motivated, derived from the nature and mission of the organization. Externally motivated or imposed accountability doesn't have the strength of accountability generated by the organization itself through the commitment of its leadership. Accountability and trust blended with talent, sufficiently well trained personnel, and an efficient and caring organization, constitute the context for a socially responsible healthcare plan or MCO.

Next, the specifics must be addressed, the bricks and mortar as it were, to be laid on the structure of trust and accountability that a socially responsible healthcare plan requires for its foundation. One of the first constants that most encounter in managed healthcare is access to their physician. A socially responsible healthcare plan should have in place some way to creates a feeling that needs will be met. This does not mean direct access to the physician at all times, but does mean access to someone in a timely fashion who can answer their questions and determine what the next step should be.

Perhaps one of the most interesting ways to discuss the development of a socially and ethically responsible healthcare plan would involve looking at those components that the public have found to be particularly troublesome. Negative perceptions may result from media perceptions, personal experience, or anticipation. Perhaps the most pronounced concern involves gatekeeping from the perspective of primary physician in terms of providing access to specialty services or getting access to the primary physician in the first place. We've seen an array of legal concerns and legal cases, and this will only continue.

It is the duty of the socially responsible MCO to provide reasonable access based on medical necessity or medical appropriateness. In a model MCO, access and availability should conform to standards of medical necessity and fairness and not be arbitrarily applied. In other words, we must be honest about how we assess what constitutes medical appropriateness. In fairness, part of the difficulty of this domain has to do with uncertainty about what and when something is medically necessary or medically appropriate. The inherent uncertainty of medicine plays a role in this. However, in ambiguous situations, the model has been to do at the very least what needs to be a done to take the patient out of danger. I think that until we have better assessment skills and outcomes data we should use the same model, which affords patient safety and protection, that we have used in the past.

Access to the primary and specialty physicians is another element that we want to examine in our socially and ethically responsible MCO. We've seen legal cases in the chapter on legal foundations and advocacy dealing with problems that arise when appropriate access to the physician is denied. In order to achieve appropriate access, is it critical that we create medical management policies and procedures to regulate what we do in the case of appeals denial, second opinions, resulting controversies, and other important facets that interface between patients, plans, and healthcare providers.

Acting on the basis of what one perceives to be ethically appropriate should always be a guide, whether it is aimed at identifying best practices and best products, or informing the patient of reasonable and probable risks, outcomes, and procedures, even when those procedures are not covered in a specific health plan. The gag rules of the past, as well as the newly enunciated idea that the plans themselves owe loyalty to their members, economic profiling, and the like need to be dealt with more carefully and honestly.

While there's nothing intrinsically negative or positive about one reimbursement system or another (except perhaps capitation, where the doctor assumes risk and must serve simultaneously as insuror, gatekeeper, and caregiver), it may very well be the case that certain types of systems may encourage abuse more than others. Managed care should not be seen as the culprit and fee-for-service is the maligned party. The advent of managed care has, however, brought attention to ethical concerns in the healthcare industry.

Another key component or ingredient to be included in our examination of a model managed-care organization is membership. There has been significant criticism associated with cherry-picking, a question involving membership which fairly represents the geographic distribution of a given market, and one which accounts for adverse selection. A model healthcare plan should provide access in equitable and fair manner, rather than sifting the population to gain unfair or inequitable advantage. This in no way suggests that creative techniques to attract healthier participants, such as adding free health club memberships for participants, should be discouraged, so long as others are not precluded or discouraged from enrollment. On the other hand, having an enrollment office up three flights of stairs with no elevator access hardly constitutes a reasonable attempt to capture a broad population. A related problem involves meeting needs of special populations. Those perceived to be at greatest disadvantage are the most disabled and those who suffer from chronic mental or behavioral health problems.

A subset of this concern involves the range and scope of services provided, which has become important bone of contention among insureds. Many legitimate denials of coverage are overridden by courts because of the invisibility of the master contract, even if provisions were clearly applied. Being informed helps the patient as well as the plan. This facet needs to be handled more effectively. Similarly, in cases of repetitive denials, in which a pattern of denials is found to be unreasonably excessive, some mechanism for identifying appropriate parties and care service providers, or innovations for locating the appropriate benefit manager at the given employer, are necessary. Plans that are unresponsive to or impede patient needs should be identified and replaced by ones that are consistent with what the employer expected to receive.

Patient confidence and satisfaction are critical issues that model MCOs should address. This should not pivot on "report cards." Report cards have not been sufficient to provide employers with this type of information. There is often a great disparity between what a report card shows as patient satisfaction and real satisfaction with various elements of a specific plan. A formal process by which timely and effective ways to evaluate and respond to appeals, as well as a fair and equitable way of evaluating and adjudicating appeals that is visible and accessible for any member or caregiver who would choose to avail themselves of this process should be the rule rather than the exception.

Specific prevailing guidelines ought to be in place to insure the manner and spirit in which a healthcare organization should operate. A pivotal element in this domain is leadership, including how leadership translates its vision to its people working in the trenches. There is nothing intrinsically good or bad about the nature of a given institution or enterprise, be it public, private, large, small, urban, rural, academic and so forth. Being proprietary or non-proprietary, for example, does not make an organization ethical or unethical; that is determined by the mission, vision and values of its leadership and its staff. This is no way suggests that underfunded or understaffed organizations are acceptable even if intentions are good. Ethical care is the combination of the provision of appropriate services and the spirit of all those are provided in the motivating principal or omission and goals of that process.

Policies and procedures that result in ethical care and deal with controversy and conflict resolution are an extension of this concern. One way to have a voice of reason and consistency among the medical staff with regard to how they interact among themselves and how appeals, second opinions, and the like are handled is by developing carefully-designed medical management policies and procedures. Medical management policies and procedures can be clear and consistent voice of the clinical standards and medical mission of a given organization. Rather than relying on ambiguity and excessive uncertainty to determine what should be done in isolated cases or in the case of a controversy, medical management policies and procedures define the manner in which the clinical integrity of the medical panels in the organization are consistently assured. As already discussed in conflict resolution sections, medical management policies can address a wide range of issues that arise between the plan and the physician, the physician and the patient, between primary care physicians and specialty physicians involving any relationship, controversy or concern that develops between the medical staff and other parties.

An element that is often added to the medical management policies and procedures is a mechanism for best practices or best products to be adopted and integrated into care plans, as they become available. If, for example, a better, safer, more efficient way of performing a specific procedure or of providing treatment than what was provided for in the original contract some mechanisms or provision to allow that procedure to be integrated and applied immediately should be afforded. This often involves no more than the insertion or inclusion of a clause inserted into medical management policies and procedures involving best practices and best products.

A formal process is needed that provides timely and effective ways to address, evaluate, and respond to appeals, as well as a fair and equitable way of evaluating and adjudicating appeals that is visible and accessible for any member or caregiver who would choose to avail themselves of this process. Formal mechanisms for the resolution of conflict are critical in the process of socially responsible healthcare plan and exemplify concrete instantiations of the organization's commitment to create upfront, in-advance, agreed-upon, fair and equitable ways of resolving a wide range of conflicts. This also involves the creation of mechanisms by which the patient can know what avenues to pursue as well as where to go and who to contact within the organization to appeal a denial. This is an important facet of a socially and ethically responsible healthcare plan. Formal mechanisms such as ethics committee, quality assurance, the medical director, or other for a resolving conflict should be easily accessible and identifiable. Conflict resolution and advocacy often go hand in hand. The plan should create ways to resolve conflict and dictate clear processes in which such actions can occur in a timely and effective manner.

Informed consent has taken quite a beating in managed care throughout its recent history. Trust and accountability regarding consent seems to have initially taken a back seat in some MCO contexts, which has fortunately improved over time and with the help of some powerful initiatives on the part of the AMA. One of its major assaults was the gag rule which fortunately is the most part entirely absent in most managed-care plans and certainly ethical plans have no place for such a rule. Informing the patient about financial incentives of physician may have any given plan that might influence his judgment had been another problem that still needs to be corrected. Informing the patient of what material considerations that affect his specific health and welfare and what options and alternatives should be considered whether or not they are covered by a specific plan remains a continuing obligation which plans and physicians owe to their patients and others whom they serve. The failure to inform patients about economic experimentation when the plan wants to "try out" something new to see whether it works puts the patient at the same risk as clinical experimentation without any of the safeguards, protections, or guidelines that clinical experimentation requires.

Personnel issues are a major consideration in assuring the quality of any healthcare organization. Certainly credentialing issues and standards must be consistent with what has been determined to constitute acceptable criteria for licensed individual practitioners or non-licensed caregivers. Provisions within medical management policies and procedures involving practitioners whose practices are considered to be substandard or suspect must be addressed within the context of the aforementioned medical management policies and procedures. The spirit with which they deal with members will spill over into the way in which business is done as well as the care provided to the patient. If members are treated as persons and not adversaries, many of these problems will evaporate. A socially and ethically responsible MCO is designed not to create adversaries.

Examining what a socially and ethically responsible healthcare plan might look like is a proactive step in this direction, rather than fault finding exercise, assigning blame to one side or the other. Yet there is a great deal of uneasiness about care needs being met, care being delayed, and increased vulnerability, particularly in the areas of caring for the disabled and in behavioral healthcare. Dramatic challenges are now the rule rather than the exception.

The primary challenge we face is to transform change into a promising tomorrow. Our goals are positive; they are utopian rather than dystopian. A dystopian approach is to focus on the bad to show how bad it can become. Instead, we want to identify ingredients, principles and models of what we want to see and what we want to be. It is important that we become active agents in the process of change and create a better world and more dependable and effective healthcare system rather than become passive victims who must inherit an unwanted future. The challenge is to be more rather than less, to exceed rather than fall short of our expectations. It is hoped that this book is a positive step in that direction.

Dennis Robbins

TOPICAL BIBLIOGRAPHY

This topical bibliography is intended as a user-friendly resource of readily available materials to assist the reader/researcher/student. It is arranged by subject categories with the major focus on Ethical and Legal Issues in Managed Care.

ADVANCE DIRECTIVES AND LIVING WILLS

Adams JG, Derse AR, Gotthold WE, Mitchell JM, Moskop JC, Sanders AB. Ethical aspects of resuscitation. Ann Emerg Med. 1992; 21:1273-1276.

Ahronheim J, Weber D. Final Passages: Positive Choices for the Dying and Their Loved Ones. New York, NY: Simon & Schuster, Inc; 1992.

Bliss MR. Resources, the family and voluntary euthanasia. Br J Gen Pract. 1990; 40(332):117-122.

Cassel CK, Hays JR, Lynn J. Alzheimer's: decisions in terminal care. Patient Care. 1991; 25(18):125-137.

Coll PP, Anderson D. Advanced directives for homebound patients. J Am Board Fam Pract. 1992; 5:359-360. Letter; comment.

Dorff EN. "A time to be born and a time to die": a Jewish medical directive for health care. United Synagogue Review. 1992; 45:20-22.

Ethical considerations in resuscitation. JAMA. 1992; 16:2282-2288.

Ethical issues of resuscitation. American College of Emergency Physicians. Ann Emerg Med. 1992; 21:1277.

Fried TR, Gillick MR. Medical decision-making in the last six months of life: choices about limitation of care. J Am Geriatr Soc. 1994; 42:303-307.

Gillick MR. Choosing Medical Care in Old Age: What Kind, How Much, When To Stop. Cambridge, Mass: Harvard University Press; 1994.

Guidelines for cardiopulmonary resuscitation and emergency cardiac care. Emergency Cardiac Care Committee and Subcommittees, American Heart Association. Part VIII. Ethical considerations in resuscitation. JAMA. 1992; 16:2282-2288. Comments.

High DM. Surrogate decision making. Who will make decisions for me when I can't? Clin Geriatr Med. 1994; 10:445-462. Review.

Iserson KV. Foregoing prehospital care: should ambulance staff always resuscitate? J Med Ethics. 1991; 17:19-24.

Iserson KV, Rouse F. Prehospital DNR orders. Hastings Cent Rep. 1989; 19:17-19. Case study and commentaries.

Compiled by Lora A. Robbins, MS, LS, HSA, Loyola University Medical Center Library, Maywood, Illinois.

Jecker NS, Schneiderman LJ. Medical futility: the duty not to treat. Camb Q Healthcare Ethics. 1993; 2:151-159.

Kapp MB. Legal and ethical issues in family caregiving and the role of public policy. Home Health Care Serv Q. 1991; 12:5-28.

Kapp MB. Geriatrics and the Law: Patient Rights and Professional Responsibilities. 2nd ed. New York, NY: Springer Publishing Co, Inc; 1992.

Kellogg FR, Crain M, Corwin J, Brickner PW. Life-sustaining interventions in frail elderly persons. Talking about choices. Arch Intern Med. 1992; 152:2317-2320.

Key ethical issues in palliative care: evidence to House of Lords Select Committee on Medical Ethics. 1993. The Council, London, England.

Krynski MD, Tymchuk AJ, Ouslander JG. How informed can consent be? New light on comprehension among elderly people making decisions about enteral tube feeding. Gerontologist. 1994; 34:36-43.

Loewy EH. Advance directives and surrogate laws. Ethical instruments or moral cop-out? Arch Intern Med. 1992; 152:1973-1976.

Loewy EH. Limiting but not abandoning treatment in severely mentally impaired patients: a troubling issue for ethics consultants and ethics committees. Camb Q Healthcare Ethics. 1994; 3:216-225.

Lynn J. Ethical issues in caring for elderly residents of nursing homes. Prim Care. 1986; 13:295-306.

Mahoney J, Singer PA, Lowy FH, Hilberman M, Mitchell A, Stroud CE, et al. Cost savings at the end of life. N Engl J Med. 1994; 331:477-478. Letters and response.

Markson LJ, Fanale J, Steel K, Kern D, Annas G. Implementing advance directives in the primary care setting. Arch Intern Med. 1994; 154:2321-2327. Comments.

Meier DE, Cassel CK. Nursing home placement and the demented patient: a case presentation and ethical analysis. Ann Intern Med. 1986; 1:98-105.

Miles SH. Advanced directives to limit treatment: the need for portability. J Am Geriatr Soc. 1987; 1:74-76. Editorial.

Murphy DJ. Improving advance directives for healthy older people. J Am Geriatr Soc. 1990; 38:1251-1256.

Olson E, Chichin E, Meyers H, Schulman E, Brennan F. Early experiences of an ethics consult team. J Am Geriatr Soc. 1994; 42:437-441. Comments.

Osman H, Perlin TM. Patient self-determination and the artificial prolongation of life. Health Soc Work. 1994; 19:245-52.

Outerbridge DE, Hersh AR. Easing the Passage: A Guide for Prearranging and Ensuring a Pain-Free and Tranquil Death via a Living Will, Personal Medical Mandate, and Other Medical, Legal, and Ethical Resources. New York, NY: HarperCollins; 1991.

Reisner A. Instructions for the Valley of the Shadow: a medical directive (living will). United Synagogue Review. 1992; 44:22-23.

Robbins DA. Edge of life. Advance directive protocols and the Patient Self Determination Act. Kentucky Hospitals Magazine. 1992; 9:26-27.

Scitovsky A, Capron AM. Medical care at the end of life: the interaction of economics and ethics. In: Breslow L, Fielding JE, Lave LB, eds. Annual Review of Public Health. Palo Alto, CA: Annual Reviews; 1994:75.

Thomasma DC. Models of the doctor-patient relationship and the ethics committee: part two. Camb Q Healthcare Ethics. 1994; 3:10-26.

Turner JF, Mason T, Anderson D, Gulati A, Sbarbaro JA. Physicians' ethical responsibilities under co-pay insurance: should potential fiscal liability become part of informed consent? J Clin Ethics. 1995; 6:68-72.

Wanzer SH. The physician's responsibility toward hopelessly ill patients: a second look. N Engl J Med. 1989; 320:844-849.

Waymack MH, Taler GA. Medical Ethics and the Elderly: A Case Book. Chicago, Ill: Pluribus Press, Inc; 1988.

Wicclair MR. Ethics and the Elderly. New York, NY: Oxford University Press; 1993.

ADVOCACY

Aroskar MA. Nursing ethics in a health reform environment: values at stake. Alumni Mag Columbia Univ Presbyt Hosp Sch Nurs Alumni Assoc 1994; 88:6-7.

Boyd CR. On timeless principles in changing times. J Trauma 1995; 39:815-817.

Bristow LR. 'David versus Goliath' merits help from government. Internist 1994; 35:9-11.

Brock DW, Daniels N. Ethical foundations of the Clinton administration's proposed health care system [see comments]. JAMA 1994; 271:1189-1196.

Brunton SA. Gag clauses in managed care. Hosp Pract (Off Ed) 1996; 31:118-119.

Carlisle D. Who will advocate for patients? [interview by Amber Stenger]. Postgrad Med 1993; 94:108-110.

Cohen ES. The elderly mystique: impediment to advocacy and empowerment. Generations 1990; 14:13-16.

Curtin L. It's not enough to be right. Fla Nurse 1995; 43:10-11.

Dallari SG, Barber-Madden R. Health advocacy post graduate education in Brazil: a response to new constitutional rights. Educ Med Salud 1993; 27:314-325.

DeHaven KE. There are things that we can do. J Bone Joint Surg Am 1996; 78:799-802.

DeJong G. The John Stanley Coulter Lecture. Health care reform and disability: affirming our commitment to community. Arch Phys Med Rehabil 1993; 74:1017-1024.

Dombi W. Chronic intensive home care: accessing non-governmental payment sources. Caring 1992; 11:58-63.

Dubler NN. Improving the discharge planning process: distinguishing between coercion and choice. Gerontologist. 1988; 3(suppl):76-81.

Fade A, Kaplan K. Managed care and end of life decisions. Health Care Law Ethics 1995; 10:97-100.

Fleck LM. Just caring: Oregon, health care rationing, and informed democratic deliberation. J Med Philos 1994; 19:367-388.

Gartner MB, Twardon CA. Care guidelines: journey through the managed care maze. J Wound Ostomy Continence Nurs 1995; 22:118-121.

Gordon S, Fagin CM. Preserving the moral high ground. Am J Nurs 1996; 96:31-32.

Hadley J. Nurse advocacy, ethics, and health care reform. J Post Anesth Nurs 1994; 9: 55-56.

Harer WB, Jr. How I spur payers to reverse bad decisions. Manag Care 1994; 3:32-33.

Hillman AL, Greer WR, Goldfarb N. Safeguarding quality in managed competition. Health Aff (Millwood) 1993; 12:Suppl:110-22.

Iezzoni LI, Greenberg LG. Widespread assessment of risk-adjusted outcomes: lessons from local initiatives. Jt Comm J Qual Improv 1994; 20:305-316.

Iglehart JK. Who spoke for the people? [editorial]. Health Aff (Millwood) 1994; 13:5-6.

Inlander CB. A vote for the single-payer system. Nurs Econ 1994; 12:104-105.

Jaklevic MC. Walking seniors through first HMO takes a personal touch. Mod Healthc 1995; 25:152.

Karpatkin RH, Shearer GE. A short-term consumer agenda for health care reform. Am J Public Health 1995; 85:1352-5.

Kelley D. Is medical care a right? The right answers. J Med Assoc Ga 1993; 82:581.

Kimaid Y, Votava KM, Myers E. Patient advocacy: one agency's positive results with the administrative law judge process. Home Healthcare Nurse 1994; 12:29-32.

Kinney ED. Malpractice reform in the 1990s: past disappointments, future success? J Health Polit Policy Law 1995; 20:99-135.

La Puma J. When it's hard to be sure of the patient's own goals. Manag Care 1994; 3:44-45.

Maguire DC, McFadden EA. Is medical care a right? The left answers. J Med Assoc Ga 1993; 82:580.

McMath SS. Insurance denial for head and spinal cord injuries: stacked deck requires health care reform. Healthspan 1993; 10:7-11.

Miles S. HealthCare Ethics Forum '94: health-care reform and clinical ethics: old values for new times. AACN Clin Issues 1994; 5:299-307.

Ortolon K. Squeeze play. Patient and physician rights could be pushed aside as state pursues Medicaid managed care. Tex Med 1995; 91:12-15.

Paris JJ, Statter M, Hebbar S, Spanknebel K, Arensman R. The "medical loss ratio": the determination of medical standards by the marketplace. J Perinatol 1995; 15: 407-411.

Paustian FF. The "any willing provider" provision and health system reform in Nebraska. Nebr Med J 1994; 79:385-386.

Quinn JB. Taking back their health care. Newsweek 1994; 123:36.

Rieger S. A profile of the Patient Protection Act. J Med Assoc Ga 1995; 84:47.

Riley PA, Fortinsky RH, Coburn AF. Developing consumer-centered quality assurance strategies for home care. A case management model. J Case Manag 1992; 1:39-48.

Rodrigue J. Patient protection rules a good first step [letter]. Tex Med 1995; 91:7.

Sabin JE. General hospital psychiatry and the ethics of managed care. Gen Hosp Psychiatry 1995; 17:293-298.

Schietinger H, Levi J. Consumer protections for people living with HIV within systems of managed care. J Acquir Immune Defic Syndr Hum Retrovirol 1995; 8:Suppl 1:S80-S84.

Sharp N. It's politics, not policy . . . people. Nurs Manage 1995; 26:18-19.

Shinn LJ. Consumers and nurses and health care reform. Gastroenterol Nurs 1994; 16:176-177.

Smith KT. Managed care safeguards sought by states. Nurs Econ 1995; 13:312-313.

Smith LJ. Poor information flow, consumer protection hurt Medicare HMO program. Bus Health 1985; 2:64.

Sofaer S. Informing and protecting consumers under managed competition. Health Aff (Millwood) 1993; 12:Suppl:76-86.

Springer A. Managed care as health care rationing. Health Pac Bull 1993; 23:26-29.

Sprung CL, Eidelman LA, Steinberg A. Is the physician's duty to the individual patient or to society? Crit Care Med 1995; 23:618-620. Editorial; comment.

Sulmasy DP. Managed care and managed death [see comments]. [Review]. Arch Intern Med 1995; 155:133-136.

Urschel HC, Jr. Put our patients first [editorial] [see comments]. Am J Cardiol 1994; 74:170-171.

Wachter MB. The Patient Protection Act: A-2928. N J Nurse 1995; 25:8.

Wenger NS, Halpern J. The physician's role in completing advance directives: ensuring patients' capacity to make healthcare decisions in advance. J Clin Ethics 1994; 5:320-323. Comments.

Wilson SA. Another view of Medicare HMOs: not always what the doctor ordered [interview by Meg Matheny]. Health Syst Lead 1995; 2:11-13.

Wolf SM. Health care reform and the future of physician ethics [see comments]. Hastings Cent Rep 1994; 24:28-41.

Yarmolinsky A. Supporting the patient. N Engl J Med 1995; 332:602-603.

CONFLICT

Bartels-Rabb L. Resolving conflicts between HMO systems and group practices. Contract Healthc 1988; 31-33.

Bartlett EE. Manage the difficult patient to reduce malpractice risk. Hmo Pract 1995; 9: 84-87.

Capilouto E, Morrisey MA. Health care reform: public views of problems and solutions. J Health Soc Policy 1994; 6:45-57.

Culliton BJ. Managed care & conflict of interest [editorial]. Nature Med 1996; 25:489.

Donaldson L. Conflict, power, negotiation. BMJ 1995; 310:104-107.

Gabin JH. Health care reformation and the need for tort reform. N J Med 1995; 92:329-332.

Glaser WA. Doctors and public authorities: the trend toward collaboration. J Health Polit Policy Law 1994; 19:705-727.

Grey JE. Conflict of interest. Part 2. Healthc Forum J 1990; 33:96-99.

Herschberg S. Potential conflicts of interest in the delivery of medical services: an analysis of the situation and a proposal. Qual Assur Util Rev 1992; 7:54-58.

Hewison A. Ethical health care management: is it possible? J Nurs Manag 1995; 3:3-9.

Hudson B. Community care. Breaks in the chain. Health Serv J 1994; 104:24-26.

Lewis AB. Psychiatric hospitalization and managed care in conflict. J Health Care Benefits 1993; 3:34-39.

Malone RE. Heavy users of emergency services: social construction of a policy problem. Soc Sci Med 1995; 40:469-477.

Mechanic D. Dilemmas in rationing health care services: the case for implicit rationing [see comments]. BMJ 1995; 310:1655-1659.

Mechanic D. Changing medical organization and the erosion of trust. Milbank Q 1996; 74:171-189.

Pellegrino ED. Allocation of resources at the bedside: the intersections of economics, law, and ethics [comment]. Kennedy Inst Ethics J 1994; 4:309-317.

Polich CL, Parker M, Fischer LR, Pastor W, Pitt L. The provision of home health care services through health maintenance organizations: conflicting roles for HMOs. Home Health Care Serv Q 1990; 11:47-61.

Rodwin MA. Conflicts in managed care. N Engl J Med 1995; 332:604-607.

Roemer R, Roemer MI, Frink JE, Kramer C. Planning Urban Health Services from Jungle to System. New York: Springer Pub.; 1975, p. 368.

Roth PA, Harrison JK. Ethical conflict in long-term care: is legislation the answer? J Prof Nurs 1994; 10:271-277.

State health reform and the role of 1115 waivers. Health Care Financ Rev 1995; 16: 139-149.

Swartz K, Brennan TA. Integrated health care, capitated payment, and quality: the role of regulation [see comments]. Ann Intern Med 1996; 124:442-448.

Tamborlane TA, Schaper T. Conflicts of interest in managed care. N J Med 1995; 92:523-525.

Wagner L. Can we make a new deal? Entitlement reform sounds alluring, but the reality is stark. Hosp Health Netw 1995; 69:24-28.

Wedding D, Topolski J, McGaha A. Maintaining the confidentiality of computerized mental health outcome data. J Ment Health Adm 1995; 22:237-244.

Wetle T. A taxonomy of ethical issues in case management of the frail older person. J Case Manag 1992; 1:71-75.

Woodhall AL. Integrated delivery systems: reforming the conflicts among federal referral, tax exemption, and antitrust laws. Health Matrix 1995; 5:181-248.

Zapka JG, Palmer RH, Hargraves JL, Nerenz D, Frazier HS, Warner CK. Relationships of patient satisfaction with experience of system performance and health status. J Ambulatory Care Manage 1995; 18:73-83.

COST AND ETHICS

Azevedo D. Are we asking too much of gatekeepers? Med Econ 1994; 71:126-128.

Caplan AL. Ethics of casting the first stone: personal responsibility, rationing, and transplants [editorial]. Alcohol Clin Exp Res 1994; 18:219-221.

Chalfin DB, Fein AM. Critical care medicine in managed competition and a managed care environment. [Review]. New Horiz 1994; 2:275-282.

Cloutier M. The evolution of managed care. Health Care Law Ethics 1995; 10:67-72.

Crane M. When doctors are caught between dueling clinical guidelines. Med Econ 1994; 71:30-32.

D'Oronzio JC. What is the good of health care system reform? N J Med 1994; 91: 451-455.

D'Oronzio JC. "Unexpected" death and other report cards on access and ethics. Camb Q Healthc Ethics 1995; 4:549-552.

Engelhard CL, Childress JF. Caveat emptor: the cost of managed care. Health Care Law Ethics 1995; 10:11-14.

Enthoven A. Alain Enthoven: father of managed competition [interview by Mike Pulley]. Integr Healthc Rep 1993; Dec: 8-12.

Garrison PJ. Care planning in integrated delivery systems: pitfalls for the unwary. Continuum 1995; 15:15-19.

Glaser RJ. Health care reform and academic medical centers [editorial]. Pharos 1994; 57:40.

Goldsmith JC, Goran MJ, Nackel JG. Managed care comes of age. Healthc Forum J 1995; 38:14-20.

Goodman JC. Health care crisis needs new approaches, not more dollars [interview by Debra Mamorsky]. J Health Care Benefits 1993; 3:15-20.

Holechek MJ. Ethical issues in drug pricing. ANNA J 1993; 20:601-603.

Jecker NS. Can an employer-based health insurance system be just? [see comments]. J Health Polit Policy Law 1993; 18:Pt 2:657-73.

Johnson JD. Some questions of ethics. Hmo Pract 1989; 3:65-67.

Kosterlitz J. Who's in charge? Natl J (Wash) 1993; 25:2414-2418.

La Puma J. Needed: clear standards for defining futile care. Manag Care 1995; 4:50-51.

Lamm RD. It is time to emerge from the trench and survey the whole battlefield. Camb Q Healthc Ethics 1994; 3:403-404.

Leri JE. The psychological, political, and economic realities of brain injury rehabilitation in the 1990s. Brain Inj 1995; 9:533-542.

Lister G. Paradise lost? J Hand Surg [Am] 1995; 20:892-901.

McArdle FB. How would business react to an employer mandate? Health Aff (Millwood) 1994; 13:69-83.

Moriarity J. Protecting patients & profits. Minn Med 1996; 79:6-8.

Morreim EH. Lifestyles of the risky and infamous. From managed care to managed lives. [Review]. Hastings Cent Rep 1995; 25:5-12.

Pomerantz JM. A managed care ethical credo: for clinicians only? [comment]. Psychiatr Serv 1995; 46:329-330.

Rodwin MA. Strains in the fiduciary metaphor: divided physician loyalties and obligations in a changing health care system. [Review]. Am J Law Med 1995; 21:241-257.

Smith AJ. Avoiding the ethical pitfalls of managed care [editorial]. Minn Med 1996; 79: 24-26.

Stein T. The ethics of managed care: profit vs. patient welfare. Calif Hosp 1995; 9:20.

Strong WB. Random and rambling thoughts on a lazy Sunday afternoon. An example of the chaos theory [editorial]. Arch Pediatr Adolesc Med 1994; 148:524.

Summers J. Substitutions and rebates: questionable material management practices in HMOs? [see comments]. J Healthc Mater Manage 1993; 11:54-55.

Summers J. Healthcare reform: beginning the ethical debate. J Healthc Mater Manage 1994; 12:52-56.

Thomasma DC. The ethics of managed care and cost control. Health Care Law Ethics 1995; 10:33-36.

Tidwell J. God, Profit, and the Newtonian laws of motion: a declaration of independence [editorial]. J Med Assoc Ga 1993; 82:477-478.

Tilford JM, Fiser DH. Futile care in the pediatric intensive care unit: ethical and economic considerations [editorial; comment]. J Pediatr 1996; 128:725-727.

Wallach SJ. Ethical issues—physicians and managed care. Hawaii Med J 1995; 54: 523-525.

Watson SD. Medicaid physician participation: patients, poverty, and physician self-interest. [Review]. Am J Law Med 1995; 21:191-220.

Weil TP, Hunt RS. Canadians write a new Rx for healthcare. Canada's healthcare system is not a panacea, but it raises interesting issues for the United States. Health Prog 1994; 75:32-38.

Wolf SM. The ethical challenge of managed care. A critique of the AMA's stance. Minn Med 1996; 79:29-32.

Wolford GR, Brown M, McCool BP. Getting to go in managed care. Hosp Mater Manage Q 1993; 15:50-68.

EMERGENCY MEDICAL SERVICES

Ethical considerations in resuscitation. JAMA. 1992; 16:2282-2288.

Iserson KV. Foregoing prehospital care: should ambulance staff always resuscitate? J Med Ethics. 1991; 17:19-24.

Iserson KV, Rouse F. Prehospital DNR orders. Hastings Cent Rep. 1989; 19:17-19. Case study and commentaries.

Koenig KL, Haynes B. Prehospital "do-not-resuscitate" orders—a new option. West J Med. 1993; 159:602-603.

Miles SH. Advanced directives to limit treatment: the need for portability. J Am Geriatr Soc. 1987; 1:74-76. Editorial.

Robbins DA. Legal and ethical dilemmas in emergency care. Emergency Medical Services. 1987; 16:19-21.

END-OF-LIFE DECISION MAKING

AMA Council on Ethical and Judicial Care Guidelines. JAMA. June 25, 1995.

Gelman D, Springen K. The doctor's suicide van. Newsweek. June 18, 1990; 46-49.

Guidelines on the Termination of Life-Sustaining Treatment and the Care of the Dying: A Report by the Hastings Center. Briarcliff Manor, N.Y.: Hastings Center; 1987.

Joint Report of the Council on Ethical and Judicial Affairs and the Council on Scientific Affairs: Persistent vegetative state and the decision to withdraw or withhold life support. Proceedings of the House of Delegates of the AMA. June 1989; 314-316.

Kass LR. Neither for love nor money: why doctors must not kill. Public Interest. 1969;94:25-46.

Office of Technology Assessment Task Force. Life-Sustaining Technologies and the Elderly. Philadelphia: Science Information Resource Center; 1988.

President's Commission for the Study of Ethical Problems in Medicine and Biomedical and Behavioral Research. Deciding to Forego Life-Sustaining Treatment: A Report on the Ethical, Medical and Legal Issues in Treatment Decisions. Washington, D.C.: Government Printing Office, 1987.

Quill TE. Death and dignity: a case of individualized decision making. N Engl J Med. 1991; 324:691-694.

Report D of the Council on Ethical and Judicial Affairs: Guidelines for the appropriate use of do-not-resuscitate orders. Proceedings of the House of Delegates of the AMA. December 1990; 180-185.

Sprung CL. Changing attitudes and practices in foregoing life-sustaining treatment. JAMA. 1990; 263:2211-2215.

ETHICS COMMITTEES

Abel E. Ethics committees in home health agencies. Public Health Nurs. 1990; 7:256-259.

Edinger W. Expanding opportunities for ethics committees: residential centers for the mentally retarded and developmentally disabled. Camb Q Healthcare Ethics. 1994; 3:226-232.

Ethical considerations in resuscitation. JAMA. 1992; 16:2282-2288.

Howe EG. Attributing preferences and violating neutrality. J Clin Ethics. 1992; 3:171-175. Comment.

Hudson T. Are futile-care policies the answer? Providers struggle with decisions for patients near the end of life. Hosp Health Network. 1994; 68:26-30.

Jecker NS, Schneiderman LJ. Medical futility: the duty not to treat. Camb Q Healthcare Ethics. 1993; 2:151-159.

Kanoti GA. Writing a proposal for determining patient decisional capacity. HEC [Hospital Ethics Committee] Forum. 1994; 6:12-17.

Kapp MB. Geriatrics and the Law: Patient Rights and Professional Responsibilities. 2nd ed. New York, NY: Springer Publishing Co, Inc; 1992.

Keffer MJ, Keffer HL. U.S. ethics committee: perceived versus actual roles. HEC Forum. 1991; 3:227-230.

Milholland DK. Privacy and confidentiality of patient information. Challenges for nursing. J Nurs Adm. 1994; 24:19-24.

Price DM. Forgoing treatment in an adult with no apparent treatment preference: a case report. Theor Med. 1994; 15:53-60.

Robbins, DA. "The Community Based Ethics Committee" in Ethical and Legal Issues in Home Care and Long Term Care. Gaithersburg, Md: Aspen Publishers, 1996.

Ross JW, Glaser JW, Rasinski-Gregory D, Gibson JM, Bayley C. Health Care Ethics Committees: The Next Generation. Chicago, Ill: American Hospital Publishing, Inc; 1993.

Rubin S, Zoloth-Dorfman L. First-person plural: community and method in ethics consultation. J Clin Ethics. 1994; 5:49-54. Editorial; comment.

Schwartz RL. Autonomy, futility, and the limits of medicine. Camb Q Healthcare Ethics. 1992; 1:159-164.

Snyder JW, Swartz MS. Deciding to terminate treatment: a practical guide for physicians. J Crit Care. 1993; 8:177-185.

Teel KW. From Quinlan to today. Camb Q Healthcare Ethics. 1992; 1:291-294.

GATEKEEPING

Azevedo D. Are we asking too much of gatekeepers? Med Econ 1994; 71:126-128.

Bahn CH. The surgeon as gatekeeper. Am J Surg 1993; 165:550-553.

Craig P. Health maintenance organization gatekeeping policies: potential liability for deterring access to emergency medical services. J Health Hosp Law 1990; 23:135-146.

Dubler NN. Individual advocacy as a governing principle. J Case Manag 1992; 1:82-86.

Felch WC. Gatekeeper: guard or guardian? An idea whose time has come? Internist 1981; 22:11-12.

Gadomski AM, Perkis V, Horton L, Cross S, Stanton B. Diverting managed care Medicaid patients from pediatric emergency department use. Pediatrics 1995; 95:170-178.

Herd B, Herd A, Mathers N. The wizard and the gatekeeper: of castles and contracts. BMJ 1995; 310:1042-1044.

Kane RA. Case management in long-term care: it can be ethical and efficacious. J Case Manag 1992; 1:76-81.

Kenkel PJ. HMOs say gatekeeper system cuts costs, boosts quality [news]. Mod Healthc 1988; 18:6.

Kranther MA. The gatekeeper in managed care. J Healthc Risk Manag 1994; 14:8-10.

Leisure LB. Managed care? Not without gatekeepers and capitation [interview]. Health Cost Manage 1988; 5:1-7.

Levinson DF. What HMOs should tell their subscribers, and what you can do about it. Consultant 1989; 29:118-120.

Menken M, Behar R, Lee P. Neurology referral patterns. Hmo Pract 1990; 4:57-60.

Nelson AR. Gatekeeper: guide or guard? Internist 1994; 35:25.

Politser P. The gatekeeper concept. Bull Am Coll Surg 1986; 71:17-20.

Pollner F. Benefits of gatekeepers unproven [news]. Med World News 1988; 29:84.

Randall VR. Impact of managed care organizations on ethnic Americans and underserved populations. J Health Care Poor Underserved 1994; 5:224-236.

Reich JS. Gatekeeping [letter]. N Engl J Med 1992; 327:1533.

Sawyer RB. General surgeons in the world of gatekeepers. Am J Surg 1995; 170:528-531.

White M, Gundrum G, Shearer S, Simmons WJ. A role for case managers in the physician office. J Case Manag 1994; 3:62-68.

GENERAL

AMA Council on Ethical and Judicial Affairs. Ethical issues in managed care. JAMA. 1995;273(4):330-335.

Annas GJ. Do feeding tubes have more rights than patients? Hastings Cent Rep. 1986; Feb.16(1):26-28.

Mill JS. Utilitarianism. Indianapolis, Ind: Hackett Publishing Co, Inc; 1979.

Rando TA. Grief, Dying and Death: Clinical Interventions for Caregivers. Champaign, Ill: Research Press; 1984.

Reiser S, Dyck A, Curran W. Ethics in Medicine: Historical Perspectives and Contemporary Concerns. Cambridge, Mass: MIT Press; 1977.

Robbins DA. Cost containment and terminal care: an essay into the ethics of appropriateness. Long Term Care Adm. 1981;9:41-47.

Robbins DA. Ethical Dimensions of Clinical Medicine. Springfield, Ill: Charles C Thomas, Publisher; 1981.

Robbins DA. Legal and Ethical Issues in Cancer Care in the United States. Springfield, Ill: Charles C Thomas, Publisher; 1983.

Robbins DA. Update: The removal of life supports in long-term care facilities. J Long Term Care Adm. 1985;13:3-5.

Robbins DA. Legal and ethical dilemmas in emergency care. Emergency Medical Services. 1987;16:19-21.

Robbins DA. Edge of life. Advance directive protocols and the Patient Self Determination Act. Kentucky Hospitals Magazine. 1992;9:26-27.

HEALTH CARE POLICY AND REFORM

Annas G. Will the real bioethics (commission) please stand up? Hastings Cent Rep. 1994; 24:19-21.

Blanchette PL. Age-based rationing of health care. Hawaii Med J. 1995; 54:507-509.

Blumenfield S, Lowe JI. A template for analyzing ethical dilemmas in discharge planning. Health Soc Work. 1987; 12:47-56.

Bovbjerg R, Held PJ, Diamond LH. Provider-patient relations and treatment choice in the era of fiscal incentives: the case of the End-Stage Renal Disease Program. Milbank Q. 1987; 2:177-202.

Chadwick R, Russell J. Hospital discharge of frail elderly people: social and ethical considerations in the discharge decision-making process. Aging & Society. 1989; 9:277-295.

Collette J, Windt PY, Jahnigen DW. Medical decision-making, dying, and quality of life among the elderly. In: Smeeding, TM, et al., eds. Should medical care be rationed by age? Totowa, NJ. Rowman and Littlefield; 1987:99-118.

Cummings NB. Social, ethical, and legal issues involved in chronic maintenance dialysis. In: Maher JF, ed. Replacement of Renal Function by Dialysis. 3rd ed. Boston: Kluwer Acad; 1989:1141-1158.

Dubler N. Individual advocacy as a governing principle. J Case Manage. 1992; 1:82-86.

Estes CL. Cost containment and the elderly: conflict or challenge? J Am Geriatr Soc. 1988;1:65-72.

Ethical considerations in resuscitation. JAMA. 1992;16:2282-2288.

Forrow L, Daniels N, Sabin JE. When is home care medically necessary? Hastings Cent Rep. 1991;21(4):36-38.

Gillick MR. Choosing Medical Care in Old Age: What Kind, How Much, When to Stop. Cambridge, Mass: Harvard University Press; 1994.

Jennings B, Callahan D, Caplan AL. Ethical challenges of chronic illness. Hastings Cent Rep. 1988;18(1)(suppl):S1-S16.

Johnson JE. Nurses vs doctors: the battle between the caregivers in health care reform. Nursing Connections. 1994;7:1-3.

Kapp MB. Are risk management and health care ethics compatible? Perspect Healthcare Risk Manage. 1991;11:2-7.

Kerschner PA. Assuring access to long-term care: legal, ethical, and other barriers. In: Kapp MB, Pies HE, Doudera A, Edward BS, eds. Legal and Ethical Aspects of Health Care for the Elderly. Ann Arbor, MI: Health Administration Press; 1986: 24-36.

Koop CE. Families caring for disabled need long-term support. Health Progress. 1986; 67(6):52-54.

Luce JM. Physicians do not have a responsibility to provide futile or unreasonable care if a patient or family insists. Crit Care Med. 1995;23:760-766. Comments.

Lumsdon K. Crash course: piecing together the continuum of care. Hosp Health Network. 1994;68:26-28.

MacMillan-Scattergood D. Ethical conflicts in a prospective payment home health environment. Nurs Economics. 1986;4:165-170.

Oppenheimer EA. Decision-making in the respiratory care of amyotrophic lateral sclerosis: should home mechanical ventilation be used? Palliat Med. 1993;7(suppl):49-64.

Paris NM, Hines J. Payer and provider relationships: the key to reshaping health care delivery. Nurs Adm Q. 1995;19:13-17.

Post SG. Justice, community dialogue, and health care. J Soc Philos. 1992;23:23-34.

Schwartzberg JG, Stein-Hulin J. Home health care: surmounting the obstacles to Medicare coverage. Geriatrics. 1991;46:28-30.

Scitovsky A, Capron AM. Medical care at the end of life: the interaction of economics and ethics. In: Breslow L, Fielding JE, Lave LB, eds. Annual Review of Public Health. Palo Alto, CA: Annual Reviews; 1994:75.

Taylor RM, Lantos JD. The politics of medical futility. Issues Law Med. 1995;11:3-12.

Weindling AM. Ethics and economics of health care. Prognosis, a traditional alternative to futility. BMJ. 1995;310:1671-1672. Letter.

HEALTH CARE TECHNOLOGY

Arras JD. The technological tether: an introduction to ethical and social issues in high-tech home care [and] executive summary of project conclusions. Hastings Cent Rep. 1994;24(5)(suppl):S1-S3.

Arras JD, Dubler NN. Bringing the hospital home. Ethical and social implications of high-tech home care. Hastings Cent Rep. 1994; 24 (suppl):S19-S28.

Brummel-Smith K. Home health care: how long will it remain 'low tech'? Southern California Law Review. 1991;65:491-502.

Ferrell BR, Rhiner M. High-tech comfort: ethical issues in cancer pain management for the 1990s. J Clin Ethics. 1991;2:108-112.

Mahoney J, Singer PA, Lowy FH, Hilberman M, Mitchell A, Stroud CE, et al. Cost savings at the end of life. N Engl J Med. 1994;331:477-478. Letters and response.

Scitovsky AA, Capron AM. Medical care at the end of the life: the interaction of economics and ethics. In: Breslow L, Fielding JE, Lave LB, eds. Annual Review of Public Health. Palo Alto, CA: Annual Reviews; 1994:75.

Stoltzfus DP, Stamatos JM. An appraisal of the ethical issues involved in high-technology cancer pain relief. J Clin Ethics. 1991;2:113-115. Commentary.

INFORMATION AND COMMUNICATION TECHNOLOGIES

Anonymous. Survey search: the status of gatekeeper systems. Health Cost Manage 1988; 5:23-28.

Anonymous. St. Joseph Health System. Center for Healthcare Ethics launches computer bulletin board. Health Prog 1992; 73:68-69.

Anonymous. Feasibility of ensuring confidentiality and security of computer-based patient records. Council on Scientific Affairs, American Medical Association. Arch Fam Med 1993; 2:556-560.

Anonymous. MTCP (Medical Transcriptionist Certification Program) to institute Code of Conduct Policy. J Am Assoc Med Transcr 1994; 13:58-59.

Arneson B. Case management services and long-term care insurance benefits [see comments]. J Case Manag 1993; 2:66-69.

Austin CJ, Sobczak PM. Information technology and managed care. [Review]. Hosp Top 1993; 71:33-37.

Benjamin CD, Baum BH. The automated medical record: a practical realization? Top Health Rec Manage 1988; 9:1-12.

Berger SH, Ciotti VG. HIS (healthcare information systems) consultants: when are they necessary, and why? Healthc Financ Manage 1993; 47:44-49.

Beto JA, Geraci MC, Marshall PA, Bansal VK. Pharmacy computer prescription databases: methodologic issues of access and confidentiality. Ann Pharmacother 1992; 26:686-691.

Blendon RJ, Szalay US, Knox RA. Should physicians aid their patients in dying? The public perspective [see comments]. JAMA 1992; 267:2658-2662.

Bodenheimer T. Insurance clerks are the real gatekeepers. Med Econ 1992; 69:29-33.

Bok S. Impaired physicians: what should patients know? Camb Q Healthc Ethics 1993; 2:331-340.

Broccolo BM, Fulton DK, Waller AA. The electronic future of health information: strategies for coping with a brave new world. J Ahima 1993; 64:38-51.

Brody H. Framing the health reform debate. Hastings Cent Rep 1994; 24:7-8.

Caputo RK. Managing information systems: an ethical framework and information needs matrix. Adm Soc Work 1991; 15:53-64.

Cassidy SO, Sepulveda MJ. Health information privacy reform. J Occup Environ Med 1995; 37:605-614.

Chenen AR. National Practitioner Data Banks's impact on medical groups. Med Staff Couns 1991; 5:65-66.

Cohen J. Share and share alike isn't always the rule in science [published erratum appears in Science 1995 Aug 25;269(5227):1120] [see comments]. Science 1995; 268:1715-1718.

Donaldson MS. Confidentiality on the information highway: balancing the needs of individual patients and society. Behav Healthc Tomorrow 1995; 4:32-36.

Douglas CW. Primary care meets managed care—who is the gatekeeper? Compend Continu Educ Dent 1995; 16:794-795.

Douglas JT. Group practice computing: the road to managing information. Med Group Manage J 1994; 41:14-16.

Dowling AF. Information management implications of federal health care reform. Healthc Inf Manage 1994; 8:7-18.

Eisner J. Need to borrow an ethical dilemma? Dial 1-800 dilemma to contact the "bank" manager. HEC Forum 1989; 1:369-371.

Epstein MH, Kurtzig BS. Statewide health information: a tool for improving hospital accountability [see comments]. Jt Comm J Qual Improv 1994; 20:370-375.

Fielder JH, Black J. But doctor, it's my hip: the fate of failed medical devices. [Review]. Kennedy Inst Ethics J 1995; 5:113-131.

Ford DE, Kissick JF. Health care financing reform in the United States: the community equity model. Aust Health Rev 1995; 18:61-81.

Gabrieli ER. Ethical-social consequences of computerized health care services. J Clin Comput 1985; 13:165-171.

Gardner SL, White R. Privacy, technology, and human services: 1984 minus one. N Engl J Hum Serv 1983; 3:12-21.

Goldstein DM. Further ethics resources [letter; comment]. Ann Intern Med 1995; 122:557.

Golembesky H. Ties that bond: going beyond simple links between hospitals & physicians. Healthc Inform 1992; 9:50-51.

Gostin LO, Lazzarini Z, Neslund VS, Osterholm MT. The public health information infrastructure. A national review of the law on health information privacy. JAMA 1996; 275:1921-1927.

Gostin LO, Turek-Brezina J, Powers M, Kozloff R. Privacy and security of health information in the emerging health care system. Health Matrix 1995; 5:1-36.

Gostin LO, Turek-Brezina J, Powers M, Kozloff R, Faden R, Steinauer DD. Privacy and security of personal information in a new health care system [see comments]. JAMA 1993; 270:2487-2493.

Grover FL. The bright future of cardiothoracic surgery in the era of changing healthcare delivery. Ann Thorac Surg 1996; 61:499-510.

Hoge SK. Proposed federal legislation jeopardizes patient privacy. Bull Am Acad Psychiatry Law 1995; 23:495-500.

Howe GE, Peddie EC, Eales HP, Swedish J, Chapman TW, Clay P, et al. CEO summit. A new breed. Hosp Health Netw 1996; 70:31-34.

James BC. Breaks in the outcomes measurement chain. Hosp Health Netw 1994; 68:60.

Keegan AJ. The need to integrate clinical and financial information. Healthc Financ Manage 1995; 49:74-76.

Leavitt M. Electronic records: better service for customers & payors. Infocare 1995; 14-16.

Love RL. Healthcare reform is already behind the times. J Am Assoc Med Transcr 1994; 13:22-23.

Parsi KP, Winslade WJ, Corcoran K. Does confidentiality have a future? The computer-based patient record and managed mental health care. Health Care Law Ethics 1995; 10:78-82.

Pitman SC. Standards in the medical transcription service industry. J Ahima 1992; 63:75-77.

Porter B. New worlds of access—but at what price? Healthc Inform 1990; 7:14-15.

Reinhardt UE. Comment on the Jackson Hole initiatives for a twenty-first century American health care system [comment]. [Review]. Health Econ 1993; 2:7-14.

Roberts J, Corrigan JM. Commentaries on public accountability [comment]. Manag Care Q 1995; 3:25-29.

Ryzen E. The National Practitioner Data Bank. Problems and proposed reforms. J Leg Med 1992; 13:409-462.

Schmitz HH, Weiss SJ, Melichar C. A systematic method of accountability. Sound policies allow facilities to account for the level of charity care they provide. Health Prog 1992; 73:46-51.

Silva JS. Information becomes lifeblood of reform [interview by Carolyn Dunbar]. Comput Healthc 1993; 14:14-15.

Siwicki B. As networks multiply, privacy concerns grow. Health Data Manag 1995; 3:57-58.

Stromberg CD. Access to hospital information: problems and strategies. Front Health Serv Manage 1987; 4:3-45.

Thacker SB, Stroup DF. Future directions for comprehensive public health surveillance and health information systems in the United States. Am J Epidemiol 1994; 140:383-397.

Thomas SP. Issues in data management and storage. J Neurosci Nurs 1993; 25:243-245.

Watson S. The marriage of financial and clinical software. Health Data Manag 1995; 3:66-70.

Weber DO. Outcry over outcomes. Healthc Forum J 1992; 35:16-26.

INFORMED CONSENT AND DECISIONAL CAPACITY

Berg JM, Karlinsky H, Lowy FH, eds. Alzheimer's: Disease Research: Ethical and Legal Issues. Toronto: Carswell; 1991:317-330.

Block JA. Evaluating the patient's capacity for making decisions. In: Dunkle RE, Wykle ML, eds. Decision Making in Long-Term Care: Factors in Planning. New York, NY: Springer Publishing Co, Inc; 1988:31-39.

Brock DW. Decisionmaking competence and risk. Bioethics. 1991;5:105-112.

Cohen CA, Meslin EM, Shulman KI. Dementia at home: ethical issues and clinical realities. In: Berg JM, Karlinsky H, Lowy FH, eds. Alzeimer's Disease Research: Ethical and Legal Issues. Toronto: Carswell; 1991: 317-330.

Downes BR. Guardianship for people with severe mental retardation: consent for urgently needed treatment. Health Soc Work. 1992;17:13-15.

Dubler NN. Improving the discharge planning process: distinguishing between coercion and choice. Gerontologist. 1988;3(suppl):76-81.

Ethical considerations in resuscitation. JAMA. 1992;16:2282-2288.

Ferrara PJ. Expanding autonomy of the elderly in home health care programs. New England Law Review. 1990;25:421-455.

High DM. Surrogate decision making. Who will make decisions for me when I can't? Clin Geriatr Med. 1994;10:445-462. Review.

Hofland BF. Autonomy in long term care: background issues and a programmatic response. Gerontologist. 1988;3(suppl):3-9.

Kanoti GA. Writing a proposal for determining patient decisional capacity. HEC Forum. 1994;6:12-17.

Igoe S, Cascella S, Stockdale K. Ethics in the OR: DNR and patient autonomy. Nurs Manage. 1993;24:112A.

Iserson KV. Foregoing prehospital care: should ambulance staff always resuscitate? J Med Ethics. 1991;17:19-24.

Kanoti GA. Writing a proposal for determining patient decisional capacity. HEC Forum. 1994;6:12-17.

Kapp MB. Who's the parent here? The family's impact on the autonomy of older persons. Emory Law Journal. 1992;41:773-803.

Krynski MD, Tymchuk AJ, Ouslander JG. How informed can consent be? New light on comprehension among elderly people making decisions about enteral tube feeding. Gerontologist. 1994;34:36-43.

Milholland DK. Privacy and confidentiality of patient information. Challenges for nursing. J Nurs Adm. 1994;24:19-24.

Murphy DJ. Improving advance directives for healthy older people. J Am Geriatr Soc. 1990;38:1251-1256.

Osman H, Perlin TM. Patient self-determination and the artificial prolongation of life. Health Soc Work. 1994;19:245-252.

Outerbridge DE, Hersh AR. Easing the Passage: A Guide for Prearranging and Ensuring a Pain-Free and Tranquil Death via a Living Will, Personal Medical Mandate, and Other Medical, Legal, and Ethical Resources, New York, NY: HarperCollins; 1991.

Smith ML. Futile medical treatment and patient consent. Cleve Clin J Med. 1993;60:151-154. Review.

Turner JF, Mason T, Anderson D, Gulati A, Sbarbaro JA. Physicians' ethical responsibilities under co-pay insurance: should potential fiscal liability become part of informed consent? J Clin Ethics. 1995;6:68-72.

Weiler K, Helms LB, Buckwalter KC. A comparative study: guardianship petitions for adults and elder adults. J Gerontol Nurs. 1993;19:15-25.

MEDICAL FUTILITY

Alpers A, Lo B. When is CPR futile? JAMA. 1995;273:156-158. Editorial; comment.

American Nurses Association. Compendium of position statements on the nurse's role in end-of-life decisions. American Nurses Association Center for Ethics and Human Rights Task Force on the nurse's role in end-of-life decisions. American Nurses Association; 1992:1-13.

American Nurses Association position statement on nursing care and do-not-resuscitate decisions. Ky Nurse. 1993;41:16-17.

Annas GJ. Do feeding tubes have more rights than patients? Hastings Cent Rep. 1986;16:26-28.

Asch DA, Hansen-Flaschen J, Lanken PN. Decisions to limit or continue life-sustaining treatment by critical care physicians in the United States: conflicts between physicians' practices and patients' wishes. Am J Respir Crit Care Med. 1995;151 (pt 1):288-292. Comments.

Brody BA, Halevy A. Is futility a futile concept? J Med Philos. 1995;20:123-144.

Capron AM. Medical futility: strike two. Hastings Cent Rep. 1994;24:42-43.

Caswell D, Cryer HG. Case study: when the nurse and physician don't agree. J Cardiovasc Nurs. 1995;9:30-42.

Curtis JR, Park DR, Krone MR, Pearlman RA. Use of the medical futility rationale in do-not-attempt-resuscitation orders. JAMA. 1995;273:124-128. Comments.

Ebell MH. When everything is too much. Quantitative approaches to the issue of futility. Arch Fam Med. 1995;4:352-356. Comments.

Ethical considerations in resuscitation. JAMA. 1992;16:2282-2288.

Gatter RA Jr, Moskop JC. From futility to triage. J Med Philos. 1995;20:191-205.

Griener GG. The physician's authority to withhold futile treatment. J Med Philos. 1995;20:207-224.

Hargrove MD Jr. A five-step approach to settling a dispute over futile care. J La State Med Soc. 1994;146:439-440.

Jecker NS, Schneiderman LJ. Medical futility: the duty not to treat. Camb Q Healthcare Ethics. 1993;2:151-159.

Jecker NS, Schneiderman LJ. An ethical analysis of the use of 'futility' in the 1992 American Heart Association Guidelines for cardiopulmonary resuscitation and emergency cardiac care. Arch Intern Med. 1993;153:2195-2198. Comments.

Jecker NS, Schneiderman LJ. Judging medical futility: an ethical analysis of medical power and responsibility. Camb Q Healthcare Ethics. 1995;4:23-35.

Jecker NS, Schneiderman LJ. When families request that 'everything possible' be done. J Med Philos. 1995;20:145-163.

Leibson CM. The role of the courts in terminating life-sustaining medical treatment. Issues Law Med. 1995;10:437-451.

Luce JM. Physicians do not have a responsibility to provide futile or unreasonable care if a patient or family insists. Crit Care Med. 1995;23:760-766. Comments.

Mahoney J, Singer PA, Lowy FH, Hilberman M, Mitchell A, Stroud CE, et al. Cost savings at the end of life. N Engl J Med. 1994;331:477-478. Letters and response.

Marsden AK, Ng GA, Dalziel K, Cobbe SM. When is it futile for ambulance personnel to initiate cardiopulmonary resuscitation? BMJ. 1995;311:49-51.

Noland LR. HealthCare Ethics Forum 94: medical futility: a bedside perspective. Clin Issues. 1994;5:366-368.

Robbins DA. Cost containment and terminal care: an essay into the ethics of appropriateness. J Long Term Care Adm. 1981;9:41-47.

Sade RM. Medical futility and ineffective care: a proposal for hospital policy. J S C Med Assoc. 1995;91:63-65.

Sprung CL, Eidelman LA, Steinberg A. Is the physician's duty to the individual patient or to society? Crit Care Med. 1995;23:618-620. Editorial; comment.

Taylor RM, Lantos JD. The politics of medical futility. Issues Law Med. 1995;11:3-12.

Teno JM, Murphy D, Lynn J, Tosteson A, Desbiens N, Connors AF Jr, et al. Prognosis-based futility guidelines: does anyone win? SUPPORT Investigators. Study to Understand Prognoses and Preferences for Outcomes and Risks of Treatment. J Am Geriatr Soc. 1994;42:1202-1207.

Tong R. Towards a just, courageous, and honest resolution of the futility debate. J Med Philos. 1995;20:165-189.

Turner JF, Mason T, Anderson D, Gulati A, Sbarbaro JA. Physicians' ethical responsibilities under co-pay insurance: should potential fiscal liability become part of informed consent? J Clin Ethics. 1995;6:68-2.

Waisel DB, Truog RD. The cardiopulmonary resuscitation-not-indicated order: futility revisited. Ann Intern Med. 1995;122:304-308.

Weindling AM. Ethics and economics of health care. Prognosis, a traditional alternative to futility. BMJ. 1995;310:1671-1672. Letter.

NEGOTIATING, CONTRACTING, PARTNERING

Aeschleman M, Koch A. Independent practice associations: risk contracting, financial controls and processes. Med Group Manage J 1993; 40:70.

Alba T, Souders J, McGhee G. How hospitals can use internal benchmark data to create effective managed care arrangements. Managed Care Q 1994; 2:79-89.

Anonymous. Physician-hospital integration and direct contracting in managed care programs. Health Care Strategic Management 1994; 12:11.

Anonymous. Becoming a 'preferred provider.' Internist 1994; 35:16-19.

Bader BS, Matheny M. Understanding capitation and at-risk contracting. Health Syst Lead 1994; 1:4-16.

Bailey C. Proposed health care reform includes changes in hospital liability. Healthtexas 1993.

Beauregard TR. Measuring the economic value of HMOs. Benefits Q 1995; 11:16-18.

Berger S, Sudman SK. Giving employers what they want. Successful CEOs read warning signs. Healthc Exec 1993; 8:12-15.

Bianculli JL. Subacute care. Signing on the dotted line. Provider 1994; 20:49-50.

Bonney RS. The art of negotiation. Getting what you want out of a managed care contract. Healthc Exec 1995; 10:12-16.

Bradman LH. Cost-cutting opportunities through direct contracting. J Health Care Benefits 1993; 3:57-60.

Brazda JF. Expect compromise, surprises in reform, history's lessons show. Mod Healthc 1993; 23:46.

Brazda JF. Too much compromise threatens to take life out of healthcare reform. Mod Healthc 1994; 24:25.

Burg B. Managed care 1995. Boost the value of your contracts. Med Econ 1995; 72:77-78.

Burke G, Lewis M. The marketplace and health care reform: the unfinished agenda of the '90s. Empl Benefits J 1995; 20:12-16.

Caesar NB. Two more snares to beware in contract boilerplate. Manag Care 1994; 3:51.

Caesar NB. "Should I join this alliance?" and other questions for your lawyer. Manag Care 1994; 3:23.

Caesar NB. Five tips for improving your negotiating skills. Manag Care 1994; 3:10,12.

Caesar NB. Six more pointers to help you prepare for effective negotiations. Manag Care 1994;3:48.

Caesar NB. How to gain leverage with a health plan. Med Econ 1994;71:32-34, 37-8, 40-1 passim.

Carter JH. Provider and subscriber education: the key to survival [comment]. Manag Care Q 1994; 2:85-86.

Casebolt JM. Taming your telephone. Physician Exec 1995; 21:28-31.

Cerny RA. Arbitration or litigation: efficacy and fairness in resolving medical malpractice disputes through arbitration proceedings. J Health Hosp Law 1994; 27:193-203.

Clark BW. Negotiating successful managed care contracts. Healthc Financ Manage 1995; 49:26-30.

Cohen RE. Commanding general. Natl J (Wash) 1994; 26:1904-1908.

Coile RC, Jr. Profits and pitfalls in direct contracting. Healthc Forum J 1992; 35:86.

Conomikes GS. Capitation strategies for your surgical practice. Bull Am Coll Surg 1995; 80:8-22.

Cook J. What to look for before you sign a contract. Internist 1994; 35:10-11.

Dechene JC. Preferred provider organization structures and agreements. Ann Health Law 1995; 35-70.

DeMuro PR. Provider alliances: key to healthcare reform. Healthc Financ Manage 1994; 48:26-30.

Denning JJ. Contracting with an MCO? Ask these 20 questions. Manag Care 1994; 3:45.

Duffy M. Clinton's plan: DOA? Time 1994; 143:20-24.

Ellenberger AR. Managed care and physician contracting skills: questions to ask. Bull Am Coll Surg 1993; 78:30-33.

Federa RD, Camp TL. The changing managed care market. J Ambulatory Care Manage 1994; 17:1-7.

Goldfield NI, Berman H, Collins A, Cooper R, Dragalin D, Kongstvedt P, et al. Methods of compensating physicians contracting with managed care organizations. [Review]. J Ambulatory Care Manage 1992; 15:81-92.

Goodroe JH, Murphy DA. The algebra of managed care. Creating physician and hospital partnerships. Hosp Top 1994; 72:14-18.

Gorman B. At-risk contracting: preparing to deliver what purchasers want. Behav Healthc Tomorrow 1994; 3:47-52.

Grimaldi PL. Navigating the waters of Medicaid managed care contracting. Healthc Financ Manage 1995; 49:72-80.

Horowitz JL, Kleiman MA. Advanced pricing strategies for hospitals in contracting with managed care organizations. J Ambulatory Care Manage 1994; 17:8-17.

Kaiser MA. Knowledge is power: a guide to fact-based managed-care negotiations. J Cardiovasc Manag 1994; 5:35-36.

Kalkhof CJ. Financial, operational issues entangle Medicaid managed care. Healthc Financ Manage 1992; 46:26-28.

Kenkel PJ. Multitude of healthcare plans may hinder direct contracting. Mod Healthc 1992; 22:32.

Kertesz L. Medicare: the final frontier for HMOs. Mod Healthc 1995; 25:76-77.

Kolb KW. Pharmacotherapy quality improvement in the managed care setting. Top Hosp Pharm.

Koller CF. Provider contracting workshop. Hmo Pract 1993; 7:186-189.

Kosterlitz J. The big sell. Natl J (Wash) 1994; 26:1118-1123.

Kosterlitz J. Guiding it through. Natl J (Wash) 1994; 26:649-654.

Kraft JG. Direct contracting with employers doesn't need to be complicated. Mod Healthc 1992; 22:42.

Krentz SE. Risk versus uncertainty in managed care contracting. Healthc Financ Manage 1994; 48:22.

Kridelbaugh WW. Reflections on the evolution of malpractice law. Bull Am Coll Surg 1994; 79:29-30.

Lane W. What the contract doesn't say. Manag Care 1994; 3:40.

Lazarus A. Using an appeals panel to mediate mental health care UR disputes. Med Interface 1994; 7:56-58.

Leeka AB. Competition in specialized managed care contracting produces bundled treatments. Health Care Strateg Manage 1995; 13:11-13.

Levine RH, Wilson JA. Physician reimbursement in Medicare risk contracting. Manag Care Q 1994; 2:62-71.

Lewis A. Appeals: the last word. Med Interface 1994; 7:50-55.

Lowes RL. Can malpractice really be kept out of court? Med Econ 1994; 71:106-107.

Madden DL. Getting paid what you're worth. Internist 1994; 35:6-9.

Marcus LJ, Wyatt JB. Negotiating the road to reform. Mod Healthc 1994; 24:26.

Masterson BJ. Important points in managed care contracts. Physician Exec 1992; 18:3-7.

Monfiletto E. When the physician's plan becomes the customer's health maintenance organization [comment]. Manag Care Q 1994; 2:83-84.

Moskowitz DB. New court rulings threaten managed care's restrictive hiring, contracting practices. J Am Health Policy 1993; 3:49-52.

Navarro RP. Capitation risks for pharmacy services. Med Interface 1994; 7:88-90.

O'Neill DD. Careers. Transitioning to managed care. Healthc Exec 1995; 10:36.

Ogden DF. Physician/hospital organizations in managed care contracting. Med Group Manage J 1993; 40:12.

Peck T, Schopp DN, Foshage DG. Hospital managed care performance standards. Manag Care Q 1993; 1:19-25.

Polich CL, Riley PA. Is Medicare contracting right for your managed care organization? Med Interface 1994; 7:78-80.

Pretzer M. Why you should watch the Senate Finance Committee. Med Econ 1994; 71:92-99.

Rice B. The malpractice shootout in Washington. Med Econ 1994; 71:106-109.

Rich A. Negotiating risk in managed care contracting. NAHAM Manage J 1994; 20:11-13.

Richardson D. Dialogue: ethical hazards of capitation contracting. Antidotes to the incentive for under-treatment. Behav Healthc Tomorrow 1994; 3:40-41.

Ronai SE, Hudner HK. Physician negotiations with managed care plans: an antitrust primer. Med Staff Couns 1993; 7:57-66.

Rothenberg N. Contracting with specialty PPOs: new cost containment options. Empl Benefits J 1993; 18:27-29.

Rothenberg N. How specialty contracts achieve savings. J Health Care Benefits 1994; 3:32-35.

Ruffin M. Managed care information needs: a summary perspective. Physician Exec 1995; 21:44-46.

Sargent SC. Dialogue: ethical hazards of capitation contracting. The dangers of at-risk contracting. Behav Healthc Tomorrow 1994; 3:40-43.

Scammon DL, Fuller DA. The management of upstream and downstream risk through selective contracting. [Review]. J Ambul Care Mark 1992; 5:209-219.

Schwartzben D. Reimbursement issues in managed care contracting. Hosp Cost Manag Account 1994; 6:1-5.

Schwartzben D. Financial, legal, and operational perils of managed care contracting. Hosp Cost Manag Account 1995; 6:1-8.

Scott RS. Why is cost a keystone to managed care contracting? Adm Radiol 1995; 14:42-43.

Scroggins ES. Employer demands lower cost [see comments]. Manag Care Q 1994; 2:72-76.

Scroggins ES, Brayer KA. How to approach managed care contracting in the 1990s. Med Group Manage J 1993; 40:70.

Seaver DJ, Kramer SH. Direct contracting: the future of managed care. Healthc Financ Manage 1994; 48:20-24.

Shapleigh C. An integrated approach to managed care contracting. Healthc Financ Manage 1993; 47:26-28.

Simione W. Capitation. Caring 1995; 14:24-28.

Solomon CM. Nation's governors demonstrate art of compromise. Health Syst Rev 1994; 27:56-57.

Stanley NR. Common road blocks to national accounts pharmaceutical programs. Med Interface 1994; 7:109-111.

Stepovich M. Department of Justice challenging big insurers' "Most Favored Nation" clauses. Health Care Law Newsl 1995; 10:3-4.

Stone DL. The health maintenance organization: guilty of complacency [comment]. Manag Care Q 1994; 2:77-79.

Theis GA. Considerations under capitated behavioral health care services. Med Interface 1994; 7:123.

Vincent DA. Integrated systems: subspecialists as capitated primary care physicians? Health Care Strateg Manage 1993; 11:12-15.

Vogel DE. The health maintenance organization must focus on maximizing value [comment]. Manag Care Q 1994; 2:80-82.

Waxman JM. Check termination rules in managed-care contract. Part two of a two-part series. Contemp Longterm Care 1994; 17:70.

Weinstein M, O'Gara N. Managed care strategies for the '90s. Healthc Financ Manage 1992; 46:42-45.

Weissenstein E. Providers fear rules will hinder Medicare direct-contracting [news]. Mod Healthc 1995; 25:28.

Weissenstein E. Groups weigh forming direct-contracting coalition [news]. Mod Healthc 1995; 25:3.

White JH. Congress and healthcare reform: divisions and alliances. Health Prog 1994; 75:12-15.

Wicks EK. Aggressive regulator or passive price-taker: what role should HIPCs (health insurance purchasing cooperatives) play? J Am Health Policy 1993; 3:21-25.

Winters RW. Home infusion therapy meets managed care: confrontation or cooperation. Med Interface 1994; 7:72-74.

Wise D. Employee assistance programs expand to fit companies' needs. Bus Health 1993; 11:40-42.

Wong LK. Specialty services capitation contracting by HMOs. Med Group Manage J 1994; 41:96.

Yedidia P. Medicare risk contracting. Early identification and follow-up of high risk enrollees are essential first steps to success. Med Group Manage J 1995; 42:46-48.

Zelenka NB, Watson K. 7 questions to answer before negotiations begin. Manag Care 1994; 3:39-42.

Zelley M, Bell C. Successful implementation of Medicare risk contracting. Med Group Manage J 1993; 40:86-90.

Zenowich C. Key strategies help providers hold winning hand in capitation game. Mod Healthc 1994; 24:40.

Zhang M. Hospitals contracting with managed care. J Hosp Mark 1995; 9:25-33.

Zhang M. Physicians contracting with managed care. Health Mark Q 1995; 12:71-83.

RESUSCITATION ISSUES

Adams JG, Arnold R, Siminoff L, Wolfson AB. Ethical conflicts in the prehospital setting. Ann Emerg Med. 1992;21:1259-1265.

Adams JG, Derse AR, Gotthold WE, Mitchell JM, Moskop JC, Sanders AB. Ethical aspects of resuscitation. Ann Emerg Med. 1992;21:1273-1276.

Alpers A, Lo B. When is CPR futile? JAMA. 1995;273:156-158. Editorial; comment.

Baskett PJ. Ethics in cardiopulmonary resuscitation. Resuscitation. 1993;25:1-8. Editorial.

Brown LM, Rousseau GK. Resuscitation status begins at home. Am J Nurs. 1990;4:24-26.

Clark GD, Lucas K, Stephens L. Ethical dilemmas and decisions concerning the do-not-resuscitate patient undergoing anesthesia. AANA J. 1994;62:253-256.

Coll PP, Anderson D. Advanced directives for homebound patients. J Am Board Fam Pract. 1992;5:359-360. Letter; comment.

Curtis LL. DNR in the OR: ethical concerns and hospital policies. Nurs Manage. 1994; 25:29-31.

Curtis JR, Park DR, Krone MR, Pearlman RA. Use of the medical futility rationale in do-not-attempt-resuscitation orders. JAMA. 1995;273:124-128. Comments.

Do-Not-Resuscitate (DNR) Decisions in the Context of Hospice Care. Arlington, Va: National Hospice Organization; 1992.

Edwards BS. When the physician won't give up. Am J Nurs. 1993;93:34-37.

Edwards BS. When the family can't let go. Am J Nurs. 1994;94:52-56.

Ethical considerations in resuscitation. JAMA. 1992;16:2282-2288.

Ethical issues of resuscitation. American College of Emergency Physicians. Ann Emerg Med. 1992;21:1277.

Finfer S, Theaker N, Raper R, Fisher M. The Hippocratic oath updated. Surrogates' decisions in resuscitation are of limited value. BMJ. 1994;309:953. Letter.

Garson KB. Do not resuscitate options in home care. Home Healthcare Nurse. 1992; 10:21-23.

Guidelines for cardiopulmonary resuscitation and emergency cardiac care. Emergency Cardiac Care Committee and Subcommittees, American Heart Association. Part VIII. Ethical considerations in resuscitation. JAMA. 1992;16:2282-2288. Comments.

Havlir D, Brown L, Rousseau GK. Do not resuscitate discussions in a hospital-based home care program. J Am Geriatr Soc. 1989;1:52-54.

Hiltunen EF, Puopolo AL, Marks GK, Marsden C, Kennard MJ, Follen MA, et al. The nurse's role in end-of-life treatment discussions: preliminary report from the SUPPORT Project. J Cardiovasc Nurs. 1995;9:68-77. Review.

Hodgson PK. Dying at home. A review of the do-not-resuscitate process. N C Med J. 1995;56:97-99.

Igoe S, Cascella S, Stockdale K. Ethics in the OR: DNR and patient autonomy. Nurs Manage. 1993;24:112A.

Iserson KV, Rouse F. Prehospital DNR orders. Hastings Cent Rep. 1989;19:17-19. Case study and commentaries.

Iserson KV. Foregoing prehospital care: should ambulance staff always resuscitate? J Med Ethics. 1991;17:19-24.

Iserson KV. The 'no code' tattoo—an ethical dilemma. West J Med. 1992;156:309-312.

Jecker NS, Schneiderman LJ. Ceasing futile resuscitation in the field: ethical considerations. Arch Intern Med. 1992;152:2392-2397. Review; comments.

Jecker NS, Schneiderman LJ. An ethical analysis of the use of 'futility' in the 1992 American Heart Association Guidelines for cardiopulmonary resuscitation and emergency cardiac care. Arch Intern Med. 1993;153:2195-2198. Comments.

Levenson JL, Pettrey L. Controversial decisions regarding treatment and DNR: an algorithmic Guide for the Uncertain in Decision-Making Ethics (GUIDE). Am J Crit Care. 1994;3:87-91.

MacLean DS, Wanzer SH. The physician's responsibility toward hopelessly ill patients. N Engl J Med. 1989;14:975-78. Letters and response.

Marsden AK, Ng GA, Dalziel K, Cobbe SM. When is it futile for ambulance personnel to initiate cardiopulmonary resuscitation? BMJ. 1995;311:49-51.

Miles SH. Advanced directives to limit treatment: the need for portability. J Am Geriatr Soc. 1987;1:74-76. Editorial.

Muller JH. Shades of blue: the negotiation of limited codes by medical residents. Soc Sci Med. 1992;34:885-898.

Orlowski JP, Collins RL, Cancian SN. Forgoing life-supporting or death-prolonging therapy: a policy statement. Cleve Clin J Med. 1993;60:81-85.

Osman H, Perlin TM. Patient self-determination and the artificial prolongation of life. Health Soc Work. 1994;19:245-252.

Robbins DA. Update: the removal of life supports in long-term care facilities. J Long Term Care Adm. 1985;13:3-5.

Rusin MJ. Communicating with families of rehabilitation patients about 'do not resuscitate' decisions. Arch Phys Med Rehabil. 1992;73:922-925.

Stein PS. Are do-not-resuscitate, do-not-intubate orders appropriate for trauma patients? AORN J. 1993;58:576-577.

Terry M, Zweig S. Prevalence of advance directives and do-not-resuscitate orders in community nursing facilities. Arch Fam Med. 1994;3:141-145.

Van Bommel H. Choices: For People Who Have a Terminal Illness, Their Families, and Their Caregivers. Port Washington, NY: NC Press; 1986.

TREATMENT REFUSAL

Ahronheim J, Weber D. Final Passages: Positive Choices for the Dying and Their Loved Ones. New York, NY: Simon & Schuster, Inc; 1992.

Cranford RE. The role of the ethics consultant in personal ethical dilemmas. In: Culver CM, ed. Ethics at the Bedside. Hanover, NH: University Press of New England; 1990:194-206.

Gillick MR. Choosing Medical Care in Old Age: What Kind, How Much, When to Stop. Cambridge, Mass: Harvard University Press; 1994.

Herr SS, Bostrom BA, Barton RS. No place to go: refusal of life-sustaining treatment by competent persons with physical disabilities. Issues Law Med. 1992;8:3-36. Review.

Mahoney J, Singer PA, Lowy FH, Hilberman M, Mitchell A, Stroud CE, et al. Cost savings at the end of life. N Engl J Med. 1994;331:477-478. Letters and response.

Price DM. Forgoing treatment in an adult with no apparent treatment preferences: a case report. Theor Med. 1994;15:53-60.

TRENDS AND THE FUTURE

Bailit H. Managed medical and dental care: current status and future directions. J Am Coll Dent 1995; 62:7-10.

Blendon RJ, Altman DE, Benson J, James M, Rowland D, Neuman P, et al. The public's view of the future of Medicare. JAMA 1995; 274:1645-1648.

Blumenthal D. Health care reform—past and future [see comments]. N Engl J Med 1995; 332:465-468.

Brooks AM, Clement JA, Billings CV, Gilbert CM. New partnerships. Creating the future. J Psychosoc Nurs Ment Health Serv 1993; 31:37-40.

Butler RN. Where is geriatrics? Our future is missing from all the proposed healthcare reform plans [editorial]. Geriatrics 1994; 49:11.

Carey WD. Humanism and professionalism in medicine's new world order. Am J Gastroenterol 1994; 89:1932-1937.

Cerne F. Dinosaur or chameleon? PPOs face a future in which survival demands risk-sharing arrangements. Hosp Health Netw 1993; 67:41-43.

Coile RC, Jr. Managed care: ten leading for the 1990s. Hosp Strategy Rep 1990; 2:1-8.

Coile RC, Jr. Future, health care reform and the outlook for long-term care. J Long Term Care Adm 1993; 21:6-10.

Coile RC, Jr. Health care 1994: top ten for the era of health reform. Hosp Strategy Rep 1994; 6:1-7.

Coile RC, Jr. Managed care outlook, 1995-2000: top 10 for the HMO insurance industry. Russ Coiles Health 1995; 7:1-8.

Coile RC, Jr. Health care 1995: top 10 for the era of capitation. Hosp Strategy Rep 1995; 7:1-8.

Coile RC, Jr. The future of American health care in the "post-reform" era. Physician Exec 1995.

Criss E. Unlocking the future. EMS must choose a path. J Emerg Med Serv Jems 1994; 19:23-24.

Curtin LL. Learning from the future [editorial]. Nurs Manage 1994; 25:7-9.

Daniels AS. The role of capitation in quality behavioral healthcare systems of the future. Behav Healthc Tomorrow 1994; 3:80.

Delaney A. The future of utilization management/review. Qrc Advis 1993; 9:1-4.

Ellwood PM. Look to the private sector for the future of managed care [interview]. Internist 1995; 36:18-20.

Ellwood PM, Jr. VIP interview: Paul M. Ellwood, Jr., M.D. Manag Care Q 1993; 1:90-92.

Ginzberg E. Lessons from 1994 point the way to future reform. Health Manage Q 1994; 16:3-4.

Goldberg RJ, Stoudemire A. The future of consultation-liaison psychiatry and medical-psychiatric units in the era of managed care. [Review]. Gen Hosp Psychiatry 1995; 17:268-277.

Graddy B. Brave new world. Young physicians bring different priorities to a whole new future in medicine. Tex Med 1994; 90:34-39.

Hadley J. Future issues in health care reform. Inquiry 1994; 31:363-364.

Hermogeno A. Consolidation. The future of HMO's. Adm Radiol 1992; 11:20-23.

Hey M. Delivery reform tops executives' concerns. Healthcare leaders focus on the move toward consolidation. Roundtable discussion. Health Prog 1994; 75:42-48.

Jenkins ER. Managed care plus (MC+): the wave of the future for Missouri Medicaid? Mo Med 1995; 92:222-223.

Kane RL, Kane RA, Finch MD. Once and future SHMOs [letter; comment]. Gerontologist 1995; 35:294-295.

Kenkel PJ. Debate will attempt to define future effects of managed care. Mod Healthc 1992; 22:62.

Kirrane DE. Healthcare reform: what the future holds. Healthc Exec 1995; 10:6-11.

Kosterlitz J. Back to the future. Natl J (Wash) 1994; 26:1039.

Kovacek PR. "The trouble with the future. . . is that it is not what it used to be [editorial]. J Orthop Sports Phys Ther 1995; 21:1.

Lamm RD. The ghost of health care future. Inquiry 1994; 31:365-367.

Lederberg J. The reform forecast for society's health care commons: heavy fog and hazardous driving conditions. Ann N Y Acad Sci 1994; 729:175-177.

Lee AJ. Key factors affecting the future of managed care. Top Health Care Financ 1992; 19:83-88.

Lewis ST. Health care reform—a look to the future. Med Group Manage J 1994; 41:70-74.

Long KA. Master's degree nursing education and health care reform: preparing for the future. J Prof Nurs 1994; 10:71-76.

Louria D. The future of health care and the medical profession in the United States. N J Med 1995; 92:667-669.

McCoy K. Views on the future of nursing. Insight 1993; 18:3.

McDermott KC. Healthcare reform: past and future. [Review]. Oncol Nurs Forum 1994; 21:827-832.

Montesano MT. Delegates proact to future environment of medicine. Pa Med 1993; 96:18-19.

Morrison JI, Morrison EM. The future of health care? Big, ugly buyers meet disintegrated systems. Hosp Health Netw 1994; 68:82-85.

Murray MJ. Changes in medical practice raise ethical questions. Minn Med 1995; 78:50.

O'Neil E. Health care reform and the future of public health. Am J Prev Med 1995; 11:Suppl):11-2.

Reinstein L. The 28th Walter J. Zeiter lecture. Facing new realities: back to the future. Arch Phys Med Rehabil 1996; 77:219-222.

Riding the wave of the future: an ET nurse's guide to surviving health care reform. J Wound Ostomy Continence Nurs 1994; 21:89-97.

Rosen D, Nichols L, Helms D, Rother J, Atkins L, Schieber S, et al. The future of employment-based health benefits. EBRI Issue Brief 1995; 1-31.

Sade RM. The Clinton health care plan: implications for the future of medicine. J Med Assoc Ga 1993; 82:667-671.

Schreter RK. Ten in managed care and their impact on the biopsychosocial model. Hosp Community Psychiatry 1993; 44:325-327.

Smith WL. Factors affecting the future numbers of diagnostic radiologists. AJR Am J Roentgenol 1994; 163:777-779.

Smyth S. President's message: the nurse of the future. Plast Surg Nurs 1993; 13:179.

Solovy A. Beyond HMOs. Backlash to the future. Is an HMO an HMO an HMO? Hosp Health Netw 1996; 70:42.

Stuart GW. Vulnerable or valuable: psychiatric nursing's future in health care reform [see comments]. J Psychosoc Nurs Ment Health Serv 1994; 32:53-54.

Swee DE. Health care system reform and the changing physician-patient relationship. N J Med 1995; 92:313-317.

Vladeck B. Medicare and managed care: working together for the future. Med Interface 1995; 8:50.

Wallerstein N, Bernstein E. Introduction to community empowerment, participatory education, and health. Health Educ Q 1994; 21:141-148.

Wilson CN. The future of U.S. hospitals is tied to an integrated health system. Hosp Pharm 1995; 30:138-135.

Wilson ME. General pediatrics in a time of change. Inventing the future [editorial]. Arch Pediatr Adolesc Med 1994; 148:243-244.

Zalta E, Eichner H, Henry M. Implications of disease management in the future of managed care. Med Interface 1994; 7:66-69.

ABOUT THE AUTHOR

Dennis A. Robbins, Ph.D., M.P.H., is a nationally recognized health systems specialist with a focus on ethical and legal issues in managed care. He serves as President of Integrated Decisions, Ethics, Alternatives and Solutions (IDEAS) in Chicago. His more than 20 years experience in the healthcare field spans the healthcare continuum.

Dr. Robbins received his Ph.D. from Boston College and his M.P.H. from Harvard University, where he served as a National Fund for Medical Education Fellow in the Kennedy Interfaculty Program in Medical Ethics. He is currently an Adjunct Associate Professor at Loyola Medical School in Chicago.

Dr. Robbins' approach is distinctive in that he works with and is respected by diverse legal, financial, and healthcare professionals. His lectures and keynotes are well received by a wide variety of healthcare professionals and executives, attorneys, insurers, medical directors, case managers, caregivers, regulators, purchasers of healthcare, and consumers. His national activity as a speaker and consultant with such organizations as the National Managed Health Care Congress, the Case Management Society of America, the American Board of QA and UR Physicians, the Joint Commission, the Healthcare Financial Management Association, the American Medical Association, Glaxo Pharmaceuticals, and the United States and Russian governments gives him a uniquely broad and integrated perspective, and enables him to approach complex issues with clarity, precision, and depth.

Dr. Robbins is the author of five books and over 150 articles dealing with innovative and controversial issues on the cutting edge of healthcare.

INDEX

AAHP. *See* American Association of Health Plans
Abuse, 125–126
  new initiatives on, 126–127
  referrals and, 129
Access, 288–289
Accountability, 17–18, 202, 287–288
Adams et al. v. Kaiser Foundation Health Plan of Georgia, 104–105
Advance directives, 261–262
  compliance with, 271
  highlighting importance of, 268–271
  orders to comply, 271–272
  polemics of, 272–273
  policies regarding, 272–273
  problems with, 266–268
  sensible, 273–274
  types, 270
Advanced procedures, 25–26
Advocacy
  AMA guidelines, 138–141
  "best practices," 133–134
  case management model, 135
  coalition for, 137
  community-based, 207–210
  conflicts in, 137–138
  discharge criteria, 143–144
  as empowerment, 134–135
  ethics committees and, 188
  formulary issues, 141–143
  managed care, 129–130
  payor-based, 131–132
  physician-based, 130–131
  public policy and, 136
  state-based consumer protection, 136–137

trade associations forums, 132
Agency for Health Policy and Research (AHCPR), 29
  performance measurement by, 48–50
Agendas, hidden, 38–39
Aggregates, ethics and, 33
AHCPR. *See* Agency for Health Policy and Research
Ambiguities, ethical, 151–152
American Association of Health Plans (AAHP), 18
  mission statement, 132–133
American Medical Association (AMA)
  Council on Scientific Affairs, 10
  managed care guidelines, 138–141
American Trail Lawyers Association (ATLA), 115
Antitrust issues, 121–122
Archiving, 85–86
Assessment, quality measurement and, 52
ATLA. *See* American Trail Lawyers Association
Audit trails, 284
Autonomy, 96

Barber case, 229–230
Benchmarking, 51–52, 284
"Best practices," 291
Bioethics, ethics and, 151–152

Capacity, consent and, 218
Capitation, 35-37
  learning curve with, 80–81
  shift from fee-for-service, 37–38

Care
    inadequate, 25
    versus services, 39–40
    -setting, 18
Caregiver
    -patient relationship, 12
    role of, 98
Carve-outs, 79–80
Case management models, 135
Case Management of America, 284
Ching v. Gaines, 101–102
Clinical judgment, *versus* cost
    containment, 109–110
Co-existence, 14–15
Common law rights, 221–222
Communication technologies, 83–85
Community, ethics and, 201–202. *See
    also* Ethics committees
Competence, 97
Confidentiality, 282, 284
    electronic medical records and,
        86–88
Conflict, adjudicating, 180–181
Conflict resolution, 254
    appeal guidelines, 183–184
    clinical guidelines, 182–183
    evaluation techniques, 181
    in managed care, 183–184
    recommendations, 184–186
    tools for, 175–176
Conroy case, 228–230
Conscience, 275
Consent, 97, 108
    confusion about, 242–243
    continuity of, 109, 248
    duty and, 243–245
    emergency, 248–249
    integrated policy, 245–247
    policies, 240–241
    procedures, 239–240
    process, 241–242
Consequentionalism, 152–153

Continuity, 203–204
    of consent, 109, 248
    patient wishes and, 205
Continuous Quality Improvement
    (CQI), 43
Controversy, documenting, 274
Cost
    containment, 12, 109–110
    -driven care, 35–37
    liability and, 112–113
    -quality interface, 29–31, 40–41
Costly procedures, 25–26
CQI. *See* Continuous Quality
    Improvement
Cruzan case, 213, 230–231

Decisional capacity, 99, 218
    patients without, 221
Decision-makers, priority of,
    247–248
Decision-making
    end-of-life, 211–212
    flowchart, 167
    framework for ethics, 157–158
    justification for, 173
    model, 165–168
    model application, 168–174
    provisional, 171–172
    sub-issues, 173
Declarant, 263
Defensive medicine, 110–112
DeMeurers v. HealthNet, 102–103
Deselection, 25, 68
    advice for physicians on, 69–70
    legal remedies and, 69
Dinnerstein case, 226
Discharge
    criteria and standards for, 143–144
    process, 145
Disclosure, 89
DNR. *See* Do Not Resuscitate
Documentation, 254

Do Not Resuscitate (DNR), 217
telephone orders to, 272
Durable powers of attorney, 263–266
Duty, consent and, 243–245

Economic profiling, 88
Effectiveness, 284
Efficiency, 8–9
quality, ethics and, 42–44
Eichner cases, 227–228
Emergency medical technicians
(EMTs), 202–203
Employee Retirement Income
Security Act (ERISA), 114–115
legal backlash, 115–117
Employer-payor model, 12
EMTs. *See* Emergency medical
technicians
End-of-life
care, cost and, 212–214
issues, 23–24
ERISA. *See* Employee Retirement
Income Security Act
Error(s), 284
electronic medical records and,
86–88
reduction, 51–52
Ethical issues
dilemmas, 170
framing, 158–159
identifying central, 168
justifying decisions, 159–160
pluralism, 153
prioritizing, 170–171
responsibility initiatives, 41–42
right and wrong answers, 160–161
sub-issues, 169
Ethics
administrative, 20–21
aggregates and, 33
application of, 149–151
audit, 176-177

bioethics and, 151–152
clarification of issues, 149–151
community-based committees. *See*
Ethics committees
component isolation, 169–170
concepts, 154
constants of, 26–27
efficiency, quality and, 42–44
integrating managed care and, 1–2
issues. *See* Ethical issues
knowledge and, 156–157
leadership and, 44
legal concepts and, 95–97
policy and, 214–216
process, 150–151
responsibility and, 41–42
theory, 150–151, 172–173
usefulness, 13–14
Ethics committees
advantages, 191–192
advocacy and, 188
case consultations, 194–195
community-based, 199
advocacy, 207–208
coordination, 207
education, 193
marketing, 200–201
membership, 205–207
scenario, 202–203
composition of, 194
history of, 187–188
home healthcare and, 189–190
long term care and, 189–190
membership, 192–194
nonhospital-based, 188–189. *See
also* Community-based
payor-based, 190–191
staff education, 193
Ethics rounds
benefits of, 178–179
clinical, 177–178
ethics committee and, 179–180

Evidence-based medicine, 30–31
    efficiency and decision-making,
        33–34
Experimental procedures, 25–26
Extraordinary measures, 263

Fee for service, 37–38
Fiscal arrogance, 54
Fiscal integrity, 32
Fluctuating capacity, 97–98,
        218–219
Formularies, 141–143
Fox v. HealthNet, 36, 100–101
Fraud, 125–127
Futility, 24
Future outcomes, 281

Gag rules, 63–64
Gaming, 14
Gatekeeping, 11
    access and, 60–61
    ethical dilemmas of, 62
    issues, 59
    negative, 61
    by physician, 61–62
    physician concerns, 64–65
Guardianship, 219–220

Harvard Community Health
        Outreach, 207
Harvard-Pilgrim Health Plan Project,
        284
HCLA. See Health Care Liability
        Alliance
Healthcare
    change implications, 11–13
    delivery in undercovered commu-
        nities, 283
    market models, 8–9
    trends, 7–8
Health Care Access and Cost
        Commission, 87

Health Care Liability Alliance
        (HCLA), 117–118, 137
Health Employer Data Information
        Sheet (HEDIS), 45
    differences between IMSystem
        and, 46–48
Health Maintenance Organizations
        (HMOs)
    defined, 4
    development of, 3–4
    limited care and financial incen-
        tives by, 67–68
HEDIS. See Health Employer Data
        Information Sheet
Hiepler, Mark, 35–36
HMOs. See Health Maintenance
        Organizations
Hold-harmless clauses, 113
Hudson Institute, 111
Hydration, withholding, 228–230

IMSystem. See Joint Commission on
        Accreditation of Healthcare
        Organizations, Indicator
        Measurement System
Independent Practice Associations
        (IPAs), 67–68
Individuals, versus populations, 22
Information
    access to, 89
    confidentiality and, 86–88
    privileged, 88
    technologies, ethical dimensions
        of, 83–85
Informed consent, 63–64, 245–246, 292
    knowledge and, 155–156
Informed decisions, 284
Integration, efficiency, quality, and
        ethics, 42–44
Integrity, fiscal, 31–32
IPAs. See Independent Practice
        Associations

JCAHO. *See* Joint Commission on
　　Accreditation of Healthcare
　　Organizations
Joint Commision for the
　　Accreditation of Health Care
　　Organizations (JCAHO), 29
　　differences between HEDIS and,
　　　46–48
　　Indicator Measurement System
　　　(IMSystem), 44
　　standards, 122–125

Kaiser Permanente, 94
Knowledge
　　ethics and, 156–157
　　informed consent and, 155–156

Lawsuits. *See also* specific cases
　　fear of, 106–107
Leadership, ethics and, 44
Legal cases, 98–106
Legal concepts
　　ethics and, 95–97
　　understanding, 154
Legal issues, 93–95
Legal legacy, 233–238
Lewin Group, 111
Liability, 62–63
　　concerns about, 118–119
　　cost and, 110–113
　　defensive medicine and, 110–112
　　fear of, 106–107
　　medical information and, 90–92
　　reducing, 184–186
　　risk management trends, 113–114
Life supports
　　AMA on, 250–251
　　cardiac, 251–252
　　in medically futile conditions,
　　　252–253
　　pulmonary resuscitation, 251–252
　　withdrawing, 249–255

withholding, 249–255
Limitations, practice, 89–90
Living wills, 262–263
Long-term care, 22–23
Lying, 14

Malpractice, 107–108
　　trends, 118–119
Managed Behavioral Health
　　Standards, 122
Managed care
　　advocacy, 129–130
　　AMA guidelines, 138–141
　　clinical standards in, 16–17
　　core ethical issues, 9–11
　　defined, 2–3
　　end-of-life and, 211–212
　　ethics committee in, 186–187
　　federal initiatives in, 5–7
　　good motivations in, 15–16
　　integration, 1–2
　　market forces in, 5
　　referrals and, 62–63
　　response to, 190
　　tort reform and, 120–121
Managed Care Organizations
　　(MCOs)
　　ethical and social challenges for,
　　　279–293
　　membership issues, 289–290
　　operations and ethics, 2
Managed Health Care Handbook,
　　183–184
Managed home care, 22–23
Management Service Organizations
　　(MSOs), 75–77
Management systems, 89–90
Maxing out, 19–20
*McClellan v. Long Beach Community
　　Hospital,* 105–106
MCOs. *See* Managed Care
　　Organizations

Measurement
  precision instruments, 34
  systems, 89–90
Media preceptions, 98–106
Medica, 116–117
Medicaid, 5–7
  fraud and abuse, 125–126
Medical arrogance, 54–55
Medical assessment, 253
Medical management determinations,
  184–186
Medical necessity, 31–32
Medical procedures, withholding or
  withdrawing, 222–232
Medical records, electronic errors,
  86–88
Medical Underwriters of Califor-
  nia, 94
Medicare, 5–7
  fraud and abuse, 125–126
Michael Martin case, 231–232
Mission, 21–22
Model advantages, 285–286
Morals, process application,
  150–151
MSOs. *See* Management Service
  Organizations

National Center for Quality
  Assurance (NCQA), 29, 132
National Patient Safety Foundation,
  141
NCQA. *See* National Center for
  Quality Assurance
Negligence, 107–108
Networks, 207
  guidelines, 20–21
  privileged information and, 88
  standards, 122–123
New England Journal of Medicine,
  121
Nonconsequentionalism, 152–153

Novel programs, 285
Nutrition, withholding, 228–230
OBRA. *See* Omnibus Budget
  Reconciliation Act (1991)
Omnibus Budget Reconciliation Act
  (1991), 213
Oregon plan, 66–67
ORYX, 45
Outcome measurement, 284
Outliers, 80

PacifiCare (Oregon), 137
Partnering, 74–75
  case management model, 135
  dimensions of, 78–79
  point of service and, 77
Patient confidence, 290
Patient Safety Foundation,
  283–284
Patient Self-Determination Act,
  155, 213
Perceptions, transforming, 281
Performance, measurement and qual-
  ity initiatives, 44–45
Personnel, 292
Physicians
  economic profiling of, 88
  practice pressures, 77–78
Point of service, 77
Policy
  consent and, 240–241
  ethics and, 214–216
  developing, 180–181
  guiding, 21–22
Populations, *versus* individual, 22
Practice, concepts and, 286
Precision instruments, 34
Privacy, 95–97
  right to, 216–217
Proactivity, 293
Problem-solving, bedside, 182
Profits, 8–9

Quality
  AHCPR measurement components,
    48–50
  assessment, 50-52
  care, 12
  efficiency, ethics and, 42–44
  ethical issues, 50–51
  improvement, 48–50
  initiatives by associations, 52–54
  liability, cost and, 112–113
  measurement, 50–52
Quality Compass, 44
Quinlan case, 187–188, 217,
    222–224

RAND Corporation, 111
Rationing, 65–66
Referrals, 62–63
  fraud, abuse and, 129
Regulatory issues, 121–122
Reimbursement, 289
Rights, 96, 154–155
  and responsibilities standards, 122
Risk
  management, 113–114
  -sharing, 202
Routine care, 65

Saikewicz case, 224–226
Security, electronic medical records
    and, 86–88

Self-determination, 95–97
Services, 290
  versus care, 39–40
Shea v. Medica, 286–287
Spring case, 226–227
Standards, 282
Suicide, physician-assisted,
    232–233
Surrogates, 246, 255, 266

Technology, role in medicine, 90
Telecare, role in medicine, 91
Telemedicine issues, 90–92
Terminal illness, 246
Terminology, 157
Tort reform
  managed care and, 120–121
  quality and, 117–118
Total Quality Management
    (TQM), 43
TQM. See Total Quality Management
Treatment, right to refuse, 221–222
Trust, 286–287

Vacco v. Quill, 232–233
Vision, 202

Washington v. Glucksberg, 232–233
Wickline v. State of California, 99
Wilson v. Blue Cross of California,
    99–100